Colección Támesis

SERIE A: MONOGRAFÍAS, 333

DIALOGIC ASPECTS IN THE CUBAN NOVEL OF THE 1990s

ÁNGELA DORADO-OTERO

DIALOGIC ASPECTS IN THE CUBAN NOVEL OF THE 1990s

TAMESIS

First published 2014 by Tamesis, Woodbridge

ISBN 978 1 85566 271 1

Tamesis is an imprint of Boydell & Brewer Ltd
PO Box 9, Woodbridge, Suffolk IP12 3DF, UK
and of Boydell & Brewer Inc.
668 Mt Hope Avenue, Rochester, NY 14620-2731, USA
website: www.boydellandbrewer.com

A CIP catalogue record for this book is available
from the British Library

The publisher has no responsibility for the continued existence or accuracy of
URLs for external or third-party internet websites referred to in this book, and
does not guarantee that any content on such websites is, or will remain, accurate
or appropriate

This publication is printed on acid-free paper

Typeset by:
The Word Service, 1 Oxford Street, Hungerford, RG17 0ET

Contents

Acknowledgements

I wish to thank Omar García-Obregón for his encouragement and expert guidance in the writing of this text, and Peter W. Evans, for his feedback and support. I am extremely grateful to Annabel Cox for reading and editing my work. Of course, if errors remain, whether linguistic or conceptual, they are wholly my own.

I would like to acknowledge the invaluable help and support of all the staff in the Department of Iberian and Latin American Studies at Queen Mary, University of London, and in particular Parvati Nair and Else Vieira, for their feedback when they read drafts of my work.

I have benefited from relevant feedback provided at conferences and seminars where I have presented my work: Universidad Iberoamericana, Mexico City; Université de Lyon, France; Círculo de Cultura Panamericano, meeting at the Institute for Cuban and Cuban-American Studies, University of Miami; the Cuban Research Institute, Florida International University; and the Departmental Research Seminar at Queen Mary. In this respect, special thanks go to Enrique Santamaría Lorenzo; Silvina Jensen; Elio Alba Buffill; Uva de Aragón, Lisandro Pérez, and everyone associated with the Cuban Research Institute; Jean-Claude Seguin and LE GRIMH (Le Groupe de Recherche sur l'Image dans le Monde Hispanique); Philippe Merlo; and to all the members of staff in Iberian and Latin American Studies at Queen Mary, past and present.

I have also benefited from teaching some of the authors included in this study at both Queen Mary and Goldsmiths, University of London. In this respect, I would like to thank my students of *Cuban Poetry and Fiction Post-1980*, which I taught when I replaced Omar García-Obregón during his sabbatical leave, and my students of *On the Road: Writing the Americas through Travel*, which I taught in the Department of English and Comparative Literature at Goldsmiths. They helped me to contextualize my work in a different light. Special thanks to those who made this teaching possible; in the case of Goldsmiths, I would like to thank Professor Peter Dunwoodie, Richard Bolley and Marian Pérez-Velázquez.

I am also indebted to the universities and institutions that funded me, and to the libraries and librarians where I carried out my research: the Cuban Heritage Collection at the University of Miami, special thanks to Lesbia Varona and Esperanza de Varona; Princeton University (Manuscripts Division); the Cuban Research Institute (Florida International University); Queen Mary and Senate House (both part of the University of London). For her ever-willing help with

Cuban research on the island, I thank Lourdes Morales. For their help in New Jersey, I thank Yolanda Vence and Marcelo Mancheno. For their help in Miami, I thank Omar García-Obregón's family.

At Queen Mary I had the privilege to share ideas with many people who contributed, in one way or another, to this work. Very many thanks to Noèlia Díaz Vicedo for her friendship and willingness to help when I needed her. Thanks also to my fellow students (past and present) and friends: Inma Alavedra, Neus Álvarez, Angeliki Assimaki, Pilar Cáceres, Axayácatl Campos García-Rojas, Enrico Chessa, Anna Hillman, Julia Pozas Loyo, Sergio Maruenda, Alejandro Melero, Aurelia Molina, Enrique Planells and Antonio Rivas. A special thank you to Robin Adams for reading drafts of my work and providing most useful critical feedback.

On a personal note, I would like to acknowledge the constant support of my family and my best friend and her family, Marina Kroyer, Colin and Uma. I would like to dedicate this book to my parents and siblings and to absent family members: my grandparents who were inspirational and supportive when I began writing this book but are no longer here to see its conclusion.

Introduction

This work focuses on six novels: Reinaldo Arenas's *El color del verano*, Leonardo Padura Fuentes' *Máscaras*, Abilio Estévez's *Tuyo es el reino*, Daína Chaviano's *Casa de juegos*, Yanitzia Canetti's *Al otro lado* and Zoé Valdés' *La nada cotidiana*. The selected novels were published during the 1990s, and in my view their authors, regardless of their place of residence, are products of the educational system of the Cuban revolution, since even those who left the island to go and live abroad did so as adults. The six novels that occupy my attention in this study share a common territorialization: their spatial constant is the island of Cuba and Cuban imagery, used as starting points. Yet the recreation of the island through the different narratives comes from different locations: Havana itself, in the case of Padura, Barcelona (Estévez), Paris (Valdés), Boston (Canetti), Miami (Chaviano) and New York (Arenas).

Yvette Sánchez has argued that the narrative written in exile attempts to create bridges that rely on nostalgia and frozen memories. In her words:

> Sin contacto directo con la vida cotidiana de aquella Isla, se sigue manteniendo y nutriendo una relación mediante la memoria, y la información actualizada de experiencias ajenas. En el destierro, se engendran recuerdos, sueños, fantasmas y proyecciones teñidos por la añoranza, que congelan una imagen propia del pasado, combinada con las impresiones de segunda mano, enviadas a través de diferentes canales, por los que se han quedado allá. La narrativa escrita en el exilio parece mostrar especial interés por recuperar el pulso diario de la tierra perdida, por luchar contra el desarraigo, y compensarlo, al menos en la dimensión ficticia. (2000: 163)

Nonetheless, I posit that this tendency to recuperate an image of the island that belongs to the past and that can only be retrieved for the present through the word is also found in writers on the island in the narratives of the 1990s. Thus cultural memory is at the core of the narratives of the 1990s, particularly in relation to an island in constant flux in terms of emigration. In this way, the concept of *cubanía* is contextualized within the parameters defined by Fernando Ortiz as 'cubanidad plena, sentida, consciente y deseada' (1991b: 14), thus challenging the state's position that *cubanía* can only be experienced in Cuba and not by exiles who, in the state's jargon, are classifed as *gusanos* (worms). As Denis Berenschot has affirmed, 'La Revolución castrista en Cuba' has dedicated part of its existence to 'la creación de *una* identidad cubana *per se*' (2003: 909); however, I agree with his observation that

> En la práctica se debe hablar de múltiples *cubanidades* y éstas no se limitan al espacio geográfico insular. En Cuba, los eventos históricos de la Revolución desde su *triunfo* en 1959 hasta el *Período Especial* en los años noventa han transformado profundamente las identidad[es] cubanas. Pero a estas versiones en perenne estado de mutación de *cubanidad* hay que añadirle las identidades cubanas que resultan de la experiencia exílica forjadas mediante el encuentro con la cultura de la patria adoptiva donde quiera que se la encuentre. (2003: 909)

I shall devote some attention to this last aspect, as some of the writers I study here lived in Cuba when I started reading them and only later became exiled. Following Ortiz, the authors that I have selected show that *cubanía* constitutes 'cubanidad plena, sentida, consciente y deseada', even if this is presented as what I would call a 'cubanía desterritorializada', with the issue of national identity in a constant process of definition and redefinition that relies on previous versions in order to construct new meanings, as in a palimpsest, which would respond to the new experiences, particularly of the exiles.

With this selection of texts, I critically examine Cuban culture as fluid and transnational, diverse and (de)centred, and I shall attempt to subvert the stereotype of Miami as the unique point of migration. As Janett Reinstädler and Ottmar Ette state in the introduction to their edited book *Todas las islas la isla*: 'la isla se ha multiplicado en muchas islas, sin perder su unidad transterritorial' (2000: 8). I analyse how the Cuban narratives of the 1990s, in response to and influenced by the hardship of the Special Period and the historical circumstances of the country, represent a turning point in the creation of the Cuban novel. This work explores how, in the relatively recent narratives of the 1990s, authors have increased their use of discursive techniques to create polyphonic novels and dialogism, in line with Bakhtinian theoretical postulates, which I shall analyse in the relevant chapters. I also examine how these polyphonic novels share common concerns when subverting homogenized views of Cuban identity and thus cross-examining the discourse of the state. I shall analyse how, in undermining monolithic representations of reality, these polyphonic texts employ discursive techniques that question absolute truths, defy established boundaries of literary genre and challenge concepts of national, gender and individual identity.

I have selected these six novels because I consider them to be representative of the new 'boom' of the Cuban novel in the 1990s, which had an international impact after four mainstream Spanish publishers (Tusquets, Planeta, Emecé and Seix Barral) published the books (either in first or second editions; the latter is particularly true of Arenas, who became an internationally studied author mostly after the posthumous publications by Tusquets, though he was already known by writers and critics). I claim that this literature responds to economic hardship, political and social changes, and issues of *cubanía* and exile, as some of the writers themselves moved abroad on a permanent basis after 1989 (Chaviano in 1991 to Miami; Canetti in 1991, first to California and then to Massachusetts; Valdés to Paris in 1995; and Estévez to Barcelona in 2000).

Through the study of the carnivalesque, the resort to masks as a performative tool, the agency of the transvestite and the use of erotic discourse, this work establishes similarities and differences in the way these authors create polyphonic texts that ridicule any hypothesis that would suggest that notions of country and nation coincide. This book further examines critically how these selected novels address the process of constructing a Barthesian 'infinite text' through intertextuality, thus creating at times a palimpsest, an overlay of writings and rewritings. I suggest that this process becomes a discursive mechanism to create a non-official history, a memory from the margins, which acts as a form of cultural resistance to monolithic representations of Cubanness. This process is a leitmotif in the six novels studied here, and I explore this topic as a process of self-knowledge and as a mechanism to get to know alterity and thus reach the Other.

These novels explore a process of reaching self-awareness in order for the subjects to understand their own circumstances and to reach a better understanding of themselves and of the Other. Hence, I suggest that the most important change in the literature of the 1990s is a shift towards a focus on the subjectivity of characters who become dialogic, in a process of becoming, and thus are presented as 'unfinalized'. At the same time, writing in these novels also becomes a site of resistance against hegemonic discourses and a way of creating, in line with oral history, a new version of history from below.

The authors studied are placed here beyond the dichotomy of outside and inside Cuba, or left (revolutionary) and right (counter-revolutionary) discourses, which I find unproductive when studying Cuban culture and the fluidity and heterogeneity that it displays. I suggest that the authors themselves, through their own displacements and relocations, have challenged the inside and outside dichotomy.

For some critics, these novelists could be considered part of a group labelled the 'novísimos', yet I would resist this generational stance, except to recognize its existence as a critical tool. Yvette Sánchez, for example, summarizes the features of the narratives of the so-called 'novísimos' and asserts that

Se cultiva una estética de lo crudo y lo soez, combinada con un discurso realista y una estructura tradicional de relato lineal en tercera persona con narrador omnisciente. Como antídoto contra las estrategias peyorativas, despreciativas, rebajadoras de la actualidad de la Isla, la mayoría de los literatos

> desterrados recurren a mitos equivalentes a la 'expulsión del edén' idílico, inocente y tropical, o de la 'tierra prometida' (de leche y miel). Se evocan las concepciones arquetípicas de las utopías regresivas (cualquier tiempo pasado fue mejor) y del paraíso (perdido y re-buscado). La pérdida de la infancia, de ideales sinestésicos, sensuales, físicos, individuales, ontogenéticos, y el anhelo de volver a ellos activa los recuerdos (a través de los olores, por ejemplo). […] panorama contradictorio y ambivalente de fuerzas, la utopista o idealizadora y la desmitificadora o de derrumbe. (2000: 175)

Although I believe labels work best in terms of marketing strategies, as was the case with the 'boom' of the Latin American novel, rather than as establishing true 'generations' of writers, I would suggest that Estévez, Valdés, Canetti, Chaviano, Padura and Arenas present certain characteristics of the so-called 'novísimos'. However, I disagree with Sánchez's oversimplified description of the discourse of the 'novísimos'.[1] I would posit that the 1990s were a period of experimentation, clearly showing a change in aesthetics in response to different realities after the changes in the international socialist camp which translated, for those in Cuba, into the Special Period of the early 1990s. In this period in particular, Cuban authors within and beyond the island managed to create polyphonic and dialogic novels that challenged any notions or portrayals of Cuban culture and identity as homogeneous.

Critics such as Gustavo Pérez Firmat and others have noted the 'transterritorialidad de la cultura cubana' (Nuez 1998: 29). As expressed well by Lillian Manzor-Coats,

> displacements, physical border crossings, and cultural discontinuities force us to theorize 'national identity' in another light, to disarticulate at the theoretical level what history has already separated: the anchoring of a national culture within one specific geographical space and within one linear history. (1995: 254)

This re-evaluation of the concept of national identity is a leitmotif of the narratives of the 1990s examined here that seek to amplify the margins of Cuban identity. In the novels of the Special Period the characters insert their subjectivity into a national discourse and demand a space within it. I believe, alongside Nanne Timmer, that

---

[1]   It is relevant to note for this study that much earlier Grisel Pujalá had referred to a generation of 'novísimos', but in a very different context. Pujalá applied this term to Cuban poets publishing particularly in the 1980s, such as Amando Fernández. She was following the label used for the 'novísimos' in Spain, mostly to identify a certain preference for baroque discourse and imagery, what for poets Amando Fernández and Lourdes Gil was 'barroco de América'. Nonetheless, even at the time, others (such as writer Belkis Cuza Malé) believed that those 'novísimos' were 'viejísimos' and refused to accept the label. See Pujalá 1993.

De manera lúdica, los textos de esta generación de escritores tratan temas social y políticamente delicados. No todos los textos, sin embargo, son tan referenciales. El rasgo principal de la literatura reciente es su gran diversidad, y aunque la crítica la coloque dentro de una misma categoría (como posmoderna, posnovísima o novísima), los rasgos textuales de las novelas de la década no coinciden tanto entre sí. Dentro de la diversidad, sin embargo, se veían ciertas constantes: la desmitificación de los grandes valores del sistema, el predominio de lo marginal, lo escatológico, del cuerpo, y particularmente algo que muchos críticos sólo mencionaron, pero que no elaboraron: el tema de la subjetividad. (2007: 123)

It is this last aspect of subjectivity, largely ignored by critics, which will occupy my attention here.

The works selected in this study show the diversity and fluidity of cultural production within and beyond the island. They share an attempt to pull away from a fixed idea of national identity, which coincides with the social changes and the narrative of the Special Period. This literature is characterized by narrative experimentation, a proliferation of intertextuality and fragmented narratives in which irony and humour permeate and subvert traditional notions of the text. The texts I study here require an active reader who will explore the signifieds of texts that are not fixed, and thus remain open to interpretation.

Antonio Vera León stresses the special use of language and swear words within the Cuban narrative of the last half of the twentieth century, which he claims constitutes the vile rhetoric of insult and vulgarity and within which he places two of the six writers that concern us here (namely Arenas and Valdés):

la maledicencia (palabrotas, lenguaje soez y obsceno) que, presente de forma menor en cierta narrativa cubana de los años sesenta, cobra un relieve notable en las dos últimas décadas y en específico en los relatos de Guillermo Cabrera Infante, Reinaldo Arenas y Zoé Valdés. Retórica soez del insulto, la palabrota y lo vulgar, se trata de un tipo perverso de decir que marca una inflexión en las convenciones y los registros literarios cubanos. (2000: 177)

I would add that the Bakhtinian heteroglossia that appears in this new narrative, in which the novels become polyphonic texts as a plurality of voices are heard, is an aesthetic that combines both high culture and popular culture in order to link the highbrow and the vulgar within Cuban society. I claim that this carnivalesque attitude allows the authors to explore subjectivities that challenge various kinds of hierarchies, be they social or political.

In chapter 1, for example, I analyse the carnival as a discursive technique that Reinaldo Arenas uses in *El color del verano* in order to subvert the established order and to denounce the state's double agenda by using and 'abusing' the discourses of power. I have chosen to begin this study with the work of Arenas, not only because he is the most famous and critically acclaimed post-

Mariel exile author, but also because he paves the way for the boom of the Cuban novel of the 1990s with his characteristic narrative dialogism, irreverence and thematic emphasis on sexuality as a site of resistance and as an excessive metaphor of freedom.[2] For Luis Manuel García Méndez, the changes that took place were mostly derived from socio-historical changes in the world scene, as he reveals in an interview with Abilio Estévez:

> Tras el desplome del comunismo en Europa del Este, Cuba se puso de moda. El público quería saber por qué no había caído la última ficha del dominó y, ante el hermetismo de los políticos y la prensa, los exploradores de la cultura compitieron por capturar músicos, artistas plásticos, narradores que ofrecieran las claves del milagro. Como saqueadores de ruinas, exponían en los circuitos del arte los restos arqueológicos de la Revolución. (2009: 115)

Even if it is true that the political and economic situation forced Cuba to renegotiate in ways it had not done before, I believe that the conditions for change and rebellion were already present before the marketable boom of Cuban literature that took off particularly after the mid-1990s. In this context, Reinaldo Arenas and Zoé Valdés, in particular, are key players in what can be seen, in hindsight, as pioneering literary ventures.

Though Arenas's writing covers various genres (he was a novelist, short story writer, poet, playwright and essayist), I believe it was his novels that had the greatest international impact and caused him the most problems in Cuba, as he defied the government's stance at the time which prevented him from publishing abroad. Arenas moved to Havana in 1962 and in 1965 won a First Mention Award at the Cirilo Villaverde National Competition with his novel *Celestino antes del alba*, which was published by Ediciones Unión of UNEAC [Unión Nacional de Escritores y Artistas de Cuba] in 1967. This was to be the only novel that he would publish in Cuba, despite his continual writing and rewriting. This was also the first of what the author considered to be his quintet or *pentagonía*, which also included *El palacio de las blanquísimas mofetas*, *Otra vez el mar*, *El color del verano* and *El asalto*. In addition, he wrote other significant works such as his second novel *El mundo alucinante*, entered in UNEAC's 1966 competition, which also received 'primera mención' (Arenas 1994: 101).

With the help of the painter Jorge Camacho, who was visiting Cuba in 1967, Arenas smuggled the manuscript of *El mundo alucinante, una novela de aventuras* out of the country, after which it was published as *Le Monde hallucinant* (Paris: Seuil, 1968). This was followed by Spanish editions in Mexico City

---

2   For Arenas's own assessment of the process of creation of this novel, see *El color del verano*'s 'Prólogo', found in the middle of the book (Arenas 1991: 246–50) and *Antes que anochezca*'s 'Introducción. El fin' (Arenas 1994: 9–16).

(Editorial Diógenes, 1969) and Buenos Aires (Tiempo Contemporáneo, 1970).[3] These editions were followed by the English translation by Gordon Brotherston, *Hallucinations: Being an Account of the Life and Adventures of Friar Servando Teresa de Mier* (New York: Harper & Row, 1971). These publications might have been indications of his success; yet, in Arenas's own words:

> En Cuba, el impacto de la crítica de la edición de *El mundo alucinante* en su versión francesa, se convirtió para mí en un golpe absolutamente negativo desde el punto de vista oficial. Fui puesto en la mirilla de la Seguridad del Estado, ya no sólo como un tipo conflictivo que había escrito novelas como *El mundo alucinante* o *Celestino antes del alba*, que eran textos irreverentes que no le hacían apología al régimen (que más bien lo criticaban), sino que, además, había cometido la osadía de sacar, clandestinamente, aquellas obras, y publicarlas sin el permiso, naturalmente, de Nicolás Guillén que era el preidente [*sic*] de la UNEAC. (Arenas 1994: 143)

Arenas's situation was complicated even further after his arrest in 1973, which he details in his autobiography (Arenas 1994: 181–4). According to Arenas, the arrest occurred after he and a friend had sex with a couple of youths at Guanabo beach, youths who allegedly ended up robbing him. When they called the police, Arenas and his friend were accused of the homosexual molestation of the young men. Arenas comments: 'olvidaba un artículo de la ley castrista que dice que, en el caso de que un homosexual cometa un delito erótico, basta con la denuncia de una persona para que él mismo pueda ser encausado' (1994: 182). To this charge was added the fact that he was publishing abroad without the required approval of UNEAC (1994: 182). Arenas initially managed to escape from prison, but was recaptured and remained incarcerated from 1974 to early 1976. During this period he had the second novel of his quintet published in France as *Le Palais des très blanches mouffettes* (Paris: Seuil, 1975). It was also published in German.[4]

Arenas was able to leave the country during the Mariel boatlift in 1980, and in 1982 his first novel was republished by Seix Barral, in Barcelona, with the new title *Cantando en el pozo*. This was followed by an English translation by Andrew Hurley entitled *Singing from the Well* (New York: Viking, 1987). In this last decade of his life, from 1980 to 1990 and now in exile, Arenas also published his poetry

---

3 Other editions in Spanish include Barcelona: Montesinos, 1981; Barcelona: Tusquets, 1997; 2001; and Madrid: Cátedra, 2008, edited by Enrico Mario Santí, among others.

4 Publications following Arenas's exile in the US include an edition of *El palacio de las blanquísimas mofetas* (Barcelona: Editorial Argos Vergara, 1983), and the English translation by Andrew Hurley, *The Palace of the White Skunks* (New York: Viking, 1990). Archival research, however, reveals that this novel dates back to a Havana version of 1966–69; see Reinaldo Arenas Papers, Manuscripts Division at Princeton University, Series I. A. Novels and Novellas, Box 10, folders 1–4. A definitve version published in Caracas by Monte Ávila Editores, in 1980, was disowned by Arenas (see Box 11, folders 1–2, used by permission of the Princeton University Libraries).

books *El Central* (Barcelona: Seix Barral, 1981), *Voluntad de vivir manifestándose* (Madrid: Betania, 1989) and *Leprosorio (Trilogía poética)* (Madrid: Betania, 1990) – completed while writing *El color del verano* – and for the theatre *Persecución (cinco piezas de teatro experimental)* (Miami: Universal, 1986). He also published the book of essays, *Necesidad de libertad* (Mexico City: Kosmos, 1986), as well as *Plebiscito a Fidel Castro* (in collaboration with Jorge Camacho) (Madrid: Betania, 1990). In addition, Arenas brought out the short story collection *Termina el desfile* (Barcelona: Seix Barral, 1981), which includes eight short stories written in the 1960s and one written in 1980 (the latter giving the title to the collection), and the narrative *La vieja rosa* (Caracas: Librería Cruz del Sur, 1980).

Arenas's typical method of writing and rewriting is documented by the author himself (1994: 249, 148) particularly with reference to the manuscript of the third novel of the *pentagonía*, *Otra vez el mar* (which he left under the roof tiles in the last place he lived before going to prison, although to his surprise the manuscript was taken, allegedly by the police). The rewritten novel was published in Barcelona by Argos Vergara in 1982, and in English translation by Andrew Hurley as *Farewell to the Sea, a Novel of Cuba* (New York: Viking, 1986). Other major publications include the short novel *Arturo, la estrella más brillante* (Barcelona: Montesinos, 1984), published in English translation by Andrew Hurley as *The Brightest Star*, in *Old Rosa: A Novel in Two Stories* (New York: Grove Press, 1989). Other publications include the novels *La loma del ángel* (Barcelona: DADOR, 1987), *El asalto* (Miami: Universal, 1990), *El portero* (Miami: Universal, 1990) and *Viaje a La Habana* (Miami: Universal, 1990); but I suggest that it is in *El color del verano o nuevo jardín de las delicias* (Miami: Universal, 1991) that Arenas particularly marks an end – the death of the author – and a beginning, which would constitute a new way of structuring his writing in line with more postmodern narrative practices. As the first publisher of this novel (Ediciones Universal, in Miami) states on the copyright page: 'Estando este libro en imprenta falleció el autor, Reinaldo Arenas [7 Dec. 1990]. Sabiendo que su salud era muy precaria, dejó instrucciones en carta del 23 de noviembre de 1990, para que las revisiones y el cuidado quedaran en manos de su amigo, Carlos Victoria. Ediciones Universal agradece a Carlos Victoria su interés y dedicación en la preparación y revisión de este libro' (Arenas 1991: copyright page). While the copyright of the novel is 1990, the year of the author's suicide, the first Spanish language edition is dated 1991, following revisions by the late Cuban novelist Carlos Victoria, mentioned above.[5] However, despite

---

5   Carlos Victoria confirmed this in conversation when I visited him at his home in Miami on 28 October 2003. Based on manuscript research, the notebook for the novel dates back to 1977 in Cuba and the final period of writing, in the US, was from 1987 to 1990 (see Reinaldo Arenas Papers, Series I. A. Novels and Novellas, Box 3, folder 1, used by permission of the Princeton University Libraries). The book was finished in 1990, as documented in folders 5–8, which include the manuscript of the first version of 1990, first published by Universal in 1991.

his success in literary terms, it was not until 1992 that Arenas was fully catapulted on to the international market in Spanish by Tusquets Editores, when they started publishing his works with the first edition of *Antes que anochezca* in April.

As he documents in his autobiography, *Antes que anochezca*, Arenas spent the last few years of his life under the shadow of death after being diagnosed with AIDS in the winter of 1987, and began writing *El color del verano* while in hospital (Arenas 1994: 12). This was meant to be the fourth novel of what he called his quintet; yet he was able to first finish what was to become the fifth novel, *El asalto*, which he had started writing in Cuba.[6] For Arenas, *El color del verano* 'resume gran parte de mi vida, especialmente mi juventud, todo desde luego en forma imaginativa y desenfadada. También es una obra que cuenta la historia de un dictador envejecido y enloquecido, y que toca descarnadamente el tema homosexual, tema tabú para casi todos los cubanos y para casi todo el género humano' (Arenas 1994: 14–15).

I have singled out *El color del verano* for this study because in its own process of writing and rewriting, and its depiction of an underground culture, it is representative of the fluidity and decentralization of Cuban culture that I put forward here. Moreover, *El color del verano* is the only novel in which Arenas uses the carnival as a narrative technique to create a polyphony that in its dialogism subverts what he sees as the monolithic discourse of the state. Arenas himself placed *El color del verano* within the context of the *pentagonía* thus:

> *Celestino antes del alba* inicia el ciclo de una pentagonía que comienza con la infancia del poeta narrador en un medio primitivo y ahistórico; continúa con la adolescencia del personaje durante la dictadura batistiana y precastrista –*El palacio de las blanquísimas mofetas*–; sigue con su obra central, *Otra vez el mar*, que abarca el proceso revolucionario cubano desde 1958 hasta 1970, la estalinización del mismo y el fin de una esperanza creadora; prosigue con *El color del verano*, novela que transcurre hacia fines del siglo XX en medio de un inmenso y alucinante carnaval en el que la juventud toma masivamente la misma Isla de Cuba, que desasida de su plataforma, parte hacia lo desconocido. *El color del verano* revela las insólitas peripecias y avatares de un dictador vitalicio, viejo y enloquecido y la vida subterránea de una juventud desgarrada, erotizada, rebelde y a veces envilecida, pero negada a aceptar la prisión marina que habita. La pentagonía culmina con *El asalto*, suerte de árida fábula sobre el destino

---

6   The manuscripts date from 1974 to 1988. See Reinaldo Arenas Papers, Manuscripts Division at Princeton University, Series I. A. Novels and Novellas, Box 1, folder 6, first version, Havana, 1974; folders 7–8, second version, 1988, up to a fifth version in folder 15, dated Havana 1974–New York 1988, and a sixth version in folders 16–17 (used by permission of the Princeton University Libraries).

del género humano cuando el estado se impone por encima de sus sueños o proyectos. (Arenas 1991: back cover)[7]

Arenas further asserts that *El color del verano*

> pretende reflejar, sin zalamerías ni altisonantes principios, la vida entre picaresca y desgarrada de gran parte de la juventud cubana, sus deseos de ser jóvenes, de existir como tales. Predomina aquí la visión subterránea de un mundo homosexual que seguramente nunca aparecerá en ningún periódico del mundo y mucho menos en Cuba. Esta novela está intrínsicamente [*sic*] arraigada a una de las épocas más vitales de mi vida [...]. *El color del verano* es un mundo que si no lo escribo se perderá fragmentado en la memoria de los que lo conocieron. (1991: 249)

In chapter 1 I analyse how in *El color del verano* Arenas creates, through carnival, an upside-down world that he uses to symbolically represent the destruction of the floating cork island, which for him is also a metaphor for the destruction of Castro's regime. He thus uses the narrative as a form of personal revenge against the state. I shall examine critically how Arenas's novel exemplifies the carnivalization of discourse. The carnival permeates the novel in its textual images, plot and language. I explore how carnival within the novel becomes a mechanism to create dialogism through the use of the grotesque, parody and the constant erasure of the boundaries between performance and reality. The textual carnival, I suggest, is a discursive technique employed to subvert the established system, and is the only chronotope where the homosexual's discourse can reach the centre, as opposed to remaining ostracized in the margins of society.

Chapter 2 focuses on *Máscaras* by Leonardo Padura Fuentes. This is the third novel of the tetralogy *Las cuatro estaciones* (*Pasado perfecto*, *Vientos de cuaresma*, *Máscaras* and *Paisaje de otoño*) although it was the first Mario Conde novel published in Spain by Tusquets in 1997. Padura has also published two more novels with the detective Mario Conde as a protagonist: *Adiós, Hemingway* (2006) and *La neblina del ayer* (2009). Each novel in the Conde series opens with a case for the detective, which functions as a pretext for Padura to explore the most obscure aspects of Cuban reality. From the Mario Conde series I have chosen to study *Máscaras* because it is the only novel in which Padura explores the figure of the transvestite, and it is also the work whose literariness, a homage to literature itself, is most explicit. This is seen in its use of intertextuality, something which I claim is representative of the writing of this period,

---

7   This text was sent by Arenas to the publisher Universal together with the manuscripts of *El color del verano* and *El asalto* and is reproduced on the back cover of this edition. The author himself places his *pentagonía* in his 'Prólogo' within the novel (1991: 249–50), where he limits the period covered in *Otra vez el mar* to a year less (from 1958 to 1969).

even if it is true that Padura, as a sanctioned writer, presents a more nuanced view of Cuban society on the island that at a first glance seems to be at odds with the more critical stance of the exile writers studied here. However, I shall explore how Padura uses both intertextuality and the figure of the transvestite as dialogic narrative strategies to subvert monolithic notions of literature, culture and identity. From this perspective he coincides with a wider aspect of Cuban literature beyond national borders, including that produced by Cuban writers in Barcelona, the US or Paris.

This chapter examines how Padura deploys the figure of the male transvestite as a dialogic voice, as a product of intertextuality, whose gender ambiguity undermines the monolithic and homogeneous idea of Cubanness recognized by the characters who represent the state. According to Martin Franzbach in his article 'La re-escritura de la novela policíaca cubana', published in *Todas las islas la isla*:

> Una de las consecuencias visibles que el 'período especial' ha tenido para la literatura cubana es la re-escritura de la novela policíaca. Por ella entiendo una inversión radical de la ideología, hasta entonces afirmativa del sistema político, expresada por este género, para, en adelante, poder competir con un estilo y paradigmas nuevos en el mercado capitalista del libro. (2000: 69)

In this sense, Padura is a pioneer in transforming the figure of the policeman of the Cuban narrative of the revolution from a closed, monologic character, who does not question either himself or the system, into a dialogic one.

Chapter 3 studies Abilio Estévez's *Tuyo es el reino* and examines the process of creating a Barthesian infinite text by means of which the island is recreated endlessly. *Tuyo es el reino* (1997) was the first and only novel written and published by Estévez during the 1990s. Following on from this successful text he published the novels *Los palacios distantes* (2002), *Inventario secreto de La Habana* (2004), *El navegante dormido* (2008), *El bailarín ruso de Montecarlo* (2010) and *El año del calipso* (2012), all with the same publishing house (Tusquets) in Barcelona. He has also published a collection of short stories, *El horizonte y otros regresos* (1998); a book of poetic prose, *Manual de tentaciones* (1999); and a collection of three pieces for theatre, *Ceremonias para actores desesperados* (2004). I examine *Tuyo es el reino* because it is here that Estévez stresses the literariness of the novel itself. *Tuyo es el reino* becomes a literary artifice through which the author explores the process of creation itself, creating a polyphonic text in which any authoritative discourse is challenged. In this novel the word acquires greater importance than the facts described. Estévez also transforms the act of creation into a political one when he describes the triumph of Castro's revolution and its consequences using the future tense. As Estévez has stated in several interviews, in *Tuyo es el reino* the author has tried to recover and recreate his childhood. This was also the only novel written by Estévez while he was in Cuba, and it was awarded the Premio de la Crítica in

Cuba in 1999 and the award for Best Foreign Book in France in 2000. Thus it is not the work of an exilic writer as such, but it is still one that shares in the dialogism of the Cuban novel of the 1990s that I examine in this study. (It also displays the introspective prose style adopted by the author himself once in exile, as seen, for example, in his *Inventario secreto de La Habana*.)

I shall show how the text/island subverts any established notion of reality, truth and national identity. This process of creation becomes a mechanism used by the characters of the novel to reach self-knowledge, and a way of inscribing the self within the collective memory of the nation. At the same time, I discuss how the notion of the author-God in the novel is challenged by means of inter-textuality and by the resulting polyphony that ultimately subverts monologic and hegemonic discourses of authority. Here, I mobilize the theoretical notions of intertextuality, palimpsest and writing in the second degree to analyse a text that subverts the traditional roles of both author and reader.

Chapters 4, 5 and 6 focus on the different erotic discourses used by three Cuban writers who now live in exile. Here I follow Julia Kristeva and Madeline Cámara, among others, in relation to feminist studies. In Cámara's words,

> De igual modo que la escritura de mujer, afirma Julia Kristeva, es intrínsicamente [*sic*] disidente del Poder, una crítica que se considere a sí misma feminista siempre efectuará una lectura reconstructora de jerarquías y binarismos, rescatando la voz o incluso lo no dicho por los marginados. (2002: 17)

It is my purpose in this study to examine critically how women novelists of the last twenty years have internalized feminist postulates and adopted a subversive feminist discourse in their creative products to refocus and challenge patriarchal concepts concerning the role of women in society. As Cámara states,

> [E]l discurso femenino subversivo es aquel que la escritora produce de modo consciente, más allá, pero incorporando implícitamente, los códigos del lenguaje pre-simbólico que provienen de la condición biológica y sicológica del ser mujer que el texto reproduce o capta. Se trata de una elaboración textual e ideológica de un mensaje cuya subversividad estaría cifrada, no sólo en su forma novedosa o en su contenido revolucionario, sino en el nuevo lugar de enunciación que crea y en las condiciones emancipadoras de recepción y circulación que propone. La escritora feminista irrumpe con su palabra desde un lugar de la tradición literaria del que ella se apropia, y se dirige a su lector/a para actuar deconstructoramente contra prejuicios establecidos que asientan una imagen discriminada/manipulada de la mujer. Su texto se escribe desde la libertad y la convoca. (2002: 19)

In order to examine this aspect of a writing that both encourages and is free to exploit new feminist viewpoints, I study in chapter 4 Daína Chaviano's

Casa de juegos. I use Kristeva's semiological concepts, based on psychoanalytic theory, to posit that in *Casa de juegos* Chaviano uses erotic discourse to represent how the feminine subject goes from the semiotic to the symbolic and how the repressive drives of the unconscious constitute a subversive force that challenges any authoritative discourse and any attempt at imposing a definition of woman. I also analyse the relevance of eroticism in this novel as an instrument to fight oppression. Chaviano's *Casa de juegos* is the second novel of a series written outside Cuba and entitled *La Habana oculta*. The novels that form this series are *El hombre, la hembra y el hambre* (Planeta, 1998), *Casa de juegos* (Planeta, 1999), *Gata encerrada* (Planeta, 2001) and *La isla de los amores infinitos* (Grijalbo, 2006). According to Chaviano's own website, *La Habana oculta*:

> Es un ciclo de novelas que Daína Chaviano comenzó a escribir después de salir de Cuba. Aunque cada obra puede leerse de manera independiente, tienen elementos que las unen. Por ejemplo, los personajes de una novela pueden aparecer brevemente en otra. [...] En estas obras, La Habana es el punto de partida para llegar a otros universos –fantásticos o mágicos– que conducen a sus personajes a descubrimientos inesperados sobre sí mismos. Cada novela explora facetas diferentes de la espiritualidad: la reencarnación, la magia celta, el espiritismo o mediumnidad, los cultos afrocubanos...
>
> Pero La Habana de estas obras no sólo oculta mundos místicos. También muestra una realidad social, a veces incomprensible y asfixiante para quienes la habitan. Las experiencias de esa realidad social impelen a sus habitantes a escapar, recurriendo a métodos de carácter mágico o paranormal que los ayudan a liberar sus espíritus, como única vía de supervivencia.[8]

Despite being part of this series, I single out *Casa de juegos* because it is the only novel that can be considered an erotic novel per se. Although in all the novels of this series love is a driving theme, it is in *Casa de juegos* that the author develops and exploits the performativity of eroticism. This eroticism in turn is developed alongside Afro-Cuban rituals, and becomes a site of resistance – in this case for the protagonist, though in general sexuality is at the core of the period that I study in this book. Here, I also examine how the author universalizes the syncretic deities or *orishas* beyond the merely Afro-Cuban context and even beyond the fluidity of names that exists in syncretism itself, in an attempt to Europeanize and universalize the island itself. Cuba as a 'casa de juegos' is also at the centre of both randomness and double moral standards, where truth and authenticity are questionable monologic stances.

---

[8]   See http://www.dainachaviano.com/pag/serieDetail.aspx? id=1&lang=esp (accessed 3 September 2013).

In chapter 5, I concentrate on a study of the erotic discourse in Yanitzia Canetti's *Al otro lado*, informed by Hélène Cixous's notion of femininity and women's writing (Cixous 1980). I claim that Canetti inscribes femininity into the world of the symbolic in order to challenge classic representations of women and patriarchal language through the use of erotic discourse. Thus I suggest that Canetti focuses on transforming her protagonist to show that she needs to recreate herself through a new language that positions woman as a producer of meaning. Women appear in this novel as fluid and as inhabiting the interstitial identity of the in-between to which Cixous refers in a theoretical context, a writing 'infinitely dynamized by an incessant process of exchange from one subject to another' (Cixous 1980: 254) that in Kristeva's work would occupy a space in a state of flux between the semiotic and the symbolic.[9] I shall consider how this feminine writing subverts the patriarchal order in a novel in which the feminine subject tries to find her place within the symbolic order and thus challenges the myths and female figures that populate the history of literature and mythology, the clear product of a masculine vision.

Canetti's *Al otro lado* was the second and last novel published by the author during the 1990s. While in *Novelita Rosa* (Versal, 1997) the author describes the life of a Latin American migrant in the United States, the setting of *Al otro lado* is Cuba. Despite the Cuban setting, Canetti has explained that the process of creation itself, in a manner that recalls Arenas's writing, took place between Cuba and the US. Therefore, the process of creation of the novel shows the fluidity and decentralization of Cuban culture as it moves beyond the shores of the island nation. I have selected this novel in order to explore how the author uses the female body as both a feminine and feminist strategy with which to undermine monologic discourses on feminine subjectivity as applied to the nameless protagonist.[10]

In chapter 6, I analyse the use of erotic language that characterizes Zoé Valdés' protagonist in *La nada cotidiana*. Valdés, who has followers and detractors perhaps in equal measure, is a pioneer in the use of vulgar language. I shall study how, through the use of humour, she challenges any possibility of having a traditional male erotic discourse. I emphasize how her gaze is genuinely feminine, more so than that of the other two women writers that I have selected, in attempting to show the plurality of voices and technical approaches at the same time as coinciding in the creation of polyphonic texts.

---

9   Eliana Rivero, for one, has referred to a post-Benedict Anderson 'new lexicon of our identity constructions' in which the 'in-between or interstitial identities, diasporas, community-building across borders, cosmopolitanisms, trans-migrants, hyphenated ethnicity', among other terms allow us to rethink place and displacement in terms of identity (Rivero 2005: 39).

10   In the first decade of the twenty-first century Canetti has also published a collection of short stories, *La muerte nuestra de cada día* (CBH Books, 2009); the novel *Adiós, best seller* (CBH Books, 2010), and a new version of *Novelita Rosa*, entitled *La vida es color de rosa* (CBH Books, 2010).

Zoé Valdés is a prolific writer who was first known as a poet in Cuba but who has made a name for herself internationally based on her novels, several of which were published during the 1990s. These include *Sangre azul* (Havana: Letras Cubanas, 1993; Barcelona: Emecé, 1996); *La nada cotidiana* (Barcelona: Emecé, 1995) – widely translated into other languages, including English, French, Portuguese, German, Italian, Dutch, Greek, Turkish, Finnish and Swedish; *La hija del embajador* (Palma de Mallorca: Bitzoc, 1995); *Querido primer novio* (Barcelona: Planeta, 1999); *Café Nostalgia* (Barcelona: Planeta, 1997); *Te di la vida entera* (Barcelona: Planeta, 1996); and *Cólera de ángeles* (Barcelona: Lumen, 1996).

I have chosen to focus on *La nada cotidiana* because it is Valdés' most successful work in terms of international impact, and marks a before and after point in terms of thematic approach which led the way for the international boom in the market for the Cuban novel in the mid-1990s. As Linda S. Howe has written,

> Even when Cuban critics describe *La nada cotidiana* as trivial and poorly written, they acknowledge the tremendous impact the work has had on European literary circles, especially in France, Spain, and Germany. The fact that Cuban officials condemned Valdés's book as a compilation of tawdry lies confirms that they found it significant enough to complain about. (2004: 63)

For Miguel González Abellás (2008), *La nada cotidiana* belongs to a *sexagonía*, a collection of six novels (*La nada cotidiana, Te di la vida entera, La hija del embajador, Café nostalgia, Querido primer novio* and *Milagro en Miami*), but I have singled out *La nada cotidiana* because in its dialogism and eroticism it marks a threshold. According to Valdés the novel was written in 1994, during and about the Special Period, just before the author left the island. I suggest that this novel anticipates and condenses the key elements of the author's narrative: the socio-political situation in Cuba, exile, eroticism and feminine subjectivity; all topics to which Valdés will return in the so-called *sexagonía*.

As José Quiroga states in his introduction to Madeline Cámara's book *La letra rebelde*,

> Por lo general, la figura intelectual con la que se comprometió la revolución era masculina, y el discurso social era producido y dirigido hacia el hombre: el guerrillero, el buen revolucionario, el patriota. Las miradas sentimentales eran dirigidas a figuras como el Che, o los Padres de la Patria. La revolución, como bien apunta Cámara, no produjo una voz autoral de mujer o un personaje femenino que pudiera plantear una política cultural en la cual el enfrentamiento se diera de forma alterna, distinta. Una historia percibida como una historia de luchas, produce entes luchadores, nunca un 'patriotismo suave', para citar una frase de Rafael Rojas. La ideología triunfante, si bien rechazaba la fácil objetivación de la mujer en una serie televisiva o en un

> bolero, por poner dos ejemplos, sí esperaba que la compañera se uniera a la lucha revolucionaria en condición de acompañante. Para el estado victorioso el espacio femenino era la contrapartida al espacio masculino y no un espacio con sus propios códigos, recursos, problemas y respuestas. Y era en el espacio masculino donde se libraba la batalla, se tomaban decisiones, o se discutía la división entre teoría y praxis. […] La Federación de Mujeres Cubanas se preocupó por las condiciones de la mujer y criticó el machismo y la misoginia. Sin embargo, en tanto la solución a estos problemas no fuera de índole estructural y no atentara contra el estado de derecho implantado en la isla, la crítica no pasaba del nivel de las formas en las cuales se llevaba a cabo el proceso. Y frente a tal proceso, y a la voz un tanto monológica que presentaba, lo único restante para la mujer era utilizar las tretas del débil. (Cámara 2002: 11)

Now, if 'the tricks of the weak', an echo of the seminal work by Josefina Ludmer, point to silence as a trick, and in particular to the use that Ludmer makes of it (exemplified by Sor Juana Inés de la Cruz), Zoé Valdés does not seek shelter in such 'tretas del débil'; rather, she does the opposite. Valdés appropriates the male-dominant discourse of the street ('la jerga de la calle') and focuses on turning the female position from one of object (the 'acompañante') to producer of feminine subjectivities and discourse, capable of challenging the traditional patriarchal space of the home that somehow continued in public life in revolutionary Cuba, and which was also exploited in Cuban film.[11]

Nissa Torrents' description of women's position in revolutionary Cuba, in what today could be seen as a dated text, is still valid in contextualizing the time up to the Special Period at least. I shall quote at length to illustrate this point concerning the role of women vis-à-vis the revolution, despite changes in the law that attempted to secure a fifty-fifty share between men and women, at least in terms of 'labores del hogar':

> It was taken for granted that all women wanted to contribute their best to the building of the 'new man'. To this day, there has been no mention of a new woman, the owners of the word sheltering themselves under the excuse that in Castilian the collective is masculine. And how better could a female contribute to the new society than by giving birth, i.e., by fulfilling her biological condition? Next to the 26th of July and the New Year, Mother's Day is Cuba's biggest holiday and today it is not a pretext for a consumer frenzy but an exaltation of women's role in society, which remains the same

---

11   We can think of films such as *Los pájaros tirándole a la escopeta* (1982), directed by Rolando Díaz; *Retrato de Teresa* (1979), directed by Pastor Vega; or the clash between generations of women in *Plaff* (1988), directed by Juan Carlos Tabío. A change of aesthetics focusing on female subjectivity can be found in the short films 'Adriana' (directed by Mayra Segura), 'Isabel' (directed by Héctor Veitía), 'Julia' (directed by Mayra Vilasís), 'Laura' (directed by Ana Rodríguez) and 'Zoe' (directed by Mario Crespo), which together form *Mujer transparente* (1990).

as in the old, patriarchal, pre-revolutionary times. As in Soviet Russia, Cuba declared the nuclear family the mainstay of revolutionary society, dismissing Engelian fears of oppression and repression. The admirable Family Code of 1975 corrected many injustices and imbalances, but the fifty-fifty share of household and parental tasks that it codified remains to this day a noble expression of wishful thinking, and the double shift, effectively, prevents women's progress and promotion in all spheres of social life. Women's magazines and mass media in general still talk about 'helping' women in their household chores, thus reinforcing the notion that they are essentially 'feminine' in nature. And Castro's definition of women as 'the workshop of life' effectively created as many obstacles as it may have aimed to demolish by 'socializing' the act of motherhood. (1991: 176–7)

Torrents' work, published in 1991, also serves to mark a pre-1990s Cuba in relation to women's writing, while I claim that women have managed to impose a new aesthetic shift in Cuban literature more recently, particularly women writers who left the island in the 1990s. In Torrents' words,

While in the advanced capitalist countries the women's movement has led to an explosion of woman writers and film makers, in Cuba they are rare not only in film making but also as novelists. Before and after 1959, women appear more often as poets and even as short-story writers, activities that do not seem to require the same level of continuity and the famous room of one's own, once longed for by the very bourgeois writer from Bloomsbury, Virginia Woolf. (1991: 178)

It is worth noting in this context that Zoé Valdés was an established poet when she left the country, and Daína Chaviano was a short story writer, while they are now mostly recognized as novelists. Having said this, it is not my purpose to undermine the importance of short fiction in the Cuban context. As Catherine Davies has rightly observed, 'Given the dearth of novels written by women, short fiction (which is cheap, easy to obtain, easy to consume, particularly by women who are short of time and space, and more readable than poetry) is likely to be the genre most popular among women readers' (1997: 145). In addition, given the current situation and political climate, censorship and the cultural divisions that persist, many of the novels published by exiles do not reach the island's readership. The same happens to be true, in reverse, for Cuban authors on the island who are unable to market their books abroad. Few writers from Cuba have managed to attract the attention of the major publishing houses in Spain so as to enjoy a wider international readership. Exceptions are Leonardo Padura (perhaps the best-known and most widely translated Cuban author living on the island at the moment), Abilio Estévez (who managed to publish with Tusquets before leaving the country) and other novelists such as Pedro Juan Gutiérrez and Ena Lucía Portela.

Overall, in relation to chapters 4, 5 and 6, I demonstrate that in the three novels written by women, eroticism rather than silence is the 'trick of the weak' that challenges any monologic attempt at labelling the feminine. All three, Chaviano, Canetti and Valdés, in their use of eroticism in their texts, adopt 'esa arma desestabilizadora del control ideológico: la comunicación desde el cuerpo' (Cámara 2002: 33). According to Madeline Cámara,

> desde los tiempos de la conquista sólo a los hombres les ha sido dado participar del Poder político y hacer circular su palabra en los discursos de la autoridad. La nueva horneada de escritoras latinoamericanas, de la cual son parte las cubanas, pretenden subvertir esa discriminación pero lo han hecho recuperando en sus nuevos modos de decir, todo aquello que ya ha sido escrito en los márgenes del Poder, haciendo su mímica y su parodia. Hablo de la literatura de memorias: diarios, crónicas, cartas, o la de corte lírico – fantástico, o incluso áquella de confesiones donde se sublimaban los deseos eróticos, que parecería restringirse a lo privado, o al dominio del sueño o la locura y que fue la práctica generalizada de la literatura femenina en las colonias latinoamericanas hasta bien entrado nuestro siglo. De esta historia de cómo burlar la censura y el silencio han salido en parte los estilos transgresores que hoy celebramos.
>   Una vez en circunstancia de exilio, también se hace notar la condición contracanónica de la escritura femenina, resultando de una lógica reacción contra el falogocentrismo. Esta puede ser una de las razones que explique porqué esta novelística cubana […] trata de buscar otros modos de nombrar la Patria que quedó atrás, o áquella adonde llegamos en busca de libertad. En estas autoras no se convierte el tema de la ciudad natal o adoptiva en la apología del pasado o del presente. La vitalidad y sensualidad de las descripciones de costumbres, cuando éstas son pertinentes, la dislocación espacio/temporal al servicio de la perspectiva fantástica y la erotización de los espacios públicos, han sido las estrategias escogidas por estas autoras. (2002: 121–2)

These strategies highlighted by Cámara occupy my attention in this book, which contextualizes this research along the lines established by Debra Castillo in *Talking Back*, where she states that

> the women writers of Latin America are in some sense privileged in their accessibility to the peripheries of culture, licensing them not only to speak of issues relating to private spaces but also to speak to and between and as intermediary for other marginalized groups: implicitly, the disadvantaged social groups. (1992: 58)

Furthermore, as Castillo argues,

> Since there is no syntax, no lexicon outside of language, women writers must refine such tools as they are given, transforming vocabularies and

focusing attention on particular usages so as to achieve a greater working knowledge of the byways of cultural production. Commentary is intended not only to describe the ellipsis but also to recuperate, reintegrate, recodify the fragmented language of the female body, to construct, if such a thing is possible, a tentative dictionary of the unspoken. (1992: 65)

I approach chapters 4 to 6 through this line of research. I suggest that the new feminine language is created through the female body. In addition, I show how Chaviano, Canetti and Valdés resignify phallocentric, patriarchal language by means of eroticism. All three women writers discussed in this study use eroticism and the sexual experiences of their characters to reflect and examine the inner workings of patriarchy and the gender struggle, in a dialogue between the private and the political spheres. I demonstrate that both the private space and the public sphere are intermingled and the criticism of patriarchy in the novels is closely related to political criticism. In these novels the protagonists undergo a process of self-awareness that goes hand in hand with their political awareness. These three authors use the revolutionary Cuba of the Special Period as the setting of their novels, and their protagonists appear as opponents of authoritarianism. The protagonists of these three novels criticize the contradictions of a social revolutionary agenda and reject the collective project in order to pay attention to their fragmented subjectivities, which inscribe the feminine in the social context of the nation. For them, sexual oppression signifies political oppression, as women are excluded from the modes of discourse production.

In conclusion, I shall show that, although in the 1990s many of the novels written by men had male protagonists and were written from a masculine point of view, there has been a clear boom in novels written by Cuban women writers from a feminist perspective. As I demonstrate in the last three chapters of this work, eroticism has become a new tool used by female writers to examine feminine subjectivity and to denounce patriarchal society. Overall, the conclusion emphasizes the main issues studied in this book with reference to dialogism and polyphony, in relation to carnival and simulacra, intertextuality, the rewriting of history and the resulting palimpsest, erotic discourse, the body as a feminine strategy used by women authors and the use of language to particular effects between the semiotic and the symbolic. It is the intention of this study to show that Cuban literature is not simply divided along political lines or binary cultural divides, and that the literature produced by Cuban writers in exile still belongs to the national discourse.

1

Carnival and Simulacra in Reinaldo Arenas's
El color del verano

This chapter focuses on an analysis of *El color del verano* in the light of Bakhtin's dialogic theory. I shall explore the Bakhtinian concepts of carnival, dialogism and the polyphonic novel, concentrating my analysis on the concept of carnival as reflected in this novel and its various functions within it. Another important aspect of my analysis is the use of the mask as a performance of identity, as it often appears related to the concept of representation, theatre and carnival.

There has been a boom in the number of critical studies focused on the life and works of Reinaldo Arenas in the last two decades, particularly by critics interested in queer studies. It is not by chance that there are over 300 entries in the MLA International Bibliography alone dedicated to works on Arenas. However, when it comes to the study of *El color del verano* in particular, the research is noticeably thinner on the ground. The most significant works are those of Rita Molinero (1994), Carmelo Esterrich (1997), Suzanne Kaebnick (1997), Humberto López-Cruz (1997b, 1998, 1999), Dinora Cardoso (2001), Enrique Del Risco (2003), Laurie Vickroy (2005), Rosa M. Díez-Cobo (2007), Roberto Ignacio Díaz (2007), Christopher Winks (2008), Daphne Grace (2009) and José Ramón Vilahomat (2010).

López-Cruz has already explored the important role played by Arenas's narrative in creating a site of resistance and subversion with reference to 'la necesidad de escribir la historia oficial' (1999: 25), although he does not connect this point in his study with the chronotope of the carnival which will be at the core of my analysis here. With reference to the narrative carnival, Díez-Cobo has noted that *El color del verano* is 'una obra plenamente postmoderna' (2007: n.p.). Most critics also agree in highlighting the importance of Menippean satire (Díez-Cobo 2007; López-Cruz 1999), with its characteristic fragmentation, in a work in which Arenas ridicules officialdom. Vilahomat has contributed a full article on the 'sujeto menipeo' (2010: 11).

These critics have also pinpointed the importance of carnival, the grotesque and the hyperbolic sexuality that abounds in this text. However, even if most of them have referred to Bakhtin's theory as a useful tool for the analysis of the novel, they seem to have forsworn a fully detailed Bakhtinian reading, which is my intention here. In this chapter I shall explore the dynamics and characteristics of Arenas's carnival, the 'upside-down world' presented in Bakhtinian theory. In doing so, I shall demonstrate how this carnival becomes the legitimated chronotope for subaltern voices, and the site of resistance and subversion of official discourses. I also document the dialogic and polyphonic nature of this novel, its multivoicedness and the mechanism of role-play permitted by the masks and the disguises used during carnival. All of these are key issues for understanding Arenas's works, and the dialogism present in more recent Cuban narratives, but surprisingly they have been largely ignored by critics.

In conjunction with Bakhtin's theory, I shall consider *El color del verano* as a paradigm of the polyphonic novel. I understand the polyphonic novel as one in which we can hear a multiplicity of voices that maintain a dialogic relationship with one another: they complement, oppose, even contradict each other and at the same time each voice shows a specific perception of reality and the world. As Bakhtin claims, the polyphonic novel is 'A plurality of independent and unmerged voices and consciousnesses, a genuine polyphony of fully valid voices' (1984: 6).

On the other hand, a monologic novel, according to Bakhtin, is one in which,

> in the objective authorial world, objective in relation to the hero's consciousness; the construction of that authorial world with its points of view and finalizing definitions presupposes a fixed external position, a fixed authorial field of vision. The self-consciousness of the hero is inserted into this rigid framework, to which the hero has no access from within. (1984: 52)

In the context of the literary production of the 1990s in Cuba, the novel *Trilogía sucia de La Habana* by Pedro Juan Gutiérrez would be a good example of a monologic novel. It has a monologic and monolithic discourse; the only voice we can perceive is the voice of the narrator and his selective ideology. In Reinaldo Arenas's literary production, however, we can only find one monologic novel, *El asalto*. In contrast to the rest of Arenas's novels, in *El asalto* we only hear the oppressor's voice (the government in this case) but not the voice of the oppressed (the people).

In *El color del verano*, Arenas introduces the reader to a diversity of voices that represent Cuban society at the end of the twentieth century. Arenas transforms Cuban society into a purely homosexual one, and gives us an account of how these characters manage to survive within a system governed by an easily recognized dictator, Fifo, a grotesque caricature of Fidel Castro. Arenas creates an environment in which his characters try to survive in a totalitarian and repressive system where communication is almost impossible and there is neither sexual freedom nor the right to self-expression. As a reaction against the imposed isolation and the resulting lack of communication and impossibility of knowing the Other, and in opposition to the monolithic discourse where the only voice we hear is that of the government, we witness in *El color del verano* the creation of a Utopian chronotope that Bakhtin calls an 'upside-down world', that is, the carnival.[1] In this carnival we can find a multiplicity of voices that function in dialogue with one another and reveal their own viewpoint and ideology. These different viewpoints subvert the discourse of power and its official version of reality. Carnival constitutes a world in itself with its own rules, rules that subvert the established order, in which people who are marginalized, reasoning that they are ignored by the official discourse, find a place where their voices can be heard.[2] During carnival these subaltern voices begin to dominate the discourse and put up resistance against the authoritative discourse in power, subverting it. As Bakhtin himself has theorized in a different context, but which is applicable here, this authoritative discourse 'is privileged language that approaches us from without; it is distanced, taboo, and permits no play with its framing context. [...] It has great power over us, but only while in power; if ever dethroned it immediately becomes a dead thing, a relic' (1981: 424).

The communion of bodies through (homo)sexual intercourse can only take place with impunity (that is, without paying as high a price as imprisonment or even death) by means of the carnival. Thus sex, the creative act and ludic activities become acts of resistance against repression and only acquire real significance as ways of exercising freedom. As Perla Rozencvaig has written,

> las novelas de Arenas, a pesar de sus diferencias semánticas y/o estructurales, constituyen un cuerpo orgánico por el que se filtra una visión del mundo en correspondencia con una ideología fija: la constante búsqueda de un espacio liberador, sede de incesantes transgresiones. (1986: 7)

Moreover, I agree with Carmelo Esterrich when he states that Arenas's protagonist refuses to be part of the nation:

> el sujeto exílico homosexual rechaza terminantemente su ciudadanía estatal. [...] No promueve su inserción ni en la nación ni en el Estado. [...] El sujeto areniano no busca en ningún momento ser incluido en la comunidad – ni siquiera pide clemencia reconocida oficialmente o la creación de un espacio legítimo propio de él – sino que se mantiene al margen de los parámetros definibles de la nación, y fuera del Estado. (1997: 180)

---

[1]   For another novel which creates an upside-down world, see Yanitzia Canetti's *Al otro lado* (1997). In this novel the author presents as an upside-down world the prison where the protagonist has been trapped, a world without any logic where the guards walk using their hands.

[2]   Francisco Soto has studied the way in which *El color del verano* allows all those voices that the official vehicle of the Cuban revolution, the documentary novel, silences. He also examines critically how, despite the revolution, we still find marginal voices in Cuba, which can be heard in *El color del verano* (see Soto 1994).

This 'proyecto anticomunitario' that Esterrich mentions, and which 'se manifiesta en el campo sexual en *Otra vez el mar* y *El color del verano*' (1997: 181),
reveals the individual's marginal position. The motivation for this position is
the existence of a repressive state. According to Esterrich, we can appreciate
'dos aspectos de la comunidad que preocupan a Arenas: la comunidad como
homogeneizante y como exclusiva' (1997: 181). The individual feels himself to
be outside the government's parameters; in this case, homosexuality is one of
the features that provoke his detachment from the community.[3] The marginal
position of Arenas's characters must be understood as a rebellion against the
system that alienates them. The carnival, however, is 'ese espacio legítimo
propio' where, in opposition to Esterrich's statement, the norm is homosexuality and where the *locas* invade the centre. Although I agree with Esterrich's view
that 'Este sujeto no se hunde en la angustia sino que arrebatadoramente se da a
una batalla campal, […] una lucha tercamente criticona y desde el margen'
(1997: 181), I disagree with his assertion that

> Su condición en la *Pentagonía* es netamente exílica y no permite que esa
> postura se suplante por otra de más centralidad en la nación o el Estado. Aquí
> no hay un intento de normalizar o legitimizar al homosexual, sino todo lo
> contrario: mantenerlo fuera de la norma que para Arenas, como veremos, es
> siempre heterosexual y moralista. (1997: 181)

I believe that this position of 'netamente exílica' is substituted by a more central
position when, throughout carnival, the main players are the producers of the
predominant discourse. This chronotope, the carnival, whose norm is homosexuality in Arenas's text, thus legitimizes the homosexual body in society. As
Suzanne Kaebnick rightly emphasizes, 'According to Arenas, the end of Cuba's
exile, or alienation from itself, will be achieved when the maricón can come to
Cuba as herself [*sic*], a maricón' (1997: 106). Contrary to Esterrich's argument,
as cited above, it is during the carnival that the *maricón* can be who he really
is, and therefore the creation of a space for the homosexual is essential and
Arenas achieves this by the use of carnival. On this topic, Rita Molinero has
argued that 'hay también en esta novela una poética muy sugerente sobre el
espacio' (1994: 32). For her, 'las locas deambulan por sus calles en busca de un
espacio, que no poseen, donde desplegar su alegría o su tristeza' (1994: 132).

---

3   This is not exclusive to Arenas, or to exile writers. A similar concern can be found in the
film *Fresa y chocolate* and the short story written by Senel Paz, 'El lobo, el bosque y el hombre
nuevo' (Mexico City: Era, 1991), on which the film is based. Here the homosexual protagonist,
Diego, has the same problem: he tries to be accepted as a homosexual, revolutionary and religious
man. The problem begins when, because of his homosexuality, he is excluded from the system,
and he is left only two choices: to leave the country or to maintain a marginal position. Diego
decides to leave; on the other hand, the protagonist of *El color del verano* decides to stay as a
marginal subject, in an attempt to subvert the dominant system.

El color del verano represents this search for and formation of a utopian space in opposition to the dominant system.

Arenas goes further in the chapter entitled 'Virgilio Piñera lee sus poemas efímeros', where Piñera reads his poems in Olga Andreu's house. According to the narrator, he will read to an audience of *locas* here empowered to see the 'country' and what he denominates the 'counter-country', thus revealing that the homosexual belongs to the country's discourse and it is the state that is relegated to the role of the 'counter-country' that attempts to regulate homosexual desire:

> Vieron en fin, el país y el contrapaís. Porque cada país, como todas las cosas de este mundo, tienen su contrario; y lo contrario a un país es su contrapaís, las fuerzas oscuras que tratan de que sólo perdure la superficialidad y el horror, y que todo lo noble, hermoso, valiente, vital (el verdadero país) desaparezcan. El contrapaís (de alguna forma lo revelaba el poema) es la ramplonería monopolítica y rígida; el país es lo diverso, luminoso, misterioso y festivo. Y esta revelación, más las imágenes de todo lo bello que habían contemplado, los invistió de una identidad y de una fe. Y comprendieron que no estaban solos, pues por encima de tanto horror – incluyendo el que ellos mismos exhalaban – una tradición hecha de belleza y de rebeldía, un país, los amparaba. (Arenas 1991: 131)

The author identifies 'el país' with all that has to do with festive elements, carnival and defiance. Again, carnival functions as a mechanism to carry out this rebellion. Moreover, 'el país' is related to the idea of diversity, that is, dialogue among several voices. The text thus suggests this multiplicity of voices, which include a centre stage for the homosexual, as an act of rebellion. Through the use of ludic elements, especially when the character of Piñera literally gags his audience (1991: 131) to prevent the intervention of the CDR (Comité de Defensa de la Revolución), Arenas once again asserts his position against what is for him the monologic and repressive voice of the state.

For Arenas, the essence of 'lo cubano', Cubanness, relies on a polysemic sign, as it did for Fernando Ortiz in his coining of the term and concept of 'transculturation'. For Ortiz, 'Cubanidad es "la calidad de lo cubano", o sea su manera de ser, su carácter, su índole, su condición distintiva, su individuación dentro de lo universal'; but at the same time he recognizes plurality by acknowledging that 'Cuba es un archipiélago' (1991b: 11). Arenas indirectly confirms Ortiz's position by highlighting in his dialogic novel that 'toda cultura es creadora, dinámica y social' (Ortiz 1991b: 14), and that the marginal is also part of that creative culture and part of the nation.

In *El color del verano* the author uses carnival as a vehicle to create a literary and alternative space, in which dialogue between different voices can take place without any kind of punishment. Outside the carnival chronotope, the search for pleasure is continually prohibited. Nonetheless, the *loca areniana* is brave enough to be in pursuit of another body, and in doing so exposes himself to endless danger. Arenas turns each member of Cuban society into a homosexual, and within a system where homosexuality is considered a crime, where the danger is considerable and the consequences are clear:[4] 'Los policías con voces y gestos de tragamundos prendieron a los jóvenes que se bañaban desnudos y a culatazos los metieron en el carro patrullero' (Arenas 1991: 65).

The police presence in the novel represents the 'formative call' to which Judith Butler refers in *Bodies that Matter*, 'precisely because it initiates the individual into the subjected status of the subject' (1993: 121). These anonymous youths (*jóvenes*) are not 'in a condition of trespass' (Butler 1993: 121) either before police intervention or during the carnival. The homosexual thus ironically becomes 'a social subject' (Butler 1993: 121) in this novel when reprimanded and thus 'subjectivated' by the state, resulting in the irony of an existence that is legitimized by the state at the same time as the state attempts to suppress it.[5]

Arenas goes on to explore how one of his subjects, identified as Oscar, witnesses how gay men are eliminated from the stage and thus hidden by the state by being sent to supposed rehabilitation units where they are forced to work in labour camps. This calls the reader's attention to the well-known years of the UMAP [Unidades Militares de Ayuda a la Producción] (1965–68) under Castro's rule:[6]

> Y Oscar desciende y toca casi rauda el suelo para presenciar la recogida de maricones más gigantesca que se ha realizado en la historia de la humanidad y de la localidad. Miles de locas son apresadas y a patadas son conducidas a guaguas, jaulas de hierro y carros patrulleros y de allí al campo de trabajo forzado. (Arenas 1991: 99)

---

4   It is worth mentioning that Arenas did not enjoy the changes that took place in Cuba in terms of the acceptance of homosexuality at official level. Even if in 1979 sodomy was no longer a crime, homosexuality could not be flaunted under laws against 'escándalo público'. Arenas left during the Mariel boatlift in 1980 and committed suicide in New York in 1990. The film *Fresa y chocolate* (1993) focused national attention on issues of homosexuality and discrimination. The CENESEX [Centro Nacional de Educación Sexual], directed by Mariela Castro Espín, states: 'Ser homosexual, bisexual, transexual o travesti no es una enfermedad, no es sinónimo de perversidad ni constituye delito alguno. No tienen su origen en la seducción a ninguna edad, no son contagiosas ni adquiridas por defectos educativos ni por malos ejemplos en el medio familiar. Son formas de expresión de la *diversidad sexual*, como lo es también la heterosexualidad' (http://www.cenesex. sld.cu/webs/diversidad/diversidad.htm [accessed 10 January 2010], emphasis in the original).

5   Butler states: 'In Althusser's notion of interpellation, it is the police who initiate the call or address by which a subject becomes socially constituted. There is the policeman, the one who not only represents the law but whose address "Hey you!" has the effect of binding the law to the one who is hailed. This "one" who appears not to be in a condition of trespass prior to the call (for whom the call establishes a given practice as a trespass) is not fully a social subject, is not fully subjectivated, for he or she is not yet reprimanded' (1993: 121).

6   On the topic of the UMAP, see Ros 2004.

For Arenas it is not only the power of the state police that is present; he also casts doubt on gender roles played by a *macho* society. Arenas uses La Tétrica Mofeta's sexual freedom to question gender, here emphasizing masculinity through the stereotypical sexual prowess of a black man, who may react after reaching orgasm by slashing the *loca*'s face:

> El sexo había sido para la Tétrica un acto de desenfado, rebeldía y libertad. [...] Conquistar a un negro en una parada de ómnibus, meterse con él en el monte Barreto, enfrentando todos los peligros incluyendo el de que el mismo negro, mientras la Tétrica se la mamaba, le diese una patada y lo desvalijara y hasta le cortara la cara: eso era un acto de libertad porque era un riesgo voluntario. (1991: 322)

On the other hand, carnival grants anonymity in which sexual desire can be expressed by the true self:

> Todos movían culos y caderas, piernas, hombros y cuellos. Los macharranes más portentosos movían sus nalgas rozando los [*sic*] de otros macharranes únicos quienes a no ser por aquella música y aquella fiesta los hubiesen descuartizado a puñetazos. [...] Siguieron retumbando las orquestas y todos, mientras bailaban, con las pintas llenas de cerveza, se excitaban. Y sin importarles qué era lo que tenían a su lado, ni quien los miraba, se palpaban, se restregaban, se apretaban. Y allí mismo, en plena muchedumbre, se enculaban o por lo menos mamaban. (1991: 408–9)

Even Castro himself, portrayed as a holy figure in a Popemobile, is part of a celebration he cannot control, and in the process Arenas questions, as he does with the rest of the nation, the leader's sexuality:

> Y en la bola gigantesca e iluminada como un resplandeciente papamóvil, Fifo, flotando a unos tres pies de la tierra, saluda a los millones de culipandeantes y él mismo, mientras saluda se menea, pero al momento se pone muy serio; pero al instante se vuelve a menear; pero otra vez recobra su compostura y pone cara de Pedro el Malo. Ay, pero al instante, sin poderse dominar, se remenea... Su tragedia es la dualidad. (1991: 409)

Carnival is the space where those activities that the government usually punishes and forbids are tolerated.

In the chapter 'Disfraces prohibidos', Arenas highlights the risk to which his character Clara Mortera is exposed in the novel, as acceptance of the forbidden at carnival time could lead to reprisals afterwards:

> Clara se dedicó afanosamente a confeccionar una inmensa y extraordinaria colección de disfraces que exhibiría durante el carnaval en *La gran competencia de disfraces prohibidos* que esa noche por ser un día especial

> Fifo había autorizado. [...] Sus disfraces serían tan irreverentes, tan
> implacables, tan reales que tal vez no habría con ella clemencia ni tolerancia.
> Hasta el mismo Fifo sería caricaturizado. (1991: 301)

Throughout the novel, the character of Clara Mortera, a caricature of the Cuban
painter Clara Morera, works as the protagonist's alter-ego. There are several moments when the narrator identifies with her and her work. Moreover, one of Clara's
paintings has the same title as this novel's subtitle: 'Nuevo jardín de las delicias',
a title that is a clear reference to Hieronymus Bosch's painting *The Garden of
Earthly Delights* in which all the sensual pleasures are represented. However,
there is a clash between this painting and the work of our protagonists. Both
Reinaldo the narrator and Clara use their art to express horror and to seek a place
like the one represented in Bosch's painting. There are further parallels between
Clara and Reinaldo: the short chapters titled 'La historia' (123–5, 163–4, 204–5,
327) are very similar to those where we hear Clara describe her paintings. Clara
and Reinaldo even die at the same time. These coincidences allow us to presume
that they complement each other. The description of one of Clara's paintings also
serves to sum up the text that we, as readers, have before us:

> La última parte del cuadro será muy oscura, casi negra, en ella se aglomerarán
> todos los expulsados, es decir, los que han intentado vivir y por lo mismo han
> sido condenados a muerte por el Dios Siniestro que rige todos los destinos
> vitales. (1991: 75)

During carnival, all those elements which are considered strange in a 'normal' context
are viewed as ordinary and become assimilated into the mass of aroused people. In
this context of 'normalization', Arenas introduces 'La dama del velo', who must be
stabbed in her genitalia by midgets ordered by Fifo to carry out this deed:

> Desde luego que los diligentes enanos no habían olvidado las órdenes de Fifo
> de matar a La Dama del Velo en pleno carnaval de una puñalada en el bollo
> para que pareciera un crimen pasional. [...] Los diligentes enanos no sabían
> a dónde se dirigía aquella mujer enloquecida envuelta en tantos trapos que
> por ser noche de carnaval, y además la última, pasaba casi desapercibida en
> medio de tantas figuras estrambóticas. (1991: 420)

The carnival is the chronotope where sexual intercourse is allowed; furthermore,
the government, while carnival is still operative, takes the opportunity to per-
petrate its misdeeds without any effect upon the international image of the
country, one of the issues that the dictator, as portrayed by Arenas in this novel,
worries about most:

> se llegaba a la conclusión de que la prueba máxima de la existencia del
> diablo era el mismo Fifo. Fifo desde luego condenó a Tomasito la Goyesca

a muerte, pero en aquel momento no podía hacerse pública ni realizarse la ejecución. Me le cortan el cuello y la lengua en pleno carnaval, le musitó a uno de sus oficiales más acuciosos quien le transmitió la orden a Raúl Kastro [*sic*]. (1991: 386)

Reinaldo, the narrator of the novel, also wants to leave the country during carnival time, and most of the characters take advantage of the specific moment; they exact revenge on one another without any danger. Violence is one of the most important features of Arenas's carnival. The government exerts violence alongside the rest of the protagonists; the use of violence thus entails a demonstration of the power one individual has over another.

El color del verano is an exaltation of the body and the desires and pleasures of the flesh. In this novel the ejection from paradise is associated with the repression of sexuality, and the quest for this lost paradise comprises the endless pursuit of another male body, the Other, in order to communicate with him. In Butler's words,

> Desire is, then, the expression of a longing for the return to the origin that, if recoverable, would necessitate the dissolution of the subject itself. Hence, desire is destined for an imaginary life in which it remains haunted and governed by a libidinal memory it cannot possibly recollect. (1999: 187)

In Arenas's case in particular, 'the subject is understood as a product of a prohibition' (Butler 1999: 187) which he highlights by mocking the political system and those who keep it afloat, despite the country (Cuba) being severed from all origins: 'La isla, desprendida de su base, partía hacia lo ignoto' (Arenas 1991: 432).

Following this argument we can deduce that carnival represents this lost paradise where carnal pleasure and delight prevail and from which human beings have been expelled. This is particularly true in the light of Arenas's own illness, AIDS, which acts as a condemnation and barrier to the achievement of his own desires: 'pues los que tenemos el virus del SIDA (yo lo tengo, desde luego) [...] Ya no podemos ni singar [...]. Vírgenes nos hemos vuelto y en espera de una muerte atroz' (Arenas 1991: 85). This letter/confession, dated Paris, May 1993, almost two years after the author's own death, is used by Arenas to foreshadow the future and claim hell as the only space present: 'Pues si existe el infierno, y es lo único que existe, ni siquiera está regido por el Diablo, sino por una Diabla' (1991: 85). Arenas presents the afterlife as a space ruled by a she-devil who takes revenge on the homosexual male. This representation of everyday life as hell is further underlined by la Reina de Holanda when she reads the following text at 'La conferencia onírico teológica político filosófica satírica', part of the 'fiesta fifal', where she describes gay men as belonging to an army of clandestine desire in continuous search for alterity:

> Se había perdido el sentido de la vida porque se había perdido el paraíso y se había perdido el paraíso porque se había condenado el placer. Pero el placer, perseguido, execrado, condenado, esquilmado y casi borrado del mundo, aún tenía sus ejércitos; ejércitos clandestinos, silenciosos y siempre en peligro inminente, pero que no estaban dispuestos, de ninguna manera, a renunciar a la vida, esto es, a hacer gozar a los demás. Ese ejército – retumbó la voz de la Reina de Holanda por todo el recinto inundado – está formado por los maricones. (1991: 388)

Arenas's clear metonymy in using a wholly homosexual society to represent the nation has not escaped critics, who have rightly seen it as a mechanism to criticize an oppressive reality and to denounce a system that at one time considered homosexuality as an aberration, even if it is 'un libro extremadamente cruel con los personajes que desfilan por él' (Nuez 1999: 226). The homosexual rebels against any kind of repression; he represents the marginalized, the oppressed and collective memory. In *El color del verano*, Arenas's *locas* write their own history, an unofficial history that undermines the government's idea that there is a monolithic and unique reality. As Iván de la Nuez has observed:

> Arenas se coloca dentro de un habla (y una trama) marginal y homosexual que fractura, precisamente, cualquier idea unívoca de un lenguaje nacional. Él no sólo recoge palabras, sino que las crea, las inventa, al punto de que podemos decir, sin exageración, que hay un lenguaje 'Arenas'. No es cubano lo que él busca, sino la posibilidad de destruir cualquier posibilidad de lo cubano como canon. (1999: 225–6)

Throughout the novel, we find allusions to the UMAP mentioned above, the Mariel boatlift and the prison in which our protagonist, like Reinaldo Arenas himself, has been incarcerated. As Humberto López-Cruz has written:

> El discurso homoerótico fraguado en *El color del verano* denuncia la condena social y oficial hacia el homosexual. La óptica narrativa se estructura desde la postura homoerótica que la mayoría de los personajes va a adoptar. Las 'locas' […] crean su submundo o su historia no oficial que legitima la denuncia y la separación entre lo aceptado oficialmente y lo mandado a repudiar por el mismo gobierno que a veces se contradice en sus decretos. (1998: 115)

Suzanne Kaebnick, in her excellent article titled 'La Loca Freedom Fighter in *Antes que anochezca* and *El color del verano*', analyses the key issues in order to understand the role of the homosexual within Arenas's *cosmogonía*. She accurately states:

> the machismo of 'the new man' of the revolution is ridiculed and the narrator / protagonist identifies himself as homosexual, as feminine, and as a Cuban citizen. Cuban nationalism celebrates male virility as the emblem of national

strength, but, like many other modern ideologies of the nation, denigrates sexual intercourse between men and constructs abject personalities supposedly pertaining to those bodies. The vilification of the homosexual in Cuba [...] has not emphasized a heterosexual versus homosexual identity, but an active masculine identity versus a passive, feminine identity [...]. The macho is presumed to be the model of strength and independence. [...] Arenas mocks masculinity's status and forces masculine (macho) desire to emerge from hiding. Because macho masculinity must be infallible, it is easy to throw into question. [...] In *El color del verano*, [the critique] is achieved in large part by transgendering the sexist and homophobic assumptions regarding the macho and the *loca*. The macho comes to resemble the *maricón* in that his erotic desire for men and his vulnerabilities are revealed. Arenas breaks down the stereotype that homosexual preference only occurs among feminine men. Furthermore, the *loca* resembles stereotypes of the macho in the self-confidence, even militancy, with which he insists on sexual and political autonomy. [...] Arenas undermines the presumptions upon which patriarchal, heterosexist knowledge and power are built and makes public their violence. (1997: 102–11)

In the novel, the homosexual appears as a martyr, as the one who makes sacrifices and is the rescuer and emancipator of society. He makes use of his freedom and will pay for this audacity with his own life. Hence, Arenas uses the homosexual in order to condemn the repression he suffered and to undermine monolithic notions of sexuality and masculinity. In this patriarchal society, where the idea of masculinity is strongly connected with the revolutionary idea of 'the new man' and the nation, Arenas challenges the establishment.

As stated by Francisco Soto, the novel has the characteristics of a documentary novel, the official vehicle of the Cuban revolution. The documentary novel, in its official role as a metonymic enterprise, must project only one voice, which at the same time, in principle, should incorporate all the voices from all strata of society. In Arenas, instead, we see how this version of the documentary novel excludes those voices that do not fit within official parameters. Those voices that are excluded in the documentary novel, for example the voice of marginalized homosexuals, can be found in *El color del verano*, a novel that thus becomes a parody of official discourse.

In *El color del verano*, with the transgression of the established order, the author breaks with the idea of reality as monolithic and having a unique and fixed meaning. As Iván de la Nuez states:

La novela es ciclónica no sólo en lo que narra, ni en el sentido de noria sin salida de los personajes, sino en su estructura toda, en esa construcción que hace de *El color del verano* un libro armado como un remolino, escrito para desolar el mundo, como buscando la fuerza suficiente para conseguir lo que su trama nos propone: desgarrar a Cuba de su plataforma insular y cercenarla radicalmente de su historia, de su fatalidad geográfica, de las ficciones de su tradición nacional, del autoritarismo de su trayectoria política. (1999: 225)

Reality is described from different perspectives and through different discourses by several voices that participate in the novel. The author refuses to
give priority to any of these perspectives; none is better than any other. Hence,
we should not be surprised when, on the one hand, we see how some characters in the novel start a dialogue with the narrator himself (they complain about
the narrator's interpretations of events) or, on the other hand, we find many
contradictions within the novel that undermine what has been already stated,
for example:

> [Tedevoro] llevaba el tomo 27 de las Obras Completas de Lenin [...] ¿Qué
> hombre iba a aceptar los parpadeos, guiños o cualquier tipo de insinuación
> de un pájaro que llevara en sus manos el tomo 26 (¡Vaya, ¿pero no dijiste que
> era el 27?). (Arenas 1991: 139)

As Francisco Soto has written in relation to the Derridean *différance* (Derrida
1982: 1–27) that allows the postponement of meaning,

> Arenas, like Borges, denies all that is stable and fixed through a derisive
> attitude that blurs genres, constantly fragments meaning, welcomes
> contradictions and delights in the use of oxymoronic combinations, all
> with the end of critically questioning the validity of final interpretations.
> (1994: 113)

Arenas himself explained his reasoning to Soto in an interview: 'Porque no creo
que exista una sola realidad, sino que la realidad es múltiple, es infinita, y además
vacía de acuerdo con la interpretación que queramos darle' (Soto 1990: 10).

Parody

In *El color del verano* there is sharp parody of official discourses, and the
author facilitates encounters between those who would generally never meet
outside the pages of the novel. As Iván de la Nuez asserts: 'Arenas hace co-
incidir sujetos marginales o "menores" con grandes hombres y mujeres de la
cultura y la política' (1999: 227). It is the carnivalesque atmosphere which is
conducive to such an encounter. As Bakhtin argues, during carnival there is a
clash between popular culture and official culture. Also, according to Bakhtin,
parody is a device that contributes to dialogism: 'To introduce a parodic and
polemical element into the narration is to make it more multi-voiced, more
interruption-prone, no longer gravitating toward itself or its referential object'
(Bakhtin 1984: 226).

> There is nothing in *parodia* that necessitates the inclusion of a concept of
> ridicule, as there is, for instance, in the joke or *burla* of burlesque. Parody,
> then, in its ironic 'trans-contextualization' and inversion, is repetition with

difference. A critical distance is implied between the background text being parodied and the new incorporating work, a distance usually signaled by irony. But this irony can be playful as well as belittling; it can be critically constructive as well as destructive. (1985: 32)

In *El color del verano* we encounter parody of three kinds of official discourse: the discourse of power (meaning that of the state), religious discourse and the discourse of the official literary canon. Here, the concept of the traditional novel is problematized and, thus, the idea of traditional genre too.

With respect to parodying the discourse of power, in this novel the discursive carnival invalidates and debunks monolithic power. Using parody, irony and carnivalesque laughter, Arenas calls into question Marxist dialectical materialism. Those chapters titled 'Una inspección' and 'La confesión de H. Puntilla' (the latter is an unequivocal reference to the famous case of Heberto Padilla and his so-called confession before the UNEAC after his arrest in 1971) are clear instances of this. In these chapters, Arenas also problematizes revolutionary obsession as anti-bourgeois discourse. This discourse presents new proposals, sometimes absurd ones, for anti-capitalist productivity: '– ¡Qué pan ni qué carajo! El pan es un prejuicio burgués y cristiano. Derrúmbenme ese monte de pan y siémbrenlo de malanga' (1991: 143).

Arenas also parodies anti-imperialist discourse which considers any reference to the United States as inimical to the Cuban revolution: '– ¿Así que nuestro clima no es propicio para que se den las manzanas de California, pero el de California sí? Está muy claro lo que ustedes están planteando: que el imperialismo es más poderoso que nosotros' (1991: 146). Arenas presents Castro as a 'maquiavelo tropical' (1991: 330) for whom the end justifies the means and the end is nothing less than: 'un estado monolítico, Fifolandia' (1991: 330).

In parodying religious discourse, irreverence is one of the features of Arenas's text. The chapter called 'La elevación del Santo Clavo' is a good example of the parody of biblical stories, for example Christ's crucifixion: 'el espectáculo de aquella cruz atravesando la multitud con un joven desnudo y erotizado cuyo falo era chupado sin cesar por reyes, obispos, obreros, militares, jóvenes comunistas [...] monjas de clausura' (1991: 427). This parody debunks and denounces an institution that also denies and disapproves of homosexuality. The Church is criticized as an institution that alienates the individual (in this case, a gay man) and prevents him from expressing himself as he really is.

Due to the carnivalization of discourse, Arenas subverts the linear diegesis of the traditional narrative, with introduction, climax and ending. According to Soto, this subversion of the sequential order of traditional narrative entails, at the same time, a subversion of Marxist discourse and its ordered concept of history. As we can appreciate, *El color del verano* has a circular structure, not a linear one; its narrative is fragmented and events are not ordered in a logical way. There are also endless transgressions of the traditional concept of time. As Arenas himself writes in the prologue of *El color del verano*, the novel has this structure because of the carnivalization of its discourse; carnival constitutes the leitmotif, the thread of the novel:

> Solamente quisiera apuntar que no se trata de una obra lineal, sino circular y por lo mismo ciclónica, con un vértice o centro que es el carnaval, hacia donde parten todas las flechas. De modo que, dado su carácter de circunferencia, la obra en realidad no empieza ni termina en un punto específico y puede comenzar a leerse por cualquier parte hasta terminar la ronda. (1991: 249)

As Arenas declares, the 'cyclonic' circularity of his novel, which ends in the same way as it begins, thus creating the 'circumference' to which the author refers, allows his text to be congruent with contemporary theories in which the text appears as 'a point where centrifugal as well as centripetal forces are brought to bear' (Bakhtin 1981: 272). Here 'every utterance participates in the "unitary language" (in its centripetal forces and tendencies) and at the same time partakes of social and historical heteroglossia (the centrifugal, stratifying forces)' (Bakhtin 1981: 272). Arenas himself presents his text 'as a contradiction-ridden, tension-filled unity of two embattled tendencies in the life of language' (Bakhtin 1981: 272), through which he empowers the marginal in the light of the canon. Thus, we are not surprised when characters who belong to the culture and history of Cuba are resuscitated. We recognize Guillén, Martí, Avellaneda, Carpentier, Lezama and Piñera among others. We even find instances of personification as in Tiburón Sangriento, and animalization, as is the case of Oscar and other *locas* who are depicted as real birds, as well as Nicolás Guillotina, a caricature of Nicolás Guillén, who is presented as a bulldog: 'Tan altos y aterradores fueron los gritos del pájaro que Nicolás Guillotina, semejante a un inmenso perro buldog [*sic*], bajó las escaleras de mármol. [...] Ya en las oficinas, Tedevoro le explicó al perro buldog [*sic*] lo que le había ocurrido' (1991: 311). By going from a simile (*semejante a*) to a metaphor (the bulldog), Arenas manages to dehumanize Guillén and thus question his status as part of official Cuban revolutionary culture in his role as a 'faithful dog' of the system, particularly in his role as president of the UNEAC.

The cruel humour at the expense of historical or literary figures in the novel, compounded by the mixture of genres, contributes to the carnivalization of discourse itself. The novel starts as theatre, an artifice that blurs the boundaries between genres; the prologue begins on page 246, while the Tétrica Mofeta's 'treinta truculentos trabalenguas' alternate with normal chapters. These thirty tongue-twisters can be understood in accordance with the analysis Soto offers, where he uses Arenas's autobiography *Antes que anochezca* to shed light on this subject:

In his autobiography, *Antes de que anochezca* [*sic*], Arenas informs the reader how he invented tongue twisters while living in Cuba as literary weapons against those individuals who betrayed him in one way or another. [...] For the most part, each tongue twister is a scathing attack directed at a given writer for his or her literary ego, sexual inclinations, or hypocrisy in supporting the Castro regime. (1994: 109–10)

The novel parodies the different literary styles of specific Cuban writers, for example Alejo Carpentier in the chapter titled 'Un paseo por La Habana Vieja en compañía de Alejo' or Lezama in 'La conferencia de Lezama'. In this way, dialogism is generated with Lezama and his novel *Paradiso*. These continual intertextual references to Cuban artists and their work[7] produce an endless dialogue between different periods of Cuban culture and history, between different characters, their works and their specific socio-political circumstances. There is also a parallelism between Martí, Lezama, Piñera and Reinaldo (the narrator) in their own condition as exiled writers (including inner exile). As Soto has stated, the presence of the character called Esteban Montejo at the beginning of the novel 'is a parodic undermining not only of Hispanic patriarchal machismo but also of the seriousness and prominence of Barnet and his famous protagonist within the canon of Cuban revolutionary letters' (1994: 47).

Arenas shows no mercy, least of all towards those figures who have been considered by official discourse as 'vacas sagradas': artists protected by the government and/or opportunists within and beyond the island. His attack, which extends to those in exile, is particularly apparent in one of the chapters, entitled 'Una carta', where La Tétrica Mofeta states:

En cuanto a las vacas sagradas del exilio, son eso, vacas. Todas se creen geniales y son muy hipersensibles en lo relacionado con su ego. Ninguna de ellas piensa ni siquiera por un instante ser de menos valía que el mismo Cervantes.
Mucho peo [*sic*] perfumado, eso es lo que abunda por aquí. (1991: 84)

As Iván de la Nuez has observed, Arenas was

Anticomunista furibundo tanto como crítico con todo el orden burgués y sus estratificaciones de las diferencias. Anticastrista feroz e igualmente crítico con los exiliados cubanos (llegó a afirmar que en Miami no hay una dictadura porque los cubanos no han podido separar la Florida de Estados Unidos). (1999: 226)

With reference to those on the island, Halisia Alonso (Alicia Alonso, Cuba's prima ballerina) is an explicit case of caricature. Arenas incessantly ridicules

---

[7]   There are even references to other novels by Arenas, such as the chapter called 'Otra vez el mar', a clear reference to the third novel of the *pentagonía.*

her dancing: 'Halisia y su cuerpo de baile interpretan "la danza del repudio". Se trata de una serie de saltos enfurecidos, patadas, escupitajos y gestos que parecen aplastar ladillas y cucarachas en pleno aire y lanzarlas al mar' (1991: 35). Alicia's portrayal reminds the reader of the Mariel boatlift and the repudiation acts of 1980 which 'led to persecution' (García-Obregón 2006a: 29) in Cuba for those leaving the country, as was Arenas's case. As García-Obregón argues: 'mass repudiation (as happened during 1980 in Cuba) was part of the mechanism of alienation and repression at large' (2006a: 35).

Rewriting and the Carnivalization of Discourse

In *El color del verano* we see the incessant rewriting of the novel, which leads to several contradictions. Following Genette's theory, we can consider the text as a palimpsest, in which

> the art of 'making new things out of old' has the merit, at least, of generating more complex and more savory objects than those that are 'made on purpose'; a new function is superimposed upon and interwoven with an older structure, and the dissonance between these two concurrent elements imparts its flavor to the resulting whole. [...] That duplicity of the object, in the sphere of textual relations, can be represented by the old analogy of the *palimpsest*: on the same parchment, one text can become superimposed upon another, which it does not quite conceal but allows to show through. (Genette 1997: 398–9)

Genette's view of the palimpsest ties in with Ortiz's concept of the *ajiaco*. For Ortiz, 'La imagen del ajiaco criollo nos simboliza bien la formación del pueblo cubano', composed of 'sustancias de los más diversos géneros y procedencias' (1991b: 15) in a process that he views as one that is 'desintegrativo e integrativo' (1991b: 16). Thus one could say that although Arenas's novel is conversant with theoretical postulates, particularly of the latter half of the twentieth century, concerning the novel, he is also creating a Cuban product of transculturation, which engages gender and sexual orientation as part of the discussion of a national project of Cubanness, in contradiction to the dynamics conditioned by the *macho* state.

   Through the carnivalization of discourse, the novel itself, in its polyphony, becomes, from a thematic and formal point of view, pure carnival. This fact explains why in Arenas's novel we find what Bakhtin encountered in Dostoevsky's novels: that the artistic key is in 'the unification of highly heterogenous and incompatible material – with the plurality of consciousness-centers not reduced to a single ideological common denominator' (Bakhtin 1984: 17). *El color del verano* shows perfectly what it means to have a carnivalization of discourse, in a world expressed through the language of the public square, as Bakhtin calls it (1984: 129–30), dominated by insults, carnal and scatological language, through which both the grotesque and carnival laughter can be expressed. This kind of discourse is pervaded by typical elements of carnival: irony, parody, satire and 'carnivalistic mésalliances' (Bakhtin 1984: 123), among other devices. A novel that has undergone a process of carnivalization can no longer belong to the category of the traditional novel. As Rita Molinero says, 'la tradición de lo grotesco se interesa por todo lo que desborda el cuerpo; lo que escapa de él y lo prolonga al unirlo a otro cuerpo, al mundo' (1994: 58).

Arenas's use of the grotesque in this novel reaches what in Valle Inclán was the theatrical *esperpento*. I assert that Arenas's characters, like those of Valle as examined by Iris Zavala, 'ingresan en un proceso intensivo de degradación paródica, de juegos especulares'[8] (Zavala 1990: 70), where 'lo esperpéntico' and 'lo grotesco' are strongly related. According to Bakhtin,

> lo grotesco se interesa por todo lo que *sale, hace brotar, desborda* el cuerpo, todo lo que busca escapar de él. Así es como las *excrecencias y ramificaciones* adquieren un valor particular; todo lo que, en suma, prolonga el cuerpo, uniéndolo a los otros cuerpos o al mundo no corporal. [...] El cuerpo grotesco es un cuerpo en movimiento. No está nunca listo ni acabado: [...] el vientre y el falo; estas partes del cuerpo son objeto de la predilección de una *exageración positiva* [...]. Después del vientre y del miembro viril, es la boca la que desempeña el papel más importante en el cuerpo grotesco, pues ella engulle al mundo; y, en seguida, el trasero. Todas estas excrecencias y orificios están caracterizados por el hecho de que son el lugar donde se superan las fronteras entre dos cuerpos y entre el cuerpo y el mundo, donde se efectúan los cambios y las orientaciones recíprocas. (1987: 285)

A good example of Arenas's use of the grotesque in the Bakhtinian sense cited above is his depiction of Ramón Sernada, la Ogresa:

> aquella loquita que era en un principio un pájaro pequeño y de pelo largo y lacio se fue convirtiendo en un ser abultado, amarillo, calvo y de ojos rojizos. [...] la Ogresa con sólo tocar la punta de un falo por encima de un pantalón se llenaba de erupciones. [...] nada más sacar la lengua a un metro de distancia de un miembro masculino la cara se le ponía completamente negra. [...] se le inflamaban las piernas y su barriga crecía hasta volverse algo descomunal. [...] Y ella, por ser loca, sólo podía ser al ser ensartada. [...] Pero no tuvo la Ogresa ni siquiera una noche de placer. El primer hombre con el que se encontró, un marinero que se veía rozagante, en cuanto la ensartó le trasmitió al pájaro todas las enfermedades contagiosas que posee el mundo. Así, repentinamente, el marinero se vio poseyendo [...] a una bola de pus. El marinero enfurecido sacó su miembro del culo de Ramón Sernada y este

---

8   For further information on the relationship between *esperpento* and carnivalization, see Zavala 1990.

(el culo) lanzó una estampida sulfurosa. Desde entonces la vida de la loca
había sido un calvario incesante, un correr de un curandero a otro curandero
y todo clandestinamente pues si Fifo se enteraba la metía en un campo de
concentración. (1991: 171)

Here, Arenas makes an indirect reference to the UMAP of the 1960s, and holds
Fidel Castro personally responsible; but, above all, this uninhibited style is a parody of social realism, as Francisco Soto has previously observed (Soto 1998: 99).

Historical Discourse

With respect to the use of historical discourse in *El color del verano*, I agree
with Humberto López-Cruz when he writes:

> La voz omnisciente del autor-narrador es la que conduce los capítulos
> designados a la historia, una voz que abandona casi completamente la
> parodia para convertirse en el analista que evalúa la tortuosa vida histórica
> de la Isla. Una voz herida pero firme que se yergue ahora como denunciante
> [...]. El discurso histórico es un elemento textual que aporta cohesión dentro
> de la estructura carnavalesca de *El color del verano*. Los capítulos dedicados
> a la historia se convierten en la voz de denuncia que ratifica la parodia.[9]
> (1997a: 4)

In the course of the novel, we find four chapters entitled 'la historia'. In these
chapters the voice of the narrator changes in tone to that of an omniscient narrator who raises his voice to denounce the 'vida histórica de la Isla'. The carnivalization of discourse disappears; parody as well as irony and carnivalesque
laughter have no place in these lines. This new serious and objective voice
denounces the existence of a totalitarian (versus authoritarian) regime on the
island. This attack complements that made by the narrator throughout the
novel and through carnival. The voices are two sides of the same coin: they
belong to the same narrator. Together they denounce dialogically the same
circumstance from different points of view.

By contrast, in all other chapters of the novel, through irony, carnivalesque
laughter and the grotesque, Arenas creates a satire with grotesque caricatures
through which real figures of the past and present of Cuban culture and politics
pass.[10] Arenas uses this satire to denounce Castro's regime, although this attack

---

[9]   For a more exhaustive study of the relationship between Arenas's novels and their referents
in the world, or between the novels and history or the documentary novel, see Soto 1994; Rozencvaig
1986 (where she suggests a new logic to examine this issue); and López-Cruz 1997a.

[10]   Linda Hutcheon, in her work *A Theory of Parody*, clarifies the differences between parody
and satire, concepts that have often been considered synonymous, but which I shall use following
Hutcheon's distinction: 'parody is by no means always satirical [...] satire frequently uses parody

extends to all forms of repression and totalitarian or authoritarian systems, regardless of political ideology. Arenas also criticizes the hypocrisy, that is, the dual morality of the leaders and of all members of Cuban society within and beyond the island as a whole. Thus, we read:

> Luego sigue *El color del verano*, retrato grotesco y satírico (y por lo mismo real) de una tiranía envejecida y del tirano, cúspide de todo el horror; las luchas e intrigas que se desarrollan alrededor del tirano (amparado por la hipocresía, la cobardía, la frivolidad y el oportunismo de los poderosos), la manera de no tomar nada en serio para poder seguir sobreviviendo y el sexo como una tabla de salvación y escape inmediatos. De alguna forma esta obra pretende reflejar, sin zalamerías ni altisonantes principios, la vida entre picaresca y desgarrada de gran parte de la juventud cubana, sus deseos de ser jóvenes, de existir como tales. (1991: 249)[11]

Arenas continues:

> Esta es la historia de una isla cuyos hijos nunca pudieron encontrar sosiego. Más que una isla parecía un incesante campo de batalla, de intrigas, de atropellos y de sucesivos espantos y de chanchullos sin fin. Nadie le perdonaba nada a nadie, mucho menos la grandeza. [...] Esta es la historia de una isla donde no cesaba nunca el girigay [*sic*], el brete, la intriga, la mala intención y las ambiciones descomunales; y quien no participaba en aquel tenebroso meneo nacional era de una u otra forma devorado por la maldición de la isla. (1991: 442)

The special hatred that the author demonstrates for Fifo, and for the soldiers and characters who represent power and exert a repressive role in society, comes as no surprise. Arenas reveals dual morality as a mechanism of survival in a monolithic system. Fifo is not aware of his own double moral standards. He rejects homosexuals, but Arenas shows him as yearning for a sexual encounter with a man; yet this is the 'instinto vital' which he must repress:

---

as a vehicle for ridiculing the vices or follies of humanity, with an eye to their correction. This very definition orients satire towards a negative evaluation and a corrective intent. Modern parody, on the other hand, rarely has such an evaluative or intentional limitation. [...] While satire can be destructive [...] there is also an implied idealism, for it is often "unabashedly didactic and seriously committed to a hope in its own power to effect change" [...]. The very positive possible marking of parody's ethos is clear in the respect that many artists show in their parodic treatment of the acknowledged masterpieces of modern art' (Hutcheon 1985: 54–9).

11   Critics have often referred to 'la picaresca' as a literary model in *El color del verano*; see, for instance, Esterrich 1997; Soto 1990. Because this novel is entirely Cuban in its context, it offers the reader a clear example of literary transculturation, as the character La Tétrica Mofeta is compared with the *pícaro* par excellence, Lazarillo de Tormes.

> Ah, si pudiera ser aquel negro que moviéndose sin cesar hace alarde de sus dotes delanteras, o aquella puta que vestida de miliciana danza sobre el muro, o aquella loca que con disimulo y pasión soba a un soldado patrio [...] Pero no, era todo eso a la vez y por lo tanto no era nada. [...] Sólo podía encontrar sosiego en la destrucción de todo instinto vital y por lo mismo auténtico. (1991: 412)

Carnivalesque codes destroy all kinds of hierarchy and produce a change of roles: those who, before carnival, had performed a repressive role, during carnival take part in activities they would have previously punished. Those who were, before carnival, victims of repression use the power that carnival confers upon them to carry out their misdeeds, their revenges and to impose their will. At the end of the novel, when the repressive regime has been abolished, those who were victims of this system are now in power; they are the new victors. In his novel, Arenas seems to apply indirectly Bakhtin's words:

> what is suspended first of all is hierarchical structure and all the forms of terror, reverence, piety, and etiquette connected with it [...]. All distance between people is suspended, and a special carnival category goes into effect: free and familiar contact among people. [...] All things that were [...] distanced from one another by a noncarnivalistic hierarchical worldview are drawn into carnivalistic contacts and combinations. Carnival brings together, unifies, weds, and combines the sacred with the profane, the lofty with the low, the great with the insignificant, the wise with the stupid. (1984: 123)

During the novel, Fifo tries to keep the carnival under his control; he says that he has to declare the carnival open and seems to lead the procession, but in the chapter titled 'El entierro de Virgilio Piñera', for example, the mass of people take no notice of the tyrant's orders and pay tribute to the dead artist as 'un acto de protesta contra Fifo' (Arenas 1991: 430). The reader realizes slowly that the carnival, with its excited multitude, is far from being under Fifo's control. The carnival has its own dynamics and life, and cannot be dominated:

> Y la gran comitiva oficial, con Fifo al frente dentro de su enorme globo rojo, tomó la Avenida del Puerto, abriendo el gigantesco desfile detrás del cual vendrían las carrozas y todas las comparsas. Quedaba pues inaugurado el gran carnaval habanero que por otra parte ya había comenzado hacía muchas horas. (1991: 90)

Arenas establishes a new dichotomy between the two important spaces where the action takes place: on the one hand, Fifo organizes 'la fiesta fifal' where every activity is controlled or else punishment will be meted out. Here the discourse is monolithic. The 'fiesta fifal' functions as a device to reinforce the established order and to justify it. Any sort of dialogue is banned. On the other hand, carnival belongs to the whole people, it is universal, everyone must participate in its familiar contact. The public square was the symbol of a communal performance. [...] Other places of action as well [...] can, if they become meeting – and contact – points for heterogeneous people – streets, taverns, roads, bathhouses, decks of ships, and so on – take on this additional carnival-square significance. (Bakhtin 1984: 128)

Carnival reaches all those places where people meet, places where contact between bodies occurs, a familiar contact where neither social class nor the status of the other is taken into account. Here, through the use of carnival, the author maintains his ambivalence as the dialogue is ensured alongside the transgression.

During this carnival, as in every carnival, we are witness to the dethroning of a system in decline. In *El color del verano*, this dethroning is symbolic. Thus, the novel becomes an omen of Castro's defeat. Arenas takes revenge in the only way he can, through the dethroning of Castro. At the end of the novel, Arenas makes no concessions and the island eventually disappears. López-Cruz states with regard to the end of the novel, 'el aura de destrucción canaliza una proyección aniquiladora del individuo y de la nación a manos de las fuerzas del poder' (1998: 117). However, I believe that Arenas wanted to go further when he wrote this ending to his novel. In *El color del verano* collective liberation takes place thanks to the carnival which produces the destruction of the totalitarian regime with Fifo's defeat: 'aquel chapuzón fúnebre era el aviso de una liberación total' (Arenas 1991: 432). Nevertheless, I agree with López-Cruz when he claims 'Arenas va a destruir al país para de este modo ofrecer a la historia una alternativa que no sea la versión oficial' (1998: 117).

Taking account of Umberto Eco's theories presented in his article 'The Frames of Comic "Freedom"' (1984), we could also find limitations to the liberation I claim for Arenas's text. Eco opposes Bakhtin's notion of the carnival as having a liberating role. Eco declares that if, during carnival, there is a violation of the established order and its rules, this entails, inevitably, the assimilation of these rules. Eco argues also that because of carnival's temporal nature, liberation is controlled and allowed, in this case by the government. Hence, after carnival, there are no changes with respect to the moment before carnival. But even if this is true, by means of ludic illusion Arenas takes the novel to its destructive limits when he eliminates the highest representative of power:

Una vez desaparecidos los enanos y los funcionarios y militares que portaban los micrófonos la voz de Fifo no podía salir de su globo lumínico que por otra parte, por esas maldiciones de la técnica contemporánea, ahora ni siquiera podía apagar. En medio de la multitud surgió un pájaro [...] y sacándose un alfiler de su atuendo pinchó el globo donde viajaba Fifo. Al instante el globo desinflándose se elevó como un cometa; luego, convertido en una suerte de preservativo gigantesco, cayó con Fifo en el mar donde Tiburón Sangriento lo esperaba con las fauces abiertas.[12] (1991: 437–8)

Nonetheless, as Eco further suggests in his article, humour is a subversive element because by using humour the individual subverts and ridicules a norm or law that he considers absurd and senseless. As we have seen, humour has such a function in *El color del verano*. This liberation requires victims, as in the case of the Tétrica Mofeta who dies when Tiburón Sangriento devours him. This is the price that he must pay for daring to be free. On the other hand, once the island has been liberated, hyper-democratic polyphony remains chaotic and destructive:

> Pero mientras iban al garete no lograban ponerse de acuerdo sobre cuál mar elegir para finalmente encallar y allí sobrevivir. Mucho menos lograban ponerse de acuerdo sobre qué tipo de gobierno iban a instaurar. [...] Cada cual quería, en fin, gobernar la isla a su manera y conducirla a un sitio diferente al elegido por el prójimo. [...] Finalmente, aquel pataleo con el que todos se manifestaban se hizo tan poderoso que la isla, que carecía de plataforma, se hundió en el mar entre un fragor de gritos de protesta, de insultos, de maldiciones, de glugluteos y de ahogados susurros. (1991: 442)

The overthrow of the monolithic system is feasible, but Arenas criticizes the nature of human beings, with their constant desire for power regardless of the means used to acquire it. Arenas uses the Cuban community to represent the whole of humankind and offers an apocalyptic vision in which the destruction of the island is caused not only by the totalitarian system under which the individual perishes but also by human mediocrity and the constant betrayals its inhabitants commit in order to reach power. Arenas himself several times expressed his discontent with the systems he experienced in Cuba as well as in the USA. Arenas destroys the island as a last resort to prevent the perpetuation of horror.

Simulacrum, Carnival and Mask

Arenas's carnival differs from the idea of simulacrum that Cuban society has turned into. If carnival in general can be taken as a simulacrum, for Arenas it is the only means to express the authentic self. Therefore, in *El color del verano*, the mask is dual: on the one hand, the protagonists must use the most convenient mask in order to survive; on the other hand, the mask they use during the carnival reflects their authentic personality. With reference to the first, that is, the symbolic mask, Arenas writes: 'Maricones de todos los tipos; algunos dis-

---

12   We should note that the Tétrica Mofeta will meet exactly the same death when he tries to leave the island; hence, the mechanism that Fifo used to spread violence and horror eventually kills him.

frazados de bugarrones; otros absolutamente tapados o tapiñados (estos eran los peores), casados, con mujeres, queridas, hijos y nietos, [...] sumidos en una renuncia bovina y beatífica' (1991: 65). For Arenas, 'Esta es la historia de una isla que mientras aparentemente se cubre con los oropeles de la retórica oficial, por dentro se desgarra y confía en la explosión final' (1991: 164). He goes further when he describes carnival thus:

> Pero no hay más que cuerpos que se retuercen, se enlazan y engarzan en medio de un carnaval sin sombras, donde cada cual se ajusta la máscara que más le conviene y la traición y el meneo forman parte de la trama oficial y de nuestra tradición fundamental. (1991: 397).

According to Baudrillard, simulacra represent a system of signs without referents; one sign leads us to another and 'lo real' no longer exists. In this novel, carnival belongs to the same kind of microcosm that Baudrillard explains through the example of Disneyland, a place that

> existe para ocultar que es el país 'real', toda la América 'real', una Disneylandia (al modo como las prisiones existen para ocultar que es todo lo social, en su banal omnipresencia, lo que es carcelario). Disneylandia es presentada como imaginaria con la finalidad de hacer creer que el resto es real. (Baudrillard 1998: 30)

In line with this perspective, we can deduce that *El color del verano* uses carnival as a metaphor for contemporary Cuban society within and beyond the island: 'Esta desolación y ese amor de alguna forma me han conminado a escribir esta pentagonía que además de ser la historia de mi furia y de mi amor es una metáfora de mi país' (Arenas 1991: 249). This is why Arenas, making reference to his own authorial self by mentioning his books (for example, 'mi libro de poemas *Voluntad de vivir manifestándose*', 1991: 345) and distancing himself by adopting the character of La Tétrica Mofeta, still in Cuba in 1999 (nine years after the author's own death), writes to his split selves in exile: 'Reinaldo, Gabriel y Mi Tétrica Mofeta':

> les pido que si todo eso se publica hagan constar que mis libros conforman una sola y vasta unidad, donde los personajes mueren, resucitan, aparecen, desaparecen, viajan en el tiempo, burlándose de todo y padeciéndolo todo, como hemos hecho nosotros mismos. Todos ellos podrían integrar un espíritu burlón y desesperado, el espíritu de mi obra que tal vez sea el de nuestro país. (1991: 345)

In *El color del verano*, the mask is not only related to the idea of simulacra and carnival, it also subverts the principle of identity. Most of the characters have more than one name; each name corresponds to a different 'self' and to a different role in society. Thus, the narrator-protagonist possesses three personalities: Reinaldo is the writer; Gabriel is the narrator in his role of ideal son, behaving as his mother would like him to; and the Tétrica Mofeta is the homosexual, the *loca* who loses control when he sees a man. Depending on the circumstances, the character will assume a specific mask. As Soto lucidly claims with respect to the duplicity of the narrator:

> In addition to underscoring how society's rejection of homosexuality forces the homosexual to protect his true identity by hiding behind a mask to avoid suspicion, Arenas's poetic trinity is also a parodic, sullen, and blasphemous (sub)version of the Catholic trinity [...] that reflects and gives voice to the very complex and contradictory human facets of the protagonist's personality. Reinaldo is the writer-creator (God the Father) who gives life to his characters. The nostalgic recollection of Gabriel (a biblical name of one of the archangels who appears as a divine messenger) must be sacrificed, like the son Jesus Christ, in order for the Tétrica Mofeta (the protagonist's vital homosexual spirit) to exist. (1994: 68)

Arenas's novel is, above all, a cry raised in complaint against oppression and a strong defence of the individual's right to self-expression and to live authentically, even if *El color del verano* is, as suggested by Iván de la Nuez, 'políticamente incorrecto hasta la médula' (1999: 226).

To sum up, in the novel I have examined in this chapter we see the appearance of recurrent notions of carnival as a subversion of official discourses and the established order, the elimination of hierarchy, and an emphasis on the fact that 'order', whether old or new, is an invention in terms of coherence and uniformity. The mask appears as a symbol of double moral standards, life as representation and simulacra. These recurrent ideas allow us to speak of a unity in Cuban discourse within and beyond the island, regardless of ideology. Arenas and, as we shall see in the next chapter, non-dissidents such as Padura Fuentes share common techniques and portray similar concerns through the mechanism of role-play permitted by masks and carnival in their respective novels.

In *El color del verano* most of the characters maintain a dialogue with their several identities or voices; thus, we can read a letter that Reinaldo the narrator sends from exile to his other self who stays in Cuba, and vice versa. In this polyphonic novel characters are constantly suffering a process of transformation, of change; their voices are completely independent from the narrator's voice. The characters reach full awareness of their subjectivities once they learn to recognize the fragmentation of their own selves and the polyphony that accompanies them; each voice has equal importance and the existence of one does not invalidate the others. In the specific case of the protagonist of *El color del verano*, this fusion can only be achieved through death. As Bakhtin expresses in another context:

Heroes are no longer diminished to the dominating consciousness of the author; secondary characters are no longer encompassed by and diminished to their usefulness to heroes – or to the author. Characters are, in short, respected as full subjects, shown as 'consciousnesses' that can never be fully defined or exhausted, rather than as objects fully known, once and for all, in their roles – and then discarded as expendable. (1984: xxiii)

In *El color del verano*, masks allow a mobility of roles and introduce simulacra, as social hypocrisy discovered through the mask. As Arenas claims in his novel, this phenomenon is the result of a long tradition of political and historical betrayals that, according to him, are part of the essence of what it means to be Cuban: 'lo cubano'.

In opposition to carnival, in everyday life in society roles are presented as fixed and there is no possibility of changing one's position. This characteristic of mobility in carnival, where one chooses the mask one wants to don, dismantles any monologic and fixed system in the novel. Thus in Arenas we find that 'Policías con casco y tolete renuncian por un momento a sus labores represivas y se agachan ante un negro heroico que viene de pelear en las guerras internacionales y trae un atraso de diez años' (1991: 417). As Padura also shows in *Máscaras*, those characters who, before carnival, had adopted a repressive role, during carnival have the chance to change these roles, even if it is true that Arenas goes further than other Cuban novelists in focusing on the sexual act to turn the whole nation into homosexuals: 'Hasta los enanos encargados de mantener el orden secreto se treparon como ardillas voraces y mamaron' (1991: 427). In this chronotope of carnival, the protagonists reflect themselves as they really are, since when they wear the disguise they recover their own identity. Disguise constitutes the true self. The carnival represents authenticity, but at the same time it is no more than a device, such as Arenas's use of literature or sexuality, to fight oppression, in what we could call 'Arenas's way'.

2

Transposed Words: Mapping Intertextuality in Leonardo Padura Fuentes' *Máscaras*

In this chapter I shall focus on the Cuban novel *Máscaras* by Leonardo Padura Fuentes in the light of intertextuality. Most critics, including Stephen Wilkinson (2000; 2006), Carlos Uxó (2006), José Antonio Michelena (2006), Sara Rosell (2006), Clemens Franken Kurzen (2009) and Antonio Aiello Fernández (2010) have focused their attention on how Padura has transformed traditional detective fiction in Cuba. Padura Fuentes himself has contributed to this approach by inserting himself in this tradition when revisiting the detective genre in his article 'Modernidad y postmodernidad: la novela policial en Iberoamérica' (1999). Some scholars have also paid particular attention to the critiques concerning political and sexual intolerance that the novel expresses (Wilkinson 2000; 2006; Aiello Fernández 2010), while a more recent study by James Buckwalter-Arias (2010: 111–51) critically examines the extent to which *Máscaras* could be considered a synthesis of political and aesthetic writing. Critics have also tried to analyse the character of Mario Conde from a psychological perpective (Wilkinson 2000; 2006; Franken K. 2009).

I am interested, however, in the increasing use of intertextuality in recent Cuban narrative, particularly post-1990, in the work of writers such as Padura Fuentes, Abilio Estévez, Reinaldo Arenas, Yanitzia Canetti and Jesús Díaz, which confirms the dialogism present in recent Cuban narrative. These authors use intertextuality for different aims, which range from the literary to the political attacks we find in Arenas's texts. I have chosen to study Padura's fourth novel, *Máscaras* (winner of the Premio Café Gijón de Novela 1995), the third of his tetralogy of 'Las cuatro estaciones', because I believe this is the Cuban novel most representative of the use of intertextuality. Together with other texts published in the 1990s *Máscaras* established a new paradigm in Cuban fiction with which to challenge the monologic positions that had been imposed upon the island, particularly in the 1970s. Abilio Estévez, for one, has participated in the polemic that ensued concerning the well-established references to and rediscovery of a possible 'quinquenio gris' and affirms, 'más de una vez he dicho que eso de "quinquenio gris" es, como bien dice Desiderio [Navarro], un eufemismo (o una burla). Ni quinquenio ni gris. Una década de horror.'[1]

As Padura himself has commented, *Máscaras* is a novel about literature and the creative process. Using intertextuality in this novel, Padura mobilizes contemporary postmodern theories of the text.[2] As Graham Allen rightly observes:

> Postmodernism is a particularly debated term. However, there are recurrent themes in these debates. Firstly, the idea that national limits for social and cultural identity have been superseded by a global environment in which multinational companies are now more important than national governments in directing social and cultural tendencies. Secondly, such a transnational system is characterized by 'empty signifiers', or representations and signs which have no base in a recognizable, lived reality. Many descriptions of Postmodernism depict a transnational cultural situation in which pastiche and parody of earlier forms and styles predominate. Postmodern art, many argue, rejects notions of originality and Modernism's desire to 'Make it New', and cultivates a wilfully derivative, mixed and thoroughly intertextual approach which attempts to capture a new age in which old certainties about historical knowledge, social progress and even the ability to represent the external world have collapsed. (2000: 217)

The novel becomes a text as Barthes himself defines it, that is, 'Woven entirely with citations, references, echoes, [...] which cut across it through and through in a vast stereophony' (1977: 160). Barthes further claims that:

> The intertextual in which every text is held, it itself being the text-between of another text, is not to be confused with some origin of the text: to try to find the 'sources', the 'influences' of a work, is to fall in with the myth of filiation;

---

1   This was published as 'Mensaje de Abilio Estévez', in *Consenso: Revista Digital* (Espacio de Reflexión y Debate del Pensamiento Progresista Cubano), in 2007 (http://www.desdecuba.com/polemica/articulos/53_01.shtml [accessed 4 September 2013]). For Ambrosio Fornet's position concerning his coining of the term 'quinquenio gris' and the uses and abuses of the term, beyond his initial intention, see his article 'El quinquenio gris: revisitando el término' (http://www.desdecuba.com/polemica/articulos/101_01.shtml [accessed 4 September 2013]).

2   In this study of intertextuality I define a text in accordance with Graham Allen and Robert Scholes. As Allen states, 'In structuralist and poststructuralist theory the "text" comes to stand for whatever meaning is generated by the intertextual relations between one text and another and the activation of those relations by a reader. "Text" becomes a term associated with the absence of stable and permanent meaning, while "work" is now associated with the idea of a stable and self-contained meaning' (2000: 220). As Scholes asserts, 'A text, as opposed to a work, is open, incomplete, insufficient. [...] As a text, however, a piece of writing must be understood as the product of a person or persons, at a given point in human history, in a given form of discourse, taking its meanings from the interpretive gesture of individual readers using the grammatical, semantic, and cultural codes available to them. A text always echoes other texts, and it is the result of choices that have displaced still other possibilities' (1982: 15–16).

the citations which go to make up a text are anonymous, untraceable, and yet *already read*: they are quotations without inverted commas. (1977: 160, original emphasis)

Despite the abundance of 'quotations without inverted commas' in *Máscaras*, there is still a traceable element that I shall pay attention to. *Máscaras* is a 'tejido', as Severo Sarduy defines it, that is, an intertext, the simultaneous text of what has been already written and what will be written, a text that 'se repite, que se cita sin límites, que se plagia a sí mismo; tapiz que se desteje para hilar otros signos' (Sarduy 1987: 66). In the 'Nota del autor' in *Máscaras*, Padura Fuentes warns us:

> Acogiéndome a ciertas libertades poéticas, en esta novela he citado, con mayor o menor extensión, textos de Virgilio Piñera, Severo Sarduy, Dashiell Hammett, Abilio Estévez, Antonin Artaud, Eliseo Diego, Dalia Acosta y Leonardo Padura, además de varios documentos oficiosos y algunos pasajes de los Evangelios. En más de una ocasión los transformé y en otras hasta los mejoré, y casi siempre les suprimí las comillas que antes se usaban en tales casos. (1997: 9)[3]

Here, Padura claims that the act of rewriting implies improvement of the original. Padura puts himself in a superior position with respect to the other authors; he is a 'bricoleur'.

In *Máscaras*, through intertextuality, the boundaries between literary genres are blurred and the traditional relationship between author and reader is subverted. Owing to its use of intertextuality *Máscaras* is not a simple detective novel. We find official documents, fragments of essays about the essence of theatre or transvestism, fragments of religious texts and even poetry, so we cannot say that *Máscaras* is simply a novel but rather that it is an amalgam of different genres. This kind of text demands a more active role for the reader and questions a traditional and fixed concept of authorship. The text is legitimized not by itself but through its relationship with other texts, both previous and future. The word, as Bakhtin claims, is never neutral (1984: 27); it is always doubled-voiced: the already written and said.[4]

---

[3] In his novel *Adiós Hemingway* (Barcelona: Tusquets, 2006), Padura Fuentes also explains in his author's note: 'el Hemingway de esta obra es, por supuesto, un Hemingway de ficción, pues la historia en que se ve envuelto es sólo un producto de mi imaginación, y en cuya escritura practico incluso la licencia poética y posmoderna de citar algunos pasajes de sus obras y entrevistas para construir la historia de la larga noche del 2 al 3 de octubre de 1958' (10).

[4] Barthes, on the other hand, in talking about the death of the author, uses Balzac's novel *Sarrasine* to affirm that 'la escritura es la destrucción de toda voz, de todo origen. La escritura es ese lugar neutro, compuesto, oblicuo, al que van [*sic*] a parar nuestro sujeto, el blanco-y-negro en donde acaba por perderse toda identidad, comenzando por la propia identidad del cuerpo que escribe' (1987b: 65).

As we shall see, Padura's use of intertextuality serves also to define Cuban culture as a product of transculturation in which both European and African elements have immense resonances. By means of intertextuality, the writer links *Máscaras* with a universal literary tradition. Culture appears as one big book that is written and constantly rewritten throughout history. Finally, intertextuality becomes a mechanism to explore different voices, and thus different views of the world, beyond the monologue of the state.

Máscaras is thus a polyphonic novel. As defined by Bakhtin, a polyphonic novel is one in which there emerge '[a] plurality of independent and unmerged voices and consciousnesses, a genuine polyphony of fully valid voices' (1984: 6). This definition, which Bakhtin applies to Dostoevsky's novels, is also applicable to Padura's novels. In a polyphonic novel such as *Máscaras* characters maintain a dialogue with other characters and with themselves. In Bakhtin's words:

> Dialogue [...] is not a means for revealing, for bringing to the surface the already ready-made character of a person; no, in dialogue a person not only shows himself outwardly, but he becomes for the first time that which he is [...] not only for the others but for himself as well. To be means to communicate dialogically. (1984: 252)

Padura's main characters are like those in Dostoevsky's novels in that:

> [They] sense their own inner unfinalizability, their capacity to outgrow, as it were, from within and to render *untrue* any externalizing and finalizing definition of them. As long as a person is alive he lives by the fact that he is not yet finalized, that he has not yet uttered his ultimate word. [...] The genuine life of the personality is made available only through a dialogic penetration of that personality, during which it freely and reciprocally reveals itself. (Bakhtin 1984: 59)

Mario Conde and Alberto el Marqués are dialogic characters who share this 'unfinalizability'. Therefore, because they are not fixed and stable, they experience a continuous process of transformation and define their identities by means of dialogue.

As in any polyphonic novel, *Máscaras* excludes any monologic and stable view of reality. As Allen has written in his study of intertextuality:

> Like the tradition of the carnival, the polyphonic novel fights against any view of the world which would valorize one 'official' point-of-view, one ideological position, and thus one discourse, above all others. The novel, in this sense, presents to us a world which is literally dialogic. And yet it is important to note that dialogism does not concern simply the clash between different character-centred discourses; dialogism is also a central feature of each character's own individual discourse. (2000: 24)

In his excellent work on intertextuality José Enrique Martínez-Fernández studies the closeness of the phenomena of dialogism, polyphony and intertextuality. Because intertextuality appears to be a dialogue among different previous discourses, we can say that Bakhtin, though he did not invent the concept of intertextuality, is one of the first theorists to have studied it. I agree with Martínez-Fernández when he says:

> [S]i la plurivocidad o polifonía revela una variedad de sociolectos y orientaciones ideológicas, la intertextualidad muestra las líneas de filiación cultural del texto; si la plurivocidad atañe a los registros y a los lenguajes de grupo, la intertextualidad lo hace a la diversidad del lenguaje literario y a los estilos individuales. Por medio de la intertextualidad el texto sale de su aislamiento y se presenta como parte de un discurso desarrollado a través de textos; además, mediante la intertextualidad, la lengua de un texto asume parcialmente como componente propio la lengua de un texto precedente. (2001: 76)

We can relate Martínez-Fernández's words to Padura's *Máscaras*. Through intertextuality Padura inserts his voice within a wider canon and he achieves what Martínez-Fernández mentions above. Because *Máscaras* is a polyphonic novel, we can find a plurality of voices that show us different views of reality, different ways of speaking and different ideologies. By means of intertextuality Padura inserts himself and his work within the universal history of literature and shows us the sources he draws from. Hence the text can no longer be considered in isolation. It is always related to previous texts and forms part of the discourse created through the history of texts.

Dialogism, polyphony and intertextuality go hand in hand. The polyphonic novel uses intertextuality as a mechanism to introduce the voice of the Other. Those voices that appear in the polyphonic novel oppose and complement each other, but without merging. As Martínez-Fernández writes with reference to Bakhtinian theory: 'El carácter dialógico del discurso (del enunciado) es la base del concepto de intertextualidad. La dialogía establece la relación de voces propias y ajenas, individuales y colectivas' (2001: 53). Because *Máscaras* is a polyphonic novel, there is dialogue between the different voices and texts that form the novel.

However, although the use of polyphony and intertextuality can be subversive, Padura does not utilize this aspect to its full extent. Padura uses the work of Sarduy and Virgilio Piñera, ostensibly rescuing the voices of these authors who had problems with Castro's regime and who suffered exile (Sarduy) or internal exile (Piñera). Although Padura maintains that *Máscaras* is a tribute to these two gay authors, I will argue that his use of their texts is not arbitrary. Padura uses the texts of two internationally known writers who had problems with Castro's government, although after the process of rectification they have been reinserted into the Cuban canon. Moreover, Sarduy and Piñera are now both dead, so they are no longer problematic, politically speaking. Padura's use of the voice of other dissidents who are still alive would have been much more problematic and subversive.[5] In this study I suggest that although Padura makes reference to certain problematic periods of recent history in Cuba, and although there is a clear reference to historical reality – to an extra-literary reality – Padura is not as subversive and critical as he pretends. Moreover, I claim that his use of intertextuality is a stratagem that prevents him from being more critical socially and politically, because this intertextual game means that 'la realidad de todo texto escrito es el texto mismo' (Levine 1976a: 97).

Therefore I suggest that Padura indirectly, with this novel, validates the so-called 'despenalización de la censura' of the 1990s, but at the same time he is only critical within the limits of what has become accepted or at least acknowledged by the state. In *Máscaras* there is no questioning of the system itself, either by its author or his characters. What we as readers see is that some individuals within the system exploit it and profit from it. Faustino Arayán is punished because he murdered his own son, but not because he has benefited from his diplomatic career within a system that supposedly promulgates the abolition of social difference. This indicates that this practice is often carried out by the Cuban elite and is not considered a crime. In this novel the reader can see the hypocrisy of the leaders who promote a specific kind of behaviour but act in a different way. Although Padura seems to denounce this hypocrisy he merely states the obvious, and does not make any statements that might challenge the system itself.

In this chapter I shall also focus on *Máscaras*'s intertextual connections with Sarduy's work on baroque and simulacra in order to use the parallelism he establishes between transvestism and intertextuality, the transvestite and writing, and the baroque and writing. By means of the principles of baroque I shall also analyse the connections between transvestism, theatre and simulacra. Padura uses Sarduy's text *La simulación* in order to introduce the subject of simulacra and transvestism, and I claim that Padura thus utilizes intertextuality to allow a more expert voice to develop the topic of transvestism. The figure of the transvestite becomes the embodiment of the collective memory, as el Marqués recalls the events of recent Cuban history and denounces the repression exerted by the state. Therefore in *Máscaras* there is an acknowledgement of the now well-known fact of the repression exerted against homosexuals and intellectuals in recent years, even if some less-acknowledged aspects of oppression under the revolution are avoided.

---

5   We could think of the work of Reinaldo Arenas, Guillermo Cabrera Infante or Zoé Valdés.

Transvestism and Hypertextuality

One of the recurrent topics in the novel is transvestism, and Padura uses the figure of the male transvestite in order to denounce the repression exerted by the state.[6] The transvestite uses his attire to define his real (sexual) identity and to practise his freedom to express himself authentically. The transvestite appears as the mimesis of the Other and represents subaltern discourse versus the state. The transvestite also appears to be the embodiment of collective memory and subverts the traditional concepts of masculinity and femininity.

Transvestism reflects how gender is a cultural construct. I agree with Judith Butler when she states that gender identity 'is performatively constituted by the very "expressions" that are said to be its results' (1999b: 33). As I shall explore during this study, transvestism embodies this idea. Because gender identity is a fabrication, I claim with Butler that 'if a true gender is a fantasy instituted and inscribed on the surface of bodies, then it seems that genders can be neither true nor false, but are only produced as the truth effects of a discourse' (1999b: 174). That is, the figure of the transvestite subverts the notion of gender as a fixed concept and undermines notions of a true or false gender. As Butler adds, 'drag [...] effectively mocks both the expressive model of gender and the notion of a true gender identity' (1999b: 174).

In my second interview with the author, I questioned Padura about the increase in the number of homosexual characters in Cuban fiction of the 1990s. I put it to him that there is a new tendency in Cuban literature 'en el uso de la figura del homosexual y/o travesti (su novela *Máscaras* forma parte de esta nueva tendencia)' and asked him to what factors he would attribute the use and abuse of this figure. He replied:

> Sin duda al hecho de que había sido una figura marginada, escamoteada, discriminada en la sociedad y en la literatura, y eso le aportaba no sólo una posibilidad de explotación artística, sino, y sobre todo, un dramatismo intrínseco generado por la marginación, el escamoteo y la discriminación de marras, que se producen en una sociedad esencialmente machista, pero además oficialmente marxista, que por años consideró al homosexual no sólo como un enfermo pervertido, sino también como un ser no compatible con la ideología oficial. (see Appendix 2)

I also asked Padura more specifically about the function of the transvestite in this novel.

> Respecto a la función del travesti en la novela es más metafórica aun que la de Mario Conde: el travesti es la representación máxima de la

---

6   It is worth noting that in this study I focus only on the male transvestite, as addressed in the novel. Hence, all references to the 'transvestite' will be in relation to male subjectivity.

> ocultación, de la transformación, de la transmutación que muchas personas han debido adoptar aquí y no sólo en Cuba para sobrevivir en una sociedad que por diversas vías lo obliga a ocultar sus verdaderos deseos y pensamientos.

In this response the author generalizes the conflict of the concealment of one's identity. Padura states that transvestism is a metaphor for the transformation some people have to carry out in order to survive. He is very careful in emphasizing that this need to conceal identity occurs not only in Cuba. Padura is not only speaking of state repression in general terms but also broadly discussing conservative views in society. Therefore *Máscaras* should not be considered a direct attack on the Cuban regime.

El Marqués tells Conde how he and his friends, el Recio and el Otro Muchacho, discovered the transvestites in the Paris of 1969. At the beginning of the novel both the reader and Mario Conde ignore the identity of el Marqués's friends. El Otro is an opportunist; he conceals his homosexuality and thus is able to become part of the Cuban elite. The fact that this character does not have a proper name but rather a general one is a method used to emphasize that there are many people like him: many people could be, then, el Otro.

Padura makes demands on his reader by voicing through el Recio the theory of transvestism offered by Sarduy in his essay *La simulación.* Thus, borrowing Gerard Genette's terminology, *La simulación* constitutes the hypotext of Padura's novel, which becomes the hypertext. In his book *Palimpsests*, Genette understands hypertextuality thus:

> By hypertextualiy I mean any relationship uniting a text B (which I call the *hypertext*) to an earlier text A (I shall, of course, call it the *hypotext*), upon which it is grafted in a manner that is not that of commentary. [...] To view things differently, let us posit the general notion of a text in the second degree [...] i.e., a text derived from another pre-existent text. [...] It may yet be of another kind such as text B not speaking of text A at all but being unable to exist, as such, without A, from which it originates through a process I shall provisionally call *transformation*, and which it consequently evokes more or less perceptibly without necessarily speaking of it or citing it. (1997: 5)

Although Padura cites extensively, he does not directly speak of a text A (that is, Sarduy's text) but inserts it without alerting his reader. According to Genette, hypertextuality is just one of the five possible relationships – the others being intertextuality, paratextuality, metatextuality and architextuality – established among texts that constitute the core of transtextuality. Genette considers that 'the subject of poetics is *transtextuality*, or the textual transcendence of the text, [...] defined roughly as "all that sets the text in a relationship, whether obvious or concealed, with other texts"' (1997: 1–2). I shall use these theories of transtextuality for the purpose of this study.

Both Padura and Sarduy consider transvestism as a strategy employed in order to permit the disappearance of the individual. Sarduy goes further in his essay when he proposes simulacra as the essence of arts and, namely, of literature. As I shall show in due course, transvestism and hypertextuality have many things in common. When Martínez-Fernández summarizes the different uses of the same terminology over the years in order to name intertextuality (part of Genette's transtextuality), he mentions how it was called 'travesty' (Martínez-Fernández 2001: 57). I will demonstrate in this study that it is not a mere coincidence.

When reading *Máscaras* and the issues it raises with reference to this topic of transvestism, we as readers can see the connection between it and Sarduy's essay. Sarduy writes:

> El travestí no imita a la mujer. Para él, à la limite, no hay mujer, sabe – y quizás, paradójicamente sea el único en saberlo –, que *ella* es una apariencia, que su reino y la fuerza de su fetiche encubren un defecto.
>
> La erección cosmética del travestí, la agresión esplendente de sus párpados temblorosos y metalizados como alas de insectos voraces, su voz desplazada, como si perteneciera a otro personaje, siempre en *off*, la boca dibujada sobre su boca, su propio sexo, más presente cuanto más castrado, sólo sirven a la reproducción obstinada de ese ícono, aunque falaz omnipresente: la madre que la tiene parada y que el travestí dobla, aunque sólo sea para simbolizar que la erección es una apariencia. (1982: 13)

On the other hand, el Marqués relates to Conde Recio's comments about transvestism:

> – No. El *travestí* no imita a la mujer – comentó entonces el Recio, como si estuviera dictando una conferencia, con esa voz y esas palabras suyas de saberlo todo-todo. Siempre usaba oraciones largas, estratificadas, barrocas y lezamianas, como caricaturas del pobre Gordo –. Para él, à la limite[,] no hay mujer, porque sabe (y su tragedia mayor es que nunca deja de saberlo) que él, es decir, ella, es una apariencia, que su reino y la fuerza de su fetiche encubren un insalvable defecto de las otras veces sabia naturaleza...
>
> Y nos explicó su teoría [that is, Sarduy's] de que la erección cosmética del *travestí* (así lo acentuaba el Recio, *travestí*), la agresión resplandeciente de sus párpados temblorosos y metalizados como alas de insectos voraces, su voz desplazada, como si perteneciera a otro personaje, siempre en *off*, la boca pretendida, dibujada sobre su boca escondida, y su propio sexo, más presente cuanto más castrado, es todo una apariencia, algo así como una perfecta mascarada teatral, dijo, y me miró, como si debiera mirarme, como si tuviera que hacerlo. (Padura 1997: 48–9)

Thus Recio, Padura's fictional character, is Sarduy's own essayist voice, here used in 'off'. Padura reproduces the style of Sarduy's essay although he transforms the earlier text considerably. Padura reworks the original and proves that texts can be relocated. He thus questions the possibility of inherent meanings.

I shall now analyse the differences and similarities between these two texts. Both Sarduy and Padura agree in considering that the transvestite does not imitate the woman. Both authors believe that transvestism is a sort of simulacrum; a phenomenon as explained by Baudrillard in his study of simulacra, that is, a system of signs without referent: one sign leads to another and reality does not exist apart from the simulacra.[7] However, both authors seem to contradict themselves because although they say that the transvestite does not imitate the woman, Sarduy proposes the mother as an icon, as a model that transvestites want to follow, and Padura shows us over the course of the novel numerous examples of transvestites who imitate famous female artists such as Marilyn Monroe, even if these imitations always have a parodic nature. They are parodies of gender, and as Judith Butler writes, 'gender parody reveals that the original identity after which gender fashions itself is an imitation without an origin' (1999b: 175). I use this theory to confirm Sarduy's and Padura's idea that transvestism lacks an original.

I agree with Butler when she states that cross-dressing is a parody of the concepts of original and copy. This idea also serves in my analysis as the first link between transvestism and an intertextual narrative such as *Máscaras*. When Padura uses different fragments of essays, biblical quotations or political speeches, the boundaries of the genres blur and the concepts of an original and a copy no longer make sense. This conforms with the view that this is 'para indicar quizás que todos los textos son uno solo: *l'écriture*. Una escritura que nunca está terminada, un libro que se escribe incesantemente' (Levine 1976b: 128–9).

In the last quotation from *Máscaras* above, when el Recio explains his theory about transvestites, Padura modifies Sarduy's text slightly, but at the same time reserves the use of the word *travestí* (accented) to identify with Sarduy's text and *travesti* for others. El Recio considers the transvestite a tragic figure because he knows his transformation will always be a failure: the device will always be discovered. However, we can say that device and discovery actually constitute the goal of the transvestite and cannot be considered his failure. Rather, I share Emir Rodríguez Monegal's viewpoint that 'el travestido es siempre una imagen doblada en que lo masculino resulta más subrayado por la misma ficción femenina' (1976: 40), and I disagree with Sarduy and Padura when they consider the transvestite a failure. I assume that the transvestite is the in-between being, who is both masculine and feminine at the same time. Transvestites do not want the full erasure of their

---

[7] The same could be said about the text. In a Derridean sense, a text does not need to have a referent in the outside world. A text is a net of signifiers that lead to other signifiers, without necessarily leading to a particular referent outside textual reality. Baudrillard has also worked on the issue of transvestism through 'La eterna ironía de la comunidad' (2000: 19–32).

masculine features. The transvestite does not want to conceal his masculine body; if that were the case he could undergo surgery as transsexuals do. Sarduy's text, however, lacks this idea.

Another difference between the two texts appears with respect to the dilemma of language. In *Máscaras* we find a recurrent concern, that is, whether or not the transvestite is a he or a she. The transvestite opens a wide range of possibilities against the traditional dichotomy of masculine and feminine, although Padura as well as Sarduy argue that transvestism is used to conceal a fault, in this case the presence of male genital organs. This view, however, has been superseded by work done in the theoretical field by Marjorie Garber. She declares that many men dress as women in order to reach an orgasm and acknowledges that many men who dress as women are in fact heterosexual (Garber 1992: 3).

Sarduy and Padura on the other hand state that attire stresses the difference between the model and the copy. Although these two writers believe that transvestism is synonymous with concealment and simulacra, their theories are totally different in terms of the essence of this phenomenon. Sarduy reads the figure of the transvestite by means of psychoanalysis; thus, as stated above, transvestites are seen as having their mothers as their icon. Using Butler's study of Julia Kristeva, I would argue, rather, that this connection between the transvestite and the maternal body enters the realm of poetic language. As Butler states, 'poetic language is the recovery of the maternal body within the terms of language, one that has the potential to disrupt, subvert, and displace the paternal law' (1999b: 102). This idea can be applied to the transvestite and his or her multiple signifiers and signifieds. The transvestite belongs to the semiotic, using Kristeva's terminology, and displaces the symbolic, that is, the univocal signifier of the paternal law.

Padura, however, points out the theatrical nature of the transvestite. In *Máscaras* the transvestite becomes the artist, the ideal actor *par excellence*: the transvestite is the artist whose artistic work appears to be his own body. El Marqués explains to Conde how he combines the idea of transvestism with the theatre: 'Una apariencia. Una mascarada. Allí había estado la esencia misma de la representación, desde que las danzas rituales se transformaron en teatro, cuando surgió la conciencia de la creación artística: el travesti como artista de sí mismo' (1997: 49). As Butler writes, 'That the gendered body is performative suggests that it has no ontological status apart from the various acts which constitute its reality' (1999b: 173). The transvestite is the actor who performs his gender and is subversive because, as Butler claims:

> As much as drag creates a unified picture of 'woman' (what its critics often oppose), it also reveals the distinctness of those aspects of gendered experience which are falsely naturalized as a unity through the regulatory fiction of heterosexual coherence. *In imitating gender, drag implicitly reveals the*

imitative structure of gender itself – as well as its contingency. […] In the place of the law of heterosexual coherence, we see sex and gender denaturalized by means of a performance which avows their distinctness and dramatizes the cultural mechanism of their fabricated unity. (1999b: 175, original emphasis).

In any case of hypertextuality there is a relationship similar to the one between the transvestite and the model. The relationship between the transvestite and his model and that between the hypertext and the hypotext is not enantiomorphic but is one of transformation, as Genette suggests above.[8] Between the male transvestite and a woman or between the hypertext and the hypotext there is never a mirror relationship. Rather, in *Máscaras*, when transvestites dress in drag imitating or pretending to be the Other, they know that they are not an exact replica of the original; rather they participate 'en la persecución de una irrealidad infinita' (Sarduy 1982: 14) and, paradoxically, 'en la persecución de una realidad infinita' (Padura 1997: 49).[9] This transvestism is also extended to the novel's writing itself. When citing Sarduy, Padura transforms the quotations, so that the intertextual fragments of *La simulación* acquire new signifieds in the context of *Máscaras*. Expanding on the relationship between copy and original, Sarduy says that the transvestite:

> [n]o copia; simula, pues no hay norma que invite y magnetice la transformación, que decida la metáfora: es más bien la inexistencia del ser mimado lo que constituye el espacio, la región o el soporte de esa simulación, de esa impostura concertada: aparecer que regula una pulsación goyesca: entre la risa y la muerte. (1982: 13–14)

Thus even if Sarduy, as previously discussed, states the possible iconicity of the mother in terms of resemblance or similitude, he negates the existence of a specific original.[10] The transvestite, then, becomes a system of signs without a referent, and transvestism appears as pure simulacra.

Sarduy uses Roger Caillois's theory of mimesis to develop his theory of transvestism. Thus Sarduy claims that:

---

8   Concerning enantiomorphism, I borrow Lotman's terminology. For him, 'El caso más simple, y a la vez el más extendido, de unión de la identidad y la diferencia estructurales es el enantiomorfismo, es decir, la simetría especular, en la cual ambas partes son especularmente iguales, pero son desiguales cuando se pone una sobre otra, o sea se relacionan entre sí como derecho e izquierdo' (1996: I, 36). I claim that in the case of the transvestite this mirror image is not achieved in the first place.

9   In theoretical terms, Baudrillard views this hyper-reality as parody: 'el maquillaje no es otra cosa: parodia triunfante, resolución por exceso, por hipersimulación en superficie de esta simulación en profundidad' (2000: 21).

10   As Robert Scholes states in terms of semiotics, 'In Peirce's theory of signs any given sign is iconic to the extent that it signifies by virtue of some resemblance or similitude between the sign and what it stands for. Pictures and diagrams are the most common iconic signs' (1982: 144). Here, for Sarduy, the mother is the iconic sign for female subjectivity in drag.

El mimetismo, para Roger Caillois, 'se presenta bajo varios aspectos diferentes, que tienen, cada uno, su correspondencia en el hombre: *travestí, camuflaje e intimidación.* Los mitos de metamorfosis y el gusto del disfrazamiento responden al travestí (*mimicry,* propiamente dicha); las leyendas de sombrero o de manto de invisibilidad al camuflaje; el terror al mal de ojo y a la mirada paralizante (médusant) y el uso que el hombre hace de la máscara, principalmente, pero no exclusivamente, en las sociedades dichas primitivas, a la intimidación producida por los ojillos (ocelles) y completada por la apariencia o la mímica aterrorizante de ciertos insectos'. (1982: 13–14)

An extended network, in line with the Barthesian concept of the infinite text, which I shall discuss below, is created through intertextuality: the novel *Máscaras* leads us to Sarduy's essay *La simulación,* which leads the reader explicitly to other texts, for example that written by Caillois, cited above, which in turn leads to animal mimicry and mirror images in the biological context, and so forth. At the same time the cultural baggage of the reader plays a role, as Baudrillard's theoretical attention to simulacra comes to mind. This text leads the reader to the reading of previous works, and thus we can say that through intertextuality we as readers participate in the process of creating a Barthesian 'infinite text'. As Barthes states:

The Text can be approached, experienced, in reaction to the sign. [...] The Text [...] practises the infinite deferment of the signified, is dilatory; its field is that of the signifier and the signifier must not be conceived of as 'the first stage of meaning', its material vestibule, but, in complete opposition to this, as its *deferred action.* Similarly, the *infinity* of the signifier refers not to some idea of the ineffable (the unnameable signified) but to that of a *playing;* the generation of the perpetual signifier (after the fashion of a perpetual calender [*sic*]) in the field of the text (better, of which the text is the field) is realized not according to an organic progress of maturation or a hermeneutic course of deepening investigation, but, rather, according to a serial movement of disconnections, overlappings, variations. The logic regulating the Text is not comprehensive [...] but metonymic; the activity of associations, contiguities, carryings-over coincides with a liberation of symbolic energy [...]. [The text] is structured but off-centred, without closure. (1977: 158–9)

In his essay *La simulación* Sarduy states that both works of art and transvestism are mere acts of simulation; thus they are metonymic acts that establish contiguities, despite the fact that he tends to emphasize the issue of resemblance which would be metaphoric.[11] We can propose that *Máscaras* is the model,

---

11 For a theoretical approach that has been applied to literature as participating in either a metonymic (contiguity) or metaphoric (substitution) process, see Jakobson's essay 'Two Aspects of Language and Two Types of Aphasic Disturbances' (in Jakobson 1990: 115–33).

the epitome of what Sarduy states: literature as simulacra. *Máscaras* focuses on how Cuban society has been transformed into pure simulacra in order to survive, a view also analysed in the previous chapter, but from a more parodic stance in relation to Arenas's carnival. From a formal point of view, *Máscaras* seems to be a completely new work but, in terms of content, other authors' works become part of it, thus implicitly questioning the novelty of any text (in its context) and the novel's own authorship. Using intertextuality Padura also tries to question the traditional and established categories of literary genre and the text in the same way that the transvestite subverts the traditional idea of sexual gender.

Returning to Caillois in this context of intertextuality, following Genette's theory we can say that when Sarduy quotes Caillois, he establishes a relationship of intertextuality, understood 'as a relationship of copresence between two texts or among several texts', which can include '*quoting* (with or without specific references)' (Genette 1997: 1–2). In addition, Padura participates in this intertextuality by quoting without quotation marks, appropriating the texts of other authors.

Sarduy seems to apply Caillois's theory, but he goes further than Caillois's mimicry, metamorphosis or 'disfrazamiento' when he relates the three types of mimesis to the figure of the transvestite. According to Sarduy, and again in terms of 'irrealidad infinita':

> El travestí humano es la aparición imaginaria y la convergencia de las tres posibilidades de mimetismo: el *travestimiento* propiamente dicho, impreso en la pulsión ilimitada de metamorfosis, de transformación no se reduce a la imitación de un modelo real, determinado, sino que se precipita en la persecución de una irrealidad infinita, y desde el inicio del 'juego' aceptada como tal, irrealidad cada vez más huidiza e inalcanzable – ser cada vez más mujer, hasta sobrepasar el límite, yendo más allá de la mujer, 'folie douce' que denunciaba un ex travestí del Carrousel[12] –; pero también el *camuflaje* pues nada asegura que la conversión cosmética – o quirúrgica – del hombre en mujer no tenga como finalidad oculta una especie de desaparición, de invisibilidad, *déffacement* y de tachadura del macho en el clan agresivo, en la horda brutal de los machos y, en la medida de su separación, de su diferencia, de su deficiencia o su exceso, también en la de las mujeres, desaparición, anulación que comunica con la pulsión letal del travestí y su fascinación por la *fijeza* a su vez fascinante; finalmente la *intimidación,* pues el frecuente desajuste o la desmesura de los afeites, lo visible del artificio, la abigarrada máscara, paralizan o aterran. (1982: 14–15)

Using this 'visible artifice' in *Máscaras*, el Marqués tells Conde the comments el Recio/Sarduy made when they saw a transvestite in Paris, and in doing so

12   A cabaret in Paris.

participates in intertextuality with Sarduy's text. I shall quote at length to illustrate this point:

> – Rey – a veces me llamaba así [el Marqués refers to el Recio], subiéndome los grados nobiliarios –, el *travestí* humano es una aparición imaginaria y la convergencia de las tres posibilidades de mimetismo – y marcó una pausa para tomarse una copa de aquel vino áspero de los Balcanes, servido en hermosas imitaciones de antiguas ánforas griegas –: primero, el travestimiento propiamente dicho, impreso en esa pulsión ilimitada de la metamorfosis, en esa transformación que no se reduce a la imitación de un modelo real y determinado, sino que se precipita en la persecución de una realidad infinita (y desde el inicio del 'juego' aceptada como tal). Es una irrealidad cada vez más huidiza e inalcanzable (ser cada vez más mujer, hasta sobrepasar el límite, yendo más allá de la mujer)...
>
> »[*sic*] Segundo, el camuflaje, pues nada asegura que la conversión cosmética (o incluso quirúrgica) del hombre en mujer, no tenga como finalidad oculta una especie de desaparición, de invisibilidad, *d'effacement* y de tachadura del macho mismo en el clan agresivo, en la horda brutal de los machos. Y por último – dijo el Recio –, está la intimidación, pues el frecuente desajuste o la desmesura de los afeites, lo visible del artificio, la abigarrada máscara, paralizan o aterran, como ocurre con ciertos animales que utilizan su apariencia para defenderse o para cazar, para suplir defectos naturales o virtudes que no tienen: el valor o la habilidad, ¿no? (Padura 1997: 49–50)

Following on from Sarduy, Padura also considers the transvestite as the figure where the three types of mimesis come together. I posit that in *Máscaras* the transvestite becomes the mimetic representation of the Other, of the in-between. In the first type of mimesis, transvestism, Sarduy and Padura address the topic in the same way. Both writers deny the existence of a specific female model for the transvestite. According to them, the transvestite follows an inaccessible ideal, on a playing field saturated by reality. Transvestism becomes a game, a limitless drive between infinite forms of 'realidad' and 'irrealidad'. Within this playing field, the male transvestite knows in advance his failure. As Johan Huizinga claims in his *Homo ludens*: 'Ese ser otra cosa y ese misterio del juego encuentran su expresión más patente en el disfraz. [...] El disfrazado juega a ser otro, representa, "es" otro ser' (2000: 27). We can see this in *Máscaras* when Conde meets el Marqués who is dressed in drag. Conde is shocked and comments: 'Y lo vio: era el mismo, pero también era otro, como si de algún modo se hubiera disfrazado para un carnaval extemporáneo' (Padura 1997: 136). In transvestism, the game of the representation exposes the authentic identity of the individual. The transvestite uses a system of signs that goes beyond the woman; this is the reason why, when Sarduy writes 'Las mujeres [...] los imitan' (1982: 62), this is obviously debatable.

Sarduy's and later Padura's negation of the existence in transvestism of a specific model, or referent, coincides with Baudrillard's negation of the existence of a referent in simulacra, in line with Derrida's concept of *différance* (Derrida 1982: 1–27).[13] Taking into account Baudrillard's view, I conceive transvestism as simulacra, although I acknowledge that many drag queens attempt to imitate, however hyperbolically, pop icons, a topic to which I shall return when el Marqués tells Conde about the imitators of Doris Day, Marilyn Monroe and Ana Magnani, for example.

For Sarduy and Padura the second type of mimesis is camouflage or *défacement*. Both authors believe that one of the main objectives of the transvestite or the transsexual is to erase from their bodies any trace of their masculine features, of their masculine condition. The most important difference between the texts is that Sarduy points out that the tremendous display of artifice or its deficiency would exclude the transvestite from the world of women as well as from the world of men. Sarduy stresses how this disappearance desired by the transvestite turns into a lethal strategy. It is arguably true that this is the case with transsexuals, that is, that they want to eliminate any trace of their masculine body and this is the reason why they undergo surgery. On the other hand, I believe that Sarduy and Padura repeat a traditional view of transvestites. Both assume that transvestites want to erase any trace of masculinity, and that because of the hyperbole of the artifice the transvestite fails to become a woman and fails to conceal his male body. However, this traditional view of transvestism has been eroded by theoretical studies, for example Butler's and Garber's. The transvestite wants to be the Other, neither a man nor a woman. When Sarduy writes in a footnote, 'como los insectos, los travestís son *hipertélicos*: van más allá de sus fines, toman un exceso de precauciones con frecuencia fatal. Esa feminidad suplementaria y exagerada los señala, los denuncia' (1982: 14), he repeats once more the idea of the failure of the transvestite. According to Sarduy, because of this exaggeration and lack of moderation the transvestite will never reach his goal, and thus his behaviour becomes a lethal drive. However, I refute the existence of the lethal drive that Sarduy sees in the figure of transvestite. This 'fijeza' mentioned by Sarduy can be understood better in light of Garber's work:

> It is a man's idea of what 'a woman' is; it is male subjectivity in drag. [...] Paradoxically, then, the male transvestite represents the extreme limit case of 'male subjectivity' [...]. Dressed in fishnet stockings, garter belt, and high heels, or in a housedress, the male transvestite is the paradoxical embodiment of male subjectivity. For it is his anxiety *about* his gender subjectivity that engenders the masquerade. (1992: 96)

---

13   Derridean *différance* relies on Saussure's work concerning the arbitrariness of the sign with reference to the relationship between signifier and signifieds, which in Derrida's view does not lead to a referent (Saussure 1945: 130–3).

The male transvestite uses his imagination and tries to imitate and represent what he considers to be a woman or being feminine.

The third kind of mimesis is intimidation. In *Máscaras*, the transvestite achieves this in drag. His 'desmesura' is not arbitrary; rather, it offers protection. Out of fear of society's vilification of the Other, would-be aggressors stay away. In the novel we see how Conde himself is in a state of shock after seeing el Marqués dressed up as a woman in order to go to a party of transvestites (Padura 1997: 136). In Sarduy we find an analogous situation when his nameless friend also suffers a similar phobia in a cabaret in Tangiers when he sees a transvestite (1982: 14–15), a topic to which I shall return. Even el Marqués confesses to Conde at the end of the novel how he exaggerated his homosexuality and his irony as a way of defending himself:

> Es que cuando uno ha recibido golpes, aprende a levantar los brazos antes de que intenten golpearlo de nuevo. Como el perro de Pavlov. Pero creo que me excedí con usted, la verdad: yo no soy tan perverso ni tan irónico, ni tan... ni tan maricón como le hice creer. No tanto. (Padura 1997: 220)

In a similar fashion, this aspect of mimesis as intimidation is applicable to the transvestism/intertextuality in the writing. The author employs other authors' discourses as a strategy of self-defence: he is using in Sarduy an internationally recognized author to represent his espoused theories of transvestism. The authorial voice mingles with the voices of other writers, thus establishing a constant dialogue, while keeping the critics at bay. Intertextuality is also used as a mechanism before the reader, who is challenged to discern the different discourses interwoven in the narrative. The reader is thus made aware of the artificiality of fiction, of its textuality. Moreover, in this case, Padura undermines the traditional idea of the author as the unique valid voice within a narration. Using intertextuality Padura rejects the traditional (masculine) idea of an author giving birth to a text in which he is meant to confer meaning and unity. In doing so, Padura exemplifies the Barthesian theory of 'The Death of the Author' (1987b).

In this essay Barthes argues that 'it is language which speaks, not the author; to write is [...] to reach that point where only language acts, "*performs*", and not "me"' (1977: 143, my italics). We can apply Barthes's words to the figure of the transvestite himself. The transvestite's performative acts, the system of signs (his dress and makeup), are the ones that speak, those which confer meaning to the transvestite and not vice versa. Barthes continues by explaining the consequences of the death of the author. For him a text is always an intertext:

> We know now that a text is not a line of words releasing a single 'theological' meaning (the message of the Author-God) but a multi-dimensional space in which a variety of writings, none of them original, blend and clash. The text is a tissue of quotations drawn from the innumerable centres of culture. (1977: 146)

Once the text is 'a tissue of quotations' and the Author-God disappears,

> the claim to decipher a text becomes quite futile. To give a text an Author is
> to impose a limit on that text, to furnish it with a final signified, to close the
> writing. [...] [W]riting ceaselessly posits meaning ceaselessly to evaporate it,
> carrying out a systematic exemption of meaning. [...] [Writing], by refusing
> to assign a 'secret', an ultimate meaning, to the text (and to the world as text),
> liberates what may be called an anti-theological activity, an activity that is
> truly revolutionary since to refuse to fix meaning is, in the end, to refuse God
> and his hypostases – reason, science, law. [...] [A] text is made of multiple
> writings, drawn from many cultures and entering into mutual relations of
> dialogue, parody, contestation, but there is one place where this multiplicity
> is focused and that place is the reader, not, as was hitherto said, the author.
> The reader is the space on which all the quotations that make up a writing are
> inscribed without any of them being lost; a text's unity lies not in its origin
> but in its destination. (1977: 147–8)

The text's meaning is endlessly deferred and thus there is no unique and fixed
meaning, Barthes giving importance to the role of the reader. Now it is not just
the author who establishes the text's meaning but also the reader who rewrites
the text at each reading. In *Máscaras* the reader is the one in charge of exploring
the different levels of readings of the novel. Depending on his or her readings
he or she will identify the texts interwoven within the novel.

Padura is inspired by the following part of Sarduy's text to recreate the environment of the cabaret called *Les Femmes*, where el Marqués, el Recio and
el Otro Muchacho see the French transvestites for the first time. Sarduy describes
his friend's phobia in the cabaret:

> cito la fobia de un amigo, falsa walkiria, en los cabarets tangerinos de los
> sixties, donde a cada noche, se desplegaban sobre la ciudad, como bandas
> fosforescentes de crisálidas recién brotadas, travestís opulentos y oxigenados;
> azafranados andaluces, de manos empalagosas y rituales, dahomeyanos
> drogados, canadienses acromegálicos que sofocaban los difíciles pasos de un
> dorisdayano *play-back*. Recuerdo el rostro demudado del temeroso, cuando lo
> rozaban, como élitros letales, las organzas almidonadas y filosas de las faldas
> plisadas, las flores envenenadas que apretaban entre las manos amarillentas y
> escuálidas, y hasta el perfume barato y dulzón que compraban en la Medina
> e inundaba, desde antes de que entraran, el tugurio, los danzantes sacudidos
> por la voz suahilí de Miriam Makeba. (1982: 14–15)

Based on Sarduy's text, el Marqués describes to Conde the terror he feels the
first time he goes in to see the transvestites:

> La luz brotaba del piso y dibujaba las volutas de un humo demasiado dulce,
> incluso para cigarros de Virginia, que mezclaba sus efluvios hipnóticos

con vahos de sudores acidulados y un incisivo perfume de esencias árabes de las que son vendidas al por mayor en los apócrifos mercados persas de París. Los oídos, mientras tanto, recibían el ritmo salvaje que imponía la voz de Miriam Makeeba (la invasión del Tercer Mundo), proyectada desde una cabina empotrada en la pared. Tuve [el Marqués] una extraña sensación de miedo al descubrirme al vórtice de aquella agresión de todos los sentidos, pero el Recio y el Otro parecían haber entrado en un sitio conocido, en el que se movían con toda naturalidad. Empecé a ver entonces unas falsas walkirias cumpliendo su ancestral función de escanciar cerveza. Parecían flotar sobre lo azul, como crisálidas fosforescentes y recién brotadas, luciendo organizas almidonadas y filosas faldas plisadas que exhibían como triunfo de un gusto retro. Cada walkiria llevaba una bandeja con copas en una mano y unas flores amarillas (¿amarillas?) en la otra. Miraba aquellas manos demasiado grandes incluso para una walkiria, incluso si original y escandinava, cuando una me rozó con el borde cortante de su saya y recibí la sensación de haber sido tocado por un insecto prehistórico. (Padura 1997: 99)

El Marqués describes how he experiences an assault against his senses. In both Sarduy's and Padura's works transvestites appear as false Scandinavian goddesses. Sarduy talks about 'canadienses acromegálicos' and Padura about the big hands of the *walkiria*. Both authors refer to the disproportion of transvestites. Both Sarduy and Padura compare transvestites with 'crisálidas'. This image of the chrysalis, which has yet to become a butterfly, draws attention to the in-between state of transvestites who are neither women nor men.

At the end of the last quotation Padura reinforces the similarity between transvestites and prehistoric insects, a similarity that both Sarduy and Padura will develop in their respective works. On the one hand Sarduy compares the world of the transvestites and the world of the insects thus:

Otro resplandor recorre simétricamente al travestí y al insecto. El hombre puede pintar, inventar o recrear colores y formas que dispone en su exterior, sobre la tela, fuera de su cuerpo; pero es incapaz e impotente para modificar su propio organismo. El travestí, que llega a transformarlo radicalmente, y la mariposa, pueden pintarse a sí mismos, hacer de su cuerpo el soporte de la obra, convertir la emanación del color, los aturdidores arabescos y los tintes incandescentes en un ornamento físico, en una 'autoplástica', aunque esas obras. [*sic*] 'indefinidamente repetidas, no pueden evitar una fría e inmutable perfección'. (1982: 15)

On the other hand, Padura uses the last fragment to reveal his own view of transvestism, returning us to the subject of transvestites using pop icons as role models to imitate. El Marqués says to Conde that while he was in the cabaret in Paris,

Haber pensado en crisálidas y haber sentido el roce de un insecto gigantesco me dio la clave de lo que estaba viviendo, viendo: una fiesta de insectos. Recuerdo que pensé, entre aquellos travestis adelantados, pioneros esforzados del movimiento, que el hombre puede crear, pintar, inventar o recrear colores y formas de los que dispone desde su exterior, y llevarlos a la tela, que está más allá de su cuerpo, pero que es incapaz e impotente para modificar su propio organismo. Sólo el travesti llega a transformarlo radicalmente y, como la mariposa, puede pintarse a sí mismo, hacer de su cuerpo el soporte de su obra máxima, convertir sus emanaciones sexuales en color, a través de los aturdidores arabescos y los tintes incandescentes de un ornamento físico. Es una autoplástica esencial, aunque esas obras, infinitamente repetidas – siete Doris Day, cuatro Marilyn Monroe, tres Ana Magnani en veinte metros cuadrados – no puedan evitar, en el mejor de los casos, una fría y nostálgica perfección. Lo más inquietante fue comprender que todo eso era la consumación del teatro consciente que se ha soñado desde los días de Pericles: la máscara hecha personaje, el personaje tallado sobre el físico y el alma del actor, la vida como representación visceral de lo soñado… Aquello era como una iluminación que hubiera estado esperándome desde siempre, agazapada en ese sucio rincón de París, y en unos minutos ya tuve planeada y montada en mi mente la solución que andaba buscando para mi versión de *Electra Garrigó*. (Padura 1997: 100–1)

Here the words taken from Sarduy's essay appear for the first time as part of the discourse of el Marqués. Because it is el Marqués who is speaking, Padura erases the accent of the 'i' in the word 'travesti'. The í becomes a sign of the identity of the speaker, as mentioned before. Sarduy and Padura emphasize the similarities between the insects and the transvestites at the same time as they separate the transvestites from men. Padura repeats Sarduy's idea that human beings are unable to modify their bodies, even if this idea finds an easy counter-argument in the figure of transsexuals who transform their bodies completely, which Sarduy acknowledges. Nonetheless, both Sarduy and Padura maintain that transvestites transform their bodies radically through the artifice which is analogous to a butterfly's mimicry. Padura, however, gives transvestism sexual connotations that Sarduy's *La simulación* lacks. Both disguise and makeup constitute the 'autoplastia' of the transvestite for Sarduy, for whom transvestism does not necessarily go hand in hand with the subject's sexuality. For Sarduy, the transvestite's body is like a blank canvas on which subjectivity is inscribed.

In Padura's novel, according to el Marqués, the transvestite transforms colours into 'las emanaciones sexuales' through the 'ornamento físico' of the dress and the makeup. Padura refers to the existence of a model that the transvestite follows and repeats infinitely, and with which he contradicts himself. This idea does not appear in Sarduy's text which refers to the repetition of the act of transformation in itself, an act that the playwright (Padura's el Marqués) sees as undefined. When Sarduy writes about the 'inmutable perfección' of the transvestite, there is an implicit allusion to the 'inmutable perfección' of God and thus he confers on the transvestite a godlike essence, an essence that Padura refuses to give to the figure of the transvestite, the false *walkiria*. Both in the essay and in the novel the result of the transformation seems to be too fixed, in *La simulación* something immutable, in *Máscaras* something nostalgic owing to the inability of the transvestite to reach the model.

Indirectly, Padura also inserts himself in a transtextual project of weaving an 'infinite text', continuing on from Sarduy's readings. Thus when Sarduy continues his analysis of transvestism, using Hugo B. Cott's work *Adaptive Coloration in Animals*, Padura also becomes part of this second-hand intertextuality. The relationship between *La simulación* and *Adaptive Coloration in Animals* is one of metatextuality. For Genette, metatextuality 'is the relationship most often labelled "commentary". It unites a given text to another, of which it speaks without necessarily citing it (without summoning it), [...] Sometimes even without naming it' (1997: 4). According to Sarduy's reading of Cott's work, which I shall quote extensively to illustrate my analysis:

Si nos atenemos al apabullante catálogo *Adaptive Coloration in Animals*, de Hugo B. Cott, y leemos en función de [*sic*] cromatismo animal la parada cosmética del travestí, esa panoplia cromática será más descifrable. Se trata, siguiendo estas reparticiones, de colores *apatéticos*, es decir, destinados a despistar y dentro de ellos, el travestí apelaría a la gama de los *pseudosemáticos*, los que advierten al revés. Si consideramos al contrario que el travestí trata de atraer al hombre, que todo el esfuerzo metamorfósico no tiene más sentido que la captación del macho – teoría más que improbable –, los colores del maquillaje y las diversas modificaciones somáticas serían *anticrípticas*, como los de la manta, que se transforma en hoja o en flor para que la presa se acerque a ella sin desconfianza. Cuando el insecto reviste una forma atractiva para la presa, el aspecto de una flor determinada donde la víctima de costumbre encuentra su botín, los colores son *pseudoepisemáticos*; se pudiera aplicar esta denominación a los travestí si se considera que imitan a la mujer, y que la mujer es el receptáculo habitual del hombre, dos premisas discutibles. El animal-travestí no busca una apariencia amable para atraer (ni una apariencia desagradable para disuadir), sino una incorporación de la fijeza para *desaparecer*.

Si he referido el travestismo humano a una pulsión letal, desde el punto de vista de la *teatralidad* animal esta pulsión emana más bien del camuflaje, que es 'una desaparición, una pérdida facticia de la individualidad que se disuelve y deja de ser reconocible' y que supone 'inmovilidad e inercia'.

En definitiva, lo letal no es a su vez más que una forma extrema, el exceso del despilfarro de sí mismo, y si se tiene en cuenta que el mimetismo animal es inútil y no representa más que un deseo irrefrenable de gasto, de lujo peligroso, de fastuosidad cromática, una necesidad de desplegar, aún si no sirven para nada – numerosos estudios lo demuestran – colores, arabescos, filigranas, transparencias y texturas, tendremos que aceptar, al proyectar este deseo de *barroco* en la conducta humana, que el travestí confirma sólo 'que existe en el mundo vivo una ley de disfrazamiento puro, una práctica que consiste en hacerse pasar por otro, claramente probada, indiscutible, y que no puede reducirse a ninguna necesidad biológica derivada de la competencia entre las especies o de la selección natural'. (1982: 15–16)

This quotation becomes a hypotext of *Máscaras*. Sarduy calls the disguise of the transvestite and his makeup 'panoplia cromática'. If we remind ourselves that 'panoplia' can literally be one of four things: '[a]rmadura completa con todas las piezas'; '[c]olección de armas ordenadamente colocadas'; '[p]arte de la arqueología, que estudia las armas de mano y las armaduras antiguas'; or '[una] [t]abla, generalmente en forma de escudo, donde se colocan floretes, sables y otras armas de esgrima' (*DRAE* 2004: 1666), we can conclude that Sarduy uses this noun to stress the dual essence of transvestism: on the one hand, as a mechanism of defence; on the other hand, as a form of attack. Sarduy refutes the idea that the justification of transvestism is the mere 'hunting' of men. Rather, he links the lethal drive of the transvestite with the baroque 'despilfarro' of his attire and colours.

This lethal drive has justification in itself but it does not respond to any natural need either of men or of animals. As Sarduy explains to the reader in a footnote:

El más concluyente es el examen de las vísceras de 80.000 pájaros, practicado desde 1885 hasta 1932 por el United States Biological Survey y publicado por W. C. McAtee y que prueba que en el estómago de los pájaros había tantas víctimas mimetizadas como no mimetizadas, según las proporciones de la región: McAtee afirma pues, la perfecta inutilidad del mimetismo. (1982: 16)

Furthermore, Sarduy believes the baroque is a key component of contemporary Latin American literature and also of transvestism. The relationship between Padura's text and Sarduy's essay is metatextual: the hypertext *Máscaras* is the result of Conde's reading of the essay on transvestism written by el Recio/ Sarduy. We have no doubt about the identity of the writer of that essay and its real title, as confirmed in the novel, which I now quote in detail and at length to demonstrate this point:

[A]quel tratado del transformismo y la autocreación corporal que había escrito el Recio, gracias al cual varias cosas iban quedando claras para el Conde: el travestismo era algo más esencial y biológico que el simple acto mariconeril y exhibicionista de salir a la calle vestido de mujer, como él siempre lo había pensado desde su machismo barriotero y visceral. Aunque nunca lo había convencido del todo, por cierto, la actitud primaria del travesti que cambia su físico para ligar mejor. ¿Ligar a quién? Los hombres-

hombres, heterosexuales, con pelo en el pecho y peste a grajo, nunca se enredarían conscientemente con un travesti: se acostarían con una hembra, y no con aquella versión limitada de la mujer, con la entrada más apetitosa definitivamente clausurada por la caprichosa lotería de la naturaleza. Un homosexual pasivo, por su parte, preferiría a uno de aquellos hombres-hombres, porque para algo eran homosexuales y pasivos. Y un homosexual activo, oculto tras una apariencia impenetrable de hombre-hombre – vulgo: bugarrón; cultismo arcaico: bujarrón –, no necesitaba de aquella exageración a veces grosera para sentir el despertar de sus instintos sodomizantes y penetrar *per angostam viam*.

El libro trataba de dar explicaciones filosóficas a aquella contradicción: el problema, creía entender el Conde, no era ser, sino parecer; no era el acto, sino la representación; ni siquiera era el fin, sino el medio como su propio fin: la máscara por el placer de la máscara, el ocultamiento como verdad suprema. Por eso le pareció lógica la identificación del travestimiento humano y del camuflaje animal, no ya para cazar o para defenderse, sino para ejecutar uno de los sueños eternamente perseguidos por el hombre: la desaparición. Porque no era probable, definitivamente, que la transformación morfológica tuviera como único sentido la captación del macho-presa, como la de ciertos insectos que varían su aspecto para simular el de flores atractivas y amadas por otros que, confundidos, caen en la trampa mortal; tampoco que el disfraz se propusiera engañar, como ciertos insectos de físico agresivo, cuya apariencia impone temor a posibles atacantes. Era, por el contrario, aquella voluntad de enmascararse y confundirse, la de negar la negación y sumarse a la tribu común de las mujeres, la que tal vez guiara un transformismo que, en tantas ocasiones, podía resultar grotesco.

Pero si la difuminación era la última razón del travestimiento, los resultados prácticos del ejercicio tenían cifras en el mundo animal que podían equipararse – haciendo más y más comparaciones – con el destino triste de esos travestis siempre descubiertos a pesar de todos sus esfuerzos: una nuez de Adán inevitable, unas manos crecidas por designio natural, una pelvis estrecha, ajena a cualquier atisbo de maternidad... El libro citaba un estudio, realizado durante cuarenta y siete años, que demostraba cómo en el estómago de los pájaros había tantas víctimas mimetizadas como no mimetizadas, según las proporciones advertidas en la región. Entonces, ¿el disfraz era inútil, vulnerable y no daba garantías de seguridad? Y el Recio concluía, citando ahora a alguien que debía saber más que él, que el travesti confirma sólo 'que existe en el mundo vivo una ley de disfrazamiento puro, una práctica que consiste en hacerse pasar por otro, claramente probada, indiscutible, y que no puede reducirse a ninguna necesidad biológica derivada de la competencia entre las especies o de la selección natural'. Y entonces, ¿a qué coño se debía? ¿Todo aquello para decir que se trataba de un simple juego de apariencias? (Padura 1997: 73–4)

The formal style of the essay of el Recio/Sarduy is interrupted by colloquial rhetorical questions posed by Conde while he is reading the essay. Although

Padura obviously borrows many of Sarduy's ideas expressed in *La simulación* (the hypotext) such as seeing transvestism as a concealment that turns out to be a hyperbole of the woman and transvestism as mere appearance whose aim is simulacra, Padura omits Sarduy's idea that Latin American baroque with its exaggeration and its characteristic *derroche* of resources is the principle that also generates transvestism. Padura also eliminates Cott's terminology as used in Sarduy's essay. However, in the fragment of *Máscaras* I am analysing we can hear the voices of Cott, Sarduy, el Recio and eventually Padura. Thus we can claim that by not always summoning Sarduy directly into the text, Padura is participating in a metatextual process.

When el Marqués describes to Conde his last visit to Paris where he saw his first show of transvestites, he claims he understood 'que había penetrado en un gigantesco *happening* de transmutación, transformismo y máscaras, menos famoso pero más intenso y real que un carnaval veneciano' (Padura 1997: 100). These lines echo the following fragment of Sarduy's essay where he also analyses the essence of transvestism. Sarduy comments:

> Como los pintores hiperrealistas, el travestí y el autor de obras manifiesta e insolentemente narcisísticas [...] obedecen a una sola compulsión: representar la fantasía. Pero con una diferencia: para el pintor, el soporte de esa representación es exterior a su cuerpo, halógeno; para el travestí, si así puede decirse, tautotópica. Pero hay otra relación, histórica: el travestismo como acto plástico es la continuación o la radicalización del *happening*; se refiere a la intensidad que se ha dado, después de la *action painting*, al gesto y al cuerpo.
> Nunca se ha tratado con más ahínco de dar a ver la fantasía, y aún más: de imponerla a la realidad: [...] El travestí, y todo lo que trabaja sobre su cuerpo y lo expone, satura la realidad de su imaginario y la obliga, a fuerza de arreglo, de reorganización, de artificio y de maquillaje, a entrar, aunque de modo mimético y efímero, en su juego. (1982: 69–70)

Sarduy and Padura emphasize the essence of transvestism as performance; they highlight its theatrical essence. Both authors find similarities between transvestism and the theatrical happening (theatre being a topic addressed in more detail in the following section of this chapter). At the same time both authors stress the idea of transvestism as a representation that seems to be unreal but that is more real than reality itself, as expressed earlier in terms of 'realidad' and 'irrealidad'. This in turn connects them with the theoretical viewpoint expressed by Baudrillard when he states that 'Incluso puede ser que la fuerza de seducción del travesti provenga directamente de la parodia – parodia de sexo mediante la sobresignificación del sexo' (2000: 20). Transvestism appears as a phenomenon which modifies and transforms reality, even as an ephemeral phenomenon.

In *Máscaras*, transvestism is linked with the idea of carnival in which the transformation undertaken is more real than so-called reality. This transformation is a simulacrum, and as Baudrillard explains when writing about Disneyland, transvestism seems to be an artifice in comparison to reality. However, on the contrary, transvestism reflects the real 'carnival' into which Cuban society has transformed, and which Arenas parodied in *El color del verano*. This is a society where, according to the novel, everybody has to disguise themselves in order to survive. Because of the state's plan of creating a monolithic and homogeneous society, individual differences have to be erased. The transvestite is unique in using a disguise to reflect his real essence.

In short, Padura follows Sarduy's *La simulación* in order to develop his own theory about transvestism. Moreover, Padura adds to transvestism a theatrical essence in which the transvestite serves to denounce the repression exerted by the state at the same time as he denounces the hypocrisy of a society that, in spite of the revolution, maintained very traditional and conservative norms. Padura uses intertextuality to put Sarduy's words into el Recio's mouth. We do not know much about the character of el Recio; we know that he has written a work about transvestism which is actually Sarduy's *La simulación*, so the reader can identify the figure, life and works of Sarduy with the character in the novel. Padura seems to rescue Sarduy's voice in order to give it centre-stage in official Cuban culture. In addition, Padura depicts Sarduy's discourse not only as part of Cuban culture but also as a producer of it.

Theatre and the Mask

Padura also uses intertextuality in order to bring his characters to life, and Alberto el Marqués is connected to the extra-literary referent of Virgilio Piñera. By revealing his notion of theatre and reality, which is actually part of Piñera's introduction to his *Teatro completo*, Padura via el Marqués establishes Piñera's work as one of the hypotexts on which *Máscaras* relies. Piñera writes in the introduction to his *Teatro completo*:

> En 1948 – fecha del estreno de *Electra Garrigó* – escribí en las Notas al programa: 'Los personajes de mi tragedia oscilan perpetuamente entre un lenguaje altisonante y un humorismo y banalidad, que entre otras razones, se ha utilizado para equilibrar y limitar tanto lo doloroso como lo placentero, según ese saludable principio de que no existe nada verdaderamente doloroso o absolutamente placentero'. [...] Para que Electra no cayera en la repetición absoluta, para que el público no se durmiese, tenía que encontrar el elemento, el imponderable que, como se dice en argot de teatro 'sacara al espectador de su luneta'. [...] Aquí tocamos con aquéllo [*sic*] de cómo es el cubano. A mi entender un cubano se define por la sistemática ruptura con la seriedad entre comillas. [...] [E]se cubano no admite cualquier imposición de la solemnidad. Aquello que nos diferencia del resto de los pueblos de América es precisamente el saber que nada es verdaderamente doloroso o absolutamente placentero. Se dice que el cubano bromea, hace chistes con lo

más sagrado. A primera vista tal contingencia acusaría superficialidad en el carácter de nuestro pueblo. […] [C]reo firmemente que dicha condición es, en el momento presente, eso que el griego Sócrates definía en el 'conócete a tí [*sic*] mismo', es decir saber cómo eres. Nosotros somos trágicos y cómicos a la vez. […] [E]n gran medida, ese chiste, esa broma perpetua no es otra cosa que evasión ante una realidad, ante una circunstancia que no se puede afrontar. Precisamente en ese elemento me detuve para escribir 'Electra'. Si algo positivo tiene esta obra es el haber captado el carácter cubano. (1960: 9–11)

El Marqués, alter-ego of Piñera, bases his work and particularly the play *Electra Garrigó* on transvestism. El Marqués's theatre is a product of a hybrid culture and of transculturation in which there is a mixture of elements of Greek, Japanese and Cuban 'bufo' theatre. Masks become the vehicle to express Cubanness, a Cubanness that Ortiz viewed as 'individuación dentro de lo universal' while also recognizing plurality (Ortiz 1991b: 11). Similarly, the mask is a plurivalent sign; it shows the hybridity of Cuban society and culture and the idiosyncrasy of the Cuban people. The mask in theatre as well as in transvestism serves to illustrate the real self:

> les comenté cómo imaginaba el escenario y los vestuarios, y sobre todo la gestualidad que quería imponer a los actores, maquillándolos como máscaras griegas pero con caras muy habaneras, de blancos, mulatos y negros habaneros, tratando que la máscara los mostrara y no los ocultara, que los revelara interiormente y no velara esa espiritualidad trágica y a la vez burlesca que quería buscar como esencia de una cubanía en la que Virgilio Piñera fungía como máximo profeta, porque para él, si algo nos distinguía del resto del mundo, era poseer esa sabiduría criolla de que nada es verdaderamente doloroso o absolutamente placentero. Mi puesta, les explicaba entonces, sería una estilización extrema de los viejos bufos habaneros del diecinueve y del vernáculo criollo del teatro Alhambra, pero asumidos desde una voluntad trágica y filosófica, hasta dejar sólo su esencia artística, pues al fin y al cabo ése ha sido el gran teatro de la idiosincrasia cubana. (Padura 1997: 165)

Following Piñera, Padura highlights in his novel the tragicomic essence of the Cuban. According to Jorge Mañach's essay 'Indagación del choteo', the *choteo* is 'la burla crónica' (1962: 82) against any kind of authority and is also a way of concealing the inner sorrow: 'El choteo viene entonces a ser como un acto de pudor, un pliegue de jocosidad que nos echamos encima para esconder nuestra tristeza íntima, y por miedo a parecer tiernos o espirituales' (1962: 84). According to Piñera and Padura life is both a tragedy and a comedy, and the *choteo* is part of the essence of Cubanness. Although the *choteo* can be considered a stereotype of the idiosyncratic behaviour of Cuban people, it is true that in recent Cuban literature humour appears as a mechanism to subvert the state's discourses.

As expressed by Piñera above, 'la broma perpetua' is also a form of evasion; hence *Electra Garrigó* both in Piñera and Padura is the result of a process of transculturation which contains the combination of tragic elements and 'la broma perpetua' that lies at the core of what these writers consider 'cubanía': Ortiz's *ajiaco*, the hybridity of the stew.[14] When el Marqués's transvestite theatre is banned by the government, the state forbids the participation of transvestites in the process of the creation of Cuban identity. El Marqués gives emphasis to language in theatre because he believes it to be an important part of Cuban identity:

> Comentaba que por eso también debía ayudarme mucho con la palabra, y no pretender, como el pobre Artaud, buscar un lenguaje escénico sólo apoyado en signos o gestos activos y dinámicos, porque uno de los rasgos más visibles de la cubanía es nuestra incontenible propensión a no cerrar la boca. (Padura 1997: 165)

Antonin Artaud's *El teatro y su doble* is where we find the theory of theatre that el Marqués is referring to:

> No se ha probado en absoluto que no haya lenguaje superior al lenguaje verbal. Y parece que en la escena (ante todo un espacio que se necesita llenar y un lugar donde ocurre alguna cosa) el lenguaje de las palabras debiera ceder ante el lenguaje de los signos, cuyo aspecto objetivo es el que nos afecta de modo más inmediato.
> Desde este punto de vista, el trabajo objetivo de la puesta en escena asume una suerte de dignidad intelectual a raíz de la desaparición de las palabras en los gestos, y del hecho de que la parte plástica y estética del teatro abandonan su carácter de intermedio decorativo para convertirse, en el sentido exacto del término, en un *lenguaje* directamente comunicativo. (Artaud 1999: 121)

Padura refers to Artaud's text on the theatre of cruelty in order to shape the way in which el Marqués conceives his theatre. Padura's character, el Marqués, also claims that language forms part of what constitutes Cubanness and thus seems

---

14   In interview I asked Padura, 'En *Máscaras*, el teatro del Marqués aparece como un producto de la transculturación en la que se mezclan elementos de teatro griego, japonés, o del teatro bufo cubano, además de aparecer la sociedad cubana como híbrida y heterogénea cultural y racialmente. ¿Considera usted que éstos son los rasgos definitorios de 'lo cubano'?' He replied: 'No, porque yo sería incapaz de decir cuales son esos rasgos definitorios. Son tantos los elementos que intervienen en la formación de lo cubano, cn épocas y situaciones tan diversas, que sólo enunciarlos sería esquemático. Aunque, por supuesto, el carácter mestizo, híbrido, multicultural, multirracial y multireligioso del cubano, de lo cubano, es indiscutible. Somos, con toda seguridad, una de las naciones más "mulatas" del mundo, gracias a una conjunción histórica, geográfica, social y cultural muy especial. Y creo que esa ha sido la gran fortuna del ser cubano, de "lo cubano": la capacidad para integrarlo todo y dar algo nuevo' (see Appendix 1).

to reject the importance Artaud gives to other sign systems in theatre. Yet in *Máscaras* el Marqués's staging of *Electra Garrigó* does not undermine the importance of paying close attention to non-verbal sign systems such as clothes, masks and gestures (see Padura 1997: 165).

According to Genette, allusion constitutes 'an enunciation whose full meaning presupposes the perception of a relationship between it and another text, to which it necessarily refers by some inflections that would otherwise remain unintelligible' (1997: 1–2). If el Marqués had not referred explicitly to Artaud's notion of theatre it would have been left to the reader to place el Marqués's aesthetic theory within a particular literary trend. In this case the author employs intertextuality as a support to define his character's transvestite theatre.

In the same way that masks and language in el Marqués's theatre express the idea that Cuban society is heterogeneous and hybrid, intertextuality in the novel also suggests that Cuban culture is hybrid. Cuban, European and African cultural elements play a part in this process of the creation of Cuban culture as we see it in the theatre developed by el Marqués. If we pay attention to el Marqués's friends, his influences and allusions, the variety is obvious; from Jean-Paul Sartre to Artaud, from Julio Cortázar to Néstor Almendros, from Pedro Calderón de la Barca to Arthur Miller. El Marqués, the epitome of Cuban culture, defines theatre thus:

> Como Artaud, eso sí, quería demostrar que, si el teatro no es un juego, sino una realidad verdadera, más verdadera que la misma realidad, debía resolver el problema que siempre significa devolverle al teatro ese rango, para hacer de cada espectáculo una especie de acontecimiento capaz de provocar la perplejidad y desatar la inteligencia, sobrepasar siempre el fácil estado de la recreación digestiva, como decía él... Y la máscara facial debía ser algo esencial en el propósito revelador de esa máscara moral con que ha vivido mucha gente en algún momento de su existencia: homosexuales que aparentan no serlo, resentidos que sonríen al mal tiempo, brujeros con manuales de marxismo bajo el brazo, oportunistas feroces vestidos de mansos corderos, apáticos ideológicos con un utilísimo carnet en el bolsillo: en fin, el más abigarrado carnaval en un país que muchas veces ha debido renunciar a sus carnavales...[15] Lo que quería [El Marqués], ni más ni menos, era darle proyección poética trascendente, fuera de un tiempo concreto, pero en un espacio preciso, a una tragedia que el autor concibió como una disyuntiva familiar: quedarse o partir, acatar o desobedecer, o lo mismo de siempre, desde Edipo y Hamlet: ser o no ser. [...] [Sartre] ¿No es demasiado complejo lo que te propones?, empezó por preguntar, para decirme que tuviera cuidado con las revelaciones, pues siempre proponen diversas lecturas y esa diversidad podía ser peligrosa para mí, igual que el fatalismo esencial que quería representar a través de una Electra cubana

---

[15] This also alludes to the cancellation of the summer carnivals in Cuba during the Special Period, because of limited resources. The novel is clearly dated by the author. The front page places it in the summer of 1989 and the last page signs it off with the date 1994–95.

del siglo veinte: ya había oído decir a ciertos burócratas insulares que el arte en Cuba debía ser otra cosa y esa otra cosa no se parecía a mi *Electra Garrigó* y su disyuntiva de ser o no ser... (Padura 1997: 165–6)

Again el Marqués identifies his conception of theatre with Artaud's. His theatre stops being a simulacrum to become 'true reality'. Theatre becomes a mechanism to make people act in response to intellectual stimulus; nobody can be a passive viewer. Theatre is also the space where the mask becomes a plurivalent sign: it reflects the hypocrisy, the 'máscara moral' that according to the novel many people use in order to pretend to be what they are not. When el Marqués talks about 'brujeros con manuales de marxismo bajo el brazo', he alludes to the historic fact that the Cuban government did not allow practitioners of any religion to become members of the Communist Party;[16] hence, el Marqués condemns the hypocrisy of those who maintain double moral standards between the private and the public. El Marqués also criticizes opportunism and those 'apáticos ideológicos' who in spite of their lack of any ideology belong to the Communist Party. El Marqués's theatre is his weapon, used to reveal the carnival of Cuban society that I have been discussing in this study, especially in terms of a *disfraz*.

El Marqués uses *Electra Garrigó* to denounce the constant repetition of tragedy throughout the years.[17] Piñera had written his *Electra Garrigó* as a criticism of pre-Castro Cuban society. When el Marqués stages the same play and makes manifest its veracity he demonstrates how Cuban society has not changed in spite of official reassurances that it has. When Sartre (in the novel) comments about the numerous readings *Electra Garrigó* can generate, he is criticizing the Cuban government's stance which favours monologic forms of social realism against any hybrid cultural phenomenon. This is historically framed by Fidel Castro's famous phrase 'dentro de la Revolución, todo; contra la Revolución nada' in his speech *Palabras a los intelectuales*, delivered in 1961 (Castro 1961: 11), to which I shall return later in this chapter.[18] We can

16   For changes in the official relationship with religious groups and the position of the state at various points, see Giuliano 1998: 140; Oppenheimer 1992: ch. 12. The major relaxation with respect to religious practices took place in the early 1990s, at a time when homosexuality was also part of the 'rectification' process of the state.

17   Piñera's play is used to reflect on the key elements of the classical tragedy, which has at its core *hamartia* (or tragic flaw) and *hubris* (pride), which cause the downfall of the protagonist through the expected nemesis.

18   García-Obregón has noted, 'Even if the Cuban revolution can be easily romanticized by the outsider for what it still means in a global struggle against imperialism, this romanticism has different consequences for the displaced individual within the nation. One needs to keep in mind that the nation has set out to exterminate the "other," because subjectivity can only be expressed within the parameters of the revolutionary nation, as expressed since 1961 by Fidel Castro in his famous speech *Palabras a los intelectuales* [...], with which he concluded the meetings with Cuban intellectuals, which took place on 16, 23 and 30 June 1961. Although he claims there will be freedom of speech, he ironically invalidates his claim by stating "dentro de la Revolución, todo; contra la Revolución nada"' (2006: 86).

thus reach the conclusion that el Marqués and Piñera share the same view of theatre and life.

We must bear in mind that el Marqués, like Piñera himself, is a homosexual and is thus doomed to disappear and to be ostracized by the censorship that prevailed in the 1970s.[19] Nonetheless, the project is an intertextual one, as el Marqués confirms in his use of Artaud, for whom theatre had a transformative power:

> Queremos transformar al teatro en una realidad verosímil, y que sea para el corazón y los sentidos esa especie de mordedura concreta que acompaña a toda verdadera sensación. Así como nos afectan los sueños, y la realidad afecta los sueños, creemos que las imágenes del pensamiento pueden identificarse con un sueño, que será eficaz si se lo proyecta con la violencia precisa. Y el público creerá en los sueños del teatro, si los acepta realmente como sueños y no como copia servil de la realidad. (Artaud 1999: 96–7)

Hence, according to Artaud, theatre would be capable of creating its own reality and dreams, as opposed to following social realism on stage. In *Máscaras* this is the case with el Marqués's transvestite theatre which becomes a threat because it can modify the notion of 'reality'.

Artaud continues by saying that the theatre of cruelty 'Incluirá no sólo el anverso, sino también el reverso del espíritu; la realidad de la imaginación y de los sueños aparecerá ahí en pie de igualdad con la vida' (1999: 140). Artaud, like el Marqués, challenges the 'teatro digestivo' with a 'teatro de la crueldad':

> Así como en el teatro digestivo de hoy los nervios, es decir una cierta sensibilidad fisiológica, son deliberadamente dejados de lado, librados a la anarquía espiritual del espectador, el Teatro de la Crueldad intenta recuperar todos los antiguos y probados medios mágicos de alcanzar la sensibilidad. [...] Y, así como no habrá sitio desocupado en el espacio, tampoco habrá tregua ni vacío en la mente o la sensibilidad del espectador. Es decir que entre la vida y el teatro no habrá corte neto, ni solución de continuidad. (1999: 142–3)

The theatre of cruelty wants to shake the viewers' consciousness. In the theatre of cruelty there are no distinctions between the stage and the audience, between reality and simulacra, and this is exploited by el Marqués in Padura's text where the transvestites act as themselves.

Artaud also proposed that one could use theatre in order to remove the individual's mask and to show him or her as he or she really is:

---

[19] To read more about Piñera's ostracism at the hands of the Cuban government, see Cabrera-Infante 1998.

[P]uede advertirse en fin que desde un punto de vista humano la acción del teatro, como la de la peste, es beneficiosa, pues al impulsar a los hombres a que se vean tal como son, hace caer la máscara, descubre la mentira, la debilidad, la bajeza, la hipocresía del mundo, sacude la inercia asfixiante de la materia que invade hasta los testimonios más claros de los sentidos; y revelando a las comunidades su oscuro poder, su fuerza oculta, las invita a tomar, frente al destino, una actitud heroica y superior, que nunca hubieran alcanzado de otra manera. (1999: 36)

It is worth keeping in mind here what Padura told me in an interview, that is, that he sees transvestism as a sign of the concealment that some individuals have adopted in order to survive in different circumstances. This is the reason why el Marqués creates his theatre based on a transvestite aesthetic. The playwright designs a space where the transvestite's voice can be heard, where the transvestite's discourse dominates, and thus the transvestite can express his real identity through the theatre.

El Marqués designs his *Electra Garrigó* as a tragedy where time does not matter. The events that take place in this play have been repeated throughout history. Moreover, el Marqués links his tragedy with classical ones and therefore examines the history of theatre from its origins and considers the history of Cuba as a cyclical tragedy that is rewritten continuously over the same palimpsest. El Marqués reinforces this view of history when he gives Conde an account of the history of the repression of homosexuals on the island and when he reads Alexis Arayán's murder as a classical tragedy in contemporary Cuba.

As an actor who chooses his characters, actor and character become mingled in the figure of the transvestite. This idea is connected to Calderón's theatre of the world, which appears very often in *Máscaras*, and with reference to the baroque that I mentioned at the beginning of this chapter. The transvestite selects the role he wants to perform and the staging of his performance in the world. Padura uses intertextuality in order to reveal to his reader the view that el Marqués has of the world and of reality itself through Sarduy's discourse and through several references to Calderón. As Padura himself replied when asked in interview: '¿Consideraría al personaje del Marqués como un ser carnavalesco? ¿Por qué?':

En el caso del Marqués creo que sí, que se pudiera considerar carnavalesco, pero mi intención es que fuera un personaje que se valiera de lo teatral [...] para representar sus papeles en la vida, antes y después de su defenestración [...] se disfraza para sentirse por encima del mundo y de esa manera esconde sus propios miedos e incertidumbres. (see Appendix 1)

El Marqués and Conde make continual references to theatre. These references give the impression that human beings are actors within the theatre of the world, where everybody has a role to play.

It is not only in el Marqués's theatre that the boundaries of stage and reality are blurred. Throughout *Máscaras* we find the same idea, which is characteristic of the baroque of the theatre of the world. The baroque is characterized by the extensive display of resources and Sarduy, as previously stated, considers transvestism and Latin American art as examples of the new baroque. The tremendous display of references and intertextual play in *Máscaras* demonstrates that this novel contains elements of this new baroque.

Conde also refers directly to Calderón, highlighting his personal view of life as a theatre, characteristic of the baroque:

> El Conde pensó otra vez que estaba en medio de una representación teatral demasiado parecida a una realidad prefabricada y en la que cada cual ya tenía asignado su papel y su asiento. *El gran teatro del mundo*, qué disparate. La Tragedia de la Vida, más disparate todavía. *¿La vida es sueño?* (Padura 1997: 170)

Through an intertextuality produced by means of continual references to Calderón and his theatre, Padura highlights Conde's and el Marqués's view of reality. El Marqués considers life as a kind of continuously rewritten tragedy and Conde feels himself trapped in a world where fate has prevented him from realizing his ambition: to be a writer. In line with Calderón's theatre of the world, as already mentioned, actors must carry out the specific roles assigned to them. Although Conde feels trapped in a role that he does not desire (as a lieutenant and police detective), in the course of the four novels that constitute Padura's tetralogy he attempts to gain control over his life and become a writer. At the end of the tetralogy Conde resigns and dedicates himself entirely to writing. This demonstrates that *El gran teatro del mundo*, where everybody has an assigned role from which they cannot escape, is a *disparate*.

Intertextuality and Dialogism: Creation and Critique

During my first interview with Padura I asked him the function of recurrent references in *Máscaras* to other authors such as Piñera, Calderón and Miller.[20] Padura replied by stating that in history and literature everything is now intertextual: there will always be a pre-text as a starting point, a pre-text that gives us an idea of structure, of the use of an adjective, of techniques to delineate a character. But one does not always recognize that one is using intertextuality. However, with reference to *Máscaras*, Padura admits he borrows without constraint and almost blatantly from other authors' texts and employs them within the story he is narrating. For him, *Máscaras* is a novel about literature, about artists, and he claims that he has assumed literary heritage as part of the arsenal that he wanted to utilize.

---

[20]   See Appendix 1 for the interview.

Through intertextuality the author recovers the voices of those Cuban writers who were excluded from the official Cuban literary canon on the island, particularly in the 1970s, such as the gay writers Piñera, Sarduy and José Lezama Lima. Although selective in his choices, Padura rescues these voices in order to allow them to participate in and belong to Cuban discourse. In interview I asked:

> Algunos críticos han negado la posibilidad de que el Marqués en su novela *Máscaras* haya sufrido represalias por su sexualidad. ¿Qué opina usted de esta lectura de la novela? A mi entender, el Marqués sufre represalias tanto por su obra, la estética travesti de su teatro, como por su sexualidad.

Padura replied:

> Estoy de acuerdo contigo. El Marqués – vaya, él también es metafórico – sufre el mismo destino que muchos artistas cubanos que a principios de los 70 fueron marginados no sólo por lo que hacían o escribían, sino también por lo que eran: religiosos, homosexuales, apáticos políticos… (see Appendix 1)

Furthermore, intertextuality helps to create a specific environment within the novel and to sketch the personality of some of the characters. When Conde arrives in el Marqués's place he realizes that the dining room is a stage:

> Entonces el Conde lo comprendió todo: había caído en medio de la escenografía de *El precio*, la obra de Arthur Miller que treinta años antes […] montara Alberto Marqués […] Había entrado a la escena en que llegan los personajes y…, claro que sí. ¿Sería posible? (Padura 1997: 43–4)

Here Padura directs the reader to establish literary links between *El precio* and *Máscaras*. Thanks to this intertextuality we can establish a parallel between the events that take place in *El precio* and the process of self-knowledge that occurs between Conde and el Marqués in *Máscaras*. Both Conde and el Marqués, like the brothers in *El precio*, have paid a high price for the choices they have made: El Marqués, in spite of being censored by the Cuban government, decides to stay in his country and refuses either to publish or to direct a play again; Conde has to give up his studies and decides to become a policeman, thus renouncing his dream of becoming a writer. Both relinquish their dreams in order to survive.

This feature of character development in Padura's intertextuality also applies strongly to the character of Alexis Arayán. Padura employs fragments of the Bible that describe the Transfiguration of Christ and references to *Electra Garrigó* in order to define Alexis. When Alexis dresses up as el Marqués's Electra Garrigó and chooses the Feast of the Transfiguration as the day of his own murder, these choices are not arbitrary. Alexis identifies with Electra Garrigó because both suffer rejection and oppression from one of their parents. Moreover, Alexis also identifies with Christ and thus chooses 6 August (the Feast of

the Transfiguration of Christ) to perform his own Calvary. By means of intertextuality the sacrifice of Christ is identified with the sacrifice of Alexis and vice
versa. Alexis's death is also related to Christ's because both are connected with
the figure of the father. However, the difference between Christ's death and
Alexis's is their effect: through his death Alexis achieves his father's destruction.

In *Máscaras*, Padura paraphrases the introduction to Piñera's *Teatro completo*, but he does not quote from Piñera's *Electra Garrigó* itself. Nonetheless,
in the novel there are many allusions to Piñera's play and the intertextual connections drawn between Electra Garrigó and Christ and the character of Alexis
are made explicit, particularly when Alexis puts a page of the Bible that describes
the Transfiguration of Christ inside Piñera's *Teatro completo*. Furthermore, when
Alexis writes in the margin of his Bible '*Dios Padre, ¿por qué lo obligas a
tanto sacrificio?*' (Padura 1997: 162, his italics) we see that transvestism and
the Transfiguration of Christ also converge in the figure of Alexis. He identifies
with Christ's suffering, which he believes to be imposed by God, his father, just
as Alexis's father, Faustino, also makes him suffer.

When Alexis suffers the contempt of his father as a result of his tranvestism,
he waits for him at the entrance of a hotel dressed as Electra Garrigó, and,
echoing both Piñera's play and the biblical text, he describes how 'Me vestí
en el baño del hotel y no me da ninguna pena… Hoy sentí que mi vida iba a
cambiar. Recibí una luz, que me ordenó: Haz lo que tienes que hacer y ve a
ver a tu padre' (Padura 1997: 214). Alexis, like Electra Garrigó, receives the
light as an epiphany:

> (Electra) […] ¡Ah, Electra…! Asciende más y más y siempre. Es hacia la
> residencia de la luz donde debes encaminar tus pasos, a fin de procurar las
> armas que necesitas. […] No avanzo, giro, siempre en el sentido de la luz.
> ¡Formas de ella, procuradme el camino y la frente que debo aniquilar! […]
> Siempre envolviendo más y más tu cuerpo en la luz. Sus dientes penetran ya
> tu carne, pero no serás despedazada, serás exaltada. (Piñera 1960: 53)

After this epiphany, both Electra Garrigó and Alexis decide to destroy their
parents, and in doing so annihilate those characters that represent the voice of
power. However, there is a difference between these two works even if they end
similarly: Electra Garrigó is responsible for the murder of her parents, for even
if she does not carry out the act itself she plans it. Although initially she gets rid
of them in order to free herself from their oppression, eventually she is unable
to leave her home because of her own fear. Alexis can only achieve his liberation
through his own death, but, in the process, he accomplishes the destruction of
his father as well. In light of the rejection of the Church and the state as represented by his father, Alexis finds only one solution to his problems: his own
death. As suicide is also condemned by Catholicism he plans his own murder,
which in turn condemns his father.

In Exodus 34, when Moses comes back from Mount Sinai after talking with Yahweh, there is also a shining, a brightness that symbolizes the divine contact between Moses and God. Furthermore, during the Transfiguration Christ's shining clothes represent his divine essence in the same way that Alexis's clothes represent his authentic self. However, in *Máscaras* it is not only Christ who appears with bright clothes after going to Mount Tabor according to the Bible: 'brilló su rostro como el sol y sus vestidos se volvieron blancos como la luz' (Matt. 17: 1). Faustino is also described in a similar way: 'Vestía una guayabera tan blanca y tan fina que el Conde no se hubiera atrevido a llevarla ni un minuto: era resplandeciente, más que blanca' (Padura 1997: 88). Rather than a divine nature, in the case of Faustino his bright clothes symbolize his many privileges and the *guayabera* his Cubanness.

In the Bible, after the Transfiguration of Christ the voice of God is heard from a 'nube resplandeciente', announcing the divine essence of his son and his unavoidable sacrifice:

> Este es mi Hijo amado, en quien tengo mi complacencia; escuchadle. [...] Elías ha venido ya, y no le reconocieron; antes hicieron con él lo que quisieron; de la misma manera el Hijo del hombre tiene que padecer de parte de ellos. (Matt. 17: 1)

In the case of Faustino, who represents the voice of power, there is no such love shown for his son:

> por ser, bueno, por ser maricón. Cada vez que podía, le hacía evidente que lo despreciaba. Imagínese usted, para un hombre tan respetable eso era la peor desgracia [...]. Pero Alexis sufría mucho, sufría por todo, y si no lo hubieran matado, yo habría dicho que se suicidó. (Padura 1997: 104)

Alexis, like Christ before him, suffers the rejection of his contemporaries and their intolerance. Both are treated as rebels and give their lives in sacrifice. The fact that Alexis is a transvestite and a Catholic in a society that is officially and theoretically atheist shows us the degree of his failure to adapt to this society as well as his rejection of official discourse. Alexis's Erinyes (or Furies) are both the Church (despite his Catholicism) and the state, as contemporary personifications of punishment.

Both institutions consider homosexuality an aberration. El Marqués himself explains to Conde:

> Gracias a él [Alexis] me aprendí la cita del Levítico que dice 'Asimismo respecto del hombre que se acostare con varón, como uno se acuesta con mujer; ambos han cometido abominación: serán muertos irremisiblemente: caiga su sangre sobre ellos'... Para un creyente no es fácil vivir sabiendo que su Dios llamó a Moisés para decirle una barbaridad así, ¿no cree? (Padura 1997: 163)

El Marqués quotes this passage of the Bible in order to demonstrate the failure of Christianity to protect everyone. On the one hand, in the last sentence quoted above, el Marqués is questioning God's piety, one of the principles of Christianity, and on the other he is extending to religious narratives responsibility for the repression exerted against homosexuals, which is not unique to Cuba. By not offering exile as an option for either Alexis or el Marqués, *Máscaras* is indirectly asserting a fatalistic viewpoint, where the only option left open for escape is death.

When Conde knows the date of the murder he immediately relates it to the Transfiguration of Christ:

> – Para que ustedes vean que haber ido al catecismo tiene sus ventajas… el 6 de agosto es la fiesta de la Transfiguración para los católicos. Según la Biblia, ese día Jesús se transformó ante tres de sus discípulos en el monte Tabor, y Dios, desde una nube de luz, les pidió a los apóstoles que lo escucharan siempre. ¿No es demasiada casualidad que aparezca un travesti muerto un 6 de agosto? (Padura 1997: 34)

Conde's Catholic education allows him to link this murder with the Transfiguration of Christ. On the one hand, contrary to the Cuban government's proclamations, Conde benefits from his Catholic background, since no-one from the police force except Conde can connect Alexis's murder with the biblical text. On the other hand, Conde's background causes him to write a short story in his school journal about his childhood, when he had to go to church instead of playing baseball with his friends. This short story is censored by his teachers because it does not respond to the needs of the times in 1970s revolutionary Cuba. Conde wanted to reflect in his short story how he felt different from the rest of his classmates because his mother was a Catholic and he was forced to go to church. The directors of the 'Preuniversitario' understood his story to be provocative and subversive. This fact is significant because Conde identifies with el Marqués not only because of their shared love of writing but also because their writings have been misunderstood and censored.

The story of the Transfiguration of Christ is also the reading that Father Mendoza had given on the day of Conde's First Communion. Twenty-eight years later, Conde meets up with Mendoza to ask him about this specific part of the Bible. In this part of *Máscaras* there is further intertextuality, since in the conversation between the priest and Conde fragments of the Bible are interwoven. Padura keeps the biblical fragments within quotation marks, which as Genette has stated is the 'most explicit and literal form' (1997: 2) of intertextuality. Padura also uses intertextuality in order to express his particular reading of the Bible through the figure of the priest, who gives Conde his interpretation of the text and, moreover, gives the Cuban reader who may not be familiar with the Bible the essential information he or she needs to understand the novel's Christian context. Father Mendoza tells Conde:

¿Sabes por qué aquel día dije en la misa el pasaje de la Transfiguración? […] Lo hice porque me sentía muy mal, y en ese pasaje, cuando Dios se le aparece a los apóstoles, Jesús comprende como pocas veces el alma humana y les dice a sus discípulos: 'Levantaos, no tengáis miedo'… Y no todo el mundo es capaz de entender las dimensiones del miedo. Y aquel día, como comprenderás, yo le tuve mucho miedo a la muerte. (Padura 1997: 84–6)

Mendoza, after the death of his own father, felt the need to talk about the Transfiguration of Christ during Conde's First Communion. He stresses the idea of the fear of human beings, and an understanding of this fear by Christ in a way that is not reflected in the Bible. The priest thus reflects on the human fear of death when he sermonizes:

'Seis días después, toma Jesús a Pedro, a Santiago y a su hermano Juan y los sube a un monte alto, a solas. Y se transfiguró delante de ellos: su rostro brilló como el sol y sus vestidos quedaron blancos como la luz. Y se les aparecieron Moisés y Elías hablando con él. Entonces Pedro dijo a Jesús: "Señor, bueno será quedarnos aquí: si quieres yo haré aquí tres tiendas, una para ti, otra para Moisés y otra para Elías". Cuando aún estaba hablando, una nube luminosa los cubrió, y se oyó una voz desde la nube que decía: "Este es mi hijo, el predilecto, en quien me he complacido: escuchadle". Al oír esto los discípulos cayeron sobre su rostro, presos de gran temor. Se acercó a ellos Jesús y, tocándoles, dijo: "Levantaos, no tengáis miedo". Y cuando alzaron los ojos no vieron a nadie, sino a Jesús solo ['].
'Al bajar del monte, Jesús les hizo este encargo: "A ninguno digáis esta visión hasta que el Hijo del Hombre resucite de entre los muertos".'
Este es el capítulo diecisiete de Mateo. Marcos y Lucas también cuentan la Transfiguración, y, oye esto qué interesante, Marcos la vio así: 'Sus vestidos se pusieron resplandecientes y muy blancos, como no los puede blanquear ningún batanero de la tierra'. […] Pero lo importante de todo esto es que en el monte Tabor ocurrió la primera revelación pública del carácter divino de Jesús, reconocido por su padre y presentado como el Mesías. Por eso los discípulos vieron cómo el aspecto de Jesús, que debía de venir sucio del largo camino recorrido por el mar y el desierto, se transformó profundamente: su ropa, su piel, su pelo brillaron, pero en realidad todo era fruto de una claridad interior necesaria para recibir la revelación del padre. Entonces es cuando se manifiesta la grandeza de Jesús: siendo quien es, presentado como ser divino, no pierde su humanidad y comprende el miedo de sus seguidores, que han sido testigos de algo que los supera infinitamente. ¿Y sabes por qué? Porque creo que Jesús presintió su propio miedo cuando les habla de cómo va a realizarse su obra: su gloria estará en su resurrección, pero antes debía pasar por el sufrimiento y el sacrificio que le esperan en la cruz, que era la prueba necesaria para que se produjera ese milagro mayor. Desgarrador y hermoso, ¿verdad? Y si El [sic] tuvo miedo, y comprendió entonces qué cosa es el miedo, ¿por qué nosotros vamos a renegar de un sentimiento tan humano? Tal vez el más humano de todos, Conde. (Padura 1997: 84–6)

According to Father Mendoza, Christ understands the fear of death and of the unknown because he himself knew his own fear at the crucifixion. If Padura through Father Mendoza points out Christ's fear of his own death, this is to emphasize human suffering and human cruelty. Christ's fear of his crucifixion humanizes him; the priest's fear of death as well as Conde's and Alexis's serve to dignify them by acknowledging their human condition.

This emphasis in Mendoza's reading is best understood in the context of fear expressed in the novel as a whole. Mendoza has previously told Conde 'Ese es tu mayor pecado, Condesito: la arrogancia. Y el otro, yo lo sé bien, es que te tienes miedo a ti mismo' (Padura 1997: 83). The priest stresses Conde's fear of himself because of the fear of many characters in the novel that they cannot express or fulfil their authentic self. For example, in *Máscaras* Conde does not dare to become a writer; Alexis prefers to die rather than to express his gender subjectivity; el Marqués does not return to the stage because he is afraid of being repressed as before; and Faustino does not show his authentic self because he is afraid of being punished for being a political traitor. Everybody in this novel has reasons to conceal their true identity.

As Stephen Wilkinson demonstrates in his book on the detective novel in Cuba, Padura employs specific Cuban legislation through the voice of Faustino Arayán and the bureaucrats who judge and condemn el Marqués (Wilkinson 2000: 248–69). Although Wilkinson affirms that Padura criticizes the Cuban system by means of this kind of intertextuality, I believe that Padura limits himself to criticizing specific historical aspects of contemporary Cuba such as the now well-documented repression of intellectuals, but, at the same time, in the course of this novel he does not question the Cuban system itself and how it functions. In his text, mistakes and failures in the system seem to be the result of the misdeeds of specific members of society such as Faustino. And these individuals are always punished for their actions or end up regretting their previous behaviour.[21]

In the Mario Conde tetralogy most of the voices that represent the state or power are revealed to follow double moral standards and to be inauthentic when claiming to know absolute truths. Those characters who exploit their position in government to obtain privileges are at the same time those who commit crimes. At the end of the novel, Faustino is sent to jail for the murder of his son, but not because he has abused his position as part of the elite of the country to obtain privileges in a society where theoretically differences of class have been erased. When Conde takes off the mask of the murderer who is punished by the state, he demonstrates the proper functioning of the system. Moreover, in *Máscaras* we can see how things have changed and how mistakes have taken place in the past. For example, Conde's investigation takes place in the summer of 1989,

---

21   A clear historical example is the Heberto Padilla affair.

while the events narrated by el Marqués occurred in 1969 and at the beginning of the 1970s. In *Máscaras* there is an explicit acceptance of the errors of the past consistent with the state's version of 'rectification'.

The novel itself tries to demonstrate the claimed openness of the system and the lack of censorship, at the same time as it uses historical documentation as hypotexts. For example, Padura told Stephen Clark in interview in 2000:

> En el año '61, se produce en Cuba una reunión cultural y políticamente muy importante en la que Fidel Castro [...] llega al final a hacer un discurso donde plantea aquellas famosas palabras 'dentro de la Revolución todo, contra la Revolución, nada'. [...] Y en Cuba, cuando comienzan a instituirse los modelos socialistas, se traen los modelos socialistas de la cultura que realmente en muchos casos fueron bastante desacertados. En los años 70 esto se puso muy de manifiesto de una manera bastante dramática – y todo eso lo cuento en mi novela *Máscaras* – cuando los intelectuales que estaban en Cuba tenían que demostrar esa posición 'a favor' mientras los que estaban fuera de Cuba para validar su posición se ponían 'en contra de' [...]. Afortunadamente mi generación, cuando comienza a escribir a finales de los 70 y a principios de los 80, una de las metas que se impone es quitarle a la política el protagonismo que había tenido dentro de la literatura cubana. [...] En la década del 90, esa opción, de hacer una literatura desde una posición esencialmente estética ha sido la que ha predominado. [...] Pienso que en los años 90 hubo un momento que marcó el hito a partir del cual se ganó definitivamente ese espacio que de alguna manera ya se había empezado a ganar; se creó un espacio a partir del cual ha sido todo diferente. Me refiero a la película *Fresa y chocolate* [...] Yo mismo me considero de alguna manera un beneficiado de la situación porque mis libros, como tú bien sabes, reflejan lados un poco oscuros de la sociedad cubana [...]. Y sin embargo los libros se han publicado en Cuba, se han divulgado, han sido leídos, todo en un ambiente mucho más sosegado. (Clark 2000: 1–2)[22]

We should bear in mind that Padura dares to criticize 'los modelos socialistas' only after the ex-USSR has collapsed and within the process of rectification. But even if it is true that Padura does not profoundly criticize the Cuban regime itself, we must say that Padura uses intertextuality in order to analyse some discourses that belong to the government, to power, and thus he can denounce the absurdity of certain proposals of the state at particular times. Padura uses intertextuality so that 'the overpowering force of heteroglossia' (Holquist in Bakhtin 1981: 426) breaks with the monologic discourse of power, as it goes against the state's insistence on transforming Cuban society into a homogeneous entity.

---

[22]   For a study that compares *Fresa y chocolate* and *Máscaras*, see 'Critiques of sexual and political intolerance in *Máscaras* and the film *Fresa y chocolate*', Wilkinson 2000: 234–69; also published in Wilkinson 2006.

According to Bakhtin, a text's dialogism has at its core centrifugal as well
as centripetal forces (1981: 272). Moreover, 'every utterance participates in the
"unitary language" (in its centripetal forces and tendencies) and at the same time
partakes of social and historical heteroglossia (the centrifugal, stratifying forces)' (1981: 272). In *Máscaras*, a polyphonic novel where language is dialogic,
Padura employs intertextuality in order to break with the 'centripetal forces' of
the monologic official discourse. The use of intertextuality as a challenge to the
state's discourse is made clear when certain characters utilize irony and sarcasm
in order to subvert political slogans that are part of the official discourse. These
official slogans are also relocated to other contexts, hence undermining their
meaning. For example, El Marqués uses political slogans and confers on them
ironic and sarcastic nuances that subvert the seriousness and official nature of
the discourse of power. We find a good example of this when el Marqués reproduces a dialogue with el Otro when they see a transvestite:

> Dios mío, ¿cómo es posible? dijo el Otro [refiriéndose al travesti], que hasta
> se permitía menciones a Dios en la lejanía libérrima de París, cuando en
> sus conversaciones habaneras aseguraba en público su ideología materialista
> dialéctica e histórica y su certidumbre de que la religión es el opio, la
> marihuana y hasta los Marlboros de los pueblos. (Padura 1997: 48)

El Marqués uses irony to make fun of the expression 'Dios mío', which has
remained in the language even though the society where it is used is theoretically secular. El Marqués emphasizes the paradox that occurs when el Otro uses
the phrase 'Dios mío' at the same time as he declares himself a Marxist. With
this joke, el Marqués points out el Otro's hypocrisy.

In the above quotation el Marqués also mocks official discourse when he
makes a pun with the Marxist slogan that states that religion is the opium of the
masses by introducing another element that symbolizes imperialism, that is,
Marlboro cigarettes. He thus mocks the Marxist discourse that the government
uses by combining it with its opposite, imperialism. El Marqués shows the absurdity of the official discourse, its use and abuse; he also stresses the hypocrisy
of the members of the Cuban government who use different discourses according
to circumstances. When Conde visits his friend Miki Cara de Jeva (Michael Girl
Face) to ask him about el Marqués, he says: 'si lo gritabas hace quince años [el
nombre de Alberto el Marqués] [...] te iban a decir [...] Es el Diablo, el enemi-
go de la clase, el apóstata, el apóstata de la próstata, buena metáfora, ¿no?'
(Padura 1997: 62). This character makes a pun with the idea that el Marqués was
considered a counter-revolutionary by the government because of his homosexuality, while on the other hand he ridicules him for his sexuality.

When el Marqués speaks about his homosexuality he states that having sex
with a man 'eso sí es mío, ayer, hoy y mañana, como dice el lema' (Padura 1997:
228). This echoes the title of the Oscar-winning erotic comedy of 1963, *Ieri, oggi*

e domani, starring Sophia Loren and Marcello Mastroianni, directed by the master of Italian neorealism Vittorio de Sica. El Marqués believes his sexuality is the only space of freedom he has within a system that in the novel is described as repressive. At the same time, with his direct reference to yesterday, today and tomorrow as a slogan, there is an elliptical allusion that undermines the political slogan made famous during the October Crisis in 1962 and thereafter, followed by 'Comandante en jefe, ordene'. This could be interpreted as a sarcastic wink to the reader where the character plays with the idea that he will never renounce his sexuality and his individuality despite the system's slogans, which also include the internationalist element popularized in the 1970s with 'donde sea, como sea y para lo que sea, Comandante en Jefe, ordene'. The slogan is thus subverted by means of the intertext used by a character, el Marqués, who expresses his rebelliousness as an act of resistance before power.

We could further claim that one of the referents in *Máscaras* is literature itself and the process of creation. The novel is full of allusions and references to texts of different styles and writers. Most of these allusions are mere phrases or even a single phrase, but they acquire a special signification that they did not have in the previous context or emphasize an idea already exposed in the hypotext. Before analysing some examples in more detail, I will pay attention to those intellectuals who are friends of el Marqués in *Máscaras* and who share his aesthetic views and thus help Padura to contextualize his text beyond his national borders. All of them are known intellectuals; some of them are foreign, and others had problems with Castro's regime. They become part of the cultural heritage of el Marqués and appear to be active voices within the continuous process of creation of a Cuban culture:

> Dos días antes yo [el Marqués] había terminado mis búsquedas de documentos sobre Artaud y también el ciclo de clases magistrales en el Teatro de las Naciones, donde expuse por primera vez en público mi nueva idea del montaje de *Electra Garrigó* a partir de lo que llamé una estética travesti. Fue un éxito, en realidad mi último gran éxito público... De Sartre a Grotowsky, pasando por Truffaut, Néstor Almendros, Julio Cortázar y Simone Signoret, me hicieron elogios públicos y privados y recibí allí mismo la invitación para presentar la obra en la temporada siguiente, con funciones en seis ciudades francesas. (Padura 1997: 222)

Furthermore, we must take into account the friends that el Marqués met in Paris, as mentioned above. These friends have an actual referent: intellectuals who in one way or another took a critical stance with respect to the Cuban revolution, such as Jean-Paul Sartre.

Piñera is the intellectual most frequently mentioned in the novel. El Marqués proposes him as the prototype of the repressed intellectual. El Marqués relates to Conde a real anecdote from Piñera's biography:

> Acuérdese que en sus últimos diez años Virgilio no volvió a ver editado un libro suyo, ni una obra de teatro representada, ni un estudio sobre su trabajo publicado en ninguna de estas seis provincias mágicas que de pronto se convirtieron en catorce y un municipio especial. Y a mí me convirtieron en un fantasma culpable de mi talento, de mi obra, de mis gustos, de mis palabras. Todo yo era un tumor maligno que debían extirpar por el bien social, económico y político de esta hermosa isla en peso. ¿Se da cuenta? Y como era tan fácil parametrarme: cada vez que me medían por algún lado, siempre el resultado era el mismo: no sirve, no sirve, no sirve… (Padura 1997: 105)

El Marqués identifies himself with Piñera and introduces into his discourse the title of Piñera's poem 'La isla en peso' (1942). It is on the island described by Piñera that both Piñera and el Marqués will be condemned, where they will become a 'tumor maligno'. The adjective 'hermosa' goes against the description that Piñera offers of his 'isla en peso', in which he provides a counter-version of the official history of Cuba, and even though the poem was published prior to the revolution it has maintained its importance and relevance in the new social and historical circumstances.

Moreover, in the summer of 1989 – at a time of political changes in the socialist bloc, and of the execution on 13 July of General Arnaldo Ochoa, Colonel Antonio de la Guardia and Captains Antonio Padrón and Jorge Martínez, all convicted of treason against the revolution for alleged drug trafficking – pervasive melancholy sets in for Conde:

> Colgado de la nostalgia, el Conde miraba el inalterable paisaje que se le ofrecía desde la ventana de su cubículo: copas de árboles, el campanario de una iglesia, los pisos altos de varios edificios, y la eterna y retadora promesa del mar, siempre al fondo, siempre inalcanzable, como la maldita circunstancia de tanta agua por todas partes de que hablara el poeta tan amigo del Marqués. (Padura 1997: 113)

In Padura's novels as well as in the works of writers such as Reinaldo Arenas, Abilio Estévez and Daína Chaviano the sea appears as a symbol of, on the one hand, the island-jail: if one wants to escape from it one has to face the ocean, with its threats. On the other hand, the sea is a symbol of a future full of promise that can only be achieved on the other side.

This latter meaning is the one that Conde gives the sea when he quotes Piñera's line 'la maldita circunstancia del agua por todas partes' from 'La isla en peso'. Moreover, Padura through el Marqués indicates explicitly the borrowing when he alludes to the author of the poem, that is, 'el poeta tan amigo del Marqués'. I shall analyse this verse in its previous context, 'La isla en peso':

> La maldita circunstancia del agua por todas partes
> me obliga a sentarme en la mesa del café.

Si no pensara que el agua me rodea como un cáncer
hubiera podido dormir a pierna suelta. [...]
Una taza de café no puede alejar mi idea fija,
en otro tiempo yo vivía adánicamente.
¿Qué trajo la metamorfosis? [...]

Esta noche he llorado al conocer a una anciana
que ha vivido ciento ocho años rodeada de agua
por todas partes. [...]

El baile y la isla rodeada de agua por todas partes:
plumas de flamencos, espinas de pargo, ramos de
albahaca, semillas de aguacate. [...]

¡Nadie puede salir, nadie puede salir!
La vida del embudo y encima la nata de la rabia.
Nadie puede salir [...]

Bajo la lluvia, bajo el olor, bajo todo lo que es una realidad,
un pueblo se hace y se deshace dejando los testimonios: [...]
un pueblo desciende resuelto en enormes postas de abono,
sintiendo cómo el agua lo rodea por todas partes,
más abajo, más abajo, y el mar picando en sus espaldas; [...]
siempre más abajo, hasta saber el peso de su isla,
el peso de una isla en el amor de un pueblo. (Piñera 2005: 24–38)

In Piñera's poem the island appears as a jail, while for Padura the ocean is full of promises. Taking into account the numerous references to Piñera and his works that appear in contemporary Cuban narratives,[23] I agree with Martínez-Fernández when he says that 'versos de creación individual pasan a ser en ocasiones patrimonio de la memoria colectiva, actualizados en cada momento' (2001: 86–7). This is exactly what happens with some of Piñera's works. The references to his texts appear as exemplary of Cuban culture or, as Padura makes apparent in *Máscaras*, as exponents of 'cubanía'. When el Marqués speaks with Conde, he refers to his friend Eligio Riego:

[T]odavía esta ciudad tiene alma, señor Conde, y no son muchas las ciudades del mundo que pueden vanagloriarse de tener el alma así, a flor de piel... Dice mi amigo el poeta Eligio Riego, que por eso aquí crece tanta poesía, aunque digo yo que éste es un país que no se la merece: es demasiado leve y amante del sol. (Padura 1997: 137)

---

[23] See, for example, *El color del verano* by Reinaldo Arenas, and *Tuyo es el reino* by Abilio Estévez, among others.

El Marqués uses Eligio Riego's words to emphasize the description of Havana as a city where constant contradictions take place.

In *Máscaras* we also find allusions to American texts, such as the film *The Color Purple* (1985), based on Alice Walker's Pulitzer Prize winning epistolary novel of the same title. When Conde asks María Antonia to come to the police station, he describes her thus: 'parecía escapada de una escena de *El color púrpura*' (Padura 1997: 204). With this referent Conde underlines the excessively servile attitude of María Antonia towards the Arayán family. What at the beginning seems to be a criticism of the persistence of servitude many years after the triumph of the revolution of 1959, and within a society where theoretically class differences have been erased, turns out to be the personal choice of an individual. María Antonia's love for Alexis makes her keep working as a servant for the family, even after the revolution, thus establishing a parallel with the situation of a black woman in the southern United States in the first half of the twentieth century in Walker's story.

Conde also views María Antonia as a character within a play: 'María Antonia permanecía de pie, como exigía su personaje de criada sumisa' (Padura 1997: 169). Once Conde discovers the identity of Alexis's killer he treats this case as if it was part of a play. Conde 'se lamentó al fin, otra vez, pues se perdería aquella última escenificación después de haber trabajado tanto en toda la obra' (1997: 212). Even when he wants to know the details of Faustino's interrogation, Conde asks Mayor Rangel: '¿Y cómo fue la función?' (1997: 214). Moreover, when Conde arrives in el Marqués's house and knocks on the door, 'esperó a que se corrieran las cortinas del teatro del mundo de Alberto Marqués' (1997: 217). According to the character Eligio Riego, el Marqués 'vivía sobre el escenario del mundo [...] es un actor nato [...] le gusta inventar sus comedias y sus tragedias particulares' (1997: 183). Therefore, it is no surprise when he offers a reading of the murder of Alexis as if it were part of a Greek tragedy:

> Porque no sé si notó que todo esto parecía una tragedia griega, en el mejor sentido de Sófocles, llena de equívocos, historias paralelas que comienzan veinte años antes y se cruzan definitivamente en un mismo día y personajes que no son lo que dicen que son, o que ocultan lo que son, o han cambiado tanto que nadie sabe ya quiénes son, y en un instante inesperado se reconocen trágicamente. Pero todos enfrentan un destino que los supera, los obliga y los impulsa en la acción dramática: sólo que aquí Layo mata a Edipo, o Egisto se adelanta a Orestes... ¿Se llamará filicidio?... Y todo se desata porque se comete *hybris*. Hay excesos de pasión, de ambición de poder, de odios enconados, y eso suele ser duramente castigado... Lo único lamentable de este juego casi teatral es que los dioses hayan escogido a Alexis para el sacrificio macabro de su destino. (Padura 1997: 220–1)

Here the tragic flaw of hubris or pride echoes the criticism of Cuban society's inability to accept its 'errors' before the rectification process, as was the case with reference to the repudiation of certain writers because of their beliefs or their sexuality, particularly in the 1970s.

When Candito el Rojo, a friend of Conde, tells him 'Tú sabes que la calle está durísima y que, si uno no tiene pesos, está fuera del juego' (Padura 1997: 23), he brings to the reading *Fuera del juego*, the poetry collection which led to the (in)famous Padilla affair. Like the poet, Candito el Rojo feels he is outside of the system, but this time it is the economic system that marginalizes the individual.[24] The dollars that Candito earns with his illegal business allow him to survive, and Conde protects him in exchange for information. Later on in the novel Conde tells him: 'El que nunca sabe soy yo, Rojo. ¿Tú sabes que me estoy sintiendo como si estuviera fuera del juego? Es una cosa rarísima, pero cada vez entiendo menos' (Padura 1997: 134). The investigation that Conde has to carry out becomes a process of self-knowledge. After talking with el Marqués, Conde discovers another reality where there is corruption and an extra-official history, where marginal beings appear as part of his reality. Prior to this new revelation, Conde has a feeling of 'extrañamiento' and inner exile while he learns more about non-official Cuban history. Therefore, Conde feels as Heberto Padilla did, 'fuera del juego', out of the game, outside the system.

Another example of the use of a well-known title within the discourse of the novel appears in the following quotation:

> Dos capitanes, vestidos de civil, habían llegado al filo del mediodía y el Conde les explicó los detalles del caso y les entregó las magras pruebas incriminatorias: [...] y una página con un par de capítulos bíblicos en los que se revelaba a los hombres la esencia divina del hijo putativo del carpintero José y se anunciaba el carácter de su sacrificio ingente, en el Reino de Este Mundo. (Padura 1997: 211)

Here, 'el Reino de Este Mundo' alludes to more than one referent: it may bring to mind the Communion prayer: 'Tuyo es el reino, tuyo el poder y la gloria por siempre, Señor'. In the Christian prayer the kingdom is heaven, in opposition to *Máscaras*, as with the word 'reino' Conde refers to the world. It also echoes the title of one of the most famous novels of Alejo Carpentier, *El reino de este mundo*. Through intertextuality the reader is able to link the figure of Alexis not only with that of Christ (as previously discussed) but also Mackandal, the protagonist of Carpentier's novel. Mackandal, like the others, sacrifices his own life for the benefit of humankind and suffers from a lack of understanding from his contemporaries.

---

[24] During the Special Period in the early 1990s, Cuba adopted multiple currencies, with pesos, US dollars (which became legal tender from 1993 until 8 November 2004), and the convertible pesos or *chavitos* (CUC) in circulation since 1994. This has limited the access of some citizens to certain goods, including basic necessities, not available in Cuban pesos, which is the currency in which state salaries are paid.

Yet another example of intertextuality appears when Conde thinks about his dream of becoming a writer:

> Entonces Mario Conde sentía que aquel desgarramiento prematuro, por el que se había dejado vencer, tal vez sólo funcionara como inhábil pretexto de su conciencia para descargar sobre algún puerto ajeno una culpa que sólo era suya: nunca había vuelto a insistir seriamente, quizá porque la única verdad fuese su incapacidad para escribir algo (que fuera escuálido y conmovedor). (Padura 1997: 113)

The closing remark connects with *Escuálido y conmovedor*, the title of a work by J. D. Salinger. Another American writer is also referenced when el Marqués mentions his experiences in Paris and says that 'París no se acaba nunca, y el recuerdo de cada persona que ha vivido allí es distinto del recuerdo de cualquier otra…' and immediately clarifies: 'Y eso es muy cierto, aunque lo haya dicho Hemingway, que ha sido el escritor más ególatra y narcisista del siglo' (Padura 1997: 46). El Marqués uses this quotation in order to make a judgement about the writer as well as to emphasize his agreement with him with respect to Paris. El Marqués considers that Paris in 1969 represented freedom and life while Havana in the 1970s represented for him repression and death in life.

When Conde is thinking about the case of the murder of the transvestite, he comments:

> La verdad podía ser aquel guagüero con cara de guagüero que había visto esa mañana, golpeando el timón con su anillo, mientras decidía si le abría o no la puerta a la muchacha que le rogaba dando saltitos frente al ómnibus. ¿Qué podría ocurrir después entre esas dos personas que no se conocían y quizá nunca se hubieran conocido si la luz roja no detiene la guagua en ese instante preciso? ¿Ese era el azar concurrente? (Padura 1997: 178)

The 'azar concurrente' is one of the topics of Lezama Lima's essay book *La cantidad hechizada*. After these thoughts, Conde will start to write again and his short story is related to Lezama Lima's 'azar concurrente'. Lezama Lima was, alongside Piñera, one of the Cuban intellectuals ostracized because of his homosexuality, and although he disappeared from the official literary canon for many years, Padura makes his voice participate in the process of the creation of Cuban culture by means of intertextuality. And the examples do not stop here. For instance, when el Marqués explains to Conde how homosexuality is condemned in the Bible, he exclaims: 'Pero eso es sólo una parte de la Tragedia de la Vida, como dice un viejo amigo mío, que por cierto no tiene nada de homosexual' (Padura 1997: 163). Here Padura alludes to Schopenhauer's philosophy of negativity and stresses the recurrent idea that we are living on a stage, the theatre of the world. As Ramón Bau rightly observes, 'en Schopenhauer el Conocimiento de la Tragedia de la Vida y la adopción de una Ética de Renuncia es lo que permite asumir lo inevitable (el tiempo y el lugar con sus consecuencias), sin pretender "comprenderlo en su ilógica material", sino superarlo por su aceptación trágica'.[25] In addition, Schopenhauer addressed homosexuality and somewhat autobiographically described it as naturally occurring in otherwise heterosexual individuals in early adolescence and late in life.[26]

The literary essence of the novel is reflected in even the smallest references. For example, when el Marqués finds the lost sheet of Alexis's Bible, as discussed earlier, and Conde asks him where he found it, el Marqués answers, 'Elemental, teniente Conde, estaba donde debía estar: dentro del *Teatro completo* de Virgilio Piñera que tengo en mis estantes' (Padura 1997: 162); he thus echoes Doctor Watson speaking to Sherlock Holmes, both characters from the detective novels of Sir Arthur Conan Doyle.[27] The same intertextual process is seen when el Marqués has to pick el Otro up at a police station in Paris. He comments, 'un sitio horrible donde no había nadie que se pareciera a Maigret y donde no entraba ni un furtivo soplo de la primavera que envolvía al resto de la ciudad' (Padura 1997: 167), making reference to the famous fictional French detective.

When Conde introduces himself to Poly and tells her he is el Conde, he cannot help but say, 'aunque no de Montecristo' (Padura 1997: 140), making an allusion to the main character of Alexander Dumas's novel. Furthermore, once el Conde has identified the murderer of Alexis, he tells Manolo, 'Llévame para mi casa, creo que me hace falta dormir. Tal vez soñar' (Padura 1997: 213), making a reference to the novel by Ray Bradbury, *Tal vez soñar.* When Conde thinks about why his friend el Flaco has to be in a wheelchair and asks '¿Por qué carajo todo tiene que ser así?' (1997: 233), he uses Don Quixote's words and asks himself '¿Será posible volver atrás y desfacer entuertos y errores y equivocaciones?' (1997: 233). This question will be answered in *Paisaje de otoño*, the last novel of the tetralogy, where according to Padura Conde 'se encierra a escribir la primera novela de la serie y cierra un círculo de fuego en cuyo interior está él, solo, independiente, escribiéndose a sí mismo, dándose forma definitiva por sí solo' (see Appendix 2).

Padura also inserts his writing within the philosophical postulates of existen-

---

25   See Ramón Bau's 'Wagner y Schopenhauer' (http://archivowagner.info/4101.html [accessed 10 February 2006]).

26   See 'The Metaphysics of Sexual Love' in Schopenhauer 1969, vol. 2; Magee 1997: 346–9.

27   Among the most important detective novel writers who have influenced him, Padura (in interview with Stephen Clark) refers to Hammett and Chandler, as well as to the Spanish writer Manuel Vázquez Montalbán, who created the famous detective Pepe Carvalho. In the Mario Conde tetralogy, as in all the novels involving Pepe Carvalho, we also find cooking recipes. In *Máscaras*, Josefina, el Flaco's mother, is in charge of these recipes.

tialism, something which has not gone unnoticed by critics (for example, see Wilkinson 2000; 2006). In Sartre's view, 'it can not [*sic*] be granted that a man may make a judgment about man. Existentialism spares him from any such judgment. The existentialist will never consider man as an end because he is always in the making' (1993: 61). In this sense, Mario Conde could be seen as an existentialist humanist. For Sartre:

> There is no universe other than a human universe, the universe of human subjectivity. This connection between transcendency, as a constituent element of man – not in the sense that God is transcendent, but in the sense of passing beyond – and subjectivity, in the sense that man is not closed in on himself but is always present in a human universe, is what we call existentialist humanism. Humanism, because we remind man that there is no lawmaker other than himself, and that in his forlornness he will decide by himself; because we point out that man will fulfill himself as man, not in turning toward himself, but in seeking outside of himself a goal which is just this liberation, just this particular fulfillment. (1993: 61)

In el Marqués's reading of Conde's short story, he stresses the idea that the story is the result of the process of transculturation, a cultural process in which he also includes existentialism:

> – ¿Conoce *El extranjero?* – el Conde afirmó y su huésped volvió a sonreír –. Bueno, es que su guagüero me recuerda al señor Meursault de *El extranjero*... Es hermosa esa posibilidad metafórica, ¿no? El existencialismo francés y las guaguas cubanas enlazados por la insistencia del sol – y volvió a sonreír y el Conde sintió deseos de agarrarlo por el cuello. El cabrón se está burlando. [...] Pero no tiene título – siguió el Marqués, [...] Pues a mí se me ocurre uno, viendo a estos personajes muertos antes de morir físicamente: *La muerte en el alma. ¿*Qué le parece? [...] Pues si lo quiere, yo se lo regalo. Total, es de Sartre [...] [Conde] pensó que no tenía sentido volver a pedirle su juicio definitivo sobre la calidad ya devaluada de aquel su cuento del alma. (Padura 1997: 218–19)

In this relationship between the established text by Albert Camus, the metanarrative offered by Padura and Conde's own writing in the novel, the different modes of approaching the literary process are mobilized. Barthes refers to 'Esa palabra transparente, inaugurada por *El extranjero* de Camus' that ultimately 'realiza un estilo de la ausencia' which is capable of giving back to the narrative 'la condición primera del arte clásico: la instrumentalidad' (2005: 79). Even if Conde tries to emulate this, there is no innocent, neutral language like that which Barthes finds in Camus. In Padura, the social character in language itself is too present, and is at times at the service of a particular ideological project in a constant state of flux.

El Marqués further uses his customary irony in order to parody the official discourse:

> Es curioso volver a leer cuentos así... En otra época seguramente lo hubieran acusado de asumir posturas estéticas de carácter burgués y antimarxista. Imagínese usted esta lectura del cuento: no hay explicación lógica ni dialéctica al irracionalismo de sus personajes ni de su anécdota; es evidente la incapacidad de estas criaturas para explicar la desorganización de la vida humana, mientras que el detallismo naturalista del narrador no hace más que reforzar la desolación del hombre que ha recibido, no se sabe de dónde, una iluminación de su existencia. Tal estética, pudiera decirse entonces (como muchas veces se dijo) no es más que un reflejo de la degeneración espiritual de la burguesía moderna. Además, su obra no ofrece soluciones a las coyunturas sociales que plantea, por no decir lo que es más evidente: que transmite una imagen sórdida del hombre en una sociedad como la nuestra... ¿Qué le parece esa lectura? Pobre existencialismo... ¿Y qué hacemos entonces con esas obras tan horriblemente bellas de Camus y de Sartre y de Simone?... ¿Y el pobre Scott Fitzgerald y el escatológico Henry Miller y los buenos personajes de Carpentier, y el mundo oscuro de Onetti? ¿Decapitar la historia de la cultura y de las incertidumbres del hombre?... (Padura 1997: 219)

Alberto el Marqués pays homage to existentialism and in doing so challenges social realism, and the official discourse of the state. Through the reading of the story Conde emphasizes the importance of all cultural influences, and thus opposes the state's Marxist focus on dialectical materialism. The transgression takes place when el Marqués reads the story using and abusing official discourse, in the process undermining it.

Padura also becomes involved in his own novel as a writer being commented on, using Conde's narrative to this effect. When Conde visits his friend Miki Cara de Jeva in the bar of the UNEAC, he overhears a conversation among three writers:

> ¡Qué imagen de una literatura! Hablaban, mal y con entusiasmo, de otro escritor que al parecer había tenido mucho éxito con una novela reciente y que escribía en los periódicos artículos muy leídos, y lo calificaban de populista de mierda. Sí, decían, destilando hiel por el suelo del local, imagínate que escribe novelas policiacas, entrevistas a peloteros y salseros, y crónicas sobre chulos y la historia del ron: lo que te digo, un populista de mierda, y por eso gana tantos premios, y cambiaban el tema para hablar de ellos mismos, que sí eran escritores preocupados por los valores estéticos y el reflejo de las contradicciones sociales, cuando regresó Miki con los dos vasos de ron. (Padura 1997: 61)

Here Padura himself is the writer who is being criticized by other members of the UNEAC, and this passage serves as a small personal revenge against those official writers who have criticized him.

The eclectic musical taste of Conde and el Flaco also serves to establish an intertextual relationship with foreign musical referents, and makes apparent the knowledge of rock music once censored in Cuba:

> El Conde se acercó a la larga hilera de casetes que ocupaban el paño superior de los estantes. Recorrió con la vista los títulos e intérpretes, y casi ni se asombró esta vez del ecléctico gusto musical del Flaco.
> – ¿Qué te gustaría oír? ¿Los Beatles? ¿Chicago? ¿Fórmula V? ¿Los Pasos? ¿Credence?
> – Anjá, Credence – fue otra vez el acuerdo: les gustaba oír la voz compacta de Tom Foggerty y las guitarras primitivas de Credence Clearwater Revival.
> – Sigue siendo la mejor versión de *Proud Mary*. […] y se sorprendieron mirándose a los ojos: en el mismo instante los dos habían sentido la agresiva certeza de la reiteración morbosa que vivían. Aquel mismo diálogo, con iguales palabras, lo habían repetido otras veces, muchas veces, durante casi veinte años de amistad, y siempre en el cuarto del Flaco, y su resurrección periódica les provocaba la sensación de que penetraban en el reino encantado del tiempo cíclico y perpetuo, donde era posible imaginar que todo es inmaculado y eterno. Pero muchas señales visibles, y otras tantas agazapadas tras la vergüenza, el miedo, el rencor y hasta el cariño, advertían que lo único permanente era la voz grabada de Tom Foggerty y las guitarras de Credence: la calvicie amenazante del Conde y la gordura enfermiza del Flaco, que ya no era flaco; la tristeza compacta de Mario y la invalidez irreversible de Carlos eran, entre otras miles, pruebas demasiado fehacientes de un desastre lamentable y para colmo ascendente. (Padura 1997: 18–19)

Thus music becomes the last link between these characters and their past – a past full of broken dreams and promises. Music also creates the space where the two friends can meet without any mask. These musical references appear to be the referents of a whole generation born within the revolutionary process, yet we must bear in mind that groups such as The Beatles were once forbidden in Cuba but still had a significant impact on a whole generation who managed illegally to listen to their music. Moreover, this scene is repeated in all four novels of Padura's tetralogy, as part of what Martínez-Fernández has observed as 'intratextualidad':

> el proceso intertextual opera sobre textos del mismo autor. El autor es libre de aludir en un texto a textos suyos pasados y aun a los previsibles, de autocitarse, de reescribir este o aquel texto. La 'obra' es, por así decir, una continuidad de textos; retomar lo que se ha dicho ya es una manera de dar coherencia al conjunto textual, a nivel formal y semántico; es una forma de lograr que el texto sea un verdadero 'tejido'. (2001: 151–2)[28]

---

28 Intratextuality in Padura's work is abundant, but it deserves separate attention that a study of this nature, because of its limits, cannot give it. Nonetheless, it is worth mentioning that themes such as the war in Angola, the past as lost innocence, and life at a crossroads where the protagonist

After this detailed enumeration of the different types of relationships that Padura's novel establishes with other texts and works of art, we can coclude that Padura utilizes this mechanism not only to pay homage to writers and their works, but to expand and push the boundaries of Cuban national discourse. This novel involves a metanarrative process, as above all it is a narrative about the process of literary creation. Moreover, when Padura introduces other voices he emphasizes the Bakhtinian idea that words are never neutral, and encourages the reader to reterritorialize his text in order to apply the words of others to the Cuban context:

> When a member of a speaking collective comes upon a word, it is not as a neutral word of language, not as a word free from the aspirations and evaluations of others, uninhabited by others' voices. No, he receives the word from another's voice and filled with that other voice. The word enters his context from another context, permeated with the interpretations of others. His own thought finds the word already inhabited. Therefore the orientation of a word among words, the varying perception of another's word and the various means for reacting to it, are perhaps the most fundamental problems for the metalinguistic study of any kind of discourse, including the artistic. (Bakhtin 1984: 202)

Thus, as I have previously mentioned, in Padura we do not find that neutral or innocent language to which Barthes refers as 'una escritura blanca, libre de toda sujeción con respecto a un orden ya marcado del lenguaje' (2005: 78).

I agree with Martínez-Fernández when he writes that 'En cualquier caso, la intertextualidad alude al hecho de que el texto no se legitima en su corporeidad o singularidad, sino por estar escrito desde, sobre y dentro de otros textos' (2001: 74). The use of the discourses of others is also a result of what Martínez-Fernández explains as 'la asunción de la tradición literaria como el Libro del que todos somos autores' (2001: 140). By means of the incorporation of the discourses of others the author reinstates voices that have been excluded from the official canon. He also questions literary categories: is *Máscaras* a novel, an essay about transvestism or a play? As Padura himself has admitted in interview (see Appendix 1), he recognizes that the salient feature of Cuban culture and society is its hybridity, which he exploits through the narrative and the various cultures and backgrounds from which he borrows in this transtextual and transcultural project.

To sum up, it is worth noting that Padura in his *Nota del Autor* limits himself to articulating the fictional realm of the novel, in which characters and events are all part of his imagination 'aunque se parezcan bastante a la realidad'. He

always seems to have chosen the wrong path and attempts to remedy this, are some of the elements that recur in his novels and short stories.

thus rejects indirectly the realist mode he openly exploits, and the non-imagined sources he uses for his book, which he claims: 'transcurre en el espacio posible de la literatura' (Padura 1997: Nota del autor).

Both the title of the novel, *Máscaras*, and the three quotations that precede the narration – quotations that belong to Piñera's *Electra Garrigó*,[29] to Artaud's *El teatro y su doble*[30] and to the famous comic *Batman*[31] – stress, summarize and prefigure the most recurrent topic in the text: the hypocrisy of a society where each individual dons the mask he or she needs in order to survive. After this analysis of the transtextual relationship of *Máscaras* with other texts, we must ask to what extent the use of this technique makes the text obscure and difficult to understand. When I asked Padura if he believed that the reader must participate actively in fixing the meaning of his works, he replied thus: 'Creo que sí, pues el lector es quien completa el ciclo de la obra literaria. Al menos yo escribo para que me lean y lo que fija el lector de mis obras es parte de ellas, sin duda' (see Appendix 1). Even if a reader is unable to unmask the interwoven voices within the narrative, he or she will still enjoy a detective novel in which the protagonist has to solve the murder of a transvestite in Havana. However, a Cuban reader or a Cubanist may bring different ideological lenses to bear on the interpretation of the text, in a socio-political context that Padura himself mobilizes through a novel that is conversant with Cuba's own 'rectification' process.

I have shown how Padura populates his novel with a multiplicity of voices that set in motion perhaps the most ambitious transtextual project in recent Cuban fiction, and this study alone cannot exhaust this analysis. Through transtextual relationships, Padura questions traditional notions of literary genre, author and reader; moreover, he establishes a dialogue between the different voices that appear in the novel. This is a dialogue that goes against any attempt to create a monologic official discourse and turn Cuban culture into a homogenized and fixed entity. With the decontextualization of official discourse, Padura shows that it is nonsense, and thus he successfully subverts the hierarchy that the state wants to establish, proposing his own unique and valid discourse.

---

29   The lines in *Electra Garrigó* are:
        'PEDAGOGO: […] No, no hay salida posible.
        ORESTES: Queda el sofisma.
        PEDAGOGO: Es cierto. En ciudad tan envanecida como ésta, de hazañas que nunca se realizaron, de monumentos que jamás se erigieron, de virtudes que nadie practica, el sofisma es el arma por excelencia. Si alguna de las mujeres sabias te dijera que ella es fecunda autora de tragedias, no oses contradecirla; si un hombre te afirma que es consumado crítico, secúndalo en su mentira. Se trata, no lo olvides, de una ciudad en la que todo el mundo quiere ser engañado. (Virgilio Piñera, *Electra Garrigó*, acto III)' (Padura 1997: n.p.)
30   'Ante todo importa admitir que, al igual que la peste, el teatro es un delirio y es contagioso. (Antonin Artaud: *El teatro y su doble*)' (Padura 1997: n.p.)
31   'Todos usamos máscaras. Batman' (Padura 1997: n.p.)

3

The Palimpsestuous (Re)writing of the Island as a Dialogic Practice: Literature in the Second Degree in Abilio Estévez's *Tuyo es el reino*

As we have seen, there has been a proliferation of the use of intertextuality in recent Cuban fiction, and the process of creation appears as a topic in all the novels studied in this book. This process of creation becomes a mechanism that the characters of the novels use to reach self-knowledge, as a way of creating a collective memory and of resisting established authority.

While Abilio Estévez has achieved international success with his novels and his writings for the theatre, critical studies of his works have been relatively few and far between. This is possibly a result of the literariness and complexity of his works, which may appeal to a limited number of readers rather than to a wider commercial readership, or to the 'lado mezquino', which Estévez identified with a lack of critical response after the success of his first novel.[1] Abilio Estévez has given several published interviews – for example with Sanjuana Martínez (1997), Armando Alanís (1998), Dean Luis Reyes (2001), Magda Resik Aguirre (2001), Eduardo Béjar (2002–03), Asunción Horno-Delgado (2006) and Luis Manuel García Méndez (2009) – in which he has shed light on important aspects of his books, including *Tuyo es el reino* (1997), the novel which occupies my attention in this chapter. In these interviews Estévez admits that he has tried to recover the happy days of his childhood in this novel, written as a homage to literature, and we can see how the writing of the novel itself is created through the narrative voice as the author attempts to apprehend the essence of 'Cubanness'. This is a topic that has not received detailed critical attention, and which I shall examine fully in this chapter.

Edna Rodríguez-Mangual has analysed the Island in the novel as part of the 'imaginario urbano' or as a site of resistance where 'la incoherencia, la fragmentación de la estructura arquitectónica y la vegetación tropical desarticulan el poder englobador de un orden físico y social impuesto de forma jerárquica', and this urban space itself permits the existence of a subject capable of reaching a Utopian state (2005: 121). As she rightly observes, 'la metáfora urbana

---

[1] See his interview in García Méndez 2009: 119–20.

articula un imaginario nacional y cultural orgánico que se escapa de la concepción racional y de lo reprimido' (2005: 121). In her study, Rodríguez-Mangual highlights the process of creation and destruction of a cosmos in constant transformation, the Island, the 'espacio arquitectónico imaginario' (2005: 126) shared by all the characters of the novel which generates a sense of community. The critic goes on to highlight the importance of memory for the reconstruction of the main protagonist's childhood, focusing on the 'cartografía [...] en tanto discursividad' (2005: 128). My study will follow on from this perspective, but concentrates on a detailed analysis of the process of writing itself that the novel engenders. While Rodríguez-Mangual understands that in this novel 'El concepto del tiempo está intrínsicamente [sic] relacionado con el espacio' (2005: 131), I shall go further by establishing a link with the Bakhtinian concept of the chronotope. This is also relevant to the literary production of the 1990s in looking at the space and time of the writing itself, a subject which occupies my attention in this study.

Overall, critics have focused on the spatiality of this novel and the roles played by cultural memory and history. For example, Armando Valdés Zamora calls attention to the fact that in this novel Estévez creates a mythic and utopian space and time, combining the Island and the time of the author's childhood. In this space, according to Valdés Zamora, there is only room for a 'temporalidad regresiva que evita la referencia al tiempo de la Historia cubana más reciente' (2009: 234, his emphasis). It is worth noting here that this lack of focus on a more immediate reality may have been influenced, in this context, by the author's place of residence on the island at the time of writing and publishing this book. As Estévez has said in an interview, recalling the words of Fernando Pessoa, 'la literatura es el modo más agradable de ignorar la vida. [...] Es un acto de soberbia, como si se tratase de un Dios que se otorga la licencia de componer la realidad de otro modo' (Resik Aguirre 2001). In this context, Matías Barchino, in his article 'El peso de la isla en la literatura cubana actual: pervivencia conjunta de las figuras de Virgilio Piñera y José Lezama Lima' (2001), has expressed the importance of both Piñera and Lezama Lima as founders of Cuban literature and their impact on Estévez's work, reiterating the notion of the Island as the paradise lost of childhood. As Estévez himself has affirmed: 'Precisamente, mi novela Tuyo es el reino es la recuperación del momento de la vida en que se define todo lo que serás después' (in Resik Aguirre 2001). Both Erika Müller (2000) and Vicente Cervera Salinas (2001) have also emphasized the insularity of Tuyo es el reino on different levels, referentially and formally, where the Island appears as a text or 'tropo preferido de la postmodernidad' (Cervera Salinas 2001: 127). My analysis, in contrast, will focus on the literariness of this text, its textuality and the connections it establishes through literature. I shall examine the process of writing and rewriting the Island in order to confirm the presence of a dialogic practice similar to that being exercised by Cuban authors in various locations throughout the 1990s, in highly polyphonic novels. I move beyond previously published studies in order to focus on how the polyphony and dialogism we find in the novel subverts any author(itative) figure and any notion of identity, be it individual, literary or national. I will pay attention here to the writing of the Island as a palimpsest that permits the creation of a non-official history, as a means of resisting monolithic representations of Cuban identity and as a way of challenging absolute truths. I claim that in this novel memory, history and culture have a literary role to play as they too become palimpsests in the process of writing and rewriting. This is also typical of Arenas's work, even if in Arenas's case the author had the real referent of having his manuscripts confiscated or stolen and an inability to publish any book on the island after his first novel.

In this chapter I shall also critically examine the dialogic relationship Estévez establishes in relation to the text, the author (as creator and demiurge) and the reader. Moreover, I shall shed light on an issue that many critics have failed to notice, namely how the process of writing the Island ends up becoming an indirect political stance, a site of resistance against oppression. Thus, instead of focusing on the role of memory as many critics have done, I shall pay particular attention to Paul Ricoeur's work in terms of the art of forgetting, which I apply to this text. I claim that in this novel Estévez constructs a narrative of forgetting in which extinction also plays a key role.

Tuyo es el reino is the novel *par excellence* of the process of creation itself. Its main subject is the creation of the novel we are reading and, as Estévez has explained, 'la novela está escrita tratando de mostrar sus costuras y eso creo que no le debe quitar para nada el placer de la lectura' (in Luis Reyes 2001: 2). *Tuyo es el reino* requires an active reader, who at times must determine the speaker in a novel that mixes first, second and third person narrative voices, and where conversations tend to happen simultaneously. The novel is set just before the 1959 Cuban revolution and takes place within the municipality of Marianao, in Havana, in a fictitious place called the Island. The Island is subdivided into Más Acá, where the houses are, and Más Allá, which is covered by overgrown vegetation and 'prácticamente intransitable' (Estévez 1997: 19) and where Professor Kingston, a Jamaican English teacher, lives. Given the numerous contradictions in the novel concerning the identifiable surface features of the region, it would be impossible for a topographer to delineate the Island with precision. The Island is in a state of disrepair and will be destroyed by an accidental fire at the beginning of the revolution on 1 January 1959. Apart from Professor Kingston, other incongruous inhabitants of the Island include Chavito (an absent character), a sculptor of clumsy replicas of Greek statues, the son of Merengue, and a *santería* practitioner who is also a street vendor of puff pastries; Casta Diva, a frustrated opera singer and her husband Chacho, a former stenographer in the Camp Columbia barracks, who leaves the Batista army to raise rabbits; the madwoman known as la Condesa Descalza, a visionary who can predict the future of the Island; Helena, who holds the keys to the Island, mother of Sebastián (the narrator-author) and sister of tío Rolo, the gay librarian; Marta, who is blind and unable to dream, and her sister Mercedes, who is the eternal dreamer; el Herido, pierced by arrows, who alludes to a representation of Saint Sebastian, found by Sebastián and Tingo-no-entiendo wrapped in a Cuban flag in a former carpentry shop in Más Allá; Irene, who nurses el Herido back to health (in a similar fashion to Irene of Rome with St Sebastian), a character traumatized by forgetting; Lucio, Irene's homosexual son; Miss Berta, a paranoid schoolteacher and her 90-year-old mother, Doña Juana, who ultimately causes the fire that will destroy the Island. These are just some of the many characters who contribute to the polyphony that characterizes this novel.

The Island was originally built by a poor Galician couple, Enrique Palacio, known as Padrino after baptizing the only daughter of his maid Consuelo, and Angelina, his sister. They are both from a fishing village near Santiago de Compostela. Enrique was born in the mid-nineteenth century and Angelina is five years younger. Enrique arrived in Cuba at the beginning of the War of Independence to fight on the Spanish side, not for patriotic reasons but with the intention of having a better future in Cuba (Estévez 1997: 178–9), which is now also named 'la Isla' in the novel: 'la Isla que, según contaban, era otro país de Jauja' (1997: 179). But upon arrival in Santiago de Cuba, 'la Isla no fue lo que Enriquillo esperaba. Tenía la misma pobreza de su aldeíta frente al mar' (1997: 179). After 1878 he settles in Havana, becomes rich, and around 1880 pays for his sister to follow him (1997: 180). After consummating their incestuous relationship, Angelina becomes pregnant and they decide to move and found the Island, where she gives birth to a monster which is allowed to be suffocated by the maid Consuelo: 'Hay quien dice que nació un minotauro. Hay quien dice que un basilisco. Otros, que una medusa. Se sabe cómo puede ser desmesurada la imaginación popular' (1997: 185). The origin of the Island is as follows:

> Enrique y Angelina decidieron abandonar la quinta y mudarse a un lugar remoto donde no los conocieran, donde el comadreo no les afectara. Vendieron la quinta de El Cerro; compraron lo que ahora es la Isla. Por esos años anteriores a la ocupación norteamericana, ni siquiera Columbia se había convertido en cuartel; Carlos J. Finlay no se había hecho famoso por descubrir en esta zona al mosquito transmisor de la fiebre amarilla. Marianao era un caserío famoso por el clima benigno, la cercanía de la playa y el Hipódromo; lo suficientemente próximo de La Habana para no sentirse en el campo, y lo suficientemente lejos como para no sufrir el espanto de la ciudad. […] [H]abía una casa donde fueron a vivir los hermanos, y una casita pequeña, apenas dos cuartos, donde una mulata hermosa y joven llamada Consuelo, vivió poco después con su marido, Lico Grande, un negro mucho más viejo, que había sido esclavo de la familia Loynaz. (1997: 184)

The Island thus originates towards the end of the nineteenth century, since the American occupation dates back to 1 January 1899; Camp Columbia barracks dates back to the same period, as in November 1898 General Humphrey acquired land in Marianao for the camp; the US military personnel that first arrived there were mostly from the District of Columbia, hence the name (Lotti 2009). Finlay's hypothesis that a mosquito was the vector for the yellow fever virus was confirmed by Walter Reed in 1900. In most non-Cuban medical history books, Reed is credited with the breakthrough in yellow fever research through the discovery that the *Aedes aegypti* mosquito was the transmitter of the infectious disease. The hippodrome was inaugurated in 1881 (Bianchi Ross 2010). And on 7 October 1886, slavery was officially abolished in Cuba. Another time marker is offered by the reference to Consuelo's daughter, who dies as a teenager, killed by a stray bullet during the 'Guerrita de Agosto' (Estévez 1997: 178). This was a short-lived rebellion by the Liberals which took place in August 1906, against the re-election of the conservative president Tomás Estrada Palma. Thus the foundational fiction has historical markers that make it abundantly clear that the 1958 setting of the novel has a late nineteenth-century and early twentieth-century background to contend with.

   This chapter will examine critically how this novel addresses the process of creating a Barthesian 'infinite text' through intertextuality, and how at times it becomes a palimpsest, as described by Genette.[2] According to Genette, drawing on Philippe Lejeune's terminology, this sort of text requires an active 'palimpsestuous reading' (1997: 398–9). The text-palimpsest is, according to Genette, always more than one. The creation of a text that is a palimpsest is exemplified within *Tuyo es el reino* through the constant writing and rewriting of the same events. Even the Island has physically a palimpsest-like essence as 'en su conjunto, la Isla [...] es muchas islas [...] para cada hora y para cada luz hay una Isla, una isla diferente' (Estévez 1997: 19). As I will analyse further on in this chapter, the topography of the Island and its palimpsest-like nature are closely related to one another.

   The palimpsest in Estévez's novel works through an overlay of writings and rewritings. This process becomes a discursive mechanism to create a non-official history, a memory from the margins, which acts as an element of cultural resistance to monolithic representations of Cuban identity. As Gerald Prince writes in the foreword to Genette's *Palimpsests: Literature in the Second Degree*: 'any writing is rewriting; and literature is always in the second degree' (Genette 1997: iv). A text in the second degree is, according to Genette, 'a text derived from another pre-existent text' (1997: 5), and Estévez's novel demonstrates this through its numerous intertextualities and its metanarrative, as the novel exploits

---

2   For a discussion of Genette's appropriation of Kristeva's intertextuality in *Palimpsestes* as 'licensed imitation', see Orr 2003: 106–12.

the many individual stories that rely on past stories while also founding a new totalizing scheme that encompasses centuries of literary creation. Thus the chronotope extends beyond the merely foundational Cuban context that the novel uses.

Tuyo es el reino, like the novels studied in previous chapters, belongs to the new boom, in the international context, of the Cuban novel in the 1990s. This novel uses the process of creation itself to subvert monolithic representations of reality and truth as well as to challenge established concepts of national, gender and individual identity. According to Estévez, the literature written in Cuba by his generation is

> bastante importante. O sea, entrando ya en el tema de las generaciones, es bastante importante, porque tienes que considerar que la década de los 70 fue una década desastrosa para la literatura cubana. Fue una década en la que todos los grandes escritores fueron marginados, y lo que se publicaba era de una medianía rayana en lo peor, de mediocre hacia abajo. De modo que cuando en el ochenta y tanto empieza a surgir una generación con Senel Paz, con Leonardo Padura, con Arturo Arango, con Miguel Mejides, lo que teníamos en frente era el páramo que dejaron los 70, y había que retomar, había que saltar por arriba de eso, e irnos a buscar a Lezama otra vez, a buscar a Virgilio Piñera, a Eliseo Diego, a buscar ese vínculo perdido, retomarlo y empezar como de cero. Yo creo que esa es la importancia de esa generación; hacer una nueva literatura en Cuba. (in Béjar 2002–03: 91–2)

When Béjar asked Estévez, '¿qué cambios ha habido en la narrativa cubana desde 1990 hasta el presente?', he replied:

> Creo que los cambios empiezan un poco antes, en el ochenta y tanto. En primer lugar, hay una necesidad de subjetivar la literatura. ¿Qué quiero decir con esto? Pues que después de una década, como ya te he dicho, que era de epopeya, de un realismo socialista peor aún que el propio soviético, puesto que no era más que triunfalismo total con una falta absoluta de subjetividad, con personajes que eran planos, externos, etc., entonces esa literatura empieza la introspección de esos personajes, que empiezan a buscar su propia vida, a psicoanalizarse. Y ya en los 90, lo que comienza en los 80 […] todo eso que no se concebía en los 70, pues después de haber entrado el personaje en sí mismo, empieza a mirar desde sí mismo a la sociedad. Esto es muy importante porque entonces, ya en los 90, se vuelve una mirada ya llena de amargura, llena de escepticismo, o también con optimismo pero ya bañada por el interior del personaje. (in Béjar 2002–03: 92)

This subjectivity permeates Estévez's novel, and the process of creation itself helps to create this subjectivity and interiority. Estévez creates, above all, atmospheres and characters; this is the reason why *Tuyo es el reino* has no linear plot. The Island is located in Havana, as an enclosure within the island of Cuba:

> A la Isla se llega por la gran puerta que da a la calle de la Línea, que está en una zona de Marianao llamada (será fácil deducir por qué) Reparto de los Hornos.[3] La entrada debió de haber sido suntuosa hace años. Tiene dos severas columnas que sostienen el frontón y la solemne verja, bastante herrumbrosa, que permanece cerrada. En lo alto de la verja, junto a unas letras retorcidas donde se lee LA ISLA, hay una campana. Si uno quiere que le abran, debe mover la verja varias veces para que las campanadas avisen, y entonces vendrá Helena con la llave y abrirá el candado. Los tiempos están muy malos, dice Helena a todo el que llega, a modo de justificación. El visitante debe reconocer que, en efecto, los tiempos están muy malos. [...] desde el zaguán no puede distinguirse la Isla porque una enorme antipara de madera interrumpe la visión. [...] De hierro, sin adornos, son las lámparas y casi ninguna tiene intactos los cristales. [...] Cuando finaliza la antipara, y se avanza unos pasos por la parte izquierda de la galería, hacia la casa de Rolo, se puede afirmar que por fin uno ha llegado a la Isla. (Estévez 1997: 18)

The main entrance to the Island was finished during Menocal's government, thus dating it between 1913 and 1921, and the reference to the Reparto Los Hornos places it between 1903 and 1915. The precarious state of things on the Island suggests that time has elapsed, and most of the events in the novel happen before 1 January 1959 when the Island will be accidentally destroyed with the coming of the revolution. The inhabitants ignore what is happening in the rest of the country:

> Ahí está, pues, la Isla ardiendo [...], y eso que ignoraban la confusión que se estaba produciendo en el resto del país en ese preciso instante, puesto que es la hora de revelar que en ese preciso instante el Señor Presidente, Fulgencio Batista, huía en un avión hacia la República Dominicana con la familia y el dinero, el cuartel de Columbia (a dos o tres cuadras de la Isla) se quedaba sin poder, y los Rebeldes, con sus larguísimas barbas vehementes, se hacían dueños de la situación. (1997: 320)

The Island is thus located within the municipality of Marianao, where the Columbia barracks were established, which were converted into the Ciudad Escolar Libertad (CEL) on 14 September 1959.[4] Despite the fluidity of the chronotope, there are enough indications in the novel to place it in Havana on the threshold of the revolution. For example, there is the reference to Merengue 'a la entrada de Maternidad Obrera', which was established in 1941,[5] and the novel in general is set in the months before the 1959 Cuban revolution.

---

3   The creation of Reparto Los Hornos dates back to the period between 1903 and 1915. See Bianchi Ross 2010.

4   For more on CEL, see Lotti 2009.

5   For more on the development of Marianao, see Bianchi Ross 2010.

The novel is fragmented and intertextuality serves as a discursive strategy that acts as a marker to identify the speaker of a particular section. Thus intertextuality is used by Estévez to identify his own characters. For example, the voice of tío Rolo is identified in the narrative through his references to Julián del Casal. Throughout the novel, Rolo refers to 'vagos dolores en los músculos y hondas tristezas en el alma', a phrase which takes the reader to the last stanza of Casal's poem 'Tardes de lluvia':

> Y, a la muerte de estos crepúsculos,
> siento, sumido en mortal calma,
> vagos dolores en los músculos,
> hondas tristezas en el alma. (Casal 1963: 193)

Estévez gives tío Rolo the attributes of melancholy and sadness found in Casal's poem, particularly because Rolo is a character in search of his younger lover, Sandokán. This indirectly connects the novel with the penultimate and antepenultimate stanzas of Casal's poem:

> Yo creo oír lejanas voces
> que, surgiendo de lo infinito,
> inícianme en extraños goces
> fuera del mundo en que me agito.
>
> Veo pupilas que en las brumas
> dirígenme tiernas miradas,
> como si de mis ansias sumas
> ya se encontrasen apiadadas. (Casal 1963: 193)

As Emilio Bejel has illustrated in his *Gay Cuban Nation* (2001: 4), following on from Agnes Lugo-Ortiz's *Identidades imaginadas: Biografía y nacionalidad en el horizonte de la guerra (Cuba 1860-1898)* and Manuel Cruz's *Cromitos cubanos (bocetos de autores hispanoamericanos)*, Casal is part of the Cuban imaginary of the 'unmanly' man, who turns away from war and politics. Here, Estévez uses Rolo to focus on this theme of the man who turns to books as a form of escapism. Rolo lives in inner exile. Bejel, with reference to Casal but also applicable here, states 'the "effeminate man" […] is constructed in Cuba to delineate the limits of the Cuban nationalist discourse; this is an excluded being that participates (by exclusion) in defining the nation to which it does not belong' (2001: 4). By means of intertextuality, the presence of Rolo in the novel confirms the existence of another subjectivity within the Cuban nation. Rolo is presented as a rejected subject, scorned by others and melancholic because of it. This characteristic of his personality is emphasized by the narrator, who presents him as if he were a victim of chance:

> [N]oches hay en que Rolo comienza a acercarse, como si no quisiera, como si fuera víctima del azar, y traería (no sería él si no) su melancolía, su aspecto derrotado, y la mirada entre apremiante y esperanzada, como si los que se reunieran en la Isla fueran criaturas superiores. Y Merengue, que lo conoce bien, se quedaría mirándolo con ojos de tristeza y exclamaría para sí, aunque tratando de que todos lo oyeran, pobre hombre, pobre hombre. Estallarían las carcajadas. Se iniciaría la conversación. (Estévez 1997: 24)

Estévez not only emphasizes the heterogeneous subjectivities present on the island but also the heterogeneity of cultures, which should embrace otherness. He achieves the latter by creating visual cues, using the statues made by Chavito, who is not himself part of the narrative although his sculptures are. His statues are fundamentally spatial. They are used within an art of memory to find directions within the Island, a sort of enclosure within the island nation. The statues take us back to ancient Greece and Rome, with the 'Victoria de Samotracia', the 'Discóbolo' and the 'Diana', which share their space with the 'Virgen de la Caridad del Cobre', the bust of Martí (a ubiquitous icon of Cuban culture) and modern foreign culture via a statue of the Swedish-born Hollywood star Greta Garbo. The statues thus form part of a visual diegesis in the novel.

The *Victoria de Samotracia*, today in the Louvre Museum in Paris, has no arms and no head. The use of this statue in the novel does not represent an arbitrary choice; it is thought to belong to the stern of a boat and the Island itself is considered a grounded vessel. As la Condesa Descalza explains:

> El hombre de la Isla se cree siempre en una balsa, se cree siempre a punto de zarpar y también a punto de zozobrar, sólo que esa balsa no surca el mar, y es en el momento en que descubre que la Isla no se moverá, en el momento en que el hombre de la Isla se percata de que su balsa está fija al fondo marino por alguna fuerza eterna y diabólica, en ese instante, corta troncos y construye la balsa y se aleja para siempre. (Estévez 1997: 174)

Myron's *Discobolus* is a long-lost Greek bronze original that is known today thanks to multiple Roman replicas. The statue highlights in the novel the role played by the simulacrum, which in a palimpsestuous way connects with the original version, echoing the writing of the novel (the hypertext) in its re(writing) of previous classics (the hypotexts). The *Discobolus* also underlines the energy and agency of the discus-thrower poised to act, mirroring the situation in which all characters seem to find themselves on the brink of the 1959 revolution. On the other hand, Diana, the hunter, the Roman virgin goddess of the moon, dwelling in the woods, is a symbol of the preservation of the Island and its vegetation until she disappears.

The balancing act between 'zarpar' and 'zozobrar' is determined in the novel by two main events: the storm that all the inhabitants of the Island are waiting for and the fire that will destroy the Island. The rest of the novel con-

centrates on the inner thoughts of the characters, their dialogues with one another and their narratives. Above all, this novel contains multiple narratives that
enter into dialogue with each other, a dialogue that is established to challenge
any attempt to present a homogenized concept of Cuban culture and identity
and to subvert any authoritative discourse of power, namely, the figure of the
Author-God that appears in the novel. Hence the novel participates in a process
of dialogization. Here I use the terminology as defined by Michael Holquist; for
him 'A word, discourse, language or culture undergoes "dialogization" when it
becomes relativized, de-privileged, aware of competing definitions for the same
things. Undialogized language is authoritative or absolute' (Holquist in Bakhtin
1981: 427).

Intertextuality: The Universal Literary Dialogue

As we have seen, intertextuality was a discursive mechanism widely used during the 1990s in Cuban narrative. Through the use of intertextuality, as in the
case of Rolo above, Estévez establishes a dialogic relationship with other texts.
On the one hand, this dialogic relationship pays tribute to the literature selected
for intertextual connections, a literature that, according to the author, has saved
him in times of crisis. As Estévez states:

> Al mismo tiempo, con *Tuyo es el reino* quería también hacer una especie
> de homenaje – la palabra me parece ridícula, pero uno a veces tiene que ser
> ridículo – a algo que es lo que me ha salvado todo el tiempo: la literatura. Si
> no hubiera sido por ella no sé qué hubiera sido de mí. (in Luis Reyes 2001:
> 2)[6]

On the other hand, Estévez uses this dialogic relationship with other works to
situate Cuban culture within a more universal literary heritage. Moreover, Estévez
has argued that 'Somos un país de poca tradición literaria, si lo comparamos
con otros. Así que nos sentimos con el lógico derecho de tomar de toda la
tradición literaria' (in García Méndez 2009: 120). Therefore, intertextuality
serves to define Cuban culture as a product of endless interactions with different
cultures. This is one of the characteristics of the Cuban novel of the 1990s, in
which Cuban culture appears in the vortex and as part of a universal heritage
that is transformed and modified within each context.

   Furthermore, intertextuality is used to establish a dichotomy between reality
and fiction in different contexts; that is, reality is fluid and based on the truth of
the speaker, which must be contrasted against other truths. As Bakhtin has

---

   6   In an interview with Eduardo C. Béjar, Estévez states in reference to his book *Los palacios
distantes*: 'Aquí se repite una idea que está en *Tuyo es el reino*, que es la salvación por la literatura, en este caso, por el arte en general' (Béjar 2002–03: 96).

stated, 'Language, no longer conceived as a sacrosanct and solitary embodiment of meaning and truth, becomes merely one of many possible ways to hypothesize meaning' (1981: 370), and Estévez puts this into practice. By means of intertextuality, Estévez suggests that the Cuban condition is created by a constant desire to escape from one's immediate environment. Estévez uses intertextuality in order to make references to other texts that highlight different realities, which the inhabitants of the Island can aspire to and indeed desire, according to the novel. This universal cultural heritage used as a contrasting background undermines any homogenized view of absolute truths presented in Cuba, challenging all dogmatic views of reality, and the author represents the island as being in a state of physical isolation from the rest of the world. Intertextuality here serves as a bridge to cross this gap.

As in Padura's novel *Máscaras*, and as Edna Rodríguez-Mangual (2005: 123–4) has observed with reference to *Tuyo es el reino*, in his use of intertextuality Estévez mobilizes postmodern theories of the text. In Barthesian terms, I suggest that this novel becomes a text 'Woven entirely with citations, references, echoes, [...] which cut across it through and through in a vast stereophony' (Barthes 1977: 160). This stereophony is also typical of Cuban narrative in the 1990s, a period when the country itself opened up to capitalist tourism after the crisis of the Special Period in 1991. This is a period when we find a proliferation of narrative experimentation, and literary work was created that, in many cases, paid particular attention to intertextuality, thus inserting Cuban narrative into a more universal dialogue.

Through intertextuality the boundaries of literary genres are blurred. For example, *Tuyo es el reino* cannot be considered a novel per se, as in it we can find essays about the process of creation, religious texts, stage directions typical of a play, and other elements that transgress the limits of the traditional novel. In this kind of text, the relationship established between the reader and the text is dialogic, and, as mentioned before, the role of the reader must be an active one. Thus, through intertextuality the rigid concept of authorship is also destabilized, even though in *Tuyo es el reino* we find the God-like Author figure.

The use of intertextuality entails this 'goce estético' (in Luis Reyes 2001: 4) that Estévez confesses he finds when he tries to apprehend in his novel the essence of Cuban identity. Thus, using intertextuality, Estévez reinforces the idea of artifice, the idea that the text is self-sufficient enough to manifest its own reality without recourse to a specific referent outside the narrative realm in order to legitimize itself. In a Derridean, deconstructive fashion, it moves instead from text to text. Hence, intertextuality becomes a mechanism to explore different voices, and different views of the world, beyond the monologic contributions of any authoritative figure, such as the God-like Author who appears in this novel.

The Palimpsestuous Intertext

In *Tuyo es el reino* the palimpsest is used as a literary technique through which to imitate the process of creation itself, whereby memories are the raw material for writing arranged anew. In this novel the narration is always part of a dialogue. The agency of the characters is in their speech acts; characters tell each other about their lives, feelings and experiences, and by doing so they become the characters of these stories. In short, they are created dialogically, that is, through discourse. With this technique, Estévez tries to highlight the textuality of life, of the sign, and blurs the boundaries between life and representation or artifice. In a postmodern metanarrative style, he revives 'the Renaissance tradition of imitation as rhetoric or poetics' (Orr 2003: 107). The words applied by Mary Orr to Genette in her study are applicable to Estévez; his concern is 'to rethink the figurative through imitation taken to other degrees' (2003: 107). Imitation allows Estévez to create a fluid topography of cultural memory that places the novel in a Cuban but also a universal context, anchored in the past, from classical antiquity until the present reality of the novel in the twentieth century.

In the novel, the palimpsest stands as well for a universal literature and culture that is part of an infinite text that is being written and will allegedly be rewritten endlessly through time. Here, the novel seems to respond to Genette's position, which as Orr convincingly argues 'leaves the Grand Narrative of mimesis and anti-mimesis intact' (2003: 112). Hence we could consider Orr's question, in relation to Genette, applicable here: 'Is there no way out of the vicious circles of mimesis and anti-mimesis that are its altogether ancient and newly towering, architextual Babel?' (2003: 112). To this, we could reply with Genette's words, also applicable to Estévez: 'This limit, happily or not, is never reached, and furthermore, I imagine that a sort of protective censorship [...] prevents the model from ever recognizing himself completely in the image that is presented to him' (Genette 1997: 79). Casta Diva, for one, will see her defacement in the mirror: 'Casta Diva corre al espejo. Nada se ve del otro lado' (Estévez 1997: 178), and the unfolding and effacement in the mirror between model and replica is a constant in the novel, reflected in the following passage which I quote at length in order to illustrate this point:

> volvió la idea de mirarse al espejo. El espejo esta vez demoró más en reflejarla, y cuando la otra que era ella misma apareció, traía expresión de sorna, o al menos así quiso interpretar Casta Diva la ligera sonrisa [...]. ¿De qué te burlas?, preguntó a la imagen. Ella ni siquiera movió los labios. [...] Ella dijo Eres [*sic*] mi imagen, te corresponde repetir cuanto hago, repetirme hasta el cansancio, es tu deber. La otra pestañeó nerviosa, la miró un segundo, para después halar la réplica de una silla que había en el cuarto [...] (¿Estará de más decir que la verdadera silla, la del cuarto, permaneció en su sitio?) No me evadas, gritó ella un tanto exasperada, no tienes derecho a evadirme.

La imagen respondió suspirando, poniéndose de pie, encaminándose a la ventana, que abrió hacia la Isla. Casta Diva pudo ver cómo miraba el día brillante. (¿Estará de más decir que la verdadera ventana siguió cerrada y que ella, considerándose la legítima, no se movió de su lugar?) Golpeó la luna del espejo, exclamó Eres irreal, aborrecible e irreal. A pesar de que la imagen permaneció quieta, supo que la había escuchado, [...] y se había llenado de ira. La suposición fue confirmada después, cuando la imagen tomó el monedero que estaba sobre la mesa de noche y salió a la Isla. (¿Estará de más decir que el verdadero monedero continuó sobre la verdadera mesa de noche?, ¿resultará inútil enfatizar que el espejo quedó vacío?)

La imagen regresó días después. Tú estabas acostada junto a Chacho poco antes del amanecer, por supuesto sin dormir, [...] cuando la viste asomar a la luna del espejo [...]. Mientras hablabas notaste que la otra tenía en la mano el abrecartas dorado, y buscaste por instinto el verdadero abrecartas y no lo encontraste, y te escondiste en un rincón, y aunque no podías ver el espejo, supiste que la otra te buscaba con la vista y sólo te alivió pensar que no podía salir del espejo, que su lugar era irremediable, que estaba condenada a ser imagen, y gracias a esa seguridad pudiste buscar el paño negro y tirarlo sobre el espejo. (1997: 121–2)

There is also an unfolding of the characters that form a motley group in the novel. El Herido, for example, evolves into multiple characters in the last part of the book. He becomes Scheherazada and el Maestro and exposes how literature can also be an expression of cultural resistance against authoritative power. It is at the end of the novel that the subversive role of literature is revealed. El Herido/Scheherazada/el Maestro tells Sebastián:

Estás autorizado a llamarme Scheherazada. Pareció que la luz se hacía íntima. Por sorpresa, el hombre rejuveneció, se convirtió para mi asombro en el Herido [...] y de ahí pasó a ser una mujer, una bellísima mujer. Como el cruel sultán es eterno, exclamó con voz potente y aún más misteriosa, Scheherazada se ha visto en la obligación de usar incontables seudónimos a lo largo de siglos incontables. [...] Tu primitivismo (eres tan joven) no te ocultará que Scheherazada fue (es, soy, seré) una mujer brillante, decidió (decidí, decido, decidiré) contar y contar y contar para salvar la vida, se dio (me doy, me daré) cuenta de que contar era (es, será) el modo único de sobrevivir, se dio (me doy, me daré) cuenta de las posibilidades salvadoras que tienen (y tendrán siempre siempre) las palabras, tuvo la iluminación de que narrar era (es, seguirá siendo) el único modo (¡el único modo!) de alcanzar la eternidad, y estuvo (estaré, quieran o no) hablando mil noches y una, ¡mil noches y una!, y más, toda una vida como aquel que dice, y como tu primitivismo no te ocultará, ¡se salvó!, ¡Scheherezada se salvó! (Estévez 1997: 330–1)

In the earlier text the Sultan of the *One Thousand and One Nights* embodies the destructive authority of power. This destructive authority existed then and is repeated throughout history in various other characters. Scheherazada's narrative, on the other hand, represents universal literature, with its power as a mechanism of resistance in order to survive oppression. Literature, according to this character, is the only element that cannot be destroyed. Narration implies freedom, resistance and eternal life in the incorporation of all the tenses: past, present and future. In the voice of the narrator, 'Una de las virtudes de la literatura es quizá que con ella se pueda abolir el tiempo, o mejor, darle otro sentido, confundir los tres tiempos conocidos en un cuarto que los abarque a todos y provoque lo que podría llamarse la simultaneidad' (1997: 220). Moreover, Scheherazada will emerge in every narrator that has been born and will ever be born:

> Y en un Segundo volvió a ser otra vez el hombre con cara Míster Poe. [...] Tenía el ceño fruncido antes de continuar: Luego, con el tiempo, a lo largo de siglos y siglos, como un personaje famoso de Mistress Woolf, Scheherazada ha cambiado de cuerpo, de sexo, de nombre, se la ha conocido como Herman Broch, Alberto Moravia, Truman Capote, Azorín, [...], Jean Genet, Vargas Llosa, Cervantes, [...], Nélida Piñón, [...], Homero, [...], Thomas Mann, José Saramago, Cirilo Villaverde [...] y *tutti quanti*, y si no los menciono a todos es por aquello de *ars longa, vita brevis*, como tú comprenderás, la vida no nos alcanzaría, y yo, tu nada humilde servidor, no soy más que una de las prodigiosas encarnaciones de esa mujer superior y por eso digo: te autorizo a llamarme por mi nombre oculto y verdadero, Scheherazada, aunque si prefieres puedes emplear también Maestro, de mayor naturalidad, rapidez, familiaridad y que al fin y al cabo significa lo mismo. El Maestro dejó que creciera otro largo y sagrado silencio. (1997: 331–2)

Focusing on a long list of authors of the Western canon, Estévez presents culture as part of a 'circular memory' that constitutes the text or the Barthesian 'infinite text' that is being written and rewritten endlessly throughout the centuries, through what could be seen as a palimpsestuous intertextuality that takes us in Derridean fashion from text to text. As Barthes defines it, the inter-text is 'the impossibility of living outside the infinite text – whether this text be Proust or the daily newspaper or the television screen: the book creates the meaning, the meaning creates life' (Barthes 1975: 36).

In the novel, culture/Scheherazada is the eternal palimpsest of different texts in history, and Cuban culture is placed in the midst of a universal cultural heritage, beyond the possibility of a unique Latin American or Caribbean construct. As Rodríguez-Mangual states, 'El personaje de Scheherazada adelanta la idea de universalidad que busca el narrador en su acción de creador' (2005: 124). However, it is only when Scheherazada/el Herido/el Maestro reads Piñera's 'La isla en peso' (1943) to Sebastián that the latter will experience his epiphany. It is with this poem (which also occupied my attention in chapter 2 in relation to *Máscaras*) that Sebastián, identified as the author of the novel we are reading, 'rediscovers' and rewrites the Island:

lo escuché leer [...]: 'La maldita circunstancia del agua por todas partes me obliga a sentarme en la mesa del café. Si no pensara que el agua me rodea como un cáncer, hubiera podido dormir a pierna suelta. Mientras los muchachos se despojaban de sus ropas para nadar, doce personas morían en un cuarto por compresión...' Y era el poder de ir entrando en la Isla casi por primera vez, sentir la compresión del mar, el encierro que cualquier isla provoca, la posibilidad de reconocerla, desvelar sus misterios, asistir a la llegada del día, de la luz que hace invisible y borra los colores, a la neblina de la luz. (1997: 332)

The process of reading Piñera's poem, which in *Tuyo es el reino* becomes prose, as quoted above, goes hand in hand with the process of (re)writing the Island.

The palimpsest in this novel undermines originality as such. Creativity lies in interacting with the past in a productive way, as Sebastián/the author does in this novel to show the power of the written word to rewrite the present. In this process, the artificial nature of narration becomes manifest. The act of literary creation itself, in portraying the fictitious subjectivity of characters who interact with the literary and historical past, constitutes the true protagonist in this novel. As expressed in the words of el Maestro, speaking with Sebastián:

En la llamada realidad (en la equívoca, en la indescifrable, en la ambigua realidad, cuyo verdadero nombre debiera ser 'fantasía'), estábamos él y yo solos. Ahora debo restringirme, sin embargo, a la inequívoca, a la poderosa fantasía, cuyo verdadero nombre debiera ser 'realidad'. Cada noche Scheherazada hacía aparecer a un personaje distinto. Así hizo aparecer a mi madre, a Irene, a Lucio, al tío Rolo, al profesor Kingston, a Merengue..., e iba volviendo a contar la historia de cada uno a su modo, como a él le hubiera gustado. ¡Míralos!, ordenó una noche. ¿A quién? ¿A quién va a ser?, a ellos. Y todos los personajes de la isla reaparecieron [...]. ¿Sabes quiénes son? Miré al Maestro lleno de sorpresa, único modo de mirar en casos como éste. Sí, Maestro, lo sé, respondí con timidez. Replicó: No vayas a cometer la vulgaridad de explicar que son Marta, Casta Diva, Chavito, Mercedes..., ese pormenor lo conoce cualquiera [...]. Volví a mirar, volví a constatar que continuaban con exacta expresión de dicha en el ocio de la tarde. Scheherazada, el Maestro, se había puesto de pie, no podía contener la ansiedad, y daba cortos paseos [...]. Y en este instante debo reconocer que el asombrado fui yo al descubrir un hecho milagroso, al comprobar que había vuelto a ser el Herido y que tenía en las manos nada menos que aquel cuaderno con el que se sentaba a escribir en el sillón de Irene. ¿De dónde sacó ese cuaderno, Maestro? Odio las preguntas tontas, respondió [...] Obsérvalos bien, [...], y ahora atiende, vas a tener una señal, voy a escribir en la libreta mientras los miras. Los personajes comenzaron a mudar el color del pelo, de los ojos, cambiaron narices, bocas, [...], eran otros, y tampoco otros, ni aquellos otros, sino otros, otros más, cambiantes, y respondieron a tantos nombres [...] Se trocaron en tantos, en tan breve tiempo, que ahora no soy capaz de dejar testimonio exacto del cambio. Hubo un momento, incluso, en que se convirtieron en réplicas exactas de mí mismo. Me vi multiplicado, cinco, seis, siete veces repetido como si la realidad se hubiera cubierto de espejos. [...] ¿Sabes lo que pasa?, gritó el Maestro con la voz de exultación propia de quien devela a otro las claves del gran descubrimiento, ¡son personajes! ¿...? (Estévez 1997: 340–1)

This act of 'invention' or creative output is crowned with an overt quotation from nineteenth-century French writer George Sand, who herself invented a male authorial persona with her pseudonym. The following statement of Sand's is used in the novel:

> '...Tampoco pinto retratos.
> No es mi estilo.
> *Invento.* El público, que no sabe en qué consiste
> inventar, trata de encontrar originales
> en todas partes.' (Estévez 1997: 341)

This quote comes from a letter to Gustave Flaubert, where Sand says 'Moi, je ne fais pas de satire. Je ne sais ce que c'est. Je ne fais pas non plus de *portraits*, ce n'est pas mon état; j'invente. Le public qui ne sait pas en quoi consiste l'invention veut voir partout des modèles. Il se trompe et rabaisse l'art' (19 March 1870, qtd in Capasso 1998: 259). Like Sand, who reacts against reading literature 'as a gossip column' (Capasso 1998: 259) and thus devaluing art, Estévez creates an intertextual connection that reflects Sand's mood when writing to Flaubert: 'Je trouve qu'avec cette habitude d'interprétation on rabaisse la profession d'écrivain et on confirme le grand public dans sa manie de deviner et de reconnaître tous les personnages de la fiction' (3 July 1870, qtd in Capasso 1998: 259). As it was for Sand, fiction for Estévez is also foundational, capable of setting its own reality without necessarily following a referential model outside of literature itself. As Orr convincingly argues in her work on the debates surrounding intertextuality, quotation 'can be a homage, an authority or a complex shorthand which also counters authenticating functions by means of parody, counter-example or ironic questioning' (2003: 130). But even if the latter is the preferred postmodern usage, as identified by Orr, here in Estévez this borrowing is part of what Orr sees in her analysis as 'layering the previous as similar and variant, part of (or for) the whole, and hence for a process of continual comparison and contrast' (2003: 130).

The structure of Estévez's novel is duplicated as if by many mirrors capable of reflecting different layers and with them multiple readings and several layers of 'reality'. Scheherazada/el Maestro/el Herido, acting as an Author-God, reveals the palimpsestuous nature of literature, whereby a single character is the foundational origin of all future characters, transformed into different subjectivities depending on the author's will. The author also recognizes the role of the active reader and not just the author's will; thus he states, 'preguntó Mandorla respetuoso o respetuosa (como quiera el lector)' (Estévez 1997: 153), and again 'gritó Mandorla indignado o indignada (como quiera el lector)' (1997: 154). Sebastián and el Maestro are fictional characters as well who establish their own 'realities'. According to el Maestro, the transcendence of these characters resides in their palimpsestuous origins, which explains the essence of all the characters who inhabit the Island within the island:

> ¿Quiere decir que no existen? ¡Qué cosas se te ocurren!, por el contrario, hijo, existen más que nosotros […] en algo, sí, son como nosotros, hay cosas en las que nos semejamos puesto que han sido hechos con alquimia rara, Sebastián, con todas las carnes y las sangres, con todas [*sic*] los huesos y arterias, con músculos y nervios, con las angustias, alegrías e incertidumbres, las nostalgias e impiedades, las grandezas y miserias, tienen, como nosotros, de Dios y del demonio, y de todos los misterios; no, al final no son, no somos, como tú: ¡poseemos brillo de eternidad! (Estévez 1997: 341)

The fictional characters exist in their own reality. Their elixir of longevity and wisdom, at the core of this alchemy that gathers elements of all human beings and characters, incorporating both good and evil, resides in being able to transcend time barriers. This becomes evident in the novel through the intertextual connections with figures such as tío Rolo (who claims to have been Charles Baudelaire in a past life) (Estévez 1997: 177–8); el Maestro (who claims to be derived in part from Piñera) (1997: 342); Mercedes who longs to be a character in a novel (197: 94) – for example, la Princesa de Clèves (1997: 93), which takes us back to the seventeenth-century French novel, set in sixteenth-century France; the singer Casta Diva, who derives her name from the famous nineteenth-century aria of the opera *Norma* by Vincenzo Bellini, here connected to the twentieth-century singer Maria Callas (1997: 217), 'la Divina', 'la Diva', here in a Cubanized version, singing before Lecuona and Rita Montaner (1997: 218); and Cuban singer Beny [*sic*] Moré as himself (1997: 148–52), among others. Here, characters and human beings retain their polyphonic essence. The only thing that, according to el Maestro, differentiates characters and human beings is death, as the characters have achieved eternal life. El Maestro shows his polyvalent essence when asserting that he is a character in Sebastián's novel, that is, the novel that we are reading. At the same time, el Maestro serves as Sebastián's alter-ego, since he is also a narrator:

> Yo mismo, ¿quién soy? ¡Tu personaje!, si vamos a ser honestos, estoy construido con entrañas tuyas, y también con entrañas de ese gran escritor, Virgilio Piñera, a quien tanto quisiste y a quien tanto debes y deberás para siempre, el escritor maldito, bendito contigo (¡ah, tenías que encontrar el modo de unirte a él!), y también estoy siendo construido con muchas otras entrañas, por supuesto, el personaje se hace con cuerpos y almas de tantos cadáveres que se van saqueando por el camino. (Estévez 1997: 342)

In the case of Estévez, as mentioned above, intertextuality also pays tribute to the authors and characters who have preceded him. The intertextual game is, then, the origin of any piece of art. El Maestro reveals the essence of literature. Alchemy becomes a metaphor for the process of writing and its palimpsestuous nature. This confirms that we are dealing with literature in the second degree, namely palimpsestuous and derived from pre-existent texts, as understood by Genette (1997: 5). And the fact that Piñera is spoken of in the past places the reader beyond 18 October 1979, the date of Piñera's death. The reference to Piñera's last unfinished play ¿Un pico o una pala? (1979) and to 'Virgilio Piñera, borrado de los diccionarios, de las antologías, de los recuentos críticos en el apartamentico de la esquina de 27 y N' (Estévez 1997: 328) sets the time of the writing in the revolutionary period as well, specifically after the censorship of Piñera in the 1970s. Nonetheless, the main story of the Island dates back to 'aquel paso de 1958 a 1959' (1997: 323) in the historical context, a topic to which I shall turn my attention in the next section.

Cuban History, Culture and Memory as Palimpsests

Even if the political element is highly nuanced in this novel, in the 'Epílogo' of *Tuyo es el reino* Sebastián reveals the purpose of the text we are reading:

> dije, quiero contar la historia de mi infancia, la historia de aquella Isla en que nací, en Marianao, en las afueras de La Habana, junto al cuartel de Columbia, narrar la historia de aquellos que me acompañaron e hicieron desdichado o feliz, regresar a los meses finales de 1958 en que estábamos próximos, sin saberlo, a un cambio tan definitivo en nuestras vidas, aquel ciclón que abriría puertas y ventanas, y destruiría techos, y echaría abajo paredes, ignorábamos entonces el poder de la Historia en la existencia del hombre común [...], ignorábamos que éramos las fichas en el tablero de un juego incomprensible, no pudimos percatarnos de que la huida del tirano con la familia hacia la República Dominicana, la entrada en La Habana de los Rebeldes victoriosos (que tomamos por enviados del Señor), transformaría tanto nuestras vidas como si hubiéramos muerto la noche del 31 de diciembre de 1958, para nacer el primero de enero de 1959 con nombres, cuerpos y almas completamente transfigurados (aunque esto, lo sé, no tendrá espacio en la novela: deberá ser narrado en otros libros). (Estévez 1997: 344)

The character speaks from revolutionary Cuba, from a moment of disenchantment and of feeling deceived by the so-called 'enviados del Señor':

> tuve la ingenuidad de creer que [...] los años por venir estarían pletóricos de paz y de bonanza. [...] Casi hubiera deseado arengar a cuantos me rodeaban, decirles No se dejen abatir, este fuego no es más que el inicio de una Nueva Era, literalmente fabulosa, donde seremos los Elegidos de la Felicidad, un

> Fuego es la puerta que se cierra para que se abran miles de puertas, la señal de una Nueva Vida Dichosa. Nada dije por fortuna (desde entonces tuve la sabiduría de reprimir las ansias de arengar, como si tuviera ya conciencia oscura de la falsedad de cualquier arenga, porque las arengas, como los jefes de Estado, son cosa del Demonio). (1997: 323)

The textuality of concepts such as memory, history and culture becomes evident when, according to the novel, these terms within the Cuban context are palimpsests. As I have already mentioned in my study of *Máscaras* in the previous chapter, the use of a text that is a palimpsest goes hand in hand with the concept of Cuban culture as hybrid. Employing Ortiz's much-used metaphor of the stew (1991b: 15), we could claim that in *Tuyo es el reino* the text-palimpsest represents an *ajiaco* of Cuban culture. The *ajiaco* complements the idea of the text as a palimpsest. In the *ajiaco* metaphor, Cuban culture is created by both an integrative and a disintegrative process whereby the first elements put in the pot precipitate to form a sediment that is transformed endlessly when new ingredients are added to the stew, while still preserving the identity of the previous ingredients. This Island, in line with Ortiz's view, 'se convirtió en tierra de tránsito […] lo que en el fondo nunca ha dejado de ser', as stated by la Condesa in the novel (Estévez 1997: 174).

In *Tuyo es el reino*, the constant writing and rewriting creates a multi-layered narrative in which the narration is transformed and challenged as new versions of the stories are superimposed on to the previous ones. This narrative technique helps to show the dialogic nature of the novel and the different points of view of the same events that appear in it, a hybridity which is epitomized in the novel by Rolo's library, which, like the textual palimpsest, challenges stable concepts of culture and identity by its wide collection of literature from East and West (Estévez 1997: 111–14).

This process of the creation of a text that is a palimpsest also undermines stable concepts of authorship. The text itself challenges the idea of an omniscient narrator by means of a polyphony of voices that give different versions of the same events, rewriting them. Eventually, the characters emerge as complex individuals who create themselves and the others dialogically. An example is el Herido, a typically unfinalized character. El Herido is the character who most presents a palimpsest-like appearance. As Rodríguez-Mangual has stated, 'el Herido es un personaje mítico ajeno a la comunidad que habita la Isla; cada personaje interpreta su llegada de modo particular' (2005: 124). The fact that all the characters of the Island see el Herido from a different perspective and in a different way provides us with information about these other characters. As Rodríguez Mangual also argues, 'Las diferentes descripciones físicas que se ofrecen del Herido reflejan la relatividad del signo, las realidades multiplicadas y las posibles lecturas que la novela ofrece' (2005: 125). Hence through the use of palimpsests, Estévez challenges the traditional notion of a text with a narrator who knows everything about his characters and who determines reality, while paradoxically having a narrator-author who is aware of controlling the narration we are reading and the agency of some characters. For example, the narrator is aware of making Doña Juana drop the candle that causes the fire which razes the Island (Estévez 1997: 320) (a point to which I shall return). Hence, in this novel, there is no place for fixed meanings and stable systems of signs.

In the novel, history is presented as the repetition of tragic events from the foundational origins of the island to the present, but the inhabitants of the Island within the island, by presenting their oral histories, are allowed to document a marginal, non-official history that defies dominant monolithic representations. Hence, Estévez focuses on what we could call, borrowing Miguel de Unamuno's term, the *intrahistórico*. For Unamuno, '[los pueblos] en sus encerronas y aislamientos hipertrofian la conciencia histórica a expensas de la vida difusa intrahistórica que languidece por falta de ventilación' (1945: 142). It is that 'vida difusa' which Estévez brings to life through his characters. In this sense, history as narration, as text, has the power that Bakhtin has granted to the novel, that is, the power of 'de-normatizing' and of being a 'centrifugal force' (Bakhtin 1981: 272–3, 425) against official histories that obviate the individual histories that inform the *intrahistórico*.

The tragic history of the Island materializes as a result of the nature of the Spanish conquest of Cuba in the fifteenth century. In a dialogue between Helena and Merengue, the latter explains his concern about Chavito's disappearance and the historic times that they are living in, when the characters of the Island are surrounded by the noise of shooting and soldiers. However, Helena links the origin of their problems to the Spanish conquest of the fifteenth century. Here is found the characteristic mixed dialogue of the novel, without the signposting of the traditional novel that would specify shifts between speakers; in this case, between Merengue, talking about his son Chavito, Helena responding, and the narrator. I will quote in detail to illustrate this point:

> Hace días que Chavito no viene, hace días que no sé de Chavito, explica Merengue. Helena lo escucha tratando de no expresar nada, tratando de mantener la serenidad, su aire de mujer fuerte. Tu hijo está en edad de desaparecer, es lo justo. Y se levanta con la conciencia de que nada que pueda decir calmará al negro, y lo único que se le ocurre es ir a la cocina y regresar con un pozuelo de natilla y una risita mentirosa Vamos, [*sic*] Merengue, los hijos no son para uno, tú lo sabes. Chavito es lo único que tengo. Por ahora, llegará el momento en que te dé nietos y biznietos y choznos, que tú, negro al fin, vas a vivir doscientos años. Merengue ríe con tristeza, sin deseos de reír, y come, también sin deseos, la natilla que tiene un fuerte gusto a canela. Nadie hace natilla como tú. Eso dice Rolo, de mi madre lo aprendí, ella la hacía mejor. Y permanecen en silencio, en la luz húmeda de la sala de Helena. Merengue termina con la natilla y la deposita en la mesa de centro. Los tiempos están malos, y la frase resulta suficiente como para que Helena

comprenda que en realidad ha querido decir otra cosa. Sí, malos, malísimos, ¿tendrías la bondad de decirme cuándo han estado buenos?, ¡esta Isla! Tienes razón: ¡esta Isla! ¿A quién se le ocurriría descubrirla? A los españoles, ellos son los culpables, ¡el espíritu aventurero, el afán de hidalguía, el ingenuo sentido del honor!, si no hubieran descubierto este pedacito de tierra, tú andarías en taparrabos por Costa de Marfil, y yo estaría limpiando los pisos de un convento de Santander. Ahora sí Merengue ríe con deseos. ¿Y no vendería dulces? Helena niega con la cabeza Andarías [*sic*] con un carro vendiendo colmillos de elefantes. (Estévez 1997: 140-41)

La Condesa Descalza also explains the essence of the Island as the result of the home seeking caused by the Spanish conquest, and the environmental circumstances of the Island that its inhabitants try to escape by prioritizing pleasure and the body at the expense of the spirit:

> *Ah, mon Dieu*, no puede ser dichoso un país fundado con la morriña de los gallegos, con la añoranza de andaluces y canarios, con la *rauxa* y la *agoixa* de los catalanes, no, no puede ser dichoso ningún lugar al que un negrero como Pedro Blanco trae miles de negros arrancados de sus tierras, maltratados, torturados, y se les vende desnudos, y se les esclaviza, y se les hace trabajar de sol a sol, esa mescolanza tiene que hacer por necesidad un pueblo triste, un pueblo maldito, y si agregas el calor, el sofoco, el tiempo que no transcurre, y los modos de evadir todo eso, el ron, la música, el baile, las religiones paganas, el cuerpo, el cuerpo en detrimento del espíritu, el cuerpo sudando sobre otro cuerpo, el ocio, ¡el ocio!, no el ocio productivo de que habla Unamuno, no, sino otro que se llama desidia, un ocio que se llama impotencia, escepticismo, falta de fe, yo quiero que me digan… Se calla bruscamente. A medida que la tarde avanza, el mar ha ido adquiriendo un intenso color violeta. (¿Añorará el nacimiento de los dioses?). (Estévez 1997: 175)

This troubled history is also epitomized – as la Condesa explains to Sebastián – by poets who are part of the nineteenth-century Cuban literary canon, including Casal (1863–93), Manuel Zequeira y Arango (1764–1846), José María Heredia (1803–39), Plácido [Gabriel de la Concepción Valdés] (1809–44), Juan Clemente Zenea (1832–71), José Jacinto Milanés (1814–63), Luisa Pérez de Zambrana (1837–1922) and José Martí (1853–95) (Estévez 1997: 176). The sufferings of these Cuban writers included illnesses such as dementia (Zequeira, Milanés) and tuberculosis (Heredia), exile (Heredia, Martí), death by firing squad (Plácido, Zenea), death of the family (Zambrana) and death on the battlefield (Martí). They all represent examples of cultural resistance. Thus it is not arbitrary that la Condesa, the only one able to foretell the Island's tragic end, happens to be suffering from dementia. As Armando Valdés Zamora has stated, this 'tragic' history is closely linked with the space of the Island and the creation of a collective memory based on twentieth-century Republican Cuba and a colonial nineteenth-century past. Valdés convincingly argues that:

> Escribir una historia es, para Abilio Estévez, imaginar la existencia de
> personajes que deambulan, deliran o reflexionan en un espacio – material o
> corporal – donde se trata de sobrevivir a la confrontación del Aquí con el Allá,
> del Interior con el Exterior, del Sujeto con el Otro. Un espacio insular desde
> el cual se enarbolan los iconos de una memoria decimonónica o republicana,
> y se imaginan desplazamientos por lugares, épocas y culturas ajenas, en un
> presente caótico desde el cual se presagia un desastre que anulará todo feliz
> desenlace del futuro. (2009: 123–4)

The Island is a fluid and hybrid entity, where the polyphony of marginal voices
invades the mainstream. And through the blur of temporal limits, history appears
as a palimpsest, eliminating the possibility of a unique creator of the Island at
a particular period of time, and thus undermining the author-narrator himself,
who states in the Epilogue:

> Se hace preciso contradecir a Flaubert: no resulta saludable que el escritor
> deba estar en su obra como Dios en la Creación: presente pero invisible. Para
> empezar, es mentira que Dios sea invisible. […] Luego, ¿Por qué debe el
> escritor imitar a Dios en el que es sin lugar a dudas el peor de sus atributos, la
> invisibilidad? Me doy el lujo de hacer una confesión: sólo yo puedo apagar el
> fuego: sólo yo soy responsable de él. Mis personajes esperan desilusionados
> a los bomberos, y rezan porque acaso aspiran, además, a un milagro, sin saber
> que depende de mí, que en este caso (sólo en este caso), venimos siendo la
> misma persona. (Estévez 1997: 319)

A somewhat fluid history is responsible for moulding the Island's topography,
whose syncretic identity has been influenced by different periods and generations. As the narrator states:

> Y nadie sabe la fecha en que la Isla fue construida, por la simple razón de
> que no fue construida en una fecha, sino en muchas, a lo largo de los años,
> en dependencia de la mayor o menor fortuna de los negocios de Padrino. Lo
> único que se sabe con certeza es que la entrada principal se terminó cuando el
> gobierno de Menocal [1913–21], en pleno brillo de las 'vacas gordas'. Lo otro
> son especulaciones. Algunos piensan que la primera casa fue la de Consuelo,
> levantada hacia 1880, […] Rolo afirma, usando datos que nadie sabe de dónde
> extrae, que buena parte de la edificación ya existía cuando el Tratado de París
> [1898]. […] De cualquier modo resulta evidente que este enorme rectángulo
> de cantería que cerca una parte de la Isla […] no fue levantado de un tirón,
> sino que se hizo a lo largo de sucesivos gustos y necesidades. Y quizá por eso
> tenga el aire de improvisación que muchos le achacan, el parecer un edificio
> que nunca se hubiera terminado. (Estévez 1997: 18–19)

On the one hand, Estévez, who published *Tuyo es el reino* when he was still
living in Cuba, assumes the existence of a tragic history that starts with the

Spanish conquest in the fifteenth century, and in doing so he absolves the revolution of 1959 of some of the responsibility for the Island's tragic fate. On the other hand, this use of the past becomes, according to the author, a mechanism to resist an arid present that, for him, is the result of the revolution.

In *Tuyo es el reino* there are several allusions to the revolution as a future event that has negative connotations. The narrator, the adult Sebastián, as we discover in the epilogue of the book, has a privileged knowledge of what belongs to the future in the novel, that is, a knowledge of the results of Castro's revolution. La Condesa Descalza, who is identified with Cassandra in the novel, foretells the future and the fall of the Island just as the mythical Cassandra predicted the fall of Troy, and in each case, nobody will believe the prediction. La Condesa refers to the future of the Island as follows:

> pronto, muy pronto, mucho más pronto de lo que hasta yo misma soy capaz de predecir, caerá la desgracia sobre la Isla, sobre la ciudad, sobre el planeta, no hay imaginación capaz de hacerse idea de la atrocidad que está por llegar, [...] cuando escampe, comenzaremos a dormirnos, un sueño paralizador será el primer síntoma, y el cuerpo tendido en la cama, el sofá o la hamaca, no se dará cuenta de cómo huye de él una luz, y esa luz será el amor encerrado en el cuarto de cada uno, el amor, que es luz, se escapará como el humo y dejará el cuerpo a oscuras, y comenzaremos a vivir en tinieblas. [...] no habrá madre que ame a su hijo, ni rey justo, ni hombre que comprenda a su semejante, nadie se amará [...] será el reino del odio, y el reino del odio es el de la traición y la mentira y la desolación y la hipocresía, la máscara ocupará el lugar de la cara, la verdadera cara desaparecerá [...] y viviremos con pistolas y cuchillos y navajas debajo de las almohadas, no dormiremos, esperando el zarpazo del amigo, del enemigo disfrazado de piadoso, las mujeres entregarán a los esposos para que el verdugo los decapite, los esposos descuartizarán a las mujeres para negarles a los verdugos el placer de la ejecución. (Estévez 1997: 102)

In contrast with the Bible, in *Tuyo es el reino* after the rain comes the fire and the destruction of the Island. As the narrator will explain to the reader, that fire is connected with the coming of the revolution of 1959. Therefore, the reader can assume that la Condesa's words refer to it as well.

As I have shown earlier, ideas of treason, masks and double standards are used by all the Cuban authors analysed in this study. Furthermore, la Condesa's discourse establishes connections with the extra-literary referent of migration and exile after the revolution; thus she claims:

> muchos huirán, miles huirán, se lanzarán al mar, nadarán y nadarán hasta dar con tierra firme, nada conseguirán, nada lograrán, un país es una enfermedad que se padece para siempre, se irán ellos, sí, y algo no los dejará dormir, llorarán por lo que han dejado aunque nada hayan dejado en realidad, que

nunca, óiganlo bien, nunca, nadie puede escapar totalmente del sitio en que
nació, un hombre que se va del sitio en que nació deja su mitad y sólo se
lleva la otra mitad que suele ser la más enferma, y cuando allá, a lo lejos, esté
donde esté, sienta la falta del brazo o de la pierna o del pulmón, se dice: Soy
un hombre que padece de nostalgia, y ya está muerto. (Estévez 1997: 102–3)

The words of la Condesa here allude to the rafters of 1994, an episode of relatively recent Cuban history. Estévez here associates Cubanness with exile.
Cubanía appears as an inherent and permanent condition that the individual
born on the island cannot escape and that follows him or her. Cubanness is still
present in the exiles; in the novel, exile is the result of the tragedy of living on
an island with a tragic history. In the polarized positions of exile as life (Victor
Hugo) or as death (Ovid), la Condesa favours the latter, without going as far as
the Socratic 'death over exile'.[7] La Condesa Descalza's prophecy seems to be
illuminated, in part, by the hindsight of the Special Period experienced in the
early 1990s in Cuba and its moral effects, the result of the loss of Soviet subsidies following an already sharp decline in the economy since the 1962 US
embargo. One also has to keep in mind that, from 1959 until relatively recently,
leaving the country was seen as an act of treason and disaffection was synonymous with counter-revolution. La Condesa argues thus:

el hambre entrará como una sombra en nuestro cuerpo en lugar del amor, y
créanme, un hombre que padece hambre es el primer candidato a la traición,
traicionar y ser traicionado, he ahí dos acciones simplísimas, como beber
agua podrida de los manantiales podridos, y junto con la traición viene
el robo […] y comenzarán las persecuciones, y los mismos que roban
vigilarán, viviremos bajo miradas persistentes, los ojos tras las ventanas,
los ojos en los techos, los ojos en la tierra, los ojos en el deseo y en la
tristeza, hasta en nuestro corazón los ojos, y al tiempo que los ojos penetran
finos como agujas en los sueños, los edificios comenzarán a derrumbarse
impelidos por ciclones imaginarios, hasta la atmósfera se cansará de tanta
atrocidad, bajo el polvo, bajo los escombros tampoco encontraremos la paz
de la muerte, hasta esa paz nos estará vedada, que habrá jueces debajo de
la tierra para juzgar y dictar sentencias, todo lo que hablamos alguna vez,
la canción más inocente, se volverá en contra nuestra […] y hay cosas
que me callo, no sé cómo decirlas, las he visto en sueños […] lo que digo
y enumero es el inicio de un espanto mucho mayor que vaticino y del
que este aguacero no es más que el inicio, llámenme loca, sí, loca, como
quieran, da igual, loco es aquel que todavía tiene valor para decir la verdad.
(Estévez 1997: 103)

---

7   On this topic, see Ángela Dorado-Otero's 'Entre Ovidio y Víctor Hugo: El exilio cubano
dentro y fuera de los discursos oficiales' (2009).

With her discourse la Condesa emerges as the personification of the history of Cuba. She represents the historical past of the country, the present at the time of the narration before the 1959 revolution, and the future which extends into post-revolutionary Cuba under the Castros.

As I have already mentioned, this novel tries to capture Sebastián/Estévez's childhood ('la historia de mi infancia', Estévez 1997: 344). Estévez uses the character of la Condesa Descalza and her omens to add a critical stance to his writing. Using the future tense, Estévez implicitly denounces the effects of the revolution of 1959 on the island. This criticism is even more explicit in his next novel, *Los palacios distantes* (2002), published after he left Cuba and moved to Barcelona. As Alejandro Fernández Diego states in his review of *Los palacios distantes*, 'el autor se ha alejado de terrenos neutros y ha optado por la denuncia de la situación cubana de hoy en día', and he continues: 'una trama urbana de marcado carácter político' (2003: n.p.).

The subtle political connotations in *Tuyo es el reino* are precursors of future, more explicit political denunciations in Estévez's writings. Nonetheless, in *Tuyo es el reino*, the political cannot be totally ignored, as the following excerpt from the narrator/author/Sebastián illustrates:

> Y aunque he tratado de mantener a los personajes al margen de la vida política, obedeciendo demasiado al pie de la letra la famosa frase de Stendhal que dice algo así como que 'la política produce en la literatura igual efecto que un pistoletazo en un concierto', la verdad es que ahora el pistoletazo me parece inevitable aun cuando se estuviera escuchando a María Callas, la Divina, en un aria de Saint-Saëns. En el fondo, alguna relación debe de tener la huida del Señor Presidente [Batista], el triunfo de los Rebeldes y el hecho de que doña Juana extienda la mano, voltee la vela y provoque el incendio que puso fin a los primeros once años de mi vida, lo que por la opinión antes expuesta, significa decir a mi vida completa. (Estévez 1997: 320)

The fire will destroy the Island, which for the author-narrator marks the only period of authentic existence, his childhood, although he will continue to live in revolutionary Cuba. However, revolutionary Cuba fails to register the existence of the Island in its history. Thus he states:

> he llegado a pensar que mi vida verdadera, la real, fue aquélla de la Isla, y que el resto, cuanto viví después, no han sido más que pobres variaciones, pretextos para hacer memoria, el mejor modo de repetirlo, unas veces bien, otras no tanto. Puede deducirse, entonces, que mi vida duró en verdad once años. Quizá no sea algo que me suceda sólo a mí, y a cada hombre le sea concedido un corto periodo de vida, un centro vigoroso de años, alrededor del cual giren los que lo anteceden y vienen después. [...] (... EL FUEGO, aun cuando la Historia no lo registre y en cambio ponga tanto énfasis en la

huida del Presidente y en el triunfo de los Rebeldes), lo cierto es que las llamaradas se alzaron. (Estévez 1997: 320–1)

The adult narrator also plays with the memory of childhood and what is inevitably forgotten in recollection, a topic to which I shall turn my attention in the next section.

Narrative Memory and Forgetting: An *Ars memoriae* and an *Ars oblivionis*[8]

As Anne Whitehead has asserted, 'In ancient Rome, memorization was raised to the level of an "art", a technique to be learned and mastered' (2009: 28). If the classical art of memory is concerned 'not with remembering past experiences but with storing away what has been learned for future recall', with a capability for demonstrating 'true understanding of the material rather than simple rote learning' (Whitehead 2009: 29), here, instead, we find a novel which subverts this technique. Repetition or memorization of fictitious events, repeated constantly so as to imprint them on long-term memory, turns fantasies or imposed memories into realities, into an act of remembering. This is taken to extremes in the changes attached to the art of memory during the Renaissance, with its call to *ingenium* at the core of the creative imagination (Ricoeur 2004: 67), which focuses on what Frances Yates calls an 'alchemy of the imagination' (1966: 224), whereby 'The imagination, freed from its service to the past, has taken the place of memory' (Ricoeur 2004: 66).

On the other hand, the art of forgetting focuses on a technique not of memorization but of extinction, of learning to forget (Whitehead 2009: 156). This extinction is taken to its limits in Estévez's novel, when Doña Juana accidentally drops a candle and starts the fire that will consume the whole Island, even though this act is performed at the command of the author-narrator who affirms, with reference to the fire:

> Y lo que me duele es que he sido yo quien lo ha provocado. Bueno, sí, doña Juana extendió la mano y derribó la vela que desató las llamaradas. Este es, sin embargo, el lado superficial del asunto. [...] Podía haberla hecho despertar, espléndida a sus noventa años, tomar la vela y salir a la Isla; [...] se me ocurrió, en cambio, el fuego. (Estévez 1997: 320)

All that will remain is the reality of the text, a self-referential world without outside referents. Hence, the narrator asserts, 'De nada valdrán los esfuerzos de los personajes. De nada servirán los gritos y la desesperación. En poco tiempo,

---

8　This title is indebted to Paul Ricoeur's work on the subject (Ricoeur 2004), following on from Frances Yates (1966) and Harald Weinrich (2004).

la Isla será un mundo arrasado, un mundo que sólo podrá encontrarse en este libro' (1997: 312). But even before the consuming fire, erasure is documented on 31 December 1958:

> El Apolo no está. Y Lucio asegura que igual sucedió al Laoconte, que él lo vio en el momento de pulverizarse. [...] Ni están el Hermes de Praxiteles, ni el busto de Greta Garbo, ni la Venus de Milo, ni la Diana, ni el Discóbolo, ni el Elegguá, ni la Victoria de Samotracia que podía verse a la entrada. Y en cuanto al busto de Martí, es como si nunca hubiera estado. Ni los crotos ni las rosas que le habían sembrado alrededor aparecen por ningún lado. [...] Se han esfumado también los caminos de piedras, gracias a los cuales era posible aventurarse por entre tantos árboles sin miedo al desastre de una desaparición, sin miedo a los fantasmas de la Isla. (Estévez 1997: 309)

The celebration of the New Year, which brings with it the Cuban revolution on 1 January 1959, facilitates the act of forgetting through erasure: 'Y resulta que hoy es 31 de diciembre, y de acuerdo con los tópicos humanos, es de suponer que los personajes de este relato celebren la llegada del Año Nuevo' (1997: 310).

The novel exploits a narrative of forgetting that swings between the literary and the historical. Focusing on the impact of the historical, German scholar Harald Weinrich, as Whitehead discusses, has argued that 'forgetting is no longer allowed' (Weinrich 2004: 184), particularly in the light of contemporary crimes against humanity. Yet, as pointed out by Whitehead, forgetting 'is an inseparable and not always sufficiently recognized aspect of memory itself' (2009: 156–7),[9] which in *Tuyo es el reino* is exemplified from the very arrival of Angelina in Cuba, when she tells her brother-lover:

> No me acuerdo de nada, de nada me acuerdo, desde ayer, desde que bajé a esta ciudad, que no es una ciudad sino el tumulto de una pesadilla deleitosa, una perturbación, no me acuerdo de nada, estoy detenida en un presente presente presente [*sic*] que no sólo carece de pasado sino también de futuro. (Estévez 1997: 182)

By suspending her ties with the past and existing in this eternal present she can become a foundational being, in this case obviating the blood links with her brother before consummating their incestuous relationship. In the words of Irene, the character who becomes the epitome of forgetting,

> yo soy una mujer con la cabeza vacía, y eso puede que algunos lo consideren una suerte, yo no, yo estimo que cada hombre vale por su pasado, será el pasado quien te redima o te condene, ya sé [...], el pasado se va urdiendo

---

[9]   Ricoeur has previously asserted, 'forgetting is bound up with memory, [...] forgetting can be so closely tied to memory that it can be considered one of the conditions for it' (2004: 426).

con los hilos del presente, observa, sin embargo, […] que cuando una mujer teje su pasado son dos hilos, nada más que eso, dos hilos, y sólo lo que deja de ser presente, lo que se hace pasado, se convierte en tela, el presente sólo sirve para hacer, es decir para el sobresalto y la incertidumbre, el pasado en cambio es lo que está hecho, mal o bien, […] el terreno firme, del futuro ni hablemos, el futuro es una ilusión, el hombre lo inventó para llenar las horas de tedio que lo conducen a la muerte. (Estévez 1997: 226)

Thus the present, forgetting the past, will allow Angelina and Enrique to found the Island itself. For the reader, the past becomes visible as a palimpsest. Therefore, in Ricoeur's words, there is 'methodical forgetting' (2004: 68) when Irene states, 'aquí tienes a Irene la Desmemoriada, la pobre Irene olvidada de cuanto le ocurrió, sé a lo sumo que mi nombre es Irene' (Estévez 1997: 226). At the core of her method is 'methodical doubt' (Ricouer 2004: 68), which allows for ambivalent interpretations. She undermines her claims by recapitulating her assertions through a strategy of forgetting, thus opening up different possible scenarios of the past, a past that she claims she has forgotten. As Ricoeur states in relation to his study of Aristotle's *De memoria et remniscentia*, 'by drawing a line […] between the simple presence of memories and the act of recollection, Aristotle has preserved for all time a space for discussion worthy of the fundamental aporia brought to light by the [Platonic] *Theaetetus*, namely, the presence of the absent' (2004: 19). The Island, with its classical statues, mobilizes a similar Platonic-Aristotelian insoluble impasse at face value, which is resolved by a hidden, palimpsestuous order. This is best expressed by Sebastián when referring to tío Rolo's bookshop, echoing the Borgesian library,[10] which acts as a microcosm of this novel: 'En este desorden, dice a menudo el Tío, impera un orden superior, detrás de la aparente falta de lógica habita el espíritu de Aristóteles' (Estévez 1997: 111).

In *Tuyo es el reino*, the palimpsest serves as a metaphor of individual memory, or, more precisely, the loss of it. Contrary to the Platonic idea that 'the use of written characters is a hindrance to memory' (Whitehead 2009: 32), Professor Kingston discovers that memory is constructed not by images but by words that fix an afterimage through a rhetoric of recollection and remembrance whereby reality and memory become subjective constructs, particularly on an island where forgetting is part of the game. The novel tries to function between the repetitions of anamnesis and the counterbalance of oblivion. As Paul Ricoeur has established in theoretical terms:

The work of anamnesis moves against the current of the river Lethe. One searches for what one fears having forgotten temporarily or for good, without being able to decide, on the basis of the everyday experience of recollection,

10   I have in mind here Jorge Luis Borges's short story 'La biblioteca de Babel'.

between two hypotheses concerning the origin of forgetting. Is it a definitive erasing of the traces of what was learned earlier, or is it a temporary obstacle – eventually surmountable – preventing their reawakening? This uncertainty regarding the essential nature of forgetting gives the search its unsettling character. (2004: 27)

In the novel, forgetting can also be a voluntary act, used as a defence mechanism against a conflictive past, in line with the avoidance of 'stimuli recalling the event' as studied in the light of memory and trauma by Cathy Caruth (1995: 4). Hence, the narrator claims, 'Hasta los niños saben que el agua de coco en esta Isla, donde el Diablo instaló las pailas del Infierno, logra que el hombre olvide cuanto le resulta incómodo. Hasta los niños saben que el agua de coco es para la Isla lo que el nepente para los griegos' (Estévez 1997: 151). In Greek mythology, Nepenthe is the potion that induces oblivion, similar to the effects produced by the waters of Lethe which the dead drink in the Underworld in order to forget their past lives on earth.[11] The coconut water is the Cuban version, in Estévez's novel, of Lethe's waters or nepenthean potions. Forgetting is part of an *ars oblivionis*, in which 'Forgetting indeed remains the disturbing threat that lurks in the background of the phenomenology of memory and of the epistemology of history' (Ricoeur 2004: 412).

In the novel, repetition of created fiction establishes reality itself, instead of an act of recollection in line with an epistemology of history. Thus Professor Kingston claims, when recalling his dead wife and their cat, 'Si soy capaz de decir que tenía expresión de dicha cuando la encontré, es porque lo he repetido y repetido a lo largo de estos años, que la frase se ha quedado ahí' (Estévez 1997: 26). And he continues: 'Son palabras, no son verdaderos recuerdos. Quiero decir, es la retórica del recuerdo lo que permite que, cuando las imágenes desaparecen, uno tenga la ilusión de que sigue recordando' (1997: 26). Here we find a subversive practice of what could be the tradition of *ars memoriae* studied by Ricoeur, which consists 'in a form of memory training in which the operation of memorization prevails over the recollection of individual events of the past' (Ricoeur 2004: 18–19). This idea brings us to Genette:

'What I tell you three times is true,' claims a character in Lewis Carroll's *Hunting of the Snark*. [...] What I have said twice or more ceases to belong to me; it now characterizes me and may be parted from me through a simple transfer of imitation; by repeating myself, I am already imitating myself, and on that point one can imitate me by repeating me. What I say twice is no longer my truth but a truth about me, which belongs to everyone. (1997: 79)

---

[11] 'Es concebida Lete como una alegoría del *olvido*, emparentada con el *sueño* y la *muerte*. Lete es el nombre de una fuente o un río existente en el mundo subterráneo donde beben o se bañan los muertos para olvidar su vida anterior. En todas las doctrinas existentes sobre la transmigración de las almas, aparecen éstas bebiendo en la citada fuente para olvidar todo lo relativo al mundo infernal' (Falcón Martínez et al. 1980: II, 387)

On the other hand, Irene, by questioning what she remembers and realizing that she has been forgetting, raises questions about memory itself and the validity of remembering as an act of faithfully re-enacting past realities in order to construct a unique national history, particularly when the memory of others contradicts one's own memories:

El jarrón significaba mucho para mí; el verdadero drama, Berta, es que he olvidado por qué.
        Primero creyó que lo había comprado para su madre en la tiendecita del judío que vivía en la carretera del cayo La Rosa. […] Sabía, sin embargo, que el anciano que veía su recuerdo tenía mucho que ver con el sastre de Santa Rosa que le hacía la ropa a Lucio. Y por otra parte, ¿no se había burlado Rita una vez diciendo que en Bauta no había ningún judío con ninguna tienda en la carretera del Cayo? […] En realidad, pensó Irene, el jarrón yo nunca lo compré en ninguna tienda, mi padre me lo regaló el día de mi cumpleaños. […] Y se dijo que si se concentraba bien […] de seguro volvería a entrar en aquella casa de su juventud y descubriría si había estado allí alguna vez el jarrón. […] Se dio cuenta de que en realidad había llegado a la casa del tío Rodrigo en la playa de Baracoa. Y eso tampoco lo pudo asegurar, que bien podía ser la casa de su prima Ernestina en Santa Fe, o cualquier otra casa que ella hubiera inventado. Entonces trató de recordar si su casa, la casa de su juventud, había sido de madera o de mampostería, y se dio cuenta de que no había manera de poder precisar el detalle. […] Durante mucho rato entró en casas ajenas, desconocidas, en casas donde sólo había estado con el pensamiento, tratando de encontrar en ellas su casa, la casa de su juventud, sin que pudiera volver con el recuerdo al lugar donde había sido feliz hasta la angustia. Y fue en ese momento cuando creyó recordar, el jarrón había sido, en realidad, regalo de Emilio el día que decidieron la fecha de la boda. Irene vio a Emilio con flus azul Prusia, el aire tímido que conservó siempre, hasta cuando reconoció que se estaba muriendo. Lo vio como debió de haber entrado la noche de 1934 en que decidieron que se casarían el primero de abril del año siguiente, […] y el jarrón envuelto en un paño de tafetán dorado. […] Había algo de falsedad en la evocación, y no sabía qué podía ser, resultaba evidente que Emilio no era Emilio, hasta que pensó que se trataba del flus. El no usaba flus, sino un vistoso traje militar, ya para entonces, luego de la caída de Machado, se había hecho ordenanza de un coronel en el campamento de Columbia. Y el flus que veía no podía ser de Emilio sino de Lucio, y en realidad no había sido Emilio quien había entrado con el jarrón sino Lucio, y creyó que estaba enloqueciendo. (Estévez 1997: 38–40)

Memory plays a role in the constant process of identity formation, which is depicted in the novel as a palimpsest in dialogue with the memory of others. Therefore the 'intrahistorical' will affect the finalized versions of 'history', which is, instead, a story in the making, situated between memory and forgetting. With reference to the latter, Ricoeur has stated: 'Ordinary forgetting is

[...] on the same silent side as ordinary memory. This is the great difference between forgetting and all the types of amnesia with which clinical literature abounds' (2004: 427).

Furthermore, in the novel, as Estévez himself states in relation to his mining of the literary past in order to survive the sterility he experienced in the Cuban literature of the 1970s, individual memory as palimpsest highlights the importance of the past in order to face the present, even if it can be romanticized in Irene's phrase 'todo tiempo pasado fue mejor' (Estévez 1997: 105). Yet the fact that she cannot accurately recall her past undermines the signified of the phrase, which becomes a rhetorical sign in the novel; the past is better because she cannot really remember it. If memory is used to construct an individual identity through narrative, then forgetting also reveals the precarious nature of human identity, distorted by narrative. Thus Irene associates the importance of the past with the possibility of narrating it, and anticipates the ideas of life as narration and human beings as characters that permeate the novel. She reflects on this issue of time thus:

> [Y]o estimo que cada hombre vale por su pasado, será el pasado quien te redima o te condene [...] cuando una mujer teje su pasado son dos hilos, nada más que eso, dos hilos, y sólo lo que deja de ser presente, lo que se hace pasado, se convierte en tela, el presente sólo sirve para hacer, es decir para el sobresalto y la incertidumbre, el pasado en cambio es lo que está hecho, mal o bien, no importa, es lo hecho y por tanto lo seguro, el terreno firme, del futuro ni hablemos, el futuro es una ilusión, [...] es la muerte, y no sé qué sea la muerte, sólo conozco que es el futuro [...], qué hago en esta Isla sin tener una historia que contar, debes saber que lo importante del pasado no es lo que enseña (la mujer teje un mal punto, se detiene, lo deshace y vuelve a tejerlo bien, ¿no?), sino lo que sirve para contar, para hacer el cuento de tu vida, y si tú no tienes nada que contar sobre ti, ¿quién eres?, nadie, por más vueltas que le des, nadie [...] tenemos que acabar de entender que la vida no puede servir únicamente para vivirla, opino que Dios nos da la vida también para que la podamos narrar como un cuento, una historia, que entretenga y sirva a otros ¿tú no crees? (Estévez 1997: 226–7)

The erasure of the subject is achieved in the absence of narrative memory. And narrative memory is at the core of any reconciliation with a traumatic past. However, beyond the individual loss of memory, or confusion, as in Irene's case, for Estévez this 'regodeo en el pasado' also has a political explanation:

> Creo que justamente porque la Revolución pretendió ser un proyecto de futuro es que nos regodeamos en el pasado. [...] Creo que con la Revolución pasa lo mismo que con el Catolicismo, en el sentido en que la vida del presente está sacrificada por el Cielo, por el Paraíso, y en el caso de la Revolución, por la vida en el futuro, que a mí no me interesa para nada.

[...] De pronto te encuentras con que no tienes a qué asirte, encuentras que no es tu lugar, y entonces, un poco por reacción rebelde o de soberbia, te vas al pasado. Al futuro, no. [...] Es una idea viejísima de Walter Scott, la de buscar en el pasado medieval, la de hacer idílico ese pasado y tratar de gozar de una sociedad que tampoco exactamente fue así. Ese es un rasgo del Romanticismo que tenemos actualmente, una reacción frente a una vida demasiado árida. (Béjar 2002–03: 94)

Thus, borrowing Ricoeur's words, we could say that Estévez puts into practice 'the reserve of forgetting', which 'is as strong as the forgetting through effacement' (Ricoeur 2004: 506). As Ricoeur concludes in his work:

> *Under history, memory and forgetting.*
> *Under memory and forgetting, life.*
> *But writing a life is another story.*
> *Incompletion.* (Ricoeur 2004: 506, his italics)

In the novel the loss of individual memory, the 'incompletion' embodied by Irene, is connected with the disappearance[12] of the statues at the end of the book, the collapse of the first house built on the Island, and the fire that will destroy it. All these events signal the beginning of the 1959 revolution, wherein collective memory and identity will be emphasized over the individual. With the arrival of the revolution, it seems that the Island and its inhabitants will sever all ties with their past and a new identity will be forged in isolation from the rest of the world. As the Tarot card reader assures Berta when she foretells the destruction of the Island: 'veo que arden el pasado y el presente, hay un jardín devastado' (Estévez 1997: 213). This fire that symbolizes the coming of the revolution appears in the novel as a breaking point with the history of the Island, and a projection towards the future in revolutionary Cuba, the larger island, in which individual memories will be displaced by a socially determined common memory based on shared experiences. This collective memory, extrapolating Ricoeur's words, 'accounts for the logics of coherence presiding over the perception of the world' (2004: 123) in post-revolutionary Cuba.

Moreover, when Estévez uses his characters to express the fragility of memory, he is pointing out the importance of discourse in re-enacting a non-extant past. The memories of the Island are the narrator's refuge and the Island can only exist as a discourse. I agree with Rodríguez-Mangual's view that

Al final cuando la isla se quema y todos los personajes desaparecen a

---

12   These disappearances are symbolic. The characters of the Island witness the disappearance of the palm trees and other plants, the Virgen de la Caridad del Cobre figure, the river, the carpenter's workplace, Martí's statue and other statues, Consuelo's place, stone pathways and the Island.

excepción de Sebastián, el Herido resulta ser el maestro que le enseñará a éste cómo escribir sus recuerdos y contar su historia [...] es a través de ese proceso de contar y recrear por medio de la escritura que se posibilita la permanencia de la memoria, y por lo tanto, la vida de la Isla y de sus personajes, la reorganización de este cosmos. [...] [L]a escritura es una manera de elevar a un nivel universal la experiencia subjetiva. [...] Esa fragmentación emula el acto de recordar. Por ejemplo, la memoria, en este caso la de uno de los personajes que recuerda su infancia (Sebastián), es selectiva y al mismo tiempo desorganizada. (2005: 124)

In the following section I shall analyse in depth the role of the author within the process of creation, and the role of the Island as incarnation of the process of creation itself within Estévez's novel.

The Author-God versus the Act of Reading: The Dialogic Practice.

As Wolfgang Iser rightly observes in his theory of aesthetic response, 'fictional language does not lead to real actions in a real context, but this does not mean that it is without any real effect' (1978: 60). In Estévez's fiction, the performativity of the text works in harmony with the process of discovery in which the reader participates. As Iser states, 'the literary work has two poles, which we might call the artistic and the aesthetic: the artistic pole is the author's text and the aesthetic is the realization accomplished by the reader' (1978: 21).

In the novel there is a tension between the reality of the text and the subjectivity of readers both within the text (in the artistic domain) and outside the text (in the aesthetic domain). The latter is how we as readers encounter the novel. Within the text, there is a further tension between those characters who believe in the existence of a male God (who even appears as a character in the novel) and those who do not. In the former group there is a constant quest for the protection of a superior being and an attempt to communicate with Him. In this context, in the novel we find the voice of an Author-God who is also one of the protagonists of the story, as if to remind the reader that he or she is participating in a dynamic process. Regarding this matter, Armando Alanís put this question to Abilio Estévez: 'En *Tuyo es el reino* se nos recuerda constantemente a los lectores que hay un autor, que se nos está contando una novela. ¿No temía usted destruir la ilusión que con frecuencia crean las novelas de que lo que se cuenta en ellas está realmente sucediendo?' Estévez replied thus:

Yo quería crear otra ilusión: la ilusión de que se está narrando. Por ejemplo, creo que Jacques el fatalista, de Diderot, es una novela extraordinaria, y todo el tiempo el autor está interviniendo. Ocurre también en Tristam Shandy. Entonces uno tiene la otra ilusión: la ilusión de que sabe que le están contando una historia. (Alanís 1998).

This awareness imposed on the reader creates a certain distancing effect that demands that the reader take an active role. Throughout the novel we hear the voice of an Author-God, identified in the Epilogue of the novel as Sebastián, who expresses, as I have mentioned before, his will to recover his childhood on the Island at the age of 11. This character, alter-ego of the author, echoes Estévez's words when he explains in interview:

> La novela es como toda novela: tiene muchos elementos autobiográficos, pero al mismo tiempo hay mucha imaginación y mucha ficción. Cuando la escribí lo que intentaba era hacer una novela donde recuperara mi infancia, una infancia que, según yo la recuerdo, fue muy feliz. (in Luis Reyes 2001: 2)

Estévez is very careful when stressing the importance of memories and differentiating them from 'reality'. Estévez continues to assert the role and the existence of the Author-God in his novel when claiming 'Que yo descubra cómo el autor me lleva por determinado camino no tiene por qué restar placer, justamente entregarse a esa mano y a esa guía es maravilloso' (in Luis Reyes 2001: 2). This Author reveals the characters' thoughts and feelings; he speaks to them and to the reader and even has influence over them, manipulating their reactions. As Iser claims, 'A reality that has no existence of its own can only come into being by way of ideation, and so the structure of the text sets off a sequence of mental images which lead to the text translating itself into the reader's consciousness' (1978: 38). From time to time, the Author in the novel also tries to fix the meanings of the narrative and claims to be the God of literature. Against this Author-God's statements I posit that the novel itself challenges them (Author and God) and the authoritative position that the Author tries to establish. Ultimately, in *Tuyo es el reino* the use of intertextuality, polyphony, heteroglossia and the role of the reader subvert the existence of an omnipresent Author and the monologic authoritative text.

In *Tuyo es el reino* Estévez uses intertextuality in a way that coincides with Barthesian postulates. For Barthes, 'writing is the destruction of every voice, of every point of origin' (1977: 142). Polyphony in this novel erases the possibility of having a unique origin assigned to the text. *Tuyo es el reino* is created via the numerous narrations of its characters and not through a unique objective narration made by an Author-God. Thus in this novel Estévez mobilizes theories and conceptions of text, textuality and authorship. In Barthesian terms, applicable here,

> Author is thought to *nourish* the book, which is to say that he exists before it, thinks, suffers, lives for it, is in the same relation of antecedence to his work as a father to his child. In complete contrast, the modern scriptor is born simultaneously with the text, is in no way equipped with a being preceding or

exceeding the writing, is not the subject with the book as predicate; there is no other time than that of the enunciation and every text is eternally written *here* and *now*. (Barthes 1977: 145)

In this sense, the Author of this novel becomes a scriptor within the 'tissue of quotations', to use Barthes's words (1977: 146).

To conclude, the dialogic relationship established through various writings and 'centres of culture' allows *Tuyo es el reino* to engage with theoretical postulates of authorship and textual production. The author seems to concur with Barthes in seeing that 'the writer can only imitate a gesture that is always anterior, never original. His only power is to mix writings, to counter the ones with the others, in such a way as never to rest on any one of them' (Barthes 1977: 146). Thus, in this respect, and against what it seems to assert at face value, *Tuyo es el reino* embodies the Barthesian death of the author because, as Barthes claims:

[Literature] by refusing to assign a 'secret', an ultimate meaning, to the text (and to the world as text), liberates what may be called an anti-theological activity, an activity that is truly revolutionary since to refuse to fix meaning is, in the end, to refuse God and his hypostases – reason, science, law. (1977: 147)

The process of creation itself is the protagonist in this novel. Meaning is created through dialogic voices that generate new meanings and subvert any (author) itative attempt at establishing a stable, monologic, ultimate signified or reality. In this novel the act of reading also becomes a dialogic practice that can in turn generate multiple meanings and thus challenge the idea of an omniscient author who masters all possible signifieds. The reader of this novel is also a producer of meaning, as the author intentionally creates confusion and open endings in the narrative. In so doing, Estévez mobilizes and challenges traditional theories of the text. We can apply to *Tuyo es el reino* Barthes's concept that 'a text's unity lies not in its origin but in its destination [the reader]' (1977: 148). In *Tuyo es el reino* the writing itself becomes a site of resistance against oppression, epitomized by the character of el Herido/Scheherazada/el Maestro, but also a site of defamiliarization for the reader, with the expectation that he or she will take an active role in the act of reading.

4

Erotic Discourse: From the Semiotic to the Symbolic in Daína Chaviano's *Casa de juegos*

In this chapter I shall focus on Daína Chaviano's novel *Casa de juegos*. I posit that the use of erotic discourse in this novel serves a foundational purpose as the site of a feminine and feminist space in the context of subaltern voices used to subvert patriarchal values and monolithic discourses of power. I start here by differentiating, like Octavio Paz, between eroticism and sexuality. For Paz, in his book *La llama doble: amor y erotismo*, 'En la sexualidad, el placer sirve a la procreación; en los ritos eróticos el placer es un fin en sí mismo o tiene fines distintos a la reproducción' (1993: 11). He continues: 'La sexualidad es animal; el erotismo es humano. Es un fenómeno que se manifiesta dentro de una sociedad y que consiste, esencialmente, en desviar o cambiar el impulso sexual reproductor y transformarlo en una representación' (1993: 106). In this novel, as well as in those analysed in chapters 5 and 6, sexuality is linked to performance, spirituality and a process of self-knowledge. Eroticism plays a central role, where reproduction is not seen as the final aim of sexual intercourse.

Chaviano was well established as an author in Cuba before moving to Miami, and is well known internationally, so it is surprising that there are almost no critical studies of her novel *Casa de juegos*. Only Anna Chover Lafarga (2006) seems to have devoted a full article to an examination of this novel, wherein she analyses the subversive essence of eroticism. My analysis intends to fill a gap in the research in terms of attention to this text. Here I shall examine critically the use of erotic discourse as a weapon to subvert patriarchal values and monolithic discourses of power, in order to demonstrate how sexuality is used in Cuban narratives published in the 1990s as a site of resistance against oppression and as an excessive metaphor of freedom. I shall examine in this context the use of eroticism as an element in a group of rituals that allows the protagonist to revisit the semiotic before re-entering the patriarchal dimension of the symbolic. I suggest that this interplay between the semiotic and the symbolic, in psychoanalytic terms, is at the core of the narratives written during the 1990s, and *Casa de juegos* is more the rule than the exception.

To contextualize my analysis I shall here provide a brief synopsis of the events in *Casa de juegos*. Gaia occupies centre stage in the novel, placed by her own name within the discourse of 'Mother Earth'. As Rosemary Radford Ruether has noted in her book *Gaia & God: An Ecofeminist Theology of Earth Healing*:

> Gaia is the word for the Greek Earth Goddess, and it is also a term adopted by a group of planetary biologists, such as James Lovelock and Lynn Margulis, to refer to their thesis that the entire planet is a living system, behaving as a unified organism.
>
> The term Gaia has caught on among those seeking a new ecological spirituality as a religious vision. Gaia is seen as a personified being, an immanent divinity. Some see the Jewish and Christian male monotheistic God as a hostile concept that rationalizes alienation from and neglect of the earth. Gaia should replace God as our focus of worship. (1993: 4)

Chaviano will not go as far as to replace a male God with a female one, but she does position her protagonist within these anti-patriarchal discourses. Gaia is placed within the context of giving a voice to the voiceless. As Radford Ruether has observed in the theological context she studies, the voice of Gaia 'has long been silenced by the masculine voice, but today is finding again her own voice', which 'does not translate into laws or intellectual knowledge' (1993: 254). However, I shall also analyse how Gaia in this novel fails to present a truly feminist viewpoint even if she seems conversant with some feminist postulates and verbalizes a woman's desires.

In the novel, Gaia, after the death of her lover, el Pintor, experiences the loss of her libido. To combat this problem Gaia does not visit the doctor but a *santera*, who advises her to find a man who can put this right. Following this 'masculinist' advice, Gaia meets Eri in a bar and agrees to meet him again. From the beginning of the novel we find Gaia following a woman sent by Eri to guide her to a house where Gaia will experience various initiation rituals, the nature of which is completely sexual and erotic. The house appears as a labyrinth in which she must overcome certain challenges. Through initiation rites, Gaia will be transformed, as will her view of society, which in this case refers explicitly to Cuba during the Special Period. While Gaia is waiting for Eri, a woman appears who invites her to a house of games, echoing David Mamet's 1987 directorial debut thriller, *House of Games*. Gaia's reply acts as temporal marker, placing the narrative well into the revolutionary process: 'Las casas de juegos se cerraron hace más de treinta años' (Chaviano 1999: 13).

Casa de juegos is a dialogic narrative. This dialogism allows us to establish different levels of readings. Dialogism is achieved through several means, including intertextuality, as studied in the previous chapters. In this novel there are several references to Greek and Roman mythology, to *santería*[1] and to

---

[1]   According to Alicia Vadillo, 'la llamada literatura de la diáspora, comienza a mostrar con más frecuencia elementos provenientes del acerbo religioso afrocubano a partir de la década de los noventa. [...] [L]a Santería, [...] comienza a integrarse a la memoria colectiva del 'exilio' y aparecen reflejados en la narrativa de escritoras jóvenes nacidas en la Isla pero que han desarrollado sus obras de este otro lado del mar. Ese es el caso de Mayra Montero, Zoé Valdés y Daína Chaviano' (Vadillo 2002: 153).

historical and literary characters. These myths are recontextualized and in their new Cuban context they acquire new meanings. Placing his discourse within the semiotic field, Bakhtin (1984) argues that everything has meaning, and that everything must be understood as part of a greater whole in which there is a constant interaction between meanings, all of which have the potential for conditioning others. This argument coincides with Chaviano's approach to narrative structure. The novel achieves its semantic conditionings and re-significations by setting in motion rhizomatic intertextualities. As suggested by Gilles Deleuze and Félix Guattari,

> Contrariamente a los sistemas centrados (incluso policentrados) de comunicación jerárquica y de uniones preestablecidas, el rizoma es un sistema acentrado, no jerárquico y no significante, sin General, sin memoria organizadora o autómata central, definido únicamente por una circulación de estados. Lo que está en juego en el rizoma es una relación con la sexualidad, pero también con el animal, con el vegetal, con el mundo, con la política, con el libro, con todo lo natural y lo artificial. (Deleuze and Guattari 2000: 49)

In Chaviano's text universal myths and archetypes appear more Cuban than ever; they have been rhizomatically displaced and recontextualized, as in the case of 'plateaus' proposed by Deleuze and Guattari in relation to Gregory Bateson's work. For them,

> Una meseta no está ni al principio ni al final, siempre está en el medio. Un rizoma está hecho de mesetas. Gregory Bateson emplea la palabra 'meseta' *(plateau)* para designar algo muy especial: una región continua de intensidades, que vibra sobre sí misma, y que se desarrolla evitando cualquier orientación hacia un punto culminante o hacia un fin exterior. [...] Nosotros llamamos 'meseta' a toda multiplicidad conectable con otras por tallos subterráneos superficiales, a fin de formar y extender un rizoma. (2000: 49–50)

I claim that Chaviano uses the equivalent of these connecting 'stalks' (*tallos*) to play different signifying intertextual roles within the narration.

When Gaia arrives for the first time in the Casa, the place is described as a hybrid of different cultures:

> Por fin se detuvieron ante un palacete versallesco, rodeado por una sólida verja de hierro. Tras la maleza del jardín se destacaba el cromatismo de los vitrales, con sus escenas inspiradas en ánforas griegas, paisajes caribeños y arborescencias al estilo *art nouveau*, donde el alma cubana revelaba sus aristas más alucinantes. Los faunos tocaban sus zampoñas entre las palmeras; ninfas amulatadas se sumergían en un río para atrapar cangrejos; varios querubes se reclinaban perezosos bajo el sol del mediodía, adormecidos por

el susurro de las malangas ornamentales que caían sobre ellos en abanico; un Mercurio en taparrabos sobrevolaba una ciénaga tropical, ignorando a los caimanes con sus fauces abiertas entre los mangles... (Chaviano 1999: 62)

The Casa appears as a chronotope in which the Cuban essence coexists with elements of Greek, Roman and European mythology that contribute to the ambience of atemporality, unreality and of being outside of history. Intertextuality in the novel is also set in motion through references to different religions in order to encompass a more heterogeneous community, and at the core of these relationships stands eroticism. However, it is worth noting that eroticism in *Casa de juegos* differs from eroticism as used by Canetti and Valdés, as I shall discuss in the next two chapters. In Chaviano, eroticism acquires religious and mystical connotations and *santería* is used as a structural feature of the narrative, in constant dialogue with other beliefs that, as in Ortiz's cultural *ajiaco*, populate the Casa/Cuba.

The sections and subsections into which the novel is divided are all related to *santería* and are clear indicators of the stages in Gaia's search for herself. The structure of this novel is also in dialogue with the *patakis* or legends of Afro-Cuban *santería*.[2] The first and second part of the novel play with the two faces of the *orisha* Elegguá. The first part is entitled *El dios que abre los caminos...* and the second *También puede cerrarlos...* According to Agún Efundé in his book *Los secretos de la santería*, Elegguá

> Es el mensajero natural que utilizan los humanos para comunicarse con los orishas. Es el que cuida los caminos. El que le cuenta a Olodumare [dios creador y supremo] quién se porta mal y quién no hace los debidos sacrificios. [...] 'el dios que representa la Casualidad, la Suerte. Cada ser tiene su destino, pero Elegguá con su influencia, puede cambiar ese destino, esa suerte.'
>
> Elegguá cuida los templos, las ciudades, las casas. [...] [es] 'el dueño de los caminos'. Con el Elegguá hay que estar siempre a bien, porque es muy entrometido, lo sabe todo, y es muy apasionado. No se le debe provocar, porque como dicen los viejos babalaos.[3] 'te cierra entonces todos los caminos que llevan a la Esperanza y a la Felicidad'. (1996: 39–40)

Above all, this novel represents a quest, expressed through Gaia as a search for hope and happiness.

Each part of the novel is in turn divided into two, making a total of four sections. The title of the first section is 'La noche de Oshún'; it starts with Gaia waiting for a person, who turns out to be Oshún, the woman/*orisha* sent by Eri

---

2   'Los Appatakis son relatos sobre los milagros y la vida de los dioses' (Efundé 1996: 28).
3   'Babalao. El hombre que tiene la facultad de adivinar mediante la cadena de Ifá, el ékuele y el *tablero de Ifá*' (Fernández Robaina 1994: 110).

to take Gaia to the Casa. The section ends with Gaia's arrival in the house. The title of the second section is 'La isla de los orishas', stressing the importance of *santería* to the plot of this narrative, and also hinting at the nature of the Casa's inhabitants. The third section is titled 'En el reino de Oyá', with clear reference to the underground world ruled by Oyá and the symbolic death Gaia will have to overcome; and the last is 'Azul Erinle o El remedio de Dios', also offering clear references to the *orisha* Inle, who has the capacity to heal. Hence, it can be argued that *santería*, with its particular cosmogony, constitutes the structural element and the leitmotif of the novel. In addition, it provides universal archetypes and shows an essential substratum of Cuban culture which in the novel becomes a site of resistance and contestation against oppression.

In her narrative Chaviano establishes rhizomatic dialogues with the *appatakis* without being faithful to the legends, yet because they are part of oral history the narrative seems to highlight the many possibilities and even contradictions of the legends which can be found in *santería* itself and the different Afro-Cuban practices.[4] Chaviano uses the figures of Afro-Cuban deities such as Oshún and Shangó as stereotypes of masculinity and femininity, stressing their erotic nature. When Gaia asks her guide for her identity, the reply is:

> – Para muchos, soy un enigma – suspiró –. Para otros, una condición.
> [...]
> – Mi nombre no significa nada – [...]
> – Lo que preguntas no tiene sentido. Me llaman de muchas formas. [...]
> – Todo depende del lugar, del momento o de las circunstancias. [...]
> – Tengo muchos nombres, y mi apellido es Andiomena... En Cuba me dicen Oshún. (Chaviano 1999: 63)

Here Oshún identifies herself with the Greek goddess Aphrodite. This fact implies the existence of common archetypes shared by different cultures but with different names. The Casa thus represents the existence of a collective substratum, a knowledge that has accumulated since the beginning of civilization. Cuban culture is, in this novel, placed in a universal context; it appears as a product of different cultural heritages, including the Greco-Roman world, the Spanish, the African and the Chinese.

On the other hand, the protagonist is also dialogic. She is the bridge between two worlds: the house and the outside world. The outside world is defined by lack of communication and death in life. The house is characterized by the erotic and its dream-like ambience. Eroticism is the main force that produces dialogism. Following Bakhtin's theory of dialogism (1984), I posit that the self is only able to know itself through encounter with the Other. According to

---

4   For different legends and *appatakis* or *patakís*, see Cabrera 1992: 221–6; Efundé 1996: 27–83.

Bakhtin, the self can only be constituted dialogically, and in *Casa de juegos* this dialogic encounter through eroticism is achieved through intercourse with the 'sacred', the 'divine'. In this novel erotic discourse develops a signifying process in which its meanings collide with monologic, undialogized language, that is, authoritative language that pretends to be absolute. Thus, the female protagonist is able to have her own voice and to subvert hegemonic male discourse, while the erotic rites undertaken by the protagonist have spiritual connotations. In speaking of rites I follow Mircea Eliade's assertion that

> Por iniciación se entiende generalmente un conjunto de ritos y enseñanzas orales que tienen por finalidad la modificación radical de la condición religiosa y social del sujeto iniciado. Filosóficamente hablando, la iniciación equivale a una mutación ontológica del régimen existencial. Al final de las pruebas, goza el neófito de una vida totalmente diferente de la anterior a la iniciación: se ha convertido en *otro*. (1975: 10)

In *Casa de juegos*, the rites of passage and the erotic experiences and discourses that accompany them appear as useful tools to subvert patriarchal and monologic myths and ideas about women. Through this relationship between the house and the outside world Chaviano exercises dialogism.

The Patriarchal Order

I shall focus now on the different sexual experiences that mould the protagonist, as she is predominantly characterized and defined by them. Through Gaia's relationships with men we can see clear traces of a patriarchal society. In the case of her relationship with el Pintor, his seduction occurs as 'un plan maestro que el propio vizconde de Valmont habría celebrado' (Chaviano 1999: 19). With the intertextual reference to this historical character the author establishes the relationship between seducer and seduced, with appropriate connotations of a power relationship. The seduction of Gaia is also described as the invasion of a fortress: 'Así llegó la tarde en que, seguro de su reacción, el Pintor se preparó para escalar la fortaleza que intuía tras la curiosidad de su amiga' (1999: 20). A clear image of the female body as a place to be penetrated, as a passive entity, is typical of patriarchal discourse.

The erotic game entails intertextual games: 'incluso inmerso en su labor seductora, no escatimaba referencias históricas ni juegos de palabras sobre sus personajes favoritos. Y ahí residía su mayor encanto. Era imposible rechazar las caricias de quien citaba a Catulo' (Chaviano 1999: 21). This intertextuality produces a dialogic game in which the lovers assume different roles. This game is emphasized by the performance that will be established between both lovers. The performativity of the erotic act is symbolized by the student dress that el Pintor gives Gaia. The erotic act appears as the 'taming' of Gaia, who assumes a passive and subjugated role, dependent on the male and without a voice: 'Fueron maestro y alumna, padre e hija, confesor y novicia' (1999: 26). Once more, the erotic relationship appears unbalanced – the man in a superior position with respect to Gaia, who appears in a situation of subordination and subjugation.

Intercourse is described through a focus on Gaia's body. Although the narration assumes Gaia's point of view, the gaze in this scene remains masculine: 'El final llegó durante la escena en que un profesor la forzaba a entregarse, a cambio de buenas calificaciones. [...] Los dedos del hombre apartaron su ropa interior para colocarle entre los muslos el duro instrumento de castigo' (Chaviano 1999: 26). This erotic scene is not only a cliché within typical male fantasies, but also fails to display a feminine gaze. There is no description of the male body and Chaviano uses traditional stereotypes of the female body. She thus reproduces a 'master-discourse'. This scene seems to be recreated for a masculine readership more than a feminine one, and most definitely not from a feminist stance. At one point the protagonist claims her right to sexual pleasure: 'Pero ella quería que la humillaran, que la empalaran como él lo estaba haciendo. [...] Porque era una gozadora innata; ya se lo había dicho su maestro' (Chaviano 1999: 27). Yet this expressed sexual desire does not prevent the scene from being a prototypical male fantasy.

The first orgasm with el Pintor has various biblical connotations. Sexual intercourse is described as a baptism ('bautizo natural') that 'sube hasta invadir cada rincón del alma' (Chaviano 1999: 28). Here orgasm is narrated in the first person, and the female protagonist announces the beginning of a new cosmogony:

> Relámpagos de éxtasis. Un temblor inagotable, como si el universo se aprestara a ser parido. Otra creación: un nuevo big bang. Los labios de la vulva son pétalos que estallan. Me inflamo. Soy de púrpura. Soy un génesis de fuego. Me vuelvo luna, me vuelvo demonia. No me alcanza el tiempo para respirar. Clavo a Dios en mi entrepierna y Él me toca con sus dedos infinitos. Perderse en la nada de otro cuerpo, en el hueco negro de una vida que parece muerte... una pequeña muerte. Sangre de mi sangre, boca de mi boca, leche de mi leche. En aquel instante mágico nació otro universo con sus dioses y sus herejías, con sus normas y sus leyes. Terminaba la prehistoria; empezaba el porvenir. Al igual que un Cristo sacrílego, el Pintor había borrado la huella de santos precedentes. A partir de entonces sería 'antes de...' y 'después de...' (Chaviano 1999: 28)

Gaia is shown as giving birth to a new universe, a feminine one in which, although el Pintor is compared with Christ – the creator of a linear history – Gaia states, 'Clavo a Dios en mi entrepierna y Él me toca con sus dedos infinitos'. The female body is the creator of a new feminine cosmos, as the symbols of the moon and fire indicate, along with her name. Here we find the typical description of orgasm as death.[5] This erotic experience which seems to have transcendental connotations later on becomes a pathology when Gaia claims 'su bien guardado secreto: a ese hombre, tan culto y elegante, se le hacía la boca agua con las niñas' (Chaviano 1999: 29). Thus, the 'sacred' act is subverted to become a 'perversión'. After el Pintor's death Gaia's libido disappears. El Pintor marks a 'before' and an 'after' in Gaia's life; hence, her subjugation to el Pintor is clear.

Further on in the novel Gaia will remember when she was raped as a child by a member of the Ballet Nacional. As an adult this fact produces in her a feeling of guilt for attracting men who love women with a childish aspect. Again, this reflects how the protagonist assumes certain patriarchal postulates characteristic of a male-dominated society. The abused assumes her guilt instead of assuming the role of the victim of an aggression.

Once more, after visiting the *santera*, Gaia meets Eri in a restaurant. After an orgiastic meal they go to his office where she is again sexually assaulted. After this encounter every time that Gaia eats or drinks something she reaches an altered state of consciousness, and has the impression that she is in another Cuba, that she has reached another dimension of it. The initial encounter with Eri is the first step in a chain of sexual rites; violence is its predominant characteristic. Gaia realizes that 'estaba siendo preparada para otro tipo de asalto' (Chaviano 1999: 55–6). Orgasm again appears described in traditional terms, but without any trace of a mystical experience:

> Pero todo en su interior se incendiaba, a merced del doble asalto donde la cosquilla masturbatoria y el empuje del miembro aceitado se fundían en una sola fuente de voluptuosidad. Luchó contra su propio placer, pero el forcejeo no hizo más que aumentarlo. Gimió hondamente. La tensión se hizo intolerable, y sus sentidos alcanzaron esa zona del cerebro donde las experiencias paranormales se funden con el nirvana. Fue inundada por elixires hirvientes. Su garganta […] pobló de quejidos la noche. (1999: 56)

Although Gaia refers to Eri as 'violador complaciente' she reveals that 'Lo peor de todo era que ni siquiera se sentía ultrajada por lo que acababa de ocurrir' (1999: 57). Again, the author states the more than polemical patriarchal idea that, as Georges Bataille once claimed, 'Many women cannot reach their climax without pretending to themselves that they are being raped' (1962: 107). In this sense, Chaviano fails to display at the beginning of the novel a feminist perspective on eroticism when she creates erotic scenes. However, her protagonist's constant demand of her right to feel pleasure entails an exploration of her sub-

---

5   Georges Bataille explains that this name usually given to orgasm as pleasure 'is so close to ruinous waste that we refer to the moment of climax as a "little death". Consequently anything that suggests erotic excess always implies disorder' (1962: 170). This squandering of resources is used in a symbolic death.

jectivity; and, as Joseph Bristow claims when he explores Jacqueline Rose's feminist theories, 'In the past, Marxist thought often believed that concentrating on subjective needs led to a narrow individualism: a preoccupation that revolutionaries regard as extremely hazardous when attention should be paid instead to collective struggles for political change' (1997: 107). Hence, as this novel's setting is Fidel Castro's Cuba and as Chaviano uses this novel to criticize his regime, the simple fact that in her novels her protagonist tries to explore her body, her sexuality and her subjectivity is a subversive act in itself.

Eroticism, Religion and Resistance in *Casa de juegos*

In this novel, Gaia's ordeals have symbolic connotations and represent a process of self-discovery. Oshún suggests this to her:

> – ¿Nunca has querido conocerte? Su voz pareció provenir de otra época.
> – Sé bien quién soy.
> – Pero no quién puedes llegar a ser – susurró la otra, reteniendo aún su mano.
> [...] No deberías renunciar al placer de ser tú misma. (Chaviano 1999: 14)

Oshún implies that this process will be one of knowledge and transformation, as is typical of an initiation rite. The Casa is also described as a labyrinth, as mentioned above, which coincides with the labyrinth the reader finds in the spiral structure of *Casa de juegos*. Several times Gaia will enter the Casa and suddenly appear outside the house. This, in addition to the use of flashbacks, creates various circles within the novel. When Gaia walks around the Casa she realizes that

> Eso eran la casa y el jardín: laberintos. Creta en La Habana. La posibilidad de hallar un Minotauro hambriento o enamorado. [...] Egipto en el Caribe. Centros iniciáticos de múltiples significados. ¿Cuál sería el de la casa? [...] Los laberintos se construían para salvaguardar el culto que se albergaba en su centro. [...] Pero los laberintos tenían otra función: preparaban el alma en la iniciación de los misterios. [...] Penetrar allí era olvidar el raciocinio y aprestarse a conocer demonios propios. Sus recovecos imitaban el caos primordial, la inconsciencia de los deseos, el abrigo incierto de la matriz. [...] En el laberinto quedaba aislada. Estaba en el centro del mundo, pero lejos de él. Era como vivir una maldición. (Chaviano 1999: 138)

The Minotaur at the centre of the labyrinth is a symbol that suggests several possible readings. On the one hand, as Paolo Santarcangeli (2002) states in his study of the mythological figure of the Minotaur, this creature can represent the animal part of the human being, the 'demonios propios' that everyone must kill in order to live in society: Gaia will, following this passage, need to reach the centre of the labyrinth through her erotic experiences in order to know her inner self before this is repressed when she re-enters society. Symbolically, she becomes aware of her subjectivity, a process that empowers her when returning to society. Also symbolically, she will kill that part of her inner self that she needs to erase in order to return and survive within the social order. On the other hand, the figure of the Minotaur can suggest a more political and contentious reading in which it represents a monstrous political system that has to be destroyed.

Following the first reading, I posit that in *Casa de juegos* Gaia performs a voyage through eroticism to the unconscious, the Casa, where the erotic games represent the drives repressed by society. As Joseph Bristow has rightly observed in relation to Sigmund Freud's *The Interpretation of Dreams*, Freud

> makes a radical claim on the ways in which the unconscious exists in parallel with the conscious mind but operates according to a distinct logic of its own. Unlike the conscious mind, which functions under the rational orders demanded by culture, the unconscious is the psychic domain that has undergone the arduous but ineluctable process of repression. To ensure the subject can function as successfully as possible in the world, mechanisms of repression necessarily come into play. It is through repression that desires and wishes forbidden to consciousness are deposited in the unconscious. (1997: 63–4)

Moreover, the Casa/unconscious in this novel resembles Kristeva's pre-linguistic *chora* (Kristeva 1974: 22–30) as the Casa can also be seen as a space where there are drives that are repressed in the Symbolic order. These drives are represented by erotic encounters and, therefore, this novel can be read as a symbolic return from the child's reign of the Semiotic to the Symbolic.[6] As is summarized well by Toril Moi,

> The endless flow of pulsion is gathered up in the *chora* (from the Greek word for enclosed space, womb), which Plato in the *Timaeus* defines as 'an invisible and formless being which receives all things and in some mysterious way partakes of the intelligible, and is most incomprehensible' (Roudiez, 6). Kristeva appropriates and redefines Plato's concept and concludes that the *chora* is neither a sign nor a position, but 'a wholly provisional articulation that is essentially mobile and constituted of movements and their ephemeral stases… Neither model nor copy, it is anterior to and underlies figuration and therefore also specularization, and only admits analogy with vocal or kinetic rhythms (*Révolution*, 24)'. (Moi 1985: 161)

The Casa is full of the movements, pulsions and vocal and kinetic rhythms of erotic encounters and is connected with the maternal body, as it appears as 'la

---

6   For a full theoretical study of the Semiotic and the Symbolic in language, see Kristeva 1974: 17–100.

matriz' (Chaviano 1999: 138). The Casa represents the *chora*/unconscious where Gaia undergoes a process in which she becomes aware of her body, its eroticism, and learns about her own sexual drives which have been repressed outside the Casa/*chora*/unconscious. With this experience of the maternal – the mother Earth that appears to be both Gaia and the Casa – Gaia is empowered to come back to the Symbolic order/patriarchal society, in order to challenge the forces that repress her. In the pre-linguistic Semiotic chora, according to Kristeva (1974: 22–30), there is no sexual difference; it is a position prior to the sign (Kristeva 1974: 26; 1980: 281). For Bataille, this sexually undifferentiated stage, equivalent to the Semiotic in Kristeva, is achieved through the erotic encounter. Bristow's comments on Bataille's *Eroticism* are revealing for this study in seeing the erotic encounter as a way of reaching the unity that human subjects long for:

> In his view, the sexual act dramatizes a deathly moment when human subjects experience what is denied elsewhere in their lives: a loss of self. [...] Since we are '*discontinuous*' individuals, Bataille asserts that there remain inescapable gulfs between each and every one of us. [...] Inevitably isolated, individuals can only eradicate the fundamental divides between the self and the other by entering into vertiginous experiences whose breathtaking dizziness provides exactly the continuity demanded by death. [...] On this basis, he examines types of physical, emotional, and ritualized eroticism which provide 'a feeling of profound continuity' in a world where each human being otherwise remains agonisingly alone. (1997: 123–4)

The sexual indifferentiation of Kristeva's *chora* that many feminists criticize is in this novel the purpose of the erotic encounter itself. Gaia reflects the indeterminacy of the Casa/*chora* when she claims that the Casa has the 'ambiente acogedor de un útero' and 'refugio que imitaba el caos primigenio, anterior al *fiat lux*' (Chaviano 1999: 89). We can see the effect of the unconscious/*chora*/the Semiotic on the conscious/outside the Casa/Symbolic order in the passage where Gaia is back in the outside world and takes a bath. The first hint that Gaia has been transformed through her experiences in the house becomes apparent in this ritual cleansing:

> Dentro del tanque flotaban algunas florecillas del naranjal vapuleado por los alisios; pero no se tomó el trabajo de apartarlas. Sabía que tanto los espiritistas como los santeros recomendaban bañarse con ciertas yerbas o flores, a manera de despojo: ebbó sagrado y rutinario que realizaban incluso quienes no practicaban ninguna de esas creencias. Remedio de brujas blancas. Magia eterna y neolítica que había sobrevivido, contra todo karma, hasta los albores de la era espacial. Allí estaban los azahares, como arrojados del cielo por la mano de un dios; aguardando su destino en esa isla, que era flotar en el agua fresca antes de precipitarse en cascada sobre los cuerpos desnudos de sus habitantes... Gaia tomó del cubo una de las flores para olerla. Sería una buena limpieza para librarse de los malos sueños. (Chaviano 1999: 104–5)

I divide the novel into three important erotic episodes: the first symbolizes Gaia's baptism, the second symbolizes Gaia's death as a rebirth, and the third and central one symbolizes Gaia's epiphany. The first two episodes are connected by the use of surrealist imagery. In interview, Chaviano has stated:

> Terror and uncertainty were elements used in the initiating rites of antiquity. I tried to construe the main character's experiences the way those ancestral rites were implemented, where experiences – erotic or not – that will lead to some final knowledge may be ambiguous and carry a fear component. But there's also such a thing as a social reading of fear. […] My childhood and adolescence were very happy, except for that ghostly element, ever□present in a child with too much imagination. But my adult life got complicated when uncertainty and fear materialized for social reasons… In Cuba, we always said we lived in a surrealistic country. We had many questions, and few answers. There was a lot of social insecurity. […] But I'd rather explore surrealism as a philosophical or stylistic format in order to create a dreamworld, search the unconscious and develop the most complex aspects of the psyche through some fantastic cosmogony. In *Casa de juegos* I use surrealism consciously, because I think the existence of that dreamworld is a very useful tool to locate reality all the more easily.[7]

Surrealism is used in *Casa de juegos* to blur the boundaries between inside and outside the Casa. For Chaviano surreal imagery actually has a very real referent: Cuba, particularly during the Special Period. To create what could be seen as controlled surrealism, based on the logic behind the imagery as opposed to automatic writing, Chaviano focuses more on creating characters and scenes that exploit the surreal than on using what in poetry could be surrealist language. The baptismal episode is achieved through the performance of a contortionist, described as follows:

> Varias mujeres admiraban las maniobras de un contorsionista que ejecutaba el arco de espalda hasta lograr con su cuerpo una O perfecta. Su miembro había crecido frente a la atenta mirada del público, que lanzó alaridos de entusiasmo cuando sus labios tocaron la punta. Instigado por las exclamaciones, redobló sus esfuerzos y logró introducirlo completamente en su boca para iniciar una masturbación lenta y gozosa de sí. (Chaviano 1999: 74)

Here the crowd of women shout out '¡Hace falta una novicia!' (1999: 74), and the contortionist proceeds to offer Gaia the first step in the process of what Chaviano presents as her sexual liberation or baptism. Yet this is far from being a feminist text. Rather, feminine initiation rites are represented through the patriarchal context of the Greco-Roman bacchanalia.

---

7   See Xurxo Fernández's interview 'Cuba in Celtic Dream', http://www.dainachaviano.com/pag/interviews.aspx (accessed 10 January 2010).

One significant feature of the novel is its sexually explicit representations, of which the following is an example that I quote at length to illustrate this point:

> Atontada por los vapores, [Gaia] no opuso resistencia cuando varias mujeres la arrastraron hacia el centro de la habitación; entre todas le sacaron el vestido y la acercaron a la boca del atleta [el contorsionista] que, manteniendo su posición en arco, atacó el sexo que se le ofrecía. Lengua y falo se alternaron para penetrarla con el tesón de dos rivales que se disputaran un botín, hasta que la boca terminó por ceder su lugar a la criatura anillada, cuya piel relucía cada vez que emergía de la gruta. Gaia cerró los ojos. Su razón se rebelaba contra aquella experiencia, pero su carne latía con un deseo nuevo que no le permitía decidir ni escoger, sólo tomar cuanto se le ofrecía.
>
> Manos poderosas la sujetaron por las caderas. Sintió la carne que pugnaba por penetrar en ese sitio al cual sólo Eri había tenido acceso, y trató de volverse hacia su agresor, tal vez con la idea de amedrentarlo; su tentativa sólo provocó que la luz se apagara dejándola a oscuras con las manos que la obligaban a doblarse y a aceptar.
>
> Dolor y caricias, suavidad y espinas: de eso estaba hecho el placer. Hubiera querido huir, pero notó que sus intentos por liberarse no hacían más que azuzar el deseo de sus dos asaltantes: el atleta, cuyo falo musculoso se distendía gloriosamente dentro de ella, y el desconocido que la atacaba sin misericordia por detrás. Hasta ella llegaban los suspiros y los gritos de la bacanal que se organizaba a su alrededor [...]
>
> Se rindió sin quejas al posesivo duelo. [...] Sintió, muy a su pesar, que gozaba hasta el paroxismo con aquella doble acometida que la mantenía clavada en su sitio, como una santa crucificada o una emperatriz que se ofreciera a sus esclavos para que éstos la disfrutaran más por ese acto de profanación que por el placer que su cuerpo les brindaba. Así soportó ella la embestida de los miembros hasta que de ambos brotó el maná, espeso y bullidor como la lava: riachuelos que la glorificaron bautismalmente. (Chaviano 1999: 74–6)

Naming the deed, in this case the rape of Gaia in the context of an orgy, could be seen as an empowering act in the context of literature dealing with the subject; that is, the woman is able to speak and perform.[8] However, if Chaviano describes what in other contexts would be gang-rape in the narratives of sexual violation, here the experience is turned into pleasure in the context of the bacchanalian orgy. This rhetoric of sexual violence, which might place Chaviano's text alongside narratives of 'realismo sucio', such as Pedro Juan Gutiérrez's novels (for example, *Trilogía sucia de La Habana*), is displaced to the Greco-Roman context. Nonetheless, I would

8   I am thinking here of Philomela in Ovid's *Metamorphoses*, for example. After the rape, her tongue is cut out so that she cannot speak the 'unspeakable' in patriarchal society. We could also think of the representation of rape in the literature of different countries, for example in J. M. Coetzee's *Disgrace* or Shakespeare's poem *The Rape of Lucrece*. On the unrepresentability of rape, see Terry Eagleton's *The Rape of Clarissa* (1989).

argue that the scripting of rape is paradoxically written from a male perspective. Scripting rape should place the voice of the woman at centre stage, yet this novel paradoxically leaves in place the patriarchal perspective. Here rape is articulated, but Chaviano performs a subversion by making Gaia enjoy her rape. Chaviano underscores the darker fantasies of the characters in a novel where abuse is represented as seduction. Having said that, the text also enters the realm of the symbolic present in the novel, and in two contexts: the rape as symbolizing entry into symbolic patriarchal language, and also Gaia as the raped Mother Earth. Nonetheless, I posit that the irony remains in expressing the enjoyment of the abuse. In the passage just cited what is represented as forced and undesired intercourse is transformed into female pleasure. This pleasure is problematically expressed as something that would have remained unknown had it not been forced. Chaviano turns the rape scene into a spectacle, thus subverting the phenomenon of silencing rape whether in literature or in the realm of real life; yet the narrative transforms rape into an aesthetic objective whereby the erotic can be explored through new perspectives.

The second important erotic episode is described again with surrealist imagery and corresponds to a rite that symbolizes Gaia's death. In the Casa, Gaia experiences a ritual in which she has sexual intercourse with death itself in the form of a skeleton and with beings of the 'underworld', a symbolic death that any 'iniciado' must overcome. This is best understood following Mircea Eliade's *Iniciaciones místicas*, where he explains that

> La mayor parte de las pruebas iniciáticas implican, de una manera más o menos transparente, una muerte ritual a la que seguirá una resurrección o nuevo nacimiento. El momento central de toda iniciación viene representado por la ceremonia que simboliza la muerte del neófito y su vuelta al mundo de los vivos. Pero el que vuelve a la vida es un hombre nuevo, asumiendo un modo de ser distinto. (1975: 12–13)

In this novel, 'una mujer nueva' appears after the initiation. Chaviano forswears a moralizing tone and focuses on the oneiric and surrealist ambience of the Casa:

> Estimulado por la visión de aquellos labios que aceptaban cualquier manjar anónimo, el espectro decidió obsequiar el suyo a la otra entrada que se ofrecía con igual pasividad y, para facilitar su tarea, le hizo abrir más los muslos. Ella soportó sus embates con el estoicismo de una Lucrecia para quien la virtud perdida no constituye una preocupación. (Chaviano 1999: 144).

With the mention of Lucrecia, Chaviano creates a rhizomatic intertext.[9] As Stanley Wells and Gary Taylor have observed in their introduction to Shake-

---

9   See, for example, Judith Still's 'Lucretia's Silent Rhetoric', which could be applicable to Chaviano's reference to Lucrecia here (Still 1984).

speare's poem *The Rape of Lucrece*, which is relevant to the intertextuality opened up here,

> *The Rape of Lucrece* is an erotic narrative based on Ovid, but this time the subject matter is historical, the tone tragic. The events took place in 509 BC, and were already legendary at the time of the first surviving account, by Livy in his history of Rome published between 27 and 25 BC. Shakespeare's main source was Ovid's *Fasti*, but he seems also to have known Livy's and other accounts.
>
> Historically, Lucretia's rape had political consequences. Her ravisher, Tarquin, was a member of the tyrannical ruling family of Rome. During the siege of Ardea, a group of noblemen boasted of their wives' virtue, and rode home to test them; only Collatine's wife, Lucretia, lived up to her husband's claims, and Sextus Tarquinius was attracted to her. Failing to seduce her, he raped her and returned to Rome. Lucretia committed suicide, and her husband's friend, Lucius Junius Brutus, used the occasion as an opportunity to rouse the Roman people against Tarquinius' rule and to constitute themselves a republic. (Wells and Taylor 1998: 237)

Chaviano inserts her narrative into a long tradition on the topos of Lucretia in the context of representation and power, but applied here to contemporary Cuba (a point to which I shall return). Machiavelli's viewpoint, as studied by Stephanie H. Jed in her book *Chaste Thinking: The Rape of Lucretia and the Birth of Humanism*, is also relevant in this context of the metaphorical account of Lucretia's rape throughout history:

> in Book III of the *Discourses*, in the chapter entitled 'How states are ruined because of women', Machiavelli classifies the rape of Lucretia as one among many examples to be found in the ancient histories of rape leading to legal and political change. His statement represents a direct cause-and-effect relation between the rape of Lucretia and Rome's change from tyranny to a republican form of government: 'the outrage done to Lucretia deprived the Tarquins of their rule (III.26)' (1989: 3)

Chaviano exploits this same context in order to represent eroticism as the only freedom expressed within the nation, almost like Arenas, though less overtly when it comes to narrating the nation.

Silence, nonetheless, is at the core of Chaviano's narrative and this invokes a rebellion even if it relies on the poetics of the dream, the most important principle of the surrealist mode as studied by Paul Ilie in the context of Spanish literature (Ilie 1968: 4). When a skeleton 'de ebúrneo falo' (Chaviano 1999: 145), symbolizing death, wants to possess Gaia,

> [E]l miedo le nubló los sentidos. Tal vez nunca gritó; tal vez sólo fue su espanto lo que desplegó aquella bandada de alaridos mentales cuando su inconsciencia la trasladó a mil años luz del horror que luchaba por poseerla. (1999: 145)

As Luce Irigaray explores in her feminist philosophy, it is worth noting that 'Becoming comprises ellipses and eclipses. Invisibility and silence take part in becoming' (Irigaray 2002: 100), and this process between 'ellipses and eclipses' is present throughout *Casa de juegos*.

I shall now move on to a secondary reading that the novel offers us, which emerges with the third episode that I have identified in it. The narrator establishes specular binarisms: inside the Casa/outside, Heaven/the Casa, the Casa/Cuba. After her first experience in the house-labyrinth Gaia witnesses the 'ceremonia de Iroko' when the *orisha* Inle deposits his semen inside some 'iniciados' (both men and women). It is in this ceremony that Gaia realizes that *santería* is a latent substratum, a rhizome, in the collective unconscious of her people. As Oshún explains to her:

> Todo en el universo tiene dos aspectos: lo esotérico y lo exotérico.[10] La gente hace sus fiestas y sus rogaciones, consulta sus oráculos, se ocupa del aspecto externo y evidente del culto, de lo exotérico; y usan esos ritos con propósitos inmediatos. Aquí nos ocupamos de la parte oculta. Es lo que en otros pueblos llaman misterios…
>   – ¿Cómo los misterios de Eleusis?[11]
>   – Y los de Isis… No puedo revelarte mucho, pero existe una conexión entre los misterios griegos y los egipcios con esta zona del Caribe. En la ceremonia de Iroko se manejan fuerzas vedadas a los seres humanos; fuerzas que, a su vez, producen otras fuerzas […] Lo que ves es un reflejo de lo que ocurre allá afuera, al otro lado de la reja. Sólo que a otro nivel. […]
>   – O una alegoría. Tómalo como quieras.

---

[10]   According to the *DRAE*, 'esotérico' means 'Oculto, reservado. // Por ext., dícese de lo que es impenetrable o de difícil acceso para la mente. // Dícese de la doctrina que los filósofos de la antigüedad no comunicaban sino a corto número de sus discípulos. // Dícese de cualquier doctrina que se transmite oralmente a los iniciados', while 'exotérico' means 'Común, accesible para el vulgo; lo contrario de esotérico. // Dícese de de lo que es de fácil acceso para la mente. // Dícese por lo común de la doctrina que los filósofos de la antigüedad manifestaban públicamente'.

[11]   Julius Evola states: 'En cuanto a la antigüedad clásica, se puede decir que en los Misterios más celebrados en ella, los de Eleusis, la unión sagrada, además de tener el valor genérico de las hierogamias simbólico-rituales, aludía al misterio del renacimiento en un contexto que es bastante probable que al principio comprendiese la sexualidad como medio; y también aquí se daba relieve al principio femenino, a la mujer divina. […] Clemente de Alejandría, Teodoreto y Psello concuerdan en afirmar que en aquellos Misterios el órgano femenino […] se presentaba a las miradas de los iniciados, como indicando el instrumento necesario para celebrar el misterio, […] Todo ello permite precisamente suponer que el sentido de la ceremonia mística simbólica […] era recordar, más allá de las propias hierogamias rituales y de una unión sexual del sacerdote con la sacerdotisa […] el misterio de la resurrección como puede efectuarse a través del sexo y de la mujer, considerada ésta encarnación de la Diosa. Así, en Eleusis, una vez que se había celebrado en la oscuridad el rito de la unión, se encendía una gran luz y el hierofante anunciaba con voz atronadora: "La gran Diosa ha parido el Hijo sagrado, la Fuerte ha engendrado al Fuerte" […] el sagrado renacimiento iniciático se pone en estrecha relación con el hombre primigenio andrógino […] y con su resurgir' (Evola 1997: 276).

> – ¿Y para qué sirve eso?
> – Para salvar o para perder.
> – ¿A quién?
> – A ti, a tus amigos, a todos los que habitan en este lugar… Para hacer un hechizo, debemos reflejar la misma realidad que queremos cambiar. Eso es la ceremonia: un acto simbólico. Después las fuerzas se pondrán en movimiento; pero ese movimiento no sirve de nada sin la voluntad. Así es que lo que hagan ustedes con esas fuerzas desatadas concierne a sus almas. (Chaviano 1999: 87–8)

The novel itself is part of this 'acto simbólico'. Through Oshún, Chaviano once more links the house with the Mysteries of Eleusis and Isis. With these inter-textual references Chaviano turns *santería* into a religion of mystery and connects the house with the spiritual world. The house becomes an allegory of the outside world, a reality that according to the character must be changed.[12] After this explanation Gaia understands for the first time that

> Un espejo refleja los objetos; reproduce lo que está frente a él y duplica la realidad. Un reflejo es un duplicado. Lo que está dentro de él es como lo que está afuera. Una parodia de la máxima hermética: lo que está arriba es como lo que está abajo. Esa ley antigua era también la base del universo, de la biología, de todo lo existente. La vida es una repetición. El macrocosmos refleja el microcosmos. La luz y la sombra son dos reflejos de una misma cosa.
>
> Observó las llamas. La dualidad sombra/luz imperaba en toda la casa… y también en esos confines. Recordó sus sentimientos mientras recorría las estancias. En contra de todo raciocinio, desconfiaba de las más iluminadas, con su infinita sucesión de lámparas que exponían cada escondrijo. Ese resplandor se le antojaba un acoso, un escrutinio sospechosamente insistente en su afán por revelar. La oscuridad, en cambio, ofrecía el ambiente acogedor de un útero; un refugio que imitaba el caos primigenio, anterior al *fiat lux* – ese punto mítico que trajera la dudosa protección de un dios –. Ella, por supuesto, prefería el ambiente subversivo de las tinieblas a la claridad. […] Trató de atrapar una idea que luchaba por emerger, pero el eco de los tambores volvió a llenar la noche. (Chaviano 1999: 88–9)

---

[12] It is worth noting that, while *santería* practitioners and religious practioners in general could not be part of the Communist Party in Cuba until the 1990s, Cubans who migrated to Florida also faced restrictions. In 1993 the US Supreme Court upheld the right of the Iglesia Lucumí in the city of Hialeah (next to Miami and with a large Cuban population) to practise animal sacri-fices, which are at the core of *santería* practices, and which the city of Hialeah (with many Cuban exiles in city government positions) had opposed. The US Supreme Court unanimously decided that the City of Hialeah had violated the freedoms guaranteed by the First Amendment of the US Constitution. See *Church of the Lukumi Babalu Aye* vs. *Hialeah*, http://www.oyez.org/cas-es/1990-1999/1992/1992_91_948/ (accessed 10 August 2009).

However, 'dos reflejos de la misma cosa' does not mean that they are 'la misma cosa'. The relationship that Chaviano establishes here is one I have examined earlier in this study in relation to Iuri Lotman's concept of enantiomorphism, that is, that mirror images are not superimposable (see Lotman 1996: I, 36). Gaia is constantly attempting to subvert patriarchal rule but somehow seems to be overwhelmed by it, by those drums capable of muffling all other sounds. In feminist terms, following Alison Martin's work on Irigaray's feminist philosophy, 'The mirror is the mechanism which establishes and consolidates the significance of the visual and of objectivity (the distinction between the subject and the instruments of reflection) for the knowledge and self-knowledge of the subject' (Martin 2000: 145); in this case a female subject – Gaia. For Gaia in the novel as for Irigaray in her philosophy, as discussed by Martin,

> only a different kind of mirror, such as a speculum [as an instrument of discourse], could represent woman and thwart the assumption of linear symmetry in the mirror metaphor. Furthermore, such a mirror would make apparent the effects of the instruments or modalities of representation in a way that the flat mirror tends to obfuscate with its deceptively accurate symmetrical image of an appearance as a copy of reality. (2000: 145)

For Irigaray, if the mother is the first home, discourse replaces her: 'Discourse becomes the world in which the subject dwells, a world that both ties the subject and separates the subject from the existing real' (Irigaray 2008: 121). Discourse is what establishes the dialogism with the Other in *Casa de juegos* as Gaia's performativity attempts to undermine the patriarchal order of the symbolic.

After this point in the novel the connections with Lucrecia and the rhizomatic intertexts have a social tone. The narrator begins to develop her criticism of revolutionary Cuba, particularly in the 1980s and early 1990s, which coincides with Chaviano's last decade on the island before joining the Cuban exiles in Miami. What was presented in a surrealistic context is now framed within a socio-political representation of what for the narrator was life in Cuba. Within this realm, the reader will notice that it is at university that Gaia shows her strongest discontent, and later displays a deep inner transformation thanks to her earlier experiences inside the house. It is in this educational space that Gaia has an epiphany, once she starts to know herself. This pushes her libido to extremes and allows her to break away from the individual prejudices (and internalized social conventions) that coerce her to act in a particular way. For the first time she becomes aware of the situation around her. In this social setting we find a banal story but one that nevertheless locates the discourse within a dialogic relationship with the state and its postulates, which are also to be observed in the classroom. Thus when Castillo, her classmate and 're-sponsable ideológico del aula' (Chaviano 1999: 110), asks Gaia to sign a document, this is her reaction:

Gaia leyó: los estudiantes se comprometían a poner al descubierto las inconsistencias filosóficas e ideológicas que atentaran contra los principios del marxismo-leninismo, en el marco de los lineamentos que velaban por la pureza de la moral comunista de la juventud...

¡Dios mío! Otra de aquellas estupideces. Esos documentos semanales provocaban el efecto de una epidemia por contagio. Por culpa de ellos tenía que esconderse para leer a Jun. Y a Blavatsky; por culpa de ellos apenas podía conseguir de contrabando ciertos filmes de Wajda y Almodóvar.

– Yo no voy a firmar nada. (Chaviano 1999: 110)

Here reference to a black market where it is possible to get certain cultural products highlights a time-frame outside the narrative itself. We should remember that Pedro Almodóvar's directorial debut, *Pepi, Luci, Bom y otras chicas del montón*, dates from 1980. Here Chaviano criticizes through her novel 'la moral revolucionaria' which she highlights as nothing more than 'doble moral' and hypocrisy, particularly in the light of what Almodóvar put forward in his early films: the break from Francoist moral values and national Catholicism in the case of Spain.

The reference to Polish film director Andrzej Wajda mobilizes many aspects of rhizomatic intertextuality as well. Wajda's own father was killed by Stalin's communist agents during the historic events that took place in Katyn in 1940.[13] Wajda was also part of the Polish resistance against the Nazis. If we think of Wajda's 1975 film *The Promised Land*, then the connection is established through the symbolic. In Wajda we find a nineteenth-century setting that alludes to the communist realities of his time, including the killing of dissident workers both in the Soviet Union and Poland. Here Chaviano's mobilization from classical antiquity to present-day Cuba has a similar allegorical effect. It was also in the early 1980s that Wajda joined Lech Walesa's 'Solidarity' labour movement and in 1989 he became a Senator in the new Poland. In his films Wajda unmasks communist propaganda (for example, *Man of Marble*, 1977, and *Czlowiek z zelaza*, 1981) and by analogy and the affiliation of Cuba with the Soviet Union, Chaviano's text reveals that Wajda was not welcome in official circles on the island.

The reference, in passing, to Helena Petrovna Blavatsky (1831–91), the founder of Theosophy and the Theosophical Society, represented as a censored writer or part of the black market in Cuba, highlights the position of the state concerning one of Chaviano's preferred topics: theosophy, that is, the knowledge of the divine that Chaviano incorporates in her text as a feminine space beyond

---

[13] Wajda returned to this subject in his 2007 Oscar-nominated film *Katyn*. It was not until the government of Mikhail Gorbachev that the Soviets officially addressed and recognized the events at Katyn as the result of Stalin's dictatorship. For more on Wajda, see Antonio Pelayo's book *Andrzej Wajda, testigo y conciencia de una generación* (1973).

the patriarchal Judeo-Christian tradition. Chaviano thus establishes a rhizomatic connection with Blavatsky's *Voice of the Silence* and her occultist writings.
In Chaviano's novel, Gaia is a disciple of sorts in terms of esoteric, spiritual
knowledge, which in the Cuban case is achieved through the syncretic practices offered by *santería*.

The reference to Jun points the reader in the direction of Japanese writer Jun
Ishikawa (1899–1987), the pen name of Ishikawa Kiyoshi, translator of Andé
Gide's *L'immoraliste* into Japanese, who lost his job as a professor of French
literature at Fukuoka University after participating in student protests. He was
censored at various times in his own country for his anti-militarist stance, but
more specifically his novel *Hakubyo* (1940) criticized Stalinism (see Tyler 1981).
This reference indirectly positions Cuba in its revolutionary period, as late as
the 1980s, as a country that was not receptive to different ideologies.

Gaia criticizes the official discourse reflected in the letter she is asked to sign,
and thus challenges the referential realm in which the text is based: revolutionary Cuba and the existence of censorship. However, the real change in Gaia is
reflected not in her criticism of this discourse but in her reaction: 'En otra ocasión
hubiera replicado "porque no me da la gana"; esta vez guardó silencio' (Chaviano 1999: 111). Here silence is used as a 'treta', a trick of the weak, to borrow
Josefina Ludmer's term (1984; 1999). When Castillo states that she must sign
because direct resistance would be equivalent to suicide, and that he himself
does not agree with the letter, Gaia realizes the possibility of a 'doble moral'
which affects Cuban society:[14]

> ¿Sería verdad que ninguno de ellos creía en lo que firmaba? ¿Bajaban la cabeza
> por conveniencia? ¿Acataban los mandatos para evitarse problemas? Repasó
> ciertos comentarios, frases intrigantes, pequeños gestos de complicidad…
> Sí, algo había cambiado. O estaba en proceso de cambiar. La hipocresía iba
> ganando terreno por doquier. La doble moral. Las máscaras. Sospechó que
> el fenómeno no era reciente, pero ella había tardado años luz en percibirlo.
> ¿Dónde estuvo metida? Mientras jugaba a los novios, sus amigos se habían
> convertido en los actores más excelsos del planeta. (Chaviano 1999: 112)

The masks thus acquire new signifieds in terms of cultural resistance, part of
'las tretas del débil' in a society that according to Chaviano is pure simulacra.
Gaia is aware of how her experiences inside the house have helped her to see
reality in a different way, but also to realize that, while the individual alone may
want to resist, such resistance in the face of the group may be futile:

---

14   This aspect of 'doble moral' is also exemplified in other cultural productions in Cuba; for
example, we can think of the film *La vida es silbar*, directed by Fernando Pérez in 1998. In the
film, just pronouncing the phrase makes certain people faint.

Se dio cuenta de que el joven aguardaba por una decisión suya, y fue como si algo se desmoronara en su interior. Comprendió que de nada valdría su resistencia aislada, si acaso para hacerla pasar por una chiquilla obtusa. Además, estaba cansada de oponerse a una fuerza que siempre terminaba por vencerla. (Chaviano 1999: 112)

Gaia at this point confirms her identification of the Casa with Cuba, where she inhabits the space of the in-between, as a fluid character. The socio-political reality of the island is as obscure as the human unconscious and she describes it thus:

La imagen de la sombría mansión brotó en su mente y, con ella, una idea se fue abriendo camino, fructificando con la pasión de una espiga que busca ansiosa la luz. Aquella casa se parecía a su país: a esa isla onírica y engañosa, seductora y fraudulenta, embustera y libertina. Sólo que para notarlo había que vivir allí, habitar sus noches y sus días, fornicar con su miseria y sus encantos, y no pasearse con el aire ausente de un turista llegado de otro mundo. Por doquier florecía una condición tortuosa que impedía saber dónde terminaba el delirio de la psiquis y dónde empezaban los absurdos de una sociedad que nadie quería, pero cuya destrucción nadie parecía dispuesto a enfrentar; una sociedad capaz de engañar al resto del mundo, pues incluso a sus propios ciudadanos le resultaba difícil descifrar los atroces mecanismos de su funcionamiento. (Chaviano 1999: 112–13)

The Casa resembles the Cuba of the 1990s, beginning a new reality with the Special Period. If the tourists before then were mostly socialists and those who had ideological connections with Cuba, after the collapse of the Soviet Union and the end of subsidies for Cuba the Special Period marked new renegotiations with capitalism that openly brought capitalist tourists to the island, particularly from Europe. The reference to the absent-minded tourist questions issues of sameness and establishes inter-subjective relationships in order to show how the performances inside the island/Casa can be both real and surreal, depending on the participants and their experiences. In the words of Irigaray: 'The other as other escapes my gaze' (2008: 126). This also establishes a similar relationship between those who inhabit the Casa and the outsiders; both are exposed to different realities which add new interpretants and meanings.[15]

Reality in the novel is encompassed by the dream poetics of the surrealist mode to which I have referred already. If Gaia depicts a Cuba of scarcity to the point where there is no bread, she focuses on entering the world of dreams by requesting a drug prescribed for the alleviation of anxiety (anxiety related to the

---

[15] I rely on Scholes's semiotic concepts, based on Peirce. As he states, 'In Peirce's theory of signs, every sign that is understood gives rise to another sign in the mind of the interpreter. This second sign is the interpretant of the first' (Scholes 1982: 145).

exam period at university). However, she cannot get any and is recommended
to take Benadryl instead:

> Buscó a su madre para pedirle un meprobramato [*sic*] […]
> – ¿Un meprobramato? […] ¿Pero en qué mundo vives, niña? Si ni siquiera
> hay pan, ¿de dónde voy a sacar un mebrobramato [*sic*]?
> – Es que ando medio nerviosa.
> – Tómate un buche de benadrilina – le dijo, volviendo a lo suyo.
> – ¡Eso es para la alergia, mami!
> – Es lo único que tengo para dormir – respondió la mujer, […] –. ¿No es
> eso lo que buscas? (Chaviano 1999: 123–4)

After taking the Benadryl, which causes drowsiness, Gaia has bisexual and
masochistic dream thoughts, with Oshún – 'emperatriz del gozo' – and Shangó
– 'señor supremo de los fuegos terrenales y celestes' – as part of the 'ilógica
conveniencia de las pesadillas' (Chaviano 1999: 125, 126), thus facilitating a
different narrative. In the dream Shangó is portrayed chasing Oshún and Gaia
through the labyrinth ('aquel negro hermoso que las persiguiera por sus pasa-
dizos', 1999: 126). Gaia finds herself the prisoner of the *orishas*: 'Y en las
brumas de ese sueño, Gaia quedó convencida de la naturaleza deífica de sus
captores' (1999: 126); she thus comes to self-realization:

> Dentro del sueño, Gaia sintió nacer esa efervescencia que es el preludio
> del orgasmo. […] el dios mantuvo su ataque hasta la eyección del magma
> que estalló con la violencia de un Vesubio negro. Corrientes telúricas se
> alojaron en su interior, la empujaron, la embistieron, amenazaron con hacerla
> pedazos. Llegó a la esencia de su nombre. Conoció los estremecimientos de
> la creación, que en la Madre Tierra adquieren connotaciones divinas. Así se
> entregaba ella, como una puta celestial. O eso le susurraba el dios mientras
> su alma escapaba y ella se unía a la nada. Ya no era ella. Ni siquiera era.
> Existía meramente en aquel murmullo. Magia de hombre. Sus sentidos se
> alejaron del mundo. Sólo entonces le desató sus muñecas y dejó que cayera
> encima del lodo, aletargada en su propio éxtasis.
>   Pero la diosa no había terminado. Sin reparar en el creciente fanguero, se
> abatió sobre la cautiva para apagar su insatisfacción atacando con su pelvis
> la entrepierna. Ebria de deseo, oculto el rostro tras los cabellos empapados,
> era la imagen rediviva de una bacante abandonada a la orgía.
>   Gaia no supo más porque el fango le tapó los ojos con tanta saña como
> cubría su cuerpo… o quizás porque el sueño ya llegaba a su fin. (Chaviano
> 1999: 127–8)

This dream expresses the process of self-knowledge that takes place throughout
Gaia's sexual experiences. In this dream she reaches an ecstatic experience, a
mystic union with both male and female deities. This mystic aspect allows for
a direct relationship with the divine that Judeo-Christian parameters would

prevent, if we follow Irigaray's belief that 'patriarchy has deprived women of the divine' (1987: 205).[16] If Irigaray's hypothesis is that 'the projection of a woman divinity could introduce sexual difference into the symbolic', as Margaret Whitford asserts (1991a: 141), in Chaviano this possibility is consolidated by the syncretism of *santería* which brings to the monotheism of Christianity both male and female deities alike.

Chaviano's narrative serves to question its own referentiality. The entire narrative could be between the dream-state and consciousness, as an attempt to create a discourse that questions the role of women in a society that follows a masculine model. As Whitford states in her study of Irigaray:

> Unless one accepts the need for women to be able to represent their relation to the mother, and so to origin, in a specific way, i.e. not according to a masculine world, then women will always find themselves devalued. Neutral/universal/single-sex models always turn out to be implicitly male ones. (1991a: 85–6).

From now on, Gaia will start a search for Eri, that is, a search for her own self, in order to know the mysteries of the Casa. There is a sharp contrast between reality, characterized by stagnation and inaction, and a house inhabited by fantastic beings. When Gaia finds Eri, he recognizes that he has submitted her to a learning process, and asks her to return to the house. She comes back guided by her special Virgilio, her 'Orfeo engañoso' (Chaviano 1999: 136), where she dies symbolically, as mentioned before. At the end of the novel Gaia's self-awareness reaches its climax when she understands the system where she lives and the way to survive and subvert it. Her fight against alienation and oppression is then a collective one. This collective fight against social oppression is not unique to women in the novel. The female body appears as the site of resistance but also of the spirituality embodied by the Afro-Cuban deities. In the Casa we witness the performance of the unity between the sacred and the profane.

The *santera* talks about the coexistence of *orishas* and human beings. We have already witnessed this through Gaia, yet we find a new element is added to the narrative: through these *orishas* and the spirituality that they teach there is a way of resistance, of survival against the biblical Apocalypse, which again can encompass a more political reading as the *santera* talks about social change as well. Thus, the rites of passage that Gaia goes through inside the Casa are confirmed to have a social and political dimension. Gaia states: 'Algún día se presentarían [los orishas] en todo su esplendor, como figuras apocalípticas y salvadoras, para culminar con un ciclo de gobierno y dar comienzo a otro' (Chaviano 1999: 188).

---

[16]   The translation is by Margaret Whitford (1991a: 141).

When Gaia meets up with Eri once again, he explains the essence of her ordeal within the social context of Cuba at the time:

> ¿Sabes que iban a expulsarte? […] De la facultad. […] Según el informe, te convertiste en una alumna problemática. […] Mi grupo tiene colaboradores en los consejos donde se decide la suerte de los estudiantes. Hemos logrado evitar la expulsión de algunos, avisándoles de manera indirecta, pero contigo no funcionó. […] no quisiste creernos. (Chaviano 1999: 161–2)

And the following dialogue between Gaia and Eri sheds light on the meaning of this novel:

> – No acabo de entender para qué montaste este teatro.
> – […] para salvarte. Te pasabas todo el tiempo cuestionando esto o aquello como si ésa fuera la única forma de rebelarse, y aquí la rebelión no sirve de nada. […] Ése es el único modo de sobrevivir: mintiendo y fingiendo las veinticuatro horas.
> – Con decírmelo habría sido suficiente.
> – Te repito que lo intentamos… en más de una ocasión; pero eres muy terca y no quisiste entender.
> – ¿Qué pinta la casa en todo eso? […]
> – Me gustaste tanto que decidí matar dos pájaros de un tiro: te curaría ese trauma de la frigidez y te haría cambiar […]
> Gaia pensó unos segundos […] Fue después de su primera experiencia en aquella casa; lo recordaba perfectamente. Había claudicado, silenciado lo que sentía… algo muy raro en ella.
> – […] te habían puesto a prueba y tus experiencias te ayudaron a pasarla. (Chaviano 1999: 164–6)

Eri continues by contextualizing the speech acts of this narrative in the social context of Cuba where sex is presented as a site of resistance:

> No hay erotismo sin audacia y no hay poder sin soberbia. A los tiranos les encanta controlar hasta los orgasmos de sus súbditos; pero no por puritanismo, sino porque no soportan que nada escape a su control. Por eso la cama es el único sitio donde los preceptos de las dictaduras son burlados a ultranza. (Chaviano 1999: 167)

In short, in this novel we witness the creation of a chronotope, the house, where resistance against a repressive system can take place. Liberation from the individual's taboos implies a place for freedom. This resistance must not be direct or it would produce political suicide and social ostracism as its end result. Nevertheless, I would argue that this novel's failure consists in not allowing the reader to see any of the real effects that this kind of resistance produces, such as we find, for example, in Arenas's *El color del verano* where the forces of carnival subvert a repressive system and lead to the destruction of the island. In *Casa de juegos* the reader only knows very late in the narrative the political implications of the erotic acts and cannot see their social dimensions reflected in the novel. As readers we only perceive Gaia's own transformation and her new point of view on the world that surrounds her:

> Tal vez el alma acudiera a esos medios para escapar de la frustración. El sexo era un recurso poderoso: al contener tabúes milenarios, resultaba también liberador; y en una prisión social podía adquirir trascendencia catártica. No importaba cuán monstruosa fuese la represión: para alguien sin posibilidades de sublevarse, forzar los límites de su erotismo se convertía en un mecanismo de cordura porque se estaba rebelando contra algo que sí podía vencer.
>
> Pensó en quienes apelaban a métodos más convencionales con un valor que a ella le faltaba; por eso sufrían golpizas y encierros interminables. Se sintió avergonzada, pero no por mucho tiempo. La misteriosa organización de Eri tampoco acudía al enfrentamiento. Su herramienta conspirativa era bastante extraña: avisaba a los descontentos, conminándolos a una aparente obediencia que, sin embargo, no cambiaba la estructura rebelde de su pensamiento. Eso habían hecho con ella. Toda la energía empleada en cuestionar órdenes absurdas había sido moldeada [...] por sus peculiares experiencias sexuales. Primero, la condicionaron a obedecer; después, tras hacerle saltar las barreras de su libido, fue liberada de esas ataduras que suelen originar mayores represiones. Su actitud cambió. Se dio el lujo de aceptar burlonamente lo que antes provocara en ella reacciones peligrosas. (Chaviano 1999: 167–8)

Gaia thus acknowledges that she has apparently learned to conform under patriarchal rule but that silence does not mean consent. In this light, Eri establishes again a connection between Gaia's sexual experiences and their individual, social and political implications:

> el suicidio social es una idiotez y no sirve de nada. Eso es lo que ibas a conseguir con tus impulsos de rebelión. [...] La única manera de tranquilizarte era hacerte sentir libre, y eso es algo que aquí sólo se puede conseguir a través de los instintos porque en la vida real es imposible. [...] La sociedad nos hace cobardes. No podemos pensar con claridad porque los prejuicios nos ciegan. Para saber quiénes somos es necesario volver a empezar, conocer en carne propia lo que significa ser libres; pero para comprenderlo, primero debemos experimentar lo que es la libertad.
> – ¿Siempre a través del sexo?
> – Por lo menos, para empezar. [...] Porque nuestra naturaleza es erótica,

y muchos de nuestros problemas se originan en esa *zona* del espíritu. […]
te aseguro que no tendremos libertad hasta que no sepamos respetarla. Nos
encanta reprimir; por eso somos reprimidos. Y la libertad debe ser entendida
hasta sus últimas consecuencias […] Eros es el dios secreto de nuestra isla.
Llevamos en la sangre el virus de la incontinencia sexual y nos empeñamos
en ser de otro modo. (Chaviano 1999: 169–70)

It is in the above citation that eroticism and the experience of freedom go hand
in hand. Repression becomes here something that is innate in every human being and is not only political. Eroticism and spirituality become weapons through
which a woman can express herself freely. Social liberation starts in this novel
with liberation from one's own taboos, and not the other way around.

Gaia agrees to a last visit to the Casa, which is in constant transformation.
There she has sexual intercourse with Inle, whom she discovers to be Eri:

[After eating in the house she wants to have a shower.] Sus percepciones
también cambiaron. Olfateó la curvatura del espacio, los colores de la
memoria, el tiempo en fuga. Luchó por aprehender las dimensiones reales
de su entorno, pero su mente se batía en retirada. Algún dios sacudía el
cosmos y lo viraba patas arriba. Se quedó inmóvil bajo la ducha para
escuchar por primera vez la penumbra. Aromas tibios y palpitaciones
doradas. Música delgada como un suspiro. El mundo susurró dentro de su
garganta y comprendió. Cada onza de aire que pasaba por sus pulmones
dejaba un rastro oleaginoso y dulce como un ciervo desbocado. Era el alfa
del misterio y ella abrió sus brazos para recibirlo. Llegó la nada. Acunó a
Dios. Una lluvia atravesó el techo, proveniente de la luna que se reflejaba
en un pedazo de espejo. Ella era la rosa mística que adoraban los monjes y
el universo se plegaba a sus deseos. (Chaviano 1999: 179–80)

Before the last erotic experience in the Casa, Gaia reaches the centre of the
labyrinth when she realizes that at the centre is only herself: she is the mystery. She has a truly mystic experience, she becomes the representation of
the sacred as she is 'la rosa mística'. She achieves union with God. Both the
symbols of the rain and the mirror represent the dissolution of Gaia's body
in her union with the sacred. This experience is conveyed using a poetic
language full of metaphors and symbols. In the words of Whitford, which I
extrapolate to this context: 'Women need a mirror too; not the one in which
they check their appearance-for-others, but a mirror that will send back to
them an image that confirms them in their autonomous subjectivity, for-
themselves, and not just in their exteriority, for-others' (1991a: 142). In
relation to the sacred, in Chaviano's work God, as in Irigaray's texts studied
by Whitford, is 'another discursive representation of the monosexual economy' which figures 'in this economy as a mirror for the male imaginary'
(Whitford 1991a: 142).

After another violent sexual act described through surrealist imagery[17] and the discovery that Eri/Inle is the same person, Gaia appears again outside the house. She is aware now of what she had learned there: 'decir que sí con ademán falsamente servil, y luego virar la espalda para hacer exactamente lo contrario... Había aprendido a no exponerse; había aprendido a desobedecer en silencio; había aprendido a sobrevivir' (Chaviano 1999: 187). Gaia's erotic pleasure becomes one of her 'tretas del débil' in order to create a space where she has none. At times, the erotic and the mystic language she uses to describe her experiences is full of symbols and metaphors that break with the linearity of the hegemonic discourses that, in this novel, attempt to homogenize a whole nation.

In her last meeting with Eri he invites her to his parents' place which, eventually, is the house of the novel. There:

> Justo en un recodo, se alzaba una ceiba rodeada por arbustos que impedían la visión de la casa. Al llegar allí, el hombre le alzó la falda y le arrancó la ropa interior. Ella quiso recoger el trozo de la tela, pero él le introdujo un dedo entre los muslos y la obligó a seguirlo. Sintió que se mojaba sin remedio. Lo obedeció sin chistar, aunque no estaba segura si la trastada de su amante terminaría al final del laberinto.
>
> De todos modos se dejó arrastrar por aquel dedo que la guiaba como un hilo de Ariadna, gozosa ante el frescor de la brisa que atravesaba sus labios entreabiertos. El soplo del céfiro le llegó hasta los ovarios, perfumándolos con aroma de rosas.
>
> Trató de consolarse, pensando que si había podido vivir en un feudo cerrado tantos años, también se adaptaría a ese otro experimento. La rebelión, por el momento, tendría que ser secreta. ¿No era lo que le habían enseñado? En su país, tales eran las reglas del juego: ocultar, mentir, simular... Por eso no había nada que hacer. Lo mejor sería fingir y seguirle la corriente a toda esa locura. Después de todo, Cuba era también una inmensa casa de juegos donde no valía la pena preguntar, porque nunca obtendría la verdadera respuesta. (Chaviano 1999: 191–2)

In the last pages of the novel Eri/Inle appears as Ariadna. The gender roles associated with the myth are subverted. Now it is the woman who has killed the Minotaur and who goes out of the labyrinth with the help of Ariadna/Eri/Inle's

---

[17]   Chaviano describes it thus: 'Se quedó inmóvil bajo la ducha para escuchar por primera vez la penumbra. [...] Nuevos seudópodos surgieron de la pared, tocaron sus pechos [...] pero ella no intentó librarse de aquella fiesta orgiástica sobre su carne. Alzó la vista hacia el espejo que le devolvía su imagen borrosa, y también la de una sombra confusa a sus espaldas. No, más que una sombra era una suma de sombras. O un ejército fantasmal. O el vapor que producía sombras... Nadie. No había nadie y era su imaginación. [...] Estaba sola, pero algo se movió detrás de ella. Le pareció que el grifo inferior de la bañera empezaba a transformarse en un pene broncíneo, en una monstruosidad que intentaba cambiar su aséptico hábitat por el fondo legamoso de su carne [...] halló gozosa su humillante servidumbre' (Chaviano 1999: 179–81).j

thread. Once Gaia has learned the lessons of the house, this new erotic experience represents her return to the outside world. She is now ready to leave the
labyrinth and integrate herself into society. In contrast with the sexual discourse
of *El color del verano*, in *Casa de juegos* the erotic discourse appears as marginal. It does not invade the discourse of the external world that it pretends to
subvert and transform, the effects of which we do not see. However, the erotic
discourse does become a feminine one, one that succeeds in giving legitimacy,
centrality and visibility to the female body. In this novel eroticism serves to
explore feminine subjectivity through a new language generated from the female
body, through which the destruction of monolithic power structures is achieved.
The feminine subject tries to find her place within the existing patriarchal society from the margins, in order to invade the centre and disrupt it. At the point
where the novel finishes, the feminine subject appears in a position of both
dependence on and subversion of the Symbolic, as a subject in the process of
becoming.

5

(Re)writing the Body as a Feminine Strategy:
Yanitzia Canetti's *Al otro lado*

One of the most complete and competent studies of Yanitzia Canetti's work is that of Yvette Fuentes (2002). Fuentes shows how Cuban women writers in the Diaspora display an isolation that challenges patriarchal discourses. She examines the three women writers that I study in this book, though the choice of novel in her study of Chaviano differs (Fuentes selects *El hombre, la hembra y el hambre* for her investigation). With reference to her analysis of Canetti's *Al otro lado*, Fuentes studies the discursive narratives (that is, fantasy, parody and allegory) that Canetti uses to undermine notions of gender and national identity. However, what for Fuentes is an *aislamiento* that allows these women to talk back 'to those wielding power' for me is a dialogic process that Canetti uses to respond to hegemonic discourses. While Fuentes considers it a feature of Cuban women writers of the Diaspora that these authors reflect in their works an 'in-betweenness', a 'continual double movement', I argue that this is a fluidity expressed by all Cuban writers, male or female, inside or outside Cuba, during the Special Period and beyond.

Rebecca Marquis (2006) has also undertaken a study focused on authority and rhetoric in confessional narratives, such as that of Canetti. Marquis considers the confession of Canetti's nameless protagonist as a strategy to assert female authorship and authority in writing within a history of women's confessional literature. Although I agree with Marquis when she states that confessional narratives are used 'to negotiate female subjectivity within patriarchal discourse' (2006: xiii), I will consider the confession of the nameless protagonist not as a real event, as Marquis proposes, but rather as a metaphor for the protagonist's self-discovery and creation. I will also explore a topic that other critics seem to underestimate, namely the role of the female body in the strategy of developing a feminine writing, that is, a dialogic practice that the protagonist undertakes through the use of masks and constant transformation during her erotic encounters. The female body appears as a site of resistance against oppression and as a weapon to renegotiate a feminine identity.

I suggest that Annegret Thiem (2004) proposes a new level of reading of *Al otro lado* by establishing a parallelism between the confession of the protagonist and the sacred history of the Bible, in what constitutes a 'mística postmoderna'.

According to Thiem, in this novel the author deconstructs the traditional mystical path. Although I agree with this viewpoint, I differ from Thiem when she
states that the author 'no intenta construir un nuevo sistema de producción de
sentido [...] un nuevo *logos* [...] es exactamente lo que niega el texto' (2004:
n.p.). Indeed, it is my intention to demonstrate the opposite in this study. According to Thiem '[la autora hace] del amor un mediador entre el cuerpo y el
espíritu en el sentido de una reconciliación de las dos existencias, siempre
separadas' (2004: n.p.). Although this reading of the novel is apt, I instead confer upon the erotic discourse in the novel a subversive essence and political
undertones. Furthermore, in a later article Thiem (2006) explains how both
memory and the use of mythology are strategies used to reconstruct an identity
in a constant process of transformation, and how the process of writing that
takes place in this novel functions as a weapon against the consequences of
exile. However, I do not consider exile but rather dialogism to be the key element of this novel, as Canetti attempts to place feminine writing at the core of
her discursive practice in the context of the 1990s.

In *Al otro lado* we witness the process of self-discovery of the nameless
protagonist, who goes to a Gothic church where she confesses to Father
Jonathan. The figure of the Father and the religious (male) imaginary function
as metaphors of the patriarchal system in which the female protagonist seems
trapped. In Michel Foucault's words, 'you will become the subject of a
manifestation of truth when and only when you disappear or you destroy
yourself as a real body and a real existence' (Foucault 1999: 179). Taken at
face value, we could conclude that this is something that the female protagonist in this novel will not do; rather, in *Al otro lado* the relationship between
the protagonist and the Father reverses the traditional mystical experience.
However, as Judith Butler asserts in relation to this model of confession proposed by Foucault, 'self-examination does not consist in self-beratement or,
indeed, the internalization of regulatory norms but becomes a way of giving
oneself over to a publicized mode of appearance' (2005: 114). Notwithstand-
ing this statement, it is worth noting that even in this mode 'a preconstituted
self is not revealed; instead, the very practice of self-constitution is performed'
(Butler 2005: 114). In the novel, this constitutive performativity will also be
achieved through writing.

In *Al otro lado*, the protagonist transforms a traditionally religious, sacred
experience into an erotic one: she will show, as the narrative progresses, an
increasing erotic attraction towards the priest. The act of crossing the church's
threshold symbolizes the protagonist's search for her inner self. I agree with
Biruté Ciplijauskaité when she states that 'Cruzar la puerta se asocia con algunos ritos de iniciación. A su vez, en las novelas femeninas frecuentemente
significa un paso hacia la liberación' (1988: 176). When the protagonist enters
the church and states '*Todo está aquí desde hace tiempo. Pero huele a nuevo
para mí, como las páginas de un libro acabado de salir de una imprenta*' (Can-

etti 1997: 11)[1] and '*Toda la iglesia huele a nueva, a libro que acaba de salir de la imprenta y cuya tinta, aún fresca, se hace apetecible a la respiración*' (1997: 13) she links the church with a brand-new book. Here the confession is a metaphor of the process of creation, 'el proceso de concienciación se vuelve doble o incluso triple: como individuo, como mujer, como creadora de un lenguaje nuevo' (Ciplijauskaité 1988: 87). As Yvette Fuentes explains, this novel

> turns to the process of writing (and rewriting) fiction and the ways in which this process is an integral element in the construction of the self. [...] [It] is a novel 'in-process' for the way it is produced, for its structure, and for the themes upon which it centers. (2002: 207)

Both the passages where she is in the church and those which constitute her confession intercalate in the novel, although the passages within the church are marked within the diegesis with italic type. The novel has a spiral structure: the protagonist is in church ready for confession, and there is a stream of consciousness in which an idea will generate the next confession. Following Butler's viewpoint (2005: 114–15), I would argue that there is a dispossession of the self and a constitution of the subject, as the protagonist is bound by a socio-historical context that she is attempting to rupture and transform. However, as Butler asserts, 'I become this self only through an ec-static [*sic*] movement, one that moves me outside of myself into a sphere in which I am dispossessed of myself and constituted as a subject at the same time' (2005: 115).

The protagonist in this novel gives us an account of her childhood and her adulthood, paying special attention to her erotic encounters. As Foucault claims about confession:

> es un ritual que se despliega en una relación de poder, pues no se confiesa sin la presencia al menos virtual de otro, que no es simplemente el interlocutor sino la instancia que requiere la confesión, la impone, la aprecia e interviene para juzgar, castigar, perdonar, consolar, reconciliar; un ritual donde la verdad se autentifica gracias al obstáculo y las resistencias que ha tenido que vencer para formularse. (2007: 78)

As Bakhtin claims, there cannot be utterance without addressivity, that is, 'the quality of turning to someone', to an addressee (Bakhtin 1986: 99). Thus, I claim that confession in Canetti's novel develops dialogism. Although the confession does not open up the dialogism itself, it gives feminine subjectivity the space needed to find a voice, to be heard.

The protagonist confesses her past to the priest. Through this confession she (re)creates herself by means of the word. Only through confession/writing will

---

[1]   All citations of the novel that appear in italics in this chapter reflect the style used in the text.

the protagonist assume her past in order to be able to look towards the future. I agree with Fuentes when she writes:

> One of the most important transgressions and one that undermines both the traditional, patriarchal family as well as the state's hold over individuals lies in her replacement of the father figure with Father Jonathan. Indeed, it is this transgression that allows the narrator-protagonist free license to 'talk back'. […] [He] is not a traditional father figure […] [He] is her creation, an androgynous figure that represents the figures of Father, Brother, Lover, Mother, Man-Woman, and Angel. His home, the Church, and more importantly the confessional, become spaces that allow the protagonist to talk back, far away from the limits imposed by society. (2002: 252)

In this novel there is a continual clash between the protagonist's dialogism and her surroundings, between the place she wants to occupy through her discourse and the place that the institutions which represent power allow her to have. The protagonist lives within a repressive society that restrains her constantly; there is also a clash between her and the state. Against a monolithic system in which there is no possibility of communication, the protagonist develops her dialogism through the constant use of masks, which are not physical like the ones used in the rituals in Chaviano's *Casa de juegos*, but symbolic. These masks are polyvalent: on the one hand they help her to encounter the Other and they are used during the protagonist's erotic encounters. On the other hand, they serve as protection; the protagonist uses them to protect herself when she is in trouble and to denounce the hypocrisy around her. The masks both cover and uncover the true self. At the end of the novel the masks appear as narrative tools to recreate/write herself and others. The masks are the product of the protagonist's writing; they are pure artifice, like the novel itself, and they activate both the intertextuality as well as the erotic game. Therefore, the confession is no more than an act of writing herself and those that surround her. The masks she uses are literary, from mythological figures to historical and literary ones. These masks' unique aim is to serve as a mechanism of self-analysis. Confession, writing and self-awareness go hand in hand. We can apply here the use Eliana Ortega makes of Rosario Castellanos's words when she claims:

> Para las mujeres en especial, recordemos las palabras de Rosario Castellanos: 'Cuando una mujer latinoamericana toma entre sus manos la literatura, lo hace con el mismo gesto y con la misma intención con la que toma un espejo para contemplar su imagen.' (Ortega 1990: 31)

This idea would explain why Canetti so often uses the symbol of the mirror as a way of reflecting her protagonist's search for herself. The protagonist's confession, therefore, equals the act of looking at herself in a mirror, though not the flat mirror criticized by Luce Irigaray (1985b) which would just give an alter-ego of the masculine, an inverted Other. As Alison Martin states in relation to this work by Irigaray,

> The only historically valorized part of her sex that cannot be represented in a flat mirror are women's sexual organs, and on one level Irigaray means quite literally that these cannot be seen in this mirror. Hence the revelation by psychoanalysis that woman is seen as castrated or as a defective male, and the representation of woman in philosophy as unformed, as nothingness or lack. For Irigaray, only a different kind of mirror, such as the speculum, could represent woman and thwart the assumption of linear symmetry in the mirror metaphor. Furthermore, such a mirror would make apparent the effects of the instruments or modalities of representation in a way that the flat mirror tends to obfuscate with its deceptively accurate symmetrical image of an appearance as a copy of reality. (2000: 145; see Irigaray 1985a)

Canetti will follow this non-linear modality in her narrative through a fragmentation that challenges linear logic and opens up new levels and possibilities of interpretation and readings. The fragmentation of the story/history becomes a centripetal force that allows us to explore different levels of interpretation. Here the protagonist stops being the source of a unique meaning and truth. I agree with Fuentes when she claims that 'contemporary Cuban women's narratives produced on and off the island display *aislamiento* (isolation) that serves as a means of "talking back" to Cuban's patriarchal discourse' (2002: ii). This isolation can be seen in the novels that I analyse in this study: Gaia in *Casa de juegos*, studied in chapter 4, the nameless protagonist within the church in *Al otro lado* in this chapter and Yocandra in her apartment, as I shall examine in chapter 6. All three spaces and times in these novels constitute private chronotopes in which the protagonists develop their erotic/feminine/feminist discourses. These chronotopes, like the female body, become sites of resistance within these narrations.

The Subversion of Official Discourses

As Madeline Cámara states, 'esta confesión, a la manera foucaultiana, resultará un discurso sobre el placer no sobre el arrepentimiento, un área peligrosa de exploración de la sensibilidad de mujer que se auto-descubre' (2002: 119). The confession thus supposes the subversion of hegemonic discourses. In Lacanian terms, the feminine *jouissance* here is attained through a transgression (Lacan 1992). She escapes any attempt to homogenize and label women, thus indirectly challenging the psychoanalytic position that there is a feminine 'supplementary *jouissance*' which focuses on the *jouissance* of the Other, similar to the mystic experience outside sex in the 'vía unitiva' (Lacan 1998: 73–6). However, in a similar vein to the latter, in the novel we also find that the protagonist makes an apology for erotic pleasure at any cost. I shall now focus on two aspects of the subversion of official discourses, namely the Church and the state.

The Church

The novel's structure not only takes the form of a confession but it is also full of intertextual references to the Bible. The concept of sin becomes one of its leitmotifs and indicates the sharp divide between the Church and the individual. The Church as a religious institution appears within this novel as an abstract entity that represents power and exerts its repression on the individual, in this case, the woman. The protagonist identifies with the biblical figure of Eve:

> Padre, cuando yo nací, ya Eva había probado del fruto prohibido. Y lo lamenté. Me hubiera gustado saber a qué sabía aquella primera fruta. Debo confesarle que de aquel fruto, yo nunca probé ni un pedacito siquiera; pero de aquel árbol fértil, creo haberme llenado la boca de jugos y sabores. Y como Eva, fui dotada de cierto entendimiento. Al menos para entender que vivir era algo supremo, el mejor de los castigos creados por ¿Dios? Y entallado a mi medida. (Canetti 1997: 22–3)

Here Canetti subverts the figure of Eve who, according to the Bible, is blamed for the expulsion from Paradise. With this identification the protagonist admits to having behaved like Eve and adds positive connotations to this biblical figure. There is a confrontation between feminine 'cierto entendimiento' and the questionable product of a more questionable male God: life appears as a punishment and as 'algo supremo', contradictions that will become characteristic of the protagonist's discourse. This discourse has pleasure as its vertex. Pleasure structures the feminine discourse in this narrative. Canetti appropriates the figure of Eve from the male religious tradition and transforms her from the despicable woman, held responsible for all our problems on Earth, into the woman who adopts as her motto the pleasure of life:

> ¡Me parece un vicio empedernido y morboso prescindir de ciertos placeres, en lugar de obedecerlos! Un placer que no florece, se nos pudre dentro. Y luego sale de algún modo – podrido de estar tanto tiempo enterrado vivo. Somos hijos legítimos del placer y lo único que podemos hacer para desentendernos de ese padre malsano y libidinoso, es sustituirlo por otro menos dañino en caso de que, ciertamente, nos dañe o dañe [sic]. A mí me complace la protección que me ofrece el placer. Me rindo y me abro como una pera. Negarme a él, es negarme a mí misma. Y yo quiero confirmarme ahora, sea cual sea el veredicto que me pueda caer encima. Venga el placer, con cualquiera de sus cabezas de dragón. Venga el placer con cualquiera de sus anillos infernales: lujuria, gula, descrédito, vanidad. Venga el placer para que me reconozca, para que me exorcice de pretender momificar mis deseos.
>
> *[...] Tiene que existir un placer. Sin un mínimo placer, sin un regocijo minúsculo, no podría el Padre soportar ni una sola de mis palabras de confesión. Creo que si mis palabras no tuvieran ese sabor escondido, él se*

aburriría de su oficio. ¡Cómo se iba a privar de ese lúdico placer de jugar a
los escondidos: él dentro de un lugar que ya yo descubrí, y yo fuera con algo
que él no ha descubierto!
   No hablamos. Nuestro diálogo fluye en una sola dirección después que él
entra al confesionario. Yo hablo. Él escucha. Los dos envueltos en un placer
redondo y compartido en dos partes iguales. [...] yo ya estoy hincada de
rodillas y con ganas de rebelar mi placer. (Canetti 1997: 26)

Confession, writing and *jouissance* appear here as a game, as ludic acts, and as
a transgresion against the hegemonic religious discourse that establishes a fixed
system of values regarding what is right and what is wrong. I agree with Foucault
when he writes:

> If sex is repressed, that is, condemned to prohibition, nonexistence, and
> silence, then the mere fact that one is speaking about it has the appearance of
> a deliberate transgression. A person who holds forth in such language places
> himself to a certain extent outside the reach of power; he upsets established
> law; he somehow anticipates the coming freedom. (1990: 6)

With her discourse, the protagonist subverts the monolithic authoritative discourse of the Church and the state which in the novel appear as repressive
entities, and escapes their power by means of the creation of a feminine discourse full of contradictions, silences, irony, humour and intertextual references. The text demands a reading between the lines in order to understand
the different levels of meaning that it offers. In the following passage, for
example, the protagonist questions the goodness of God, the existence of God,
and recontextualizes the biblical account in Genesis (1: 27) which says that
God created 'man' ('human beings' in the era of political correctness)[2] in his
own image. In a text about pleasure, once again the intertextual reference
acquires subversive connotations:

> El sofá también tenía brazos de madera. Caoba. [...] fui tan diestra en hallar
> placer en aquel mullido mueble [...] Yo le juro, Padre, que nunca he sabido
> por qué sentí aquellos primeros impulsos, ni por qué no he podido prescindir
> de ellos para calmar los latidos de mi cuerpo. ¿Y cómo considerar pecado el
> placer? ¿Acaso aquello era una revelación de mi desamor por el prójimo? Si
> he amado al prójimo con tanta vehemencia – y perdone usted, Padre – ha sido
> por la manera violenta en que me he amado a mí misma. Conocí el placer
> físico antes que ningún otro placer y nunca privaría a otro ser de ese don
> que Dios puso en nuestros cuerpos... porque, ¿no dijo usted hoy en la misa
> que Dios nos creó a su imagen y semejanza? ¿Y por qué nos dispuso para el

---

2   'So God created human beings' is the new version found, for example, in the *Holy Bible,*
New Living Translation (Carol Stream, IL: Tyndale House Publishers, 2007).

placer, si no quería que lo sintiéramos? ¿Para torturarnos? ¿Para obligarnos a ganar una vida mejor… sin placer? ¿Y por qué iba a querer yo una vida sin placer? (Canetti 1997: 28)

Here the biblical Scripture that sums up 'toda la ley', all the comandments, into 'amarás a tu prójimo como a ti mismo', which is repeated several times in the Bible (Lev. 19: 18; Gal. 5: 14; Rom. 13: 9; Jas. 2: 8), is challenged to justify erotic encounter and gratification. In the fragment quoted above we find already the idea that pervades the whole narrative, that is, the idea of the erotic encounter as a way to encounter the Other.

The title of the fourth chapter of the novel, 'La mentira, otra vez', has a special meaning when we read the following fragment of this narrative:

> *No estoy segura de lo que estoy haciendo en este lugar. No me acostumbro a estar escoltada por estatuas sufrientes ni a pisar una alfombra de terciopelo falso. No creo en la santidad de los apóstoles ni en la virginidad de la Virgen. Creo en la virginidad de su alma callada. Veo más casta su maternidad consciente, que su coito con un espíritu alado. ¡Qué perversión han admitido durante siglos! Y después de todo, ¡qué dulce perversión! La madre del Señor sigue siendo pura para mí, pero pura por su dolor y por amamantar a un hombre bueno. No creo que la fricción de las carnes sea más impura que la eyaculación de una paloma enviada por Dios. No creo en la pureza...* (Canetti 1997: 29)

Once more the protagonist subverts Christian dogma; in this case she questions the virginity of the Virgin Mary. She establishes her own notion of purity from a female perspective. Against the demand of the Scriptures – 'no mentirás' – she denounces what we find in the Bible as lies, and considers those alleged lies a perversion which ultimately relies on patriarchal discourse. As Fuentes explains, this sort of confession 'reveals the way in which individuals continually reconstruct their beliefs, therefore hinting in yet another way at identity "in-process"' (2002: 219). Against the alleged lie, the protagonist stresses the erotic nature of her relationship with the Father, at times hesitating between simultaneous exclamation and question marks:

> *Dios mío, ahora veo su boca. Es divina. Con razón este hombre intercede entre el cielo y yo. ¡¿Cómo no advertirla antes?! ¡¿Cómo pudieron sus ojos abismales ocultarme la línea tenue de su boca?! Tal vez no sea un cura. Tal vez sea un impostor como su madre. Tal vez sea un ángel. [...] Son labios tan rojos como los que sólo existen en los cuentos de hadas. Son labios finos y pulposos como una rodaja de sandía. Son una herida abierta y leve en pleno rostro. [...] Su cuello es otra de sus espadas. [...] un cuello así no podría hacerlo Dios dos veces. Es un cuello de seda mojada, de rocío, de temblor cabizbajo. Tendré que hacer un esfuerzo para olvidar que esos ojos, esa boca y ese cuello están refugiados en el confesionario, dispuestos otra vez a ser golpeados por mi culpa y mi descrédito.*

No sé cuál es el camino de la mentira, no sé cuál es, pero sí sé que el
cuello del Padre es una verdad rotunda y convincente. No ha nacido aún una
mentira para desmentir el cuello del Padre. Ni una sola mentira...
  La hermosura del Padre no es una verdad relativa. Es una verdad
absoluta. (Canetti 1997: 31)

The narrator describes the priest's body with a poetic language full of eroticism.
We witness the eroticization of discourse while the narrator begins to describe
the priest's body. The priest's beauty is her only truth. She thus transforms the
essence and nature of religious confession and the role of the priest.

The State
The setting of *Al otro lado* is not unknown. Although the protagonist does not
mention the place where she was born explicitly, the narrator gives us enough
hints to be able to identify her island with Cuba. Although in this novel we find
a denunciation of the hegemonic official discourse of the Cuban state, that is,
revolutionary discourse, Canetti tries to go beyond the anecdotal example and
to narrate the individual search from a universal perspective.

Vivo a finales de siglo en una isla bien poblada y condenada por algún
pecado en su otrora encarnación. Somos el pueblo elegido por Dios para
competir con el Infierno. Ni Dante pudo jamás imaginar la tan prolífera sarta
de diabluras que abundan en esta isla diminuta del Caribe. Dicen que es por
la lluvia torrencial y porque los huracanes nos adiestran en transgredir los
límites de lo posible. Yo pienso que es porque tenemos dentro ríos de sangre
tirando en todas direcciones. Somos una raza de muchas razas. Y por una
de las calles de la isla, ando yo buscándome por aquí y por allá. Yo ¿dónde
estás, eh? ¿Dónde te has metido? Anda, sal, que llevo rato buscándote y
no te encuentro. Que ya estás muy grandecita para estos juegos. Sal de tu
escondite, y dime quién eres. (Canetti 1997: 10)

Like most of the authors studied here, Canetti repeats the idea of Cuban culture
as an *ajiaco* of cultures and races. Both Canetti and Chaviano compare Cuba
with Dante's inferno and stress the capacity of Cuban people to 'transgredir los
límites de lo posible'. The three female authors studied in this work (Chaviano,
Canetti and Valdés) perpetuate the stereotypes of Cuban essence as erotic. It is
through eroticism and sexuality that transgression takes place.
  The state's discourse appears in this novel as what Bakhtin denominates
authoritative discourse, that 'privileged language' which 'permits no play
with its framing context' and that has power only while in power (Bakhtin
1981: 424), as discussed in chapter 1 in relation to Arenas's *El color del*
verano. The monologic characters that represent power, such as Torquemada,
uphold their power through a discourse in which they assure us that they
produce and hold the truth.

We find the protagonist in prison, where she loses her voice: 'Noches enteras estuve gritando y gritando y gritando y gritando hasta que perdí la voz' (Canetti 1997: 83). In front of an 'hombre de cara verde' (1997: 76), the man who comes to her house to take her to prison – Julio César, el Capitán Aquino or el Capitán Torquemada; all related to her stay in prison and representatives of the voice of the state – the protagonist wears the mask of Juana de Arco. These names function as symbolic masks that establish clear parallels between the historical characters and the literary ones created by Canetti in this novel.

I agree with Fuentes when she writes 'Canetti returns to a figure tied to both religious and political history [...] [and] fictionalizes the life of controversial historical figures as a way of commenting on the particular social and political situation the main protagonist faces within society' (2002: 241). And when the inquisitor Torquemada questions the martyr Juana de Arco, there is no dialogism:

> Y ese jovencito promiscuo, ladrón, timador, estrafalario, delincuente, enfermo mental, mentiroso, grosero, infeliz, hijo de mala madre, adúltero, jodido ideológicamente, perverso y corrupto es tu novio. ¿Vamos bien? [...] No, Capitán – me atreví a decir otra vez –, el que usted dice no es mi novio. Mi novio se llama Calígula y siempre me espera en las escaleras, y cuando me abraza hay eclipses de astros y todas las estrellas se me enredan en el pelo y... (Canetti 1997: 85)

In this quotation there is an opposition between the two versions of reality that confront the subject and the state. The protagonist rejects the labels associated with Calígula and emphasizes her own masks. The protagonist's confessions reveal that the questions that represent the state's discourse are absurd:

> Bueno, voy a ayudarte para que veas que no soy tan malo. ¿Qué piensas de los homosexuales? [...]
> – ¿De qué? – no comprendía qué era lo que quería saber el Capitán sobre los hombres a los que les gustaba su mismo sexo.
> – Por lo visto estás muy de acuerdo con la mariconería y la corrupción – concluyó –. ¿Te parece bien que un hombre, lo que se dice un hombre, esté pensando en falos en vez de estar ayudando a la patria, haciendo deportes o cortando caña?
> Yo no sabía qué tenían que ver los falos con la patria, con los deportes o con la caña, ni por qué el Capitán mezclaba aquellas cosas como si todas estuvieran atadas por un denominador común y procesadas en el mismo central azucarero.
> – Depende – dije.
> – ¿De qué? ¿De qué? Continúa, continúa – su cara se iluminó como la de un detective que ya casi está descubriendo a los autores del crimen y su caso va a salir en todos los periódicos [...].
> – Del hombre – dije, y al ver la mueca oblicua en la faz recta del Capitán Torquemada, intenté explicarme mejor –. Si un hombre quiere pensar en

falos, pues que piense en falos y si quiere hacer deportes, que los haga, y si decide ayudar a la patria, pues que la ayude.

- ¿La anarquía, no?
- La libertad.
- Lo supuse desde el principio – sentenció –. Tú eres una de ellos. [...]
- ¿Quién iba a suponer? – se decía el Capitán –. Que una joven de padres tan correctos iba a tener pensamientos tan sucios. Pero, claro, ¿qué se iba a esperar si andaba con ese Calígula? En fin, no veo posibilidad de sanar el problema. Cuando la corrupción entra en la cabeza es como el cáncer, ya no hay quien lo detenga ni quien lo cure. Tendremos que extirparlo a como dé lugar – se decía –. Tendremos que sacrificarte en la hoguera – me pareció que decía. [...]
- Tú eres una espía, una maldita espía del imperialismo que se hace pasar por mosquita muerta, pero yo te voy a desenmascarar o me dejo de llamar Tomás – y así diciendo, se marchó. (Canetti 1997: 85–7)

The protagonist's discourse does not coincide with the state's and echoes the scene of an interview with writer Ana María Simo in the 1984 documentary *Mauvaise conduite* (*Conducta impropia*), directed by Néstor Almendros and Orlando Jímenez Leal. The state's discourse is used by Canetti with irony, and through several references within the narrative to 'la patria', to homosexuals and to the cutting of sugar cane and imperialism, the reader discovers the historic and extra-literary referent to which the novel refers: Cuba. The references to homosexuals and the cutting of sugar cane in particular echo the witch-hunts in revolutionary Cuba against homosexuals, first sent to the UMAP in the mid-1960s, as discussed in chapter 1. According to the position of the state, those 'desviaciones' such as homosexuality had to be eliminated from revolutionary society; thus the narrative enters the debate on sexuality which took place in Cuba and which reached its climax for an international audience through the 1993 film *Fresa y chocolate*.[3] The fact that Torquemada accuses Juana de Arco of being 'espía del imperialismo' also recalls the official discourse of the Cuban government[4] and places it in the context of the Spanish Inquisition, as Torquemada emphasizes his first name as Tomás. The name alludes to the historical first Inquisitor General of Spain, Tomás de Torquemada (1420–98), confessor to Queen Isabella. In the novel, this accusation, which appears nonsensical, helps to ridicule Torquemada and all allegorical Torquemadas throughout history. This caricature of the Grand Inquisitor Torquemada is related to the upside-down world of the prison. None of the characters who inhabit the prison can escape this carnivalization, not even the protagonist. The last sentence pronounced

---

[3]   On the topic of homosexuality in Cuba in the first two decades of the revolution, see Young 1981.

[4]   For the typical labelling of dissidents as CIA agents or 'agentes del imperialismo', see Arrabal 1983.

by Torquemada in the citation above has special connotations when we are aware of the multiple masks that the protagonist uses. I agree with Fuentes when she states: 'Torquemada's words "claim to speak the truth" [...] and by doing so warn that sexual deviances are a *treta* to the individual and society' (2002: 243). The novel highlights how the state establishes what is appropriate sexual behaviour to display in society and attempts to control individual desires. After thirty-three days in prison the protagonist returns home, but this time she seems to be suffering the effects of trauma at the hands of power; she cannot remember what she has just experienced (Canetti 1997: 87) and loses her capacity to talk. This means that back at home monologism is reinstated. Language fails as an instrument of communication:

> Un día su curiosidad pudo más que su prometida misión de no hacerme recordar los terribles momentos:
> – ¿Es cierto que tú estuviste en orgías? ¿De qué corrupción hablaba el Capitán Torquemada?
> No pude responder enseguida, Padre, no sabía nada de nada. Traté de recordar. ¿Habría estado en orgías? ¿A qué orgías se refería mi padre? Calígula y yo habíamos hecho el amor muchas veces y con mucha gente a la vez, sí, pero sólo los días de luna en cuarto menguante. Esos días hacíamos el amor con mucha gente y con muchas cosas a la vez: algunos fantasmas, ánimas en pena, muebles, estatuas de porcelana, diosas del Olimpo que danzaban en los bajorrelieves de madera y sádicos centauros que cabalgaban en los dibujos de mi sobrecama. Fuera de ellos, con nadie más.
> – No, no estuve en orgías y no sé de qué corrupción me hablas – le respondí a mi padre tras avivar mi memoria, pero desde entonces tuve la sensación de decepcionarlo con mi respuesta. Y lamenté no haber estado en las orgías en las que él creía que yo había estado.
> – Está bien – me dijo con aire resignado y compasivo –. Si no quieres contarme, no me cuentes.
> Meses después fui recobrando las imágenes que había dejado sepultadas bajo el cemento gélido de la celda. (Canetti 1997: 87–8)

She begins to recall the sexual abuses she suffered in prison at the hands of the prison doctor. On the day of the trial of the protagonist words seem unable to challenge the discourse of power; it is then that the female body becomes the site of resistance. The Oráculo, the lawyer who represents her case, is an allusion to Ancient Greece, although in this case he is not able to foretell the future and is instead a representative of the power of the state. Thus silence is a form of resistance:

> Padre, antes de que me pusieran las esposas y me amordazaran, ya yo sabía que debía vivir ciega, sorda y muda. El oráculo me advirtió de todo y hasta me dio muy buenos consejos. El oráculo era un hombre que ejercía leyes desde que era mozuelo y era tan ducho en materia de balanzas y legislaciones,

que me puse en sus manos sin rechistar. Pero ocurrió que las brujas de mi conciencia luchaban por zafarse y decir toda la verdad. (Canetti 1997: 94)

But once again feminine discourse, tormented by the demons of her conscience that are trying to make a public appearance, clashes with the official patriarchal discourse of the state:

Finalmente, el oráculo me explicó con cifras, estadísticas y acápites la ventaja de decir la verdad, es decir, de decir algo que convenciera a los demás de que era la verdad, porque la verdad verdadera no sería en estos casos muy convincente y daría lugar a malos entendidos. [...] Me aseguró que todo sería bien fácil porque sólo debía limitarme a decir la verdad y demostrar mi inocencia. [...] que llorara en los momentos culminantes, que me vistiera de blanco y con falda desahogada para que no mostrara mis protuberancias y contornos porque contrastaban mucho con mi inocencia, que negara rotundamente mi amor hacia el otro implicado, Calígula, y que si todo salía bien, como estaba seguro que saldría, volvería a ser la misma de antes y aprendería a no cometer los mismos errores.

Eso último no lo comprendí en aquel momento, Padre. Y tampoco lo comprendo ahora, ¿sabe?, yo nunca he sido ya la misma y he cometido los mismos errores que no había cometido antes. (Canetti 1997: 95–6)

Here the protagonist establishes a division between 'verdad' and 'verdad verdadera'. Confession is part of a 'verdad' which is not necessarily the real truth; it is presented as a subject construct. The protagonist, with the references to Torquemada and Caligula, seems to take the place of Milonia Caesonia, Caligula's last wife, who offered her neck as well after her husband was killed by assassins while attending a private theatrical function. The protagonist inserts herself into the debate that brings into question transhistorical subjectivity as posed by Foucault in 'How Much Does It Cost for Reason to Tell the Truth?' (1989). Just as Foucault questions 'Can a transhistorical subject [...] be accounted for by a history of reason?' (1989: 238), the protagonist has come to question whether truth can be accounted for in her 'confession'. As Butler has observed in Foucault's argument, this implicitly questions whether 'the transhistorical subject accounts for all experience and knowledge, that it is the ground of knowing' (Butler 2005: 115). If Butler argues that, in Foucault's case, 'asking what accounts for this "ground" [...] implicitly argues that this ground is no ground' and 'comes to appear as a ground only after a certain historical process has taken place' (Butler 2005: 115), in the novel we find the ground of the Oráculo's discourse is based on numbers and statistics that uphold the patriarchal discourse of the state as the only truth, and only confessions that conform with it can be accepted as 'truth'. In this sense, the ground that Canetti is exploring is a feminine one that, extrapolating the words of Hélène Cixous, 'bear[s] the mark of our time – a time when the new breaks away from the old, and, more precisely, the (feminine) new from the old' (Cixous 1980: 245). As Cixous continues: 'Thus, as there are no grounds for establishing a discourse, but rather an arid millennial ground to break, what I say has at least two sides and two aims: to break up, to destroy, and to foresee the unforeseeable, to project' (1980: 245). Canetti's text seems congruent with this feminist project. As a character who represents power, the Oráculo attempts to impose his own view of reality. He prevents the protagonist from using her own words to defend her own truth. He also tries to erase her feminine appearance which, according to the Oráculo, confirms that she is guilty. The Oráculo's idea of femininity is a patriarchal and monologic concept that does not coincide with the subjectivity that the protagonist reflects in her confession. According to the Oráculo, if she wants to avoid a prison sentence she must negate her love for Calígula, her real love. The protagonist stresses the significance of her relationship with the depraved Calígula. Yet the experience transforms her. The second time she is released from prison, she is a different person. In terms of her trial:

> El juicio fue a puertas cerradas porque, según el magistrado, el asunto era altamente bochornoso e indecente, y los casos de corrupción no deben corromper a los demás, que no tienen la culpa de que haya gente en este mundo tan perversa como yo. Sí, Padre, se me acusaba de cosas que yo no sabía ni imaginar en aquel momento: complicidad, encubrimiento, corrupción, espionaje, y todo ello con premeditación y alevosía, morbo y crueldad, mala intención, sagacidad y astucia. (Canetti 1997: 96)

In Freudian terms, the state is attempting to prevent the spread of the disease ('el contagio') and thus must eliminate that which could lead to an infringement of social taboos (Freud 1970: 48) – in this case the protagonist herself, representative of the 'diversionismo ideológico' of the time. Moreover, the Oráculo states: 'pareces muy cuerda y aunque tu cara de niña te favorece, tu cuerpo y tu pretensión de quererlo saber todo son un atentado a tu inocencia' (Canetti 1997: 96). The female body is criminalized from a patriarchal point of view. The female protagonist will be punished for her desire to know, as well as for her body.

The scene on the day she has to go in front of the judge is described as a theatre (echoing the place where Caligula was killed), where the protagonist must know the script in order to survive. The protagonist confesses: 'Me porté bien pero no pude llorar al final de ninguno de los actos. El auditorio era insuficiente y, por otra parte, no me sabía muy bien el libreto, pese a que el oráculo me insistió que lo ensayara' (Canetti 1997: 97). A woman's crying is meant to manipulate the judge, but she fails to perform; she has her own script. She realizes that 'la verdad los decepcionaría mucho a pesar de ser limpia como el agua de un arroyuelo; lo que decía aquel papel resultaba más interesante, más condenable, y los hacía sentir verdaderos apóstoles del bien (1997: 99). To preserve the morality of the state and, in doing so, undermine it, she decides to go on with the farce and to sign the official statement; but before doing so she asserts: 'Lo que yo decía era lo de menos. Lo que decía el papel parecía verdad. En vano me empeñé en explicar que yo jamás haría algo así [...] tan morboso con tal lujo de detalles [...] Mientras más explicaba, más incredulidad sembraba en los presentes' (1997: 99). The roles of the confessor and judge in this novel seem to demand a morbid story and the protagonist learns her lesson:

> Mi madre sabía que la balanza no siempre se inclina del lado frágil sino del que tiene mayor peso, y mi padre creía que mi madre deliraba, porque la justicia era ciega... mucho más la justicia revolucionaria. Ésa no ve ni lo que está delante de sus ojos.
>   Yo, Padre, sé que la justicia no es sólo ciega, también es sordomuda y mutilada por el exceso de papeles y contiendas. (Canetti 1997: 97)

Here the protagonist mocks the discourse of the state. She includes a clear reference to revolutionary justice. The narrator makes a pun on the saying 'love is blind' and the well-established representation of justice in the form of Justitia, the blindfolded statue holding a scale. She, instead, asserts that justice is actually blind and that her blindfold, instead of representing fairness and moral justice, means that she cannot see the truth. Once the protagonist momentarily gets free, 'Todos salieron hacia la luz. Menos yo. Yo salí hacia las tinieblas, al mundo de la irrealidad que aún no había conocido. Al mundo de lo predecible pero que tenía que tomar como impredecible' (1997: 100). She highlights the huge gap between her subjectivity and society, and the blurred boundaries between reality and unreality.

The title of the twelfth chapter, 'Cárcel', makes reference to the protagonist's new stay in prison. This chapter is placed in the middle of a novel of twenty-five chapters and becomes the axis upon which the narrative revolves. This chapter will inform the rest of the narrative, as it moulds the scripting of the female subject. Before she goes to prison her parents take her to see the General. In her confession and explanation of the facts we find the constant contradictions that characterize the protagonist's speech acts:

> Volví a contar, Padre, la historia que tantas veces había contado ya y que casi me sabía de memoria. Pero entre la historia original y la reciente, habían pasado cuatro años y en cuatro años hay muchos detalles que se van agregando y otros muchos que se van olvidando. Así que no supe si lo que yo contaba era la reproducción de la *Odisea* o de un cuento de hadas. Posiblemente, incluso, maticé la historia para que el General creyera en mi inocencia, lo cual me hacía – ante mí misma – menos inocente que cuando ocurrieron los hechos. Mientras iba hablando, el General me miraba y de vez en cuando – y de una manera involuntaria, supongo – miraba el retrato de su joven esposa. (Canetti 1997: 110)

This narrative becomes a palimpsest as she rewrites herself as the protagonist of *The Odyssey* or of a fairy tale. Writing the female body entails this body becoming a palimpsest. The words recreate the female body through a discourse full of contradictions, silences, irony and intertextuality. Once the protagonist comes back to prison, she recounts:

> Padre, en ese momento, justo en ese momento, me pareció que la Tierra giraba al revés. Todo se puso patas arriba. [...] Apenas se hubo alejado mi padre, la mujer gruesa se paró de cabeza y se puso a caminar con las dos manos. [...] Pero, por primera vez, comencé a saber algo de algo, después de aquel inmenso vacío que me producía el no saber nada de nada y presentirlo todo. El mundo me mostró su cara oscura y las nubes se atrincheraron aún más de lo que estaban. Y yo empecé a ver en la oscuridad y a descubrir la forma de los objetos con sus dimensiones reales. Había entrado a la cárcel y había comenzado mi peregrinación por 'la vida al revés', que así me encapriché en llamarla en ese momento de naciente lucidez. (Canetti 1997: 111)

The prison becomes an upside-down world, a carnivalized world in which the workers walk with their hands and hurt each other in order to generate pleasure. This carnival is Bakhtinian in the sense that there is a momentary break in the power relationships established outside the chronotope of the prison. The absurd and surrealist scenes emphasize the absurdity of what the protagonist experiences in the social order, which is palimpsestuously inscribed in all the histories of atrocities and corruption of power. Although the power of institutions outside the prison is not challenged by this carnival, this chronotope allows the existence of a matriarchy in which woman and, particularly, the protagonist, exerts her power and is crowned. Within the prison system the female body acquires visibility and power. She feels as if she is in Dante's inferno, where she meets 'las hijas legítimas de Nerón ... en coincidencia y sin ponerse de acuerdo, habían quemado a sus maridos, vivos' (Canetti 1997: 114). The matriarchy established in a female prison community paradoxically eliminates the figure of man, the phallocentric order that put them there in the first place and keeps them incarcerated. Instead, prison creates a space for women.

> A mi paso se interpuso Vesta, una muchacha de perfil romano y cabellos de querube: 'Yo soy la jefa de la celda y te voy a besar en la frente', y me besó en la frente. Luego se aproximó una mujer morena de ojos almibarados: 'Yo soy Judit y te voy a besar en la mejilla', y me besó en la mejilla. 'Y yo soy Clitemnestra y te voy a besar una oreja'. Y la mujer de labios canela llamada Clitemnestra me besó una oreja. Después se abrió paso una grácil muchacha de ojos olivos, que sostenía en un brazo sus cabellos negros para que no arrastrasen por el piso: 'Yo soy Eva y te voy

a besar el corazón', y me besó el lado izquierdo del pecho.

Se presentaron luego otras jóvenes, igualmente envueltas en un halo de gracia y crueldad. Una a una me fueron besando cada trozo de piel como si se tratara de una iniciación sagrada o de un bautismo secreto. Salomé y Deyanira parecían ser las últimas de la fila.

Cuando creí que el ritual iba a terminar, Padre, apareció una anciana voluminosa, negra y con voz de gruta que al verme, rompió la paz del recinto con un grito volcánico: 'Ay, Dios mío, arrodíllense que Ella ha venido'. Todas se arrodillaron al mismo tiempo, luego besaron el suelo, y luego me pidieron perdón por sus pecados. Yo no entendía. Pensé que era parte de la liturgia para llevarme a la pira de fuego. Pero no era así, Padre. Ellas no pretendían quemarme viva ni arrojarme a la piedra del sacrificio. Ellas creían firmemente que yo había venido a salvarlas y que era la Virgen de la Caridad del Cobre. (Canetti 1997: 116)

Canetti mixes here Roman and Greek mythology with the Catholic Cuban version of the Virgin Mary: la Virgen de la Caridad del Cobre. In this inter-textual contextualization,[5] it is worth remembering that Vesta is the virgin goddess of the home and family in Roman mythology. Judith (which means Jewish woman) is the biblical heroine who decapitated the Assyrian general Holofernes (Jdt. 13: 1–10). In Greek mythology, Clytemnestra is Helen of Troy's sister, who married Agamemnon who had murdered her first husband. Clytemnestra and her lover (Agamemnon's cousin) kill Agamemnon to prevent him from finding out about her infidelities. Her youngest son, Orestes, kills her in revenge for his father's murder. Deianira is a mythological figure who commits suicide after attempting to kill her husband Heracles. Eve seduces Adam and convinces him to try the apple, thus making him break the Edenic covenant. Salome is the Idumean princess responsible for the death of John the Baptist. All these masks make reference to female characters who in one way or another represent the subversion of the patriarchal system. These figures crown the protagonist, in a sacred and carnivalesque ritual, as the Virgen de la Caridad, the patron saint of Cuba, and although the protagonist attempts to 'persuadirlas de que estaban equiv-ocadas' (1997: 117) 'era la única forma de no morir acuchillada o quemada. De cualquier forma, si les decía la verdad no me hubieran creído. Ellas necesitaban que yo fuera la Virgen de la Caridad y... y yo también necesi-taba serlo para salir de allí con un poco de vida' (1997: 117). She confesses that 'Me dejé coronar y asumí el trono', thus becoming the new carnival queen who exerts her power within her kingdom through the ability to use the word:

---

5   I rely here on the *Diccionario de mitología clásica* by Constantino Falcón Martínez et al. (1980).

Corrió la voz por toda la prisión. Se me acercaban no sólo las asesinas, sino también las ladronas, las homicidas, las pervertidas sexuales, las malversadoras, las cómplices, las conspiradoras, las prostitutas, las malasmadres, las hijasde..., en fin, las marginadas del Paraíso y las violadas por Lucifer. Todas acudían con la mirada mansa y las carnes rotas. Escuchaban con atención cuanto les decía. Les leía cuentos, les recitaba versos, les cantaba canciones y ellas se quedaban embelesadas, sumergidas en un sueño. (Canetti 1997: 117–18)

As a Cuban Scheherazade her discourse occupies the centre of the microcosm of the prison. In prison:

Habían pasado sólo cinco días que a mí me parecieron cinco siglos, cuando me tuvieron que llevar a la enfermería a causa de un desmayo repentino que tuve y que se produjo después de ver a Eva ahorcada con sus cabellos y haber leído sobre sus senos el nombre del marido masacrado por ella, seguido de un mensaje que no entendí: 'Devuélveme mi costilla'. (Canetti 1997: 120)

This last statement reveals the feminine demand and search for her own subjectivity, independent of men and of the religious tradition that makes her an appendix, a rib of man. Women reject their subordination to the father-figure that prevails outside prison. When the protagonist leaves prison, representing a baptism of sorts, she returns to a different reality, transformed by the experiences at the core of her subjectivity:

El mundo comenzó a girar con su ritmo habitual. [...] La tierra giraba con su ritmo habitual. [...] Yo no supe nunca si mi delito fue amar o fue no saber nada de nada. Yo no supe por qué me encarcelaron, primero bajo la tierra y luego en 'un mundo al revés'. Yo no supe nunca por qué tanta rabia se confabuló en mi contra. Yo no supe qué delito pudo ser tan grande para ser esclavizada a tal pesadilla. Yo quería que mi madre tuviera razón cuando me dijo que yo olvidaría pronto la amarga experiencia. Pero algo falló, porque no lo he olvidado. Ya no puedo decir, sin sentir que miento, que no sé nada de nada. Ahora sé.
    Lo que yo leí en los rostros de las reclusas, Padre, no lo he leído en ningún libro. Y lo que allí aprendí, no lo hubiera aprendido aunque me hubiera leído todos los libros del mundo y hubiera vivido mil años. Es una lección que no se puede transmitir porque se queda sembrada dentro y no sabe uno cómo sacarla. Pero está aquí, Padre, aquí dentro de mí, y ya no va a salir nunca de ahí, se me clavó como una espina negra. Y mientras más trato de desenterrarla, se clava más, se hunde más, y me crece más. Voy a morir con esa espina llena de raíces dentro de mi cuerpo. ¿Voy a morir, dije? No, Padre, los muertos no pueden morir. (Canetti 1997: 122)

In the chapter entitled 'La resurrección de Leda' Canetti continues her intertextual game with her referent from Greek mythology. According to the
Diccionario de la mitología clásica,

> Fue Leda madre de cuatro importantes personajes: Clitemnestra, Helena,
> Cástor y Pólux. La leyenda atribuye a Zeus la paternidad de alguno de
> ellos. Según unos, Zeus, enamorado de la extraordinaria belleza de Leda,
> la habría conseguido, tomando la forma de cisne. De esta unión habrían
> nacido dos huevos: de uno habrían salido Helena y Clitemnestra, y del otro
> Cástor y Pólux, los llamados Dioscuros. Helena y Pólux serían hijos de
> Zeus, mientras Cástor y Clitemnestra lo serían de Tindáreo, que también
> esa misma noche se había unido a Leda. (Falcón Martínez 1980: 383)

This myth is in a paratextual relation with the image on the cover of the
novel – Leonardo da Vinci's painting of Leda. This is the painting Freud
(2005) used to demonstrate da Vinci's homosexuality. In this chapter the
protagonist arrives in church, which appears to have been destroyed by fire.
As the title indicates, the main subject of the chapter is resurrection. The
church becomes an allegory of the protagonist: there is a comparison between
Christ's resurrection and the protagonist's, between the church and Leda.
They are all symbolized by the figure of the Fénix. All these figures have
suffered abuse from those who have power.

> Fue aquel día de abril, frente al jarrón de porcelana griega, que renuncié
> a mi vida de muerta. Abrí puertas y ventanas, dejé que entrara toda la luz
> del cosmos, que los rayos invadieran toda la casa y se metieran por todas
> partes sin pedirme permiso. Y uno de ellos me atravesó de lado a lado y
> me dijo: 'estás viva, Leda, estás viva y lista para engendrar más vida aún'.
> Me miré al espejo durante veinticinco horas seguidas y descubrí muchas
> mujeres del otro lado. Unas hermosas y otras más hermosas. Unas desnudas
> y otras más desnudas. Unas suspirantes, otras sofocadas; unas enfurecidas,
> otras doblegadas; unas poderosas, otras amedrentadas. Unas seductoras y
> otras seducidas. Y todas con cara de hembra en celo, dispuestas a llenarse
> el vientre de placeres. Nunca me asusté, Padre, de las imágenes que
> caprichosamente me devolvía el espejo. Todas me gustaban, todas, todas.
> Perdone, usted, esta confesión. Es inevitable para mí querer estar viva con
> tanta insistencia. Y, aunque mi sino me muestre lo contrario, yo no creo
> estar nacida para un sufrido peregrinaje. Algo hay en el fondo de mi sangre
> que clama siempre por ser resucitado. Quizás no sea yo, sino lo que hay al
> otro lado de mí. ¿Será mucho pecado querer vivir? (Canetti 1997: 134)

There is a reference here to the act of creation that the narrator identifies as
a female characteristic. Confession/writing and maternity are interconnected
in the novel. It is her erotic desire that makes her want to live. The narrator
is aware of her polyphony and assumes her masks.

The Process of Self-Knowledge: Masks, Performativity and Intertextuality

In *Al otro lado* we find a polyphonic novel that is also a 'novela de concienciación', a novel in which we witness the formation of a female adult. In this study I understand the concept of 'novela de concienciación' as Ciplijauskaité does. She explains in her book *La novela femenina contemporánea (1970–1985): Hacia una tipología de la narración en primera persona*:

> En el siglo XX es muy frecuente la pregunta '¿quién soy?', '¿cuál es mi papel en el mundo?'. Se podría considerarla como el punto de partida de la novela de concienciación, que se desarrolla como una especie de *Bildungsroman*, pero usando técnicas más innovadoras. Desplaza el énfasis del devenir social, activo al cuestionamiento interior. Para saber quién soy debo saber quién he sido y cómo he llegado al estado actual. De aquí la abundancia de novelas que reevalúan el pasado desde el presente, es decir, desde una conciencia ya despierta. Esto no es un fenómeno nuevo: lo hacía ya el héroe-narrador picaresco, pero con el propósito de justificar sus actos; la mujer contemporánea sigue preguntándose por su propia esencia, buscando su identidad, se acentúa el proceso abierto. (1988: 34)

As Bakhtin claims, 'To be means to communicate dialogically' (1984: 252). Only through dialogism among her different selves and with the Other can the protagonist exist. Dialogism can only be established in this novel through the erotic encounter in which the lovers use different masks attributed by the protagonist. The fact that the protagonist is the one to recreate herself and the one who assigns masks to the Other(s) implies her agency. She is the producer of meaning and therefore she can transform her reality.

Canetti uses masks throughout the narrative; thus the text becomes full of historical, literary and mythological references and the masks themselves are turned into pure signifiers without a stable signified. Hence, the text is in a constant process of transformation and becoming, as is its protagonist. In *Al otro lado* we find different levels of readings, and hence this novel is a text in the way Barthes understands it: 'The logic regulating the Text is not comprehensive [...] but metonymic; the activity of associations, contiguities, carryings-over coincides with a liberation of symbolic energy' (1977: 158–9). In this novel the text becomes 'off-centred, without closure' (Barthes 1977: 159).

The erotic game can only take place by means of the masks, through which dialogism between the bodies is possible. The masks highlight the performativity implied in every erotic act: reality, theatre and ritual are concepts whose boundaries are constantly challenged within this novel and reflect the fact that gender itself 'is performatively constituted by the very "expressions" that are said to be its results' (Butler 1999b: 33). As Fuentes writes, 'Rather than essentialize identity, Cuban women argue its constructedness' (2002: 2–3), and this 'leads to an undoing of fixed notions of nation and national identity' (2002: 217). *Al otro lado* undermines the notion of confession itself as well as notions of reality and truth: 'each telling/retelling through the confession undermines previous tellings, previous "truths"' (Fuentes 2002: 216).

The deployment of masks opens up the dialogism of the novel by means of a continuous intertextual game. The nameless protagonist acquires multiple masks/names depending on her specific situation. Thus, she becomes a polyphonic character and the intertextuality recreated through her body is her strategy to subvert patriarchy. I agree with Lucía Guerra when she states:

> De manera similar, en el texto producido por la mujer se observa una diglosia fundamental en la cual la escritura adopta y se asimila a un espacio intertextual de carácter masculino y dominante estratégicamente ubicando elementos de una visión de mundo subordinada a través de márgenes, vacíos, silencios, inversiones y mímicas con valor subversivo. (1990: 77)

And as Debra Castillo rightly points out:

> The revolutionary response to silencing is resemanticization: to use silence as a weapon (to resort to silence) or to break silence with hypocrisy. One scenario for a response of the repressed to the represser may take form in the strong woman whose mode of resistance consists in playing with the cherished myths of the dominant society and secretly reversing their charge. (1992: 38)

In addition, Toril Moi explains in relation to Sandra Gilbert and Susan Gubar's book *The Madwoman in the Attic*:

> The female textual strategy, as they [Gilbert and Gubar] see it, consists in 'assaulting and revising, deconstructing and reconstructing those images of women inherited from male literature, especially... the paradigmatic polarities of angel and monster'. (1985: 60)

Thus, the construction of a feminine identity is produced by discourse and through endlessly playing roles by means of masks. The concept of identity itself is constantly questioned and appears as a social construct in the novel. The protagonist appears in a process of constant becoming, 'unfinalized' as a proper dialogic character. As discussed previously in this chapter, her confession is full of silences and contradictions that she resignifies throughout her erotic encounters, 'concealing a coded speech between the lines of the said and the unsaid' (Castillo 1992: 41).

Through the use of irony and humour the protagonist shows that the very concepts of masculinity and femininity are social constructs that have no real essence in the world. In this novel, the endless game that the protagonist develops with masks during her sexual relationships serves to create a palimpsest-like character; this interaction and dialogue among the different masks acquired in erotic intercourse erases, re-establishes and challenges notions of masculinity and femininity. According to Fuentes:

> [T]he humor within the novel serves to free the narrator-protagonist from certain societal restraints; on the other hand, humor clears reader(s) from particular expectations or ideas regarding acceptable individual behavior as well as particular modes of narration. [...] [and] serves to expose particular contradictions within society and as a means of escape, via laughter, from that society. [...] humor, within the confession, becomes an option for the narrator-protagonist, a personal recourse that allows her to talk back to a restrictive society. [...] the same humor, no doubt as a means of undermining those in a position of power. (2002: 220)

The protagonist deconstructs through her discourse monolithic stereotypes of femininity as established by patriarchal discourse. As Moi explains in relation to *The Madwoman in the Attic* (Gilbert and Gubar 1979):

> behind the angel lurks the monster: the obverse of the male idealization of women is the male fear of femininity. The monster woman is the woman who refuses to be selfless, acts on her own initiative, who *has* a story to tell – in short, a woman who rejects the submissive role patriarchy has reserved for her. [...] The monster woman for Gilbert and Gubar is *duplicitous*, precisely because she has something to tell: there is always the possibility that she may choose *not* to tell – or to tell a different story. The duplicitous woman is the one whose consciousness is opaque to man, whose mind will not let itself be penetrated by the phallic probings of masculine thought. (1985: 58)

In this novel feminine identity and feminine writing are based on the endless enactment of desire that becomes part of the narrative we are reading through the duplicitous confessions of the protagonist. The eroticism established between the protagonist and her lovers blurs hierarchies and power relations. And through the narrative Canetti makes it evident that the woman who challenges these power relations is seen by patriarchy as part of a monstrous femininity because patriarchy denies women's autonomy. In this novel the protagonist places emphasis on the illusory status of identity.

I posit that the protagonist of this novel, through the use of masks, the writing of herself through the erotic experience and intertextuality, develops what Cixous has denominated écriture feminine, as in her confession/writing of herself she 'inscribes femininity'. Although it is not my intention to present an exhaustive account of feminine writing, as my main focus in this study is dialogism, I shall emphasize here some of those characteristics that Cixous identifies with feminine writing and that I find used by the protagonist in her discourse to recreate herself. In 'The Laugh of the Medusa' Cixous says:

> I shall speak about women's writing: *about what it will do*, Woman must write her self: must write about women and bring women to writing, from which they have been driven away as violently as from their bodies – for the same reason, by the same law, with the same fatal goal. Woman must put herself into the text – as into the world and into history – by her own movement. (1980: 245)

In *Al otro lado* the nameless protagonist places her body at the centre of her discourse. She is the subject of her confession/writing and her body is the site from which the narrative develops through the use of intertextuality. As I have shown in this chapter, the protagonist's confession clashes with official discourse. History becomes a text that the protagonist rewrites from her own perspective. History appears as a palimpsest when characters such as Torquemada, the historical Spanish inquisitor, reappear in the Cuba of the twentieth century. When the protagonist gives masks to other characters she starts a process of rewriting history. We can apply Cixous's words to this novel in relation to feminine writing. She claims that 'Her [woman's] speech, even when "theoretical" or political, is never simple or linear or "objectified", generalized: she draws her story into history' (Cixous 1980: 251). Cixous continues by exploring the characteristics of feminine writing, which we find in the heterogeneity that Canetti explores in this novel. Cixous argues:

> there is, at this time, no general woman, no one typical woman [...]. But what strikes me is the infinite richness of their individual constitutions: you can't talk about a female sexuality, uniform, homogeneous, classifiable into codes – any more than you can talk about one unconscious resembling another. Women's imaginary is inexhaustible, like music, painting, writing: their stream of phantasms is incredible. (1980: 245–6)

In *Al otro lado* the protagonist uses masks that create intertextuality. These masks form part of her discourse, of her confession/writing, and they highlight what Cixous mentions above, namely that feminine subjectivity is fluid, heterogeneous. Like Cixous, Canetti's protagonist rejects any attempt to label the feminine as something homogeneous and monolithic. Cixous continues her definition of feminine writing thus:

> By writing her self, woman will return to the body which has been more than confiscated from her, which has been turned into the uncanny stranger on display [...] Censor the body and you censor breath and speech at the same time. [...] your body must be heard. Only then will the immense resources of the unconscious spring forth. [...].

> To write. An act which will not only 'realize' the decensored relation
> of woman to her sexuality, to her womanly being, giving her access to her
> native strength; it will give her back her goods, her pleasures, her organs, her
> immense bodily territories which have been kept under seal; it will tear her
> away from the superegoized structure in which she has always occupied the
> place reserved for the guilty [...] tear her away by means of this research,
> this job of analysis and illumination, this emancipation of the marvellous text
> of her self that she must urgently learn to speak. A woman without a body,
> dumb, blind, can't possibly be a good fighter. She is reduced to being the
> servant of the militant male, his shadow. We must kill the false woman who
> is preventing the live one from breathing. Inscribe the breath of the whole
> woman. [...] To write and thus to forge for herself the anti-logos weapon. To
> become *at will* the taker and initiator, for her own right, in every symbolic
> system, in every political process. (1980: 250, her italics)

Once more, the protagonist of *Al otro lado* makes use of écriture féminine as Cixous
understands it. Throughout the novel we witness the constant repressions exerted
over the protagonist's body and language: on the one hand, the protagonist's desires
are censored when she wants to kiss and caress her neighbour or her cousin – to do
so she has to hide; on the other hand, her discourse is ignored and manipulated when
she goes to court or when she is in front of the policemen. Only when the protagonist starts her confession, her writing of herself, can she liberate herself from the
censorship suffered within patriarchal society. In the passage cited above, Cixous
stresses the importance of the unconscious and the possibility of opening it up through
the female body and through writing. In Canetti's novel the protagonist develops
her writing through the constant descriptions of her erotic encounters. Through the
confession of these erotic encounters the female body is heard, the sexual drives
that were kept hidden and repressed in the unconscious are released and the links
between feminine subjectivity, her body and her sexuality are re-established. The
'superegoized structure in which she has always occupied the place reserved for the
guilty' that Cixous mentions above appears reflected in the novel by means of the
protagonist's confession. However, through her confession of her erotic encounters
the protagonist subverts the religious discourse of the guilty sinner; she uses and
abuses this discourse to continuously challenge its validity through eroticism. The
protagonist of *Al otro lado* is, in Cixous's terms, a good fighter: her writing of her
body is her narrative technique to create a new logos, her own cosmogony against
phallocentrism. She is thus the producer of a discourse that, as Cixous states, subverts
the established symbolic order. And, as we have already examined above, in this
novel feminine discourse has its effect on 'every political process'. Cixous emphasizes further the importance of the maternal body:

> In women's speech, as in their writing, that element which never stops
> resonating, which, once we've been permeated by it, profoundly and
> imperceptibly touched by it, retains the power of moving us, that element

is the song: first music from the first voice of love which is alive in every woman. [...] a woman is never far from 'mother' (I mean outside the role functions: the 'mother' as nonname and as source of goods). There is always within her at least a little of that good mother's milk. She writes in white ink. (1980: 251)

In fact, in this novel, if we use Kristeva's terminology, we see how the protagonist goes from the Semiotic to the Symbolic, and how écriture féminine is part of the novel. Here the maternal body is a keynote and will affect the protagonist's life. The protagonist recalls her stay in the maternal womb:

> Pensé que era el mismísimo infierno, Padre. Todo era oscuro oscuro. Pero cuando sentí que estaba protegida por el vientre de mi madre, supe que el Paraíso era oscuro también.
> El vientre de mi madre era un lugar pequeño pero en aquel momento era un planeta provisto de todo lo necesario para vivir. Me sentía cómoda. Daba vueltas y estiraba los pies. ¡De maravilla! Un calorcito húmedo, un sentirme apretadita, así, bien abrigada y querida... Son sensaciones que han quedado en mí aunque no las recuerde. (Canetti 1997: 15)

The protagonist's language is, then, affected by this maternal experience. As Kristeva has claimed, maternal language also can affect the language of the individual. After she was born,

> Todo comenzó entonces. Yo no sabía lo que hacía, Padre. Sólo salí detrás del agua y porque mi madre me empujó con todas sus fuerzas. Pero yo no sabía lo que hacía. Fue un salto al que fui empujada por una fuerza más fuerte que yo. Y le digo que hasta intenté regresarme a mi lugar de agua y esfera, pero las aguas se arremolinaron y me arrastraron por un túnel de luz, un túnel que nunca antes crucé y que, sin embargo, me parecía transitado en sentido opuesto. (Canetti 1997: 17)

However, as soon as she is born she begins to feel the impositions she will suffer when she becomes an adult:

> Me envolvieron en telas blancas. Yo quise quedarme desnuda: me sentía comprimida entre tantos trapos... Pero ellos hicieron caso omiso a mi llanto y me envolvieron como un paquete de regalo. Y pusieron el paquete en los brazos de mi madre.
> La leche de mi madre estaba calentita y fresca [...] ¡Y para colmo siempre alguien me desprendía, incluso mi madre, en el momento más divertido! (Canetti 1997: 17)

She also recalls her mother's songs: 'Duérmete mi niña; duérmete mi amor [...] Arrurú, dormir dormir dormir dormir' (Canetti 1997: 17). She rejects 'el suicidio del durmiente' (1997: 17) and 'En un principio todo fue así, Padre' (1997: 18); thus the protagonist's Genesis becomes the genesis of the text. It is not surprising that 'Saberme viva fue el pecado original' (1997: 21) and the special link between her and her mother. From the very beginning the protagonist will position herself within society as female; her gender influences her point of view and her language – the same language that her mother uses:

> Mi madre necesitó mucho de mí para ser madre. Gracias a mí lo era. Eso me lo tendría que agradecer toda la vida. Ella también disfrutó adivinar mi sexo, tocar cada espacio de mi espacio y decirme todas aquellas palabras que ella sabía que yo nunca le diría a nadie.
> Y jamás he dicho nada de aquello. Lo he guardado tanto que ni siquiera lo recuerdo. Mi madre tampoco ha mencionado nada, como si jamás hubiera hablado conmigo. [...] Debí retenerlo tan fresco y claro como cuando mi madre me lo dijo. [...] Pero mi madre se aseguró bien y me lo dijo apenas nos dejaron solas en una salita del hospital. Estuvo un buen rato contándome todas las cosas que sentía y todo lo que pensaba de mí. Y todo lo que pensaba del mundo. Y cómo le había impactado conocerme. Pero hubo algo que nunca me dijo porque yo la interrumpí con mi llanto. (Canetti 1997: 21–2)

This feminine cosmogony pervades the whole novel. The protagonist asserts: 'no conocía el idioma que hablaba mi padre, pero sí lo entendí cuando pasó sus dedos rocosos por mi frente y acercó su nariz de montaña para olerme' (Canetti 1997: 23). When the protagonist is a baby, her acts are defined by her sexual drives; the Semiotic will still affect her behaviour in adulthood. Even as a child she discovers the pleasure of masturbation:

> Tenía sabe Dios si dos o tres años o si todavía no había cumplido el primero, cuando descubrí los milagros de mi cuna. [...]
> Tal vez yo sí luché por salir de la cuna alguna vez y en esa lucha de mis piernas con los barrotes de madera, descubrí una rara sensación de placer de apenas unos segundos. No sé por qué intuición ancestral callé el secreto. Entré al pecado por la puerta ancha. Con el placer y con el secreto.
> Aprendí a sentir la diferencia entre los pasos de mi abuela y los de mi madre, y a reconocer las pisadas fuertes de mi padre. Cuando no escuchaba ni unas ni las otras, me dejaba poseer, tranquilita como yo era, por uno de los barrotes de la cuna. Quise denominar aquella sensación de alguna manera, como mismo había aprendido a decir 'mamá', 'papá' y 'leche'. Pero tarde aprendí que las sensaciones no tienen nombre, pues si no, ya no serían sensaciones. (Canetti 1997: 27)

When the protagonist enters the Symbolic order she finds her drives repressed by the Law of the Father, represented here by the members of her family. She establishes a sharp difference between her erotic pleasure and language and thus she places feminine *jouissance* within the Semiotic, using Kristeva's terminol-

ogy. Through her discourse, this character challenges the notion of sin established
in society and instead she contrasts sin and pleasure. Her parents and grandparents are monologic characters who symbolize the repression exerted against the
individual once he or she is part of society. We should bear in mind how the
protagonist substitutes the figure of her father with the figure of the Father, the
priest. Later on in the novel, the policeman who comes to her home to arrest
her, Torquemada, behaves in a paternal, patronizing way – a substitution of the
biological father by the state as father-figure. The three paternal figures attempt
to subjugate her under their power.

Canetti also expresses through her novel the fluidity of feminine writing, in
this case through the protagonist's confessions. In this, she concurs with Cixous's view concerning the concept of écriture féminine, which she claims cannot be fixed:

> It is impossible to define a feminine practice of writing, and this is an
> impossibility that will remain, for this practice can never be theorized,
> enclosed, coded – which doesn't mean that it doesn't exist. But it will always
> surpass the discourse that regulates the phallocentric system; it does and will
> take place in areas other than those subordinated to philosophico-theoretical
> domination. It will be conceived of only by subjects who are breakers of
> automatisms, by peripheral figures that no authority can ever subjugate.
> (Cixous 1980: 253)

According to Cixous both the feminine and feminine writing share their inability to be defined. Again, in *Al otro lado* Canetti explores the inability to apprehend what the feminine essence and language is. The protagonist is presented
in a constant process of becoming. She subverts any authoritative discourse that
tries to define her. Her language is fluid, full of erotic imagery that breaks with
the linearity of patriarchal discourse. From the margins, the protagonist's discourse will occupy the centre through her confession. The female body also
acquires visibility as the centre of all meaning. Applying Cixous's words, and
as we witness through the entire novel, the protagonist and her language can
never be subjugated by authority, although this is not for lack of effort on its
part, as is constantly reflected in the narrative.

Cixous links the fluid essence of the woman with her heterogeneous erogenous
organs and highlights the feminine capacity to know the Other:

> Heterogeneous, yes. For her joyous benefits she is erogenous; she is the
> erotogeneity of the heterogeneous: airborne swimmer, in flight, she does not
> cling to herself; she is dispersible, prodigious, stunning, desirous and capable
> of others, of the other woman that she will be, of the other woman she isn't,
> of him, of you.
>
> Woman be unafraid of any other place, of any same, or any other. (Cixous
> 1980: 260)

Canetti's novel is the perfect example of what constitutes écriture féminine. Its protagonist recreates herself through the erotic act, as a way to get closer to her body and her sexual drives. She also epitomizes the capacity that, according to Cixous, woman has to encounter the Other. She is a polyphonic character who develops the dialogism between her different selves through the erotic act in which she deploys several masks. She also meets the Other in her erotic encounters. The protagonist's confession is 'just like the desire to write: a desire to live self from within, a desire for the swollen belly, for language, for blood' (Cixous 1980: 261).

Overall, I have tried to compare Cixous's concept of écriture féminine with the language used by the protagonist of *Al otro lado* who recreates herself using a language of her own. For Cixous, feminine writing has to challenge male images of the female body with the exploration of her sexual experiences, of her body, her femininity, the erotic. Cixous connects language with the body; language is a body function. For her, the repression of the body implies the repression of writing, and if women allow this repression to stand it will translate into producing a false writing. Cixous, like Kristeva, stresses the function of the maternal body in feminine writing, the pre-Oedipal rhythms. The articulations of the maternal body will influence women's writing and will serve to challenge the patriarchal order and the relationship of the subject with the Other, with the world. The love of the mother is for Cixous, as for Kristeva, a model for the relationship between the subject and the Other. That special relationship between the woman and the Other appears inscribed in language. This revolutionary language subverts male narcissism. As Susan Sellers explains, 'For Cixous, this willingness to encounter and "sing" the other, without seeking to appropriate or annihilate the other's difference in order to construct and glorify the self, is the keynote of écriture féminine' (1991: 141).

Against those characters who represent power, the narrator expresses her own language, her own cosmogony and her particular view of the world. Her language, then, has a different syntax, a different meaning that the others cannot understand. In the following quotation we see how this language clashes with the rest:

> Me temo haber dicho demasiada verdad, Padre. Aunque yo no tenga bien claro los límites entre lo cierto y lo incierto de la vida, juro que me esmeré en decir lo que sentía – del corazón a la boca. Quizás mi mente nunca quiso ver la realidad. Quizás. Y fui castigada por eso hasta que finalmente aprendí la lección: debo decir la verdad de los demás y no mi propia verdad; debo ver con los ojos de los demás y no con mis propios ojos; debo decir lo que los demás esperan y no alterar su noción exacta de las cosas; debo creer en lo que veo y no en lo que imagino. ¡Pero cuánto lo lamento, Padre! Yo veía flores donde los otros veían vegetales. Yo veía trinos donde los otros veían pájaros. Yo veía caballos de espuma galopante donde los otros veían nubes. Y con el tiempo aprendí a ver solamente vegetales, pájaros y nubes, porque eso de mentir era muy feo – según los otros – y porque debía ver las cosas tal

cual eran y no cambiarlas a mi antojo. Mi pecado es que hasta hoy mezclo todo en mi mente, Padre, y veo nubes que cantan entre pájaros galopantes y vegetales floridos.

Nunca me perdonará mi madre por aquella verdad que le dije y que luego resultó ser mentira porque ella me lo dijo bien clarito, que era una mentira y que me lo metiera bien en mi cabeza. Aquel día yo lloraba y lloraba postrada de rodillas frente a la tierra del patio. (Canetti 1997: 32)

The narrator shows the contradictions between her world, created through her own language, and the imposition of the social hegemonic discourse. She challenges the established notions of reality and truth. She also denounces social hypocrisy as well as displaying her need to be hypocritical in order to survive. Although she pretends to have learned the lesson, to have accepted the restrictions exerted over her, she admits that 'hasta hoy mezclo todo en mi mente, Padre' (1997: 32), as a way of showing that she imposes her own truth, her difference. Her subjective world contrasts with the view of 'todos', an abstract entity that tries to alienate her. Once the narrator enters the realm of language, new restrictions take place; the characteristic sexual indifferentiation of the semiotic *chora*, following Kristeva's theory, is repressed once the female character becomes part of society. It is in this moment that the protagonist has to differentiate between the meaning of the words 'woman' and 'man':

> Yo nunca supe hallar la diferencia entre hembra y varón. Ni creo que nadie haya nacido con tan acertado instinto. Nací con el instinto de amar y con la certeza de que el placer existía en algún lugar del amor. Muchas veces quise besar a mi madre en los labios... y a mi abuela y a mi padre y a mis amigos. Los amaba tanto que quería llenarme de ellos completamente y coserlos a mi piel de algún modo mágico. Pero mi temeridad fue rápidamente atiborrada de tabiques y muros. Por aquí, por allá, esto no, esto sí. Entonces comencé una de las escuelas más difíciles: encontrar las diferencias, adivinar qué era correcto y qué era incorrecto, hasta dónde llegaba el bien y hasta dónde llegaba el mal, qué cosas serían aprobadas y cuáles no. […] oculté placeres y miedos, desenfrenos y locuras que sabía me llevarían al cadalso paterno. […] no ocurrió así con mi prima, a quien sí besé en los labios, y quien me respondió con una caricia. Teníamos tres o cuatro años. Solamente. […] la alegría nos hacía besarnos y acariciarnos. Era tan agradable sentir el alma vulnerable y abierta. Nada nos hacía sentir culpables ante nosotras mismas, pero sí sentíamos culpa ante el mundo. Luego fue con la vecina. (Canetti 1997: 39)

Notions of femininity and masculinity appear as rigid social constructs that clash with the fluidity of the nature of the protagonist, her 'alma vulnerable y abierta'. It is only with a child of her own age that the narrator can erase the rigid, binary categories that society tries to impose on her. From this point onwards in the novel there is a significant break between private space and public space.

The narrator moves between them, and this explains her fragmented subjectivity. Once the distinction between the concepts of masculinity and femininity is established, the protagonist will use her fantasy to invent platonic lovers. She is still a child and describes her lovers with childish language. This language is closer to the maternal body and serves to criticize the colossal gap between her world and that of the adults. In the end, she learns the lesson: 'Padre, siempre lo supe. A pesar de no conocer la diferencia, estaba escrito en mi piel. Me gustaban los varones, mucho más los guerreros' (1997: 43-44). When a real man appears in her life, the masks begin to work in every relationship:

> Un día un hombre apareció ante mí y rompió mi desenfreno con una sonrisa. […] No, Padre, no me hizo el amor. Tan sólo me besó de una manera desconocida. Me besó como si me estuviera haciendo el amor. Lo peor es que ambos lo sentimos a pesar de la distancia que nos separaba. Yo tenía doce años y él tenía veintidós. […] El muchacho se llamaba Donaciano Sade, pero todos lo apodaban 'el Marqués'; quizás por la estirpe de su madre, una de las consentidas del gobierno en mi isla. ¿Yo? Me llamaba Teresa, Teresita, Teresita del niño Jesús, y andaba descalza con sólo doce años de mirar el mundo. (Canetti 1997: 56–7)

Here Canetti uses humour and anachronism to good effect, mixing the famous libertine the Marquis de Sade (1740–1814) with Saint Thérèse of Lisieux (Teresita del niño Jesús) (1873-–97), a French Carmelite nun whose name echoes that of Santa Teresa de Ávila, the Spanish mystic. This mask highlights the virginity and naivety of the narrator in contrast to the perversity of the male character, whose mask is Sade. Both the protagonist and Saint Thérèse write about their lives: Saint Thérèse's spiritual autobiography, *The Story of a Soul*, published posthumously after her death from tuberculosis, had a great impact which led to her canonization in 1925 by the Catholic Church. In this context, the protagonist's confession acquires a religious overtone when she recalls her sexual evolution, thus subverting religious norms. The male character in the novel belongs to the country's elite, which echoes Sade's aristocratic rank, although the latter was imprisoned for his writings. Here the narrator leaves the reader to establish the possible connections, including the suggestion that the masks of elite members of society hide the libertine sexual drives which are examined in the private spaces that the novel explores.

   In the light of Kristeva's essay 'Romeo and Juliet: Love-Hatred in the Couple', published in her book *Tales of Love* (Kristeva 1987: 209–33), I suggest that it is not by chance that the first sexual encounter of Canetti's protagonist in this novel is with Romeo, and that the protagonist dons Juliet's mask:

> Sus besos me envolvieron en otros besos y en más besos, largos y cortos, secos y mojados, suaves y violentos, tenues y bruscos, dulces y amargos, fríos y ardientes, mudos y ruidosos, mullidos y desplumados, besos, y besos

y besos y besos [*sic*]. Y antes de que pudiera darme cuenta, los besos fueron quitándome la ropa. Y el silencio de la sala se hizo cómplice. El silencio conspiraba silenciosamente. Con el silencio, me estremecí. Sin saber cómo, abrí las piernas. Con el silencio, grité. Sin saber cómo, mi aliento y mi sangre se precipitaron y me dejaron al borde de una playa. Con el silencio, mis besos se perdieron, sin eco. Sin saber cómo, estaba desnuda como un caracol. Con el silencio y sin saber cómo, me dejé comprimir contra el sofá, en la arena de la playa en donde fui abandonada como un caracol desnudo. Me dejé besar y oler. Y me volví flor y me volví lirio y me dejé deshojar. (Canetti 1997: 64)

The use of Romeo and Juliet in the text sets in motion what Kristeva identifies as the 'incompatibility between idealization and the law' (1987: 209). But Canetti breaks again with the stereotype of idealized love that the two Shakespearean characters represent when the protagonist, although a virgin, does not bleed after she first has sexual intercourse. The first sexual act is described as a battle where 'Mi novio (el primero) me miraba casi furioso, y mi cuerpo obediente fue acuchillado una y otra vez, deshojado, mutilado, mordido y, finalmente dominado y vencido' (Canetti 1997: 65). Here again is the idea of the female body as mutilated, and this imagery reflects the patriarchal society in which the protagonist lives. In Kristeva's words:

> It is a fact that the lover (especially the woman lover) desires his or her passion to be legal. The reason may be that the law, which is external to the subject, is an area of power and attraction [...]. Nevertheless, once instituted for the subject, the law reveals its no longer ideal but tyrannical facet, woven with daily constraints and consonant hence repressive stereotypes. (Kristeva 1987: 209)

The lack of blood that infuriates Romeo allows the female character to subvert his rigid notions of the female body and assume her agency when she lies to Romeo, saying: 'Ni te creas que fuiste el primero' (Canetti 1997: 66). In a reversal of Shakespeare's play, this Juliet rejects her passive role and disrupts the patriarchal notion of virginity. Juliet breaks up with Romeo, in this case not because of familial rivalries but because of Romeo's *machismo*, and because monologism prevails in him. It is not until the narrator meets Calígula that dialogism is possible.

> No era ni un ángel ni un demonio, Padre, era un hombre. Un hombre. Se llamaba Calígula [...] Su mirada era mansa y lejana como la de Cristo, con el brillo cercano de los ojos del... de usted. No tenía boca. O sí, sí tenía algo así como una boca borrosa. Tan flagelado y huesudo era, que no sabía si postrarme ante él o amarlo. Opté por amarlo, por amarlo infatigable y poderosamente. Por odiarlo de tanto amarlo. Por amarlo con sólo una palabra inexpresiva y con infinitas expresiones que jamás sabría encerrar ningún

idioma. ¡Cuánto cuánto [*sic*] lo amé, Padre, cuánto! Llegó a ser mi religión. Mi altar. Perdóneme, perdóneme [*sic*], pero si usted lo hubiera conocido, si usted… Perdóneme, no quise decir eso. (Canetti 1997: 68)

Once more, as when Chaviano describes her protagonist's first love in *Casa de juegos*, here in Canetti's text the narrator links the figure of Calígula with God. In this case the comparison has two readings. First, Calígula changes the essence of the protagonist's erotic experiences. Secondly, he will be the cause of her imprisonment. Hence, Calígula marks a before and an after point in the life of the female character. Both the protagonist and Calígula will be sacrificed by society as Christ was: 'Pero a Calígula no le importó haber sido asesinado alguna vez en un lejano imperio de nuestra era; se dispuso a hacer su última y más condenable locura, la que nos costaría la vida: amarme' (1997: 68–9). In this relationship, dialogism is produced by bodies and by the constant use of masks:

> Los días siguientes se rompen en mi mente como algunas olas antes de llegar a la orilla, Padre. Pero recuerdo que un día Calígula decidió que yo fuera el sol azteca y me puso a girar por diferentes estaciones y a contorsionarme como los códices místicos de la gran piedra solar; y que otro día fuera una amazona estrepitosa, y que otro día fuera tan sólo yo, y que al día siguiente fuera un ánima desconsolada y sin reposo que vagaba en pena y gritaba por las calles, y que un día después me volviera un hada milagrosa que convertía la frigidez en orgasmos sin usar la varita mágica y sin ungüentos de jazmín. Fui muchas cosas, y otra vez yo; y muchas cosas más, y otra vez yo. Sobre el cuerpo delgado y curvo de Calígula estuvo Perséfone venida de ultratumba y le pidió al oído que, después de revivirla, la llevara de regreso a su hogar. Yo era ella, Perséfone, y también Artemisa y Minerva y Venus y Dafne y Clío y todas y ninguna. Fui un árbol que se atrevió a hacer el amor con un hombre, Calígula, y cuyas ramas fueron vilmente podadas por eyaculaciones violentas. Ay, Calígula mío, aburrido de aburrimiento, que inventaste el mundo otra vez y te salió torcido como tu cuerpo. Me multipliqué para ti, me deshice para ti, me hice hombre para ti, envejecí para ti. He existido sólo para reencontrarme contigo en todos los mundos maltrechos en el que equivocadamente resucitamos para no olvidarnos de hacer el amor y para devolvernos luego, y otra vez, a la penumbra de la travesía infinita. Ay, mi Calígula, ¿en qué otro mundo vivo he de hallarte nuevamente? (Canetti 1997: 75)

The process of creation is the only way the narrator can recover her relationship. The confession becomes the recovery of her voice and the creation of her version of reality:

> [Calígula] – Me busca la policía.
> [She] – ¿Qué?
> – Eso, que me busca la policía. Tú no sabes nada de nada. ¿De acuerdo?
> – ¿De qué? – yo realmente no sabía nada de lo que hablaba.

– Nada de nada. ¿De acuerdo? – me repitió.
Nada de nada, nada de nada. Nada de nada, Padre, yo nunca supe nada de
nada hasta el día de hoy, hasta ahora. Le digo, le confieso de rodillas, que yo
nunca supe nada de nada, Padre. Pero bueno, ya de qué podría valer, salvo
de confesión. Quizás hubiera sido mejor que supiera algo de nada. O nada
de algo. Algo de algo. Pero, tristemente, no supe nada de nada, y ahora no
tengo qué confesar. Sólo esto: no sabía nada de nada. Se da cuenta, Padre,
se da cuenta que hasta me mutilaron la confesión, que hasta me quitaron el
derecho de expiar mi pecado, el pecado de no saber algo, cualquier cosa,
algo? (Canetti 1997: 76)

In *Al otro lado* the protagonist uses those discursive techniques that Josefina
Ludmer has detected in the narrative of Sor Juana Inés de la Cruz. Our nameless
protagonist separates the field of knowledge and the field of saying. She says
that she does not know and that she says all that she knows, but at the same time
we do not know if she is saying all that she knows. Although the protagonist's
main act throughout the novel is confession, silence forms part of her discourse
as well. For example, the reader never knows the exact reason for Calígula's
prosecution or how much the protagonist knows about him and his supposed
corruption. Like Sor Juana, the narrator claims that she does not know but she
wants to know; in this case, she wants to know herself. We can apply Ludmer's
words to the protagonist here: 'Her story, narrated as the history of her passion
for knowledge, strikes the reader as a typical popular autobiography, or autobiography of a marginalized figure: an account of the practices of resistance vis-
à-vis power' (1999: 88–9). Like Sor Juana, the narrator's trick of the weak
consists in separating 'the field of saying (the law of the other) from the field of
knowing (my law), [that] combines, as in all tactics of resistance, submission
to and acceptance of the place assigned to one by the other, with antagonism
and confrontation, retreat from collaboration' (Ludmer 1999: 91).

As Fuentes states with reference to *Al otro lado*, in the chapters that centre
on the protagonist's university years, those in which she is arrested and sent to
jail, we find that 'the national first begins to appear in more detail. In these
chapters, the female protagonist confesses her social and political problems'
(2002: 236). The confession is the protagonist's revenge against the abuses
inflicted on her by the characters who represent power. It is not by chance that
when the narrator is released from prison she participates in an orgy, where she
arrives in 'heaven', in a hotel called Edén. It is in this hotel with its orgiastic
and festive ambience that she 'por primera vez en la vida no tenía nombre. O
al menos nadie, ni yo, lo sabía. Era una más. Un cuerpo más. Una hembra más
de las tantas que allí había. Simplemente una más' (Canetti 1997: 142).

The role of the orgy is transgression. As Georges Bataille writes, 'In the orgy
the celebration progresses with the overwhelming force that usually brushes all
bounds aside. In itself the feast is a denial of the limits set on life by work, but
the orgy turns everything upside-down' (1962: 112). After her stay in prison the

protagonist has the most subversive erotic encounter. As Fuentes claims, 'the lack or apparent loss of a fixed identity in an orgy reveals the constructive nature of identity. In an orgy, participants lose a sense of their selves, names and nationalities are absent, as sexuality takes precedence […] she is abject for participating in a deviant act, abject within the act itself […] abject for narrating her participation to a Catholic Priest' (2002: 247). Both Chaviano and Canetti choose surrealist language to depict erotic intercourse; thus they stress the close connection between sexuality and the unconscious. As the narrator explains: 'Después de salir de la cárcel, hice todo lo que no hice antes. Ya puedo decir que sí sé, y que he hecho de todo… y con todos' (Canetti 1997: 149). In her next relationship, her boyfriend and his friend become Tristán and Cástor, Zaratrusta and Fausto, Don Juan and Casanova, Bécquer and Byron, Rómulo and Remo, Menelao and Pólux, Hunahpú and Ixabalanque, Caín and Abel, Jacob and Esaú. At the same time the protagonist is Celestina, Margarita Gautier, Sor Juana Inés, Helena. With the use of these masks the author reinforces the importance of literature, and writing becomes the product of endless intertextualities that rely on the realm of the real, myths, biblical scriptures and literary history. Literature appears as a force that feeds the relationship between the three characters (the protagonist, her boyfriend and his friend). 'Sí, Padre, sí amé a Tristán, como bien hubiera amado a cualquiera de los personajes que él traía a casa bajo el brazo y con los que infaliblemente yo debía copular cuando él los evocaba en nuestra cama' (Canetti 1997: 160).

From the long list of her lovers throughout the novel, Antonio is one of the most important. Antonio has the body of a woman but feels she/he is a man. This is the only character within the novel, apart from the narrator, who recreates herself/himself through continuous dialogue with her and the use of masks. She/he is the dialogic character *par excellence*. She/he creates and recreates herself/himself through the word and the use of masks and she/he gives masks to others as a way of knowing them, as the narrator does. The transgressive essence of this character becomes apparent when the protagonist confesses that 'las palabras de Antonio me ponían demasiado nerviosa' (Canetti 1997: 172). Although Antonio is biologically a woman, the narrator attributes masculine features to her:

> Hice un último intento por implantar mi estirpe de experta vividora y otra vez fui enmudecida por esa seguridad que Antonio tenía en sí mismo, como ese don al que parecen haber dotado a los del sexo opuesto, y que yo – muy a mi pesar – no tengo. (Canetti 1997: 174)

The protagonist calls Antonio 'Antonio de Erauso', and she/he calls herself/himself 'la monja de Alférez' (the nun lieutenant), a transparent mask that refers to the historic figure of Catalina de Erauso (1592–1650), a nun who escaped from the convent of Dresde disguised as a man. Using male names such as Antonio de Erauso, she went to the Spanish colonies in the 'New World' and fought in Chile against the Mapuches. Because of her skills in war, both Felipe IV and Pope Urban VIII allowed her to dress as a man and to use male names (Erauso 1996). In Foucault's words we could say that characters such as Antonio, because of 'their anatomical disposition, their very being', 'confounded the law that distinguishes the sexes and prescribed their union' (Foucault 1990: 38). The subversive elements of this character and the social constraints she/he faces are obvious. In the convent, she/he becomes transgressive against the monologism that governs such a place, in which the Mother Superior requires the erasure of her/his body (Canetti 1997: 179):

> Después que colgó los hábitos, Antonio decidió no discutir más con la estructura física en la que estaba entrampado. Sí, definitivamente era un hombre con cuerpo de mujer, pero a partir de ahora creería que así fue siempre, que algunas personas andan en el cuerpo que no les pertenece. Y tampoco renunciaría a esos ademanes blandos y a esa ambigüedad que lo hacía igual de apetecible para hombres y mujeres. Trató de pisar con el pie y pensar con el cerebro, de decir y hacer lo que pensaba y sentía, sin que afectara demasiado lo que pensaba y sentía otra persona. Y sobre todo, seguiría cantando a todo pulmón y con todas las ganas, sin importarle que alguien suspirara con carita de ganado vacuno. (Canetti 1997: 180)

Canetti repeats the idea that a homosexual is trapped in the wrong body, a mistake of nature, a stereotype also used by Padura Fuentes.[6] Nonetheless, Canetti reverses this stereotype (we should remember that Padura's transvestites could not seduce the heterosexual man) when 'this mistake' constitutes Antonio's appeal to people of both sexes. The narrator resolves the 'mistake' of nature, naming this character with the masculine pronoun. The protagonist is also seduced:

> […] [Ante la pregunta de Antonio de si le gustaba] – Sí – dije con miedo y la respuesta me zumbó en los oídos mientras mil pájaros me revoloteaban en la cara.
> – No tengas miedo, muchacha, no soy un hombre para que te pongas así – me dijo con gracia y ternura.
> – No sé, no sé a qué tengo miedo. Pero sí, tengo miedo. Tengo miedo de tus veinte años y de tu condición de mujer sin sexo.
> – Oye, no exageres – rió –. Sí tengo sexo, carajo. […]
> Antonio tocó mi pelo mojado y lo exprimió un poco con la mano. Mientras me sujetaba la muñeca con la mano empapada en agua, se acercó para chupar más del agua de mi pelo y la dejó caer sobre la parte de la toalla que envolvía mi pubis. Me eché hacia atrás y me atrajo con ambas manos por las caderas, por las que fue escalando luego con los dedos hasta llegar a mi boca y apretarla a la suya con extrema suavidad.

---

6   'defecto de las otras veces sabia naturaleza' (Padura 1997: 48–9).

> Me besó con los ojos abiertos, con sus ojos negros sin cerrarlos, y me
> pidió que hiciera yo lo mismo, que la mirara mientras la besaba y que no
> dejara de besarla ni de mirarla porque ella no era Antonio, sino Catalina.
> Catalina de Erauso. Que así era como la habían bautizado su madre y su
> abuela y su bisabuela.
> – Catalina – dije –, yo también te bautizo con el agua de mi pelo. (Canetti
> 1997: 183–4)

Sexual intercourse between the protagonist and Antonio is not described in
detail but has, according to the narrator, the connotations of a baptism ritual,
although this time the one who is baptized and initiated is not the female protagonist but Antonio/Catalina de Erauso. By the end of this chapter, we can
recontextualize its title, 'Ella y yo: el mismo vientre', as it acquires a different
meaning: it does not refer to the reproductive function of the female body but
to the love between two women. I posit that Antonio represents what Cixous
calls bisexual writing whose characteristic is its subversiveness. With the appearance of Antonio in the novel, we can apply here what Susan Rubin Suleiman
states about Cixous's work. Antonio represents with his/her body the kind of
writing Cixous calls bisexual writing. As Suleiman explains:

> Cixous […] insisted on the potential bisexuality in writing […] she was
> careful to point out that the bisexuality she had in mind was not that of the
> hermaphrodite, who represents a 'fantasy of unity' or a myth of totality, but
> rather the bisexuality of a 'dual' or even multiple subject, who is not afraid to
> recognize in him or herself the presence of both sexes, not afraid to open him
> or herself up to the presence of the other, to the circulation of multiple drives
> and desires. She then went on to say, however, that for historical and cultural
> reasons, it is women who today have the greatest potential for realizing this
> kind of bisexuality, and for practicing the kind of writing that results from
> it. (1986 16)

However, in the novel, social constraints are maintained in Cuba. It is in exile
that the protagonist tears off the masks:

> Adiós, mi isla. Adiós, mi país hermoso en el que dejé veinte y tantos años.
> Adiós, pedacito de tierra de la que crecí. Ahora yo no te pertenezco ni me
> perteneces. Ahora vivo en otro país. Viajé como mis antepasados en busca
> de mí y, también como mis antepasados, sigo sin encontrarme. No sé por qué
> me fui lejos; sólo tengo la certeza de que era necesario (Canetti 1997: 216).

Once in exile we no longer have the confession of the protagonist to the priest,
and the pages written in italics disappear from the novel. In exile there is no
longer any need for masks/characters, although the polyphony that structures
the protagonist continues. She does not stop being a dialogic voice, even if her
environment is, as it was in her country, completely monologic:

Estoy sola. Solitaria y sola. Consulto libros y no encuentro una voz gemela. Acudo a los recuerdos y nadie me estira la mano. Miro al horizonte y no veo más que mar y después mar. Llamo por teléfono y nadie contesta del otro lado. O sí, contesta una voz grabada con la que cualquier papagayo podría competir y resultar más original y caluroso. Escribo y las letras se paran de cabeza o se enroscan como culebrillas en invierno. Evoco a todos los dioses, y las nubes se apoltronan sobre mí como una amenaza. Consulto horóscopos, adivinos, brujos, buenos samaritanos, guías espirituales, *babalaos*, mensajeros extragalácticos, seres iluminados, hijos elegidos, profetas contemporáneos, y estafadores de todo tipo. Acudo, por honrar siglos de sabiduría y creer que quizás en estas tierras haya alguien diferente, a un psicólogo. (Canetti 1997: 219–20)

In the face of the monologism that she must confront, the protagonist is aware again of the need for an interlocutor:

Quiero hablar. Quiero decir algo. Las ideas quieren salirse pero mi frente es un muro de carne que las aprisiona y tiene a las más valiosas de rehenes. Las ideas chocan con mi frente y se deshacen. Alguna logra escapar por los poros pero se esfuma, raquítica, en el aire. Y otras, las más rezagadas, emergen de la garganta y se hacen palabras que al ordenarse en perfectas oraciones gramaticales, ya no serán nunca más la idea que fueron. (Canetti 1997: 221)

Confronting the absence of an interlocutor, the protagonist loses the skill of her verbal confessions. The few confessions that we have in exile are in written form. This is the first time in the novel when we can read explicitly what the protagonist writes. In her writing, she turns again to questions of finding herself. She finds the need to rescue her interlocutor. This time exile is the cause, that is to say, it produces the fragmentation of the subject:

Tengo que ir a buscarme. Yo me quedé del otro lado del mar. Yo debo estar todavía caminando por la isla. Debo ir a buscarme antes de que otra persona se apodere de mí. Yo no estoy aquí frente al mar. Yo estoy allá, en la isla. Posiblemente sea ésa la razón por la que no me encuentro aquí, en otro país, donde la soledad grita desde varias bocinas colgadas del cielo. (Canetti 1997: 224)

And she continues:

Quiero que hablemos ahora, solos, y sin intermediarios. Cansada estoy de andar y tengo el suelo de mis pies hecho pedazos. Aún quedas Tú. Escúchame, estoy lejos de mi sacerdote. Lejos de mi infancia, lejos de lo que he sido, de lo que soy, de lo que pude ser. Lejos muy lejos. Perdida entre el mar y la tierra, la tierra y el cielo. El cielo y Tú. Quiero un respiro, Dios. Detenerme o dejarte decidir que éste es el final del camino y hay que darse la vuelta otra vez; ¡a empezar!

He amado y ya lo sabes. He amado aunque diga y repita que no he amado a nadie, o que quien amó no fui yo, sino uno de mis tantos personajes. Pero todo eso son pretextos que me invento a mitad de camino. En realidad, he amado y punto. Bueno ¿para qué te lo digo…? Ya lo sabes, ¿no? (Canetti 1997: 238)

In exile the only person to whom she can talk is Christ. She confesses her use of her characters to Him and also to them being part of herself. The protagonist, who feels completely alone, is thinking about the existence of God when a man appears to repair her telephone. He tells the yet nameless protagonist: 'He venido para que se comunique por fin' (Canetti 1997: 239). This telephone repairman is the first person with whom the protagonist establishes a dialogue in exile, which I will quote at length to illustrate this point. He will be Father Jonathan's alter-ego to her and he facilitates communication once again:

Esa sonrisa. Esa sonrisa. La he visto millones de veces. La he soñado otras tantas. ¿No le habré confesado nada a este desconocido? ¿No habrá arreglado antes mi teléfono? […] Me come. Me desea.
   Qué digo. Qué hago ahora. Sin sacerdote, sin psicólogo, sin un Dios que me socorra, sin familia ni amigos, sin idea ni ideales, sin confesores ni confidentes, sin personas ni personajes, sin otros y sin mí, y tan distante de mi isla… ¿cómo se puede andar? ¿Cómo se puede confiar en esa visión viril que tengo enfrente? […] [hablando con él] Y sí, tengo miedo. Tengo un dolor comiéndome las vísceras. Miedo de llegar hasta las últimas consecuencias. Me aterra tocar en la última puerta, confirmarme en mi descrédito, adherirme a la no-religión como a otra religión.
   – Es parte del proceso, y requiere dolor – dice, y me hace creer que él ya ha saltado esa verja –. Somos esclavos del yo desconocido que llevamos dentro. Ignoramos lo que él sabe y por eso él ha tomado el reino de nuestro ser […] ¿A eso temes?
   Vuelvo a sentir que este hombre disfrazado de técnico de teléfonos no es otro que mi cura, más viejo, menos tímido, más dispuesto ahora a llegar hasta el final. Confiada, me voy dando. Lentamente.
   – Tengo miedo de lo que soy, de lo que puedo desencadenar si no me recojo y me vuelvo discípula de algún credo legendario o histórico – sigo […] Tengo que escucharme cuando digo esto. […] La creación suprema de Dios hemos sido nosotros – dice, concluyente, y me intenta besar.
   – La creación suprema de nosotros ha sido justamente Dios – me dejo besar una esquina de los labios, y lo aparto. […] [Él hablando con la protagonista] […] No nos gusta abandonarnos a nosotros mismos. Queremos buscar fuera de nosotros porque subestimamos que dentro de cada uno pueda estar eso que llamamos Dios. Vemos hacia fuera para no ver hacia adentro. Huimos y huimos de nuestra limitación y vulnerabilidad en busca de la perfección

y la inmoralidad, en busca de lo que no somos. [...] No tengo a nadie – le digo al desconocido [...] Te tienes a ti, ¿no te parece suficiente? [...] Mi cuerpo vibra, ya indomable. Veo que es necesario hacerlo ahora. Dilatarlo sería prolongar, como siempre, mi agonía.

— Vete ahora – digo muy serena.

Mi desconocido espera eso de mí. En vez de ofendido, lo sorprendo orgulloso de mi reacción brusca. [...] Se va, pero deja la puerta abierta.

Cierro. (Canetti 1997: 241–5)

The protagonist assumes the role of God: she becomes the creator. Through the creation of masks she formulates her own self. In this role she makes carnal a symbolic union with God the Son in Christian terms. The symbolic union with Christ in a church in exile also implies the position of the woman as goddess, usurping the role of God the Father in Christianity. After this union with the divine, the protagonist realizes that effectively she does not need anyone else but herself and is fully in control of language and the creative enterprise that comes with it. Hence, she begins a dialogue with herself:

Es cierto. No necesito nada. Me tengo completita, pedacito por pedacito. [...] No estoy sola. Estoy conmigo. Hablo conmigo. Me estoy tratando de decir algo. Sigue, sigue. Dime algo, Yo, sácalo de adentro y dímelo tal y como te venga a la cabeza. No lo pienses, por favor, dímelo, no me tengas miedo, soy yo misma, no te voy a hacer daño, dímelo y verás que te comprendo, y verás que te tolero. Vamos, habla, ya se fue el desconocido. Estamos a solas. Habla de una vez, habla, por favor, habla.

— Te amo, Yo misma, aunque dejes de amarme y aunque dejes de confiar en mí, que soy yo y tú a la vez. Me amo a mí que es la mejor forma que conozco de amarte y me considero literalmente feliz y bendecida por la gracia de todos los espíritus, porque tengo un don que me hace libre. Puedo amarte [*sic*]. Así lo proclamo hoy, el día de mi nacimiento. ¡Sea mi voluntad! (Canetti 1997: 246)

The protagonist assumes her polyphonic identity and she is reborn completely aware of this gift that now she sees as something positive. That is, the quest for her self will be eternal, because she is a fluid character who cannot be fixed with ultimate signifieds. The protagonist, as the polyphonic character that she is, will always be in a process of 'becoming': 'Characters are, in short, respected as full subjects, shown as "consciousnesses" that can never be fully defined or exhausted, rather than as objects fully known, once and for all, in their roles – and then discarded as expendable' (Bakhtin 1984: xxiii). The protagonist admits that identity 'is always in transit, in process, like the novel itself' (Fuentes 2002: 254). Once abroad the protagonist realizes that there is no answer to her questions and that her life in itself is already a permanent quest. In sum, the confession-writing and the protagonist are metaphors of life as a constant flow, open to permanent transformation. And the protagonist appears also as the representative of all women through time. Her trick of the weak, again, is 'changing, from within one's assigned and accepted place, not only its meaning but the very meaning of what is established within its confines' (Ludmer 1999: 93).

6

Language Unbound: Zoé Valdés' *La nada cotidiana*

Zoé Valdés is one of the best-known Cuban writers of her generation. She was born in Havana in 1959 and left Cuba as an adult. She is well known internationally as an outspoken opponent of the Castros' regime. As Catherine Davies pointed out shortly after Valdés settled in Europe, she 'has made a reputation for herself by criticizing the Cuban government and writing novels that some would call erotic and others pornographic' (1997: 223–4). Valdés is well known for the use of explicit sexual language in her novels. She is actually a pioneer in doing so, and opened up a new chapter in the creation of the so-called Cuban literature boom of the 1990s. In *La nada cotidiana* the author clearly criticizes the socio-political situation in Cuba during the Special Period. According to Miguel González Abellás, Valdés 'a juicio de algunos críticos, supuso un momento clave en el reciente bum de la narrativa cubana que existe entre finales del siglo XX y comienzos del XXI, sobre todo en Europa' (2008: 17).

La nada cotidiana marks a turning point in the Cuban narrative of the Special Period and beyond, and as such has received substantial critical attention. Most critics – for example, Perla Rozencvaig (1996), Cristina Ortiz Ceberio (1998), Carmen Faccini (2002), María de la Cinta Ramblado Minero (2006), Isabel Álvarez Borland (2007), Liliana Soto Fernández (2008) and Elena Lahr-Vivaz (2010) – have emphasized the vulgar use of language in this novel, its open and detailed use of sexuality, and apparent criticism of the Cuban regime. Though all the critical works of the above authors can be considered key texts that contribute to the body of research on *La nada cotidiana*, one study in particular stands out, that written by González Abellás: *Visiones de exilio: Para leer a Zoé Valdés* (2008). Here, the critic explores the socio-political background of Valdés' fictions and contextualizes them in the light of her own biography. González Abellás analyses the importance of concepts such as exile and inner exile, Cubanness, race, sex and gender, and pinpoints the dichotomy between urban and rural spaces and the use of intertextuality as key elements in Valdés' narratives. He also stresses the public figure of Valdés as an outspoken critic of the Castros' Cuban regime.

Another prominent analysis in the critical bibliography on Valdés' work is that of Yvette Fuentes (2002). Fuentes stresses how Valdés challenges revolutionary icons and patriarchal values. According to Fuentes, Valdés proposes

a transportable Cuban identity, independent of where the individual lives.
While I draw on all of these studies, at the same time I propose a different
analysis. In this novel I will consider once more the strategic use of language,
paying particular attention to the use of erotic discourse in order to reveal the
polyphonic and dialogic nature of this language when it is subversive. This
point has been repeatedly ignored by other critics, and I will suggest that
Valdés' novel is central in terms of offering a feminine and feminist gaze and
a counter-erotic discourse.

La nada cotidiana has a circular structure. It starts and finishes with the
story of a woman who has died trying to leave Cuba. Once in Purgatory she
has another chance to return to life and to her island. This story is presented
in italics and constitutes the story that the narrator/protagonist begins to write
and that frames this circular novel.[1] This metafiction marks the beginning of
the process of writing that the protagonist starts as she recalls her birth and
past. She is able to recall very important episodes from her life and analyses
them from a more mature point of view.[2] The process of writing occurs when
the female protagonist acquires agency and her discourse takes on a central
position. The process of writing parallels the process of self-discovery that
the protagonist undertakes simultaneously. When the character from the
metafiction appears on the beach, the next chapter starts with an account of
the protagonist's birth, her insertion into society, or, using Kristeva's terminology, into the Symbolic. The novel we are reading ends/starts when the
process of creation is made possible, when the female's voice can be heard.
I agree with González Abellás in considering Valdés' narratives an example
of feminist writing:

> Sus obras son feministas a varios niveles, puesto que se centran en el papel
> de la mujer dentro de la familia y la sociedad y también en el control y la
> exploración de su sexualidad. El cuerpo femenino se convierte en receptor
> del contexto socio-histórico y también en un elemento de autodefinición
> de la mujer, que descubre el placer del juego sexual y el gusto por la
> experimentación como una manera, muchas veces, de escapar al tedio
> cotidiano. (2008: 59)

La nada cotidiana is the 'inicio de una escritura antipatriarcal, antiautoritaria y
subversiva' (González Abellás 2008: 61). In addition, I posit that it is the erotic
and dialogic essence of this novel that makes it subversive. I disagree with some

---

[1]   Some other critics consider this story a part of the novel itself; see, for example, Ortiz
Cebeiro 1998.

[2]   Isabel Álvarez Borland states: 'Valdés's first-person narrators, like Canetti's and Chaviano's,
are often transgressors and outlaws who emerge transformed by their power of witnessing what
has happened in Cuba. Instead of taking refuge in exotic realities, most of these novels are anchored
in Cuba and become testimonies of the failed project of the revolution' (2007: 255).

critics such as Carol Wasserman (2000) who consider Valdés' texts as monologic, too focused on the sexual in general, and on the sexual life of her protagonists more particularly. In *La nada cotidiana* the use of erotic discourse is
dialogic and 'esta sexualidad desbordante es también un discurso alternativo a
la precariedad con que se vive en la Cuba del periodo especial y al discurso
oficial "gris", serio y político' (González Abellás 2008: 61). For the protagonist,
the erotic encounter is a deliberate choice, because this is what she wants. She
becomes thus a subject of her conscious actions.

La nada cotidiana is a polyphonic and dialogic novel. It is polyphonic because
it shows the range of voices that represent different points of view concerning
'reality'. It becomes dialogic from the moment when the protagonist's discourse
is double-voiced, and the novel is full of asides, comments and judgements made
by the older protagonist who is recalling her past from a retrospective and thus
privileged point of view. The narrator-protagonist presents events that had
taken place but that do not belong to the narrative we are reading, or that will
take place later on in the narration. The protagonist is in constant dialogue with
the other voices that form part of the narration. Although formally speaking
most of the time we hear the others' voices through letters and calls that the
protagonist recalls, the protagonist is created dialogically; her discourse is in
constant interaction with that of others. She is a character in constant transformation and development. The inclusion of other voices, such as la Gusana's and
el Lince's, has as its function the expression of different perspectives about
Cuba. All of these characters have left Cuba and live abroad and, therefore, they
analyse the Cuban situation from other perspectives and contexts. These voices
in constant dialogue with the protagonist's voice confirm the polyphony and
dialogism in *La nada cotidiana.*

Dialogism is further produced by means of intertextuality. The novel is
full of references to other works, not limited to literature. As González Abellás states, 'se mencionan películas, actores y directores como elementos
cuya función es referencial, ya que sirven como fuentes para que el lector
se haga una idea de la persona o de la situación' (2000: 45). Dialogism goes
beyond the limits of this novel when, as González Abellás claims, the protagonist of *La nada cotidiana* appears in other novels written by Valdés.
Yocandra appears, for example, in *Te di la vida entera* as a friend of Cuca,
the protagonist of this novel. This dialogism between the different texts[3]
written by Valdés destroys the boundaries of a particular piece of work and
defies the limits on the existence of characters. Reading *Milagro en Miami*
we know that Yocandra will leave Cuba on a raft and will be found on a
beach by el Lince, who is living there. Valdés uses this 'internal' intertex-

---

[3]   González Abellás labels these dialogic relationships in Valdés' texts 'autocanibalismo
textual' (2008: 44).

tuality to continue and develop the lives of protagonists which she has left open in previous novels. Thus, Valdés stresses the impossibility of giving a fixed and monologic, finalized description of dialogic characters. Valdés shows the 'inner unfinalizability' of her characters, to use Bakhtin's terminology (Bakhtin 1984: 59). Moreover, I agree with González Abellás when he states that 'a través de la creación de un grupo estable de personajes que aparecen sucesivamente en varias obras, se ofrecen diferentes perspectivas sobre la situación de Cuba' (2008: 22).

The double-voiced discourse is also created by the constant use of humour and irony. Valdés subverts official and patriarchal discourses and any monolithic notion of femininity and reality through language, humour and irony. We can apply Antonio Vera León's words, referring to *La hija del embajador* and Valdés' use of humour in that narrative, to *La nada cotidiana* as well:

> uno de los recursos del humor en Zoé Valdés: [es] el contraste de registros linguísticos que coloca, en impúdica promiscuidad, la expresión sublimada y espiritualizada de una retórica literaria originaria del modernismo al lado de expresiones obscenas que se refieren al cuerpo y que son propias del lenguaje coloquial cubano. (2000: 180)

In addition, I agree with González Abellás when he states that 'No cabe duda que el humor es fundamental en la obra de Valdés, en muchas ocasiones con un componente de crítica política añadido en su propósito de desarticular el discurso oficial del gobierno cubano' (2008: 50). Through the use of humour and irony the word, as Bakhtin (1984) suggests, is never neutral but is double-voiced. However, I disagree with Carmen Faccini's statement that in this novel, 'la ironía se vuelve sarcasmo, para hiperbolizarse hasta convertirse en un discurso del absurdo' (2002: n.p.). I shall posit that irony does not create a discourse of the absurd but rather denounces the nonsense of hegemonic discourse. As Jorge Mañach has stated in his 'Indagación del choteo', humour can be considered an essential characteristic of Cuban culture and is, according to Mañach, a strategy used to criticize and denounce (1962: 81–7). This is actually the role played by humour in *La nada cotidiana*.[4] Moreover, I shall argue that through the use of humour Valdés produces a carnivalization of sexual difference and gender roles.

In *La nada cotidiana* the author establishes a dialogism that links the time when the author's writing takes place and the fictional time of the narrative. Furthermore, the reader plays a role in this dialogism, by adding the time of his or her reading of the novel, which is framed within a particular socio-political context. The referent of the narrative is Cuba in the early 1990s, during the Special Period.

---

4   This point has already been studied by other critics such as González Abellás (2008).

In this chapter I shall focus on Valdés' use of erotic discourse.[5] In contrast with Chaviano's and Canetti's erotic discourse, Valdés depicts sexual intercourse between her protagonist and her partners from a genuinely female perspective.[6] Eroticism is used to demonstrate the protagonist's subjectivity and agency, as well as her different gaze. The woman's body is not subjugated to the male gaze, and instead the male body is objectivized, and thus becomes her object of desire. Therefore, she becomes the subject who desires and ceases to be only the object of desire. In this way, eroticism serves to reverse gender roles.

Unlike Chaviano and Canetti, Valdés does not use either symbolism or poetic or surrealist language to describe episodes of sexual intercourse. Her language is crude, vulgar and even obscene and sexuality lacks any spiritual nuance.[7] Valdés tends to reinforce the idea of a crude reality that itself lacks any romanticism and where survival becomes the basic instinct that prevails. When creating an erotic narrative or an erotic scene, Valdés uses a counter-erotic discourse that challenges traditional male discourses and also literature in which romanticism means that women adopt the passive role. Valdés uses humour to prevent a sexual scene from turning into a romantic one.

---

5   It is important here to highlight, as Vera León has done, the existence in Valdés' and Arenas's works of obscene discourse. I agree with Vera León when he claims that 'Lo obsceno literario de Cabrera Infante antecede a Zoé Valdés y a Reinaldo Arenas [...] en Arenas y Valdés estamos ante un obsceno literario que parte de la oralidad popular revolucionaria, el lenguaje oral del "hombre nuevo", siendo especialmente pertinente esto a los relatos de Zoé Valdés, donde a veces la fecha y el lugar de nacimiento de la narradora casi coinciden con celebraciones revolucionarias, como en *La nada cotidiana* (1995): el 1 de mayo en la Plaza de la Revolución, donde además el Che Guevara deposita una bandera cubana sobre la barriga de la futura madre. El pasaje es notable porque inscribe el origen y el inicio de la narración en una zona excremental, de ahí que la narración sea por definición escatológica. No es la única vez que un escrito de Zoé Valdés asocia de raíz la narración a explosiones de flujos corporales' (2000: 185). Vera León continues: 'es la mirada escatológica, excremental, que carnavaliza la oratoria pública revolucionaria a partir del lenguaje oral del "hombre nuevo", dando lugar a lo obsceno literario en Zoé Valdés. Es notable la relación establecida entre la narración y el cuerpo. En todos los casos, lo obsceno literario se asocia a una descarga corporal o a una descomposición del cuerpo' (2000: 186).

6   It is worth noting that, as Madeline Cámara suggests, Yocandra is a character who has been created using 'los modelos estructurales del género picaresco en voz femenina' (2002: 34). Cámara adds: 'De existir en *La nada* y en otras novelas de los 90 una forma novelística que pudiéramos llamar picaresca, no es porque la [*sic*] autoras hayan copiado el modelo español. [...] Las nuevas escritoras se han reapropiado de la picaresca con intenciones de parodiar su añejo afán didáctico-moralizante y reorganizar creativamente unas estructuras narrativas significantes que le son válidas para contar sus propias cóleras y desilusiones' (2002: 34). Cámara continues by analysing *La nada cotidiana* as 'una actualización del modelo de la picaresca femenina que se desarrolló en España, en el barroco, pero ahora dentro de las condiciones de postmodernidad dadas en Cuba' (2002: 61).

7   Vera León claims: 'En la literatura cubana, la obscenidad no tiene una función dominante en el lenguaje de un texto literario hasta la publicación de la obra de Guillermo Cabrera Infante, y en especial *La Habana para un infante difunto* (1979), uno de los grandes relatos de la literatura cubana contemporánea' (2000: 183).

Erotic discourse and sexuality are monologic when they are metaphors of repression within a patriarchal and repressive society. One of the privileges of men in a patriarchal society is their capacity to name everything.[8] In this novel the protagonist rejects the name that her father has chosen for her, not only for ideological reasons but also because her first love rejects it. Ironically, this demonstrates her subjugation to the patriarchal order, represented here by the figure of her first love as a substitute for the paternal figure:

> Y no me llamo más Patria porque siempre odié ese nombre, porque en la primaria se burlaban de mí, porque en el fondo respeto profundamente el significado de esa palabra. Pero además, ¿qué sentido tiene llamarse así? Y porque fue él, mi primer amor, el de mis dieciséis años, el que me desposó, y después nos divorciamos, y me casé tres veces más (en el trópico uno empieza desde muy temprano a casarse y a divorciarse, es como tomarse un vaso de agua). Y al cabo del tiempo, y de tantos maridos, ahora es mi amante, el que alterno con el Nihilista, el otro, el joven, al que de verdad amo hoy por hoy. [...] Al principio fue eso, cuando me presenté se rió a carcajadas. ¿Cómo podía él acostarse con la Patria? ¡Ni muerto! Esa noche, él mismo me vistió correctamente con mi uniforme escolar, y añadió que cuando me cambiara el nombre regresara a verlo. [...] Esa noche iniciática, cuando no quiso hacerme el amor a causa de mi nombre, lloré como una magdalena, sin consuelo. (Valdés 1995: 29–31)

This subjugation is inverted in the actual novel when the protagonist grants names to her lovers or to those characters that form part of her text: el Nihilista, el Traidor, la Militonta, la Macha Realista Socialista. Although González Abellás (2008) gives these comic nicknames a symbolic role, they are also textual masks through which the protagonist not only ridicules and makes fun of the characters, but also shows their real nature; once more masks do not just conceal but also reveal the real self. Hence, the protagonist adopts and claims her role as a subject and creates in the novel her own feminine cosmogony, turning the power relationships in place within it upside-down. As Madeline Cámara rightly observes, in the change of her name we can see 'la primera señal de que estamos ante un personaje literario que, al construirse desde la primera persona, optará por la libertad de la ficción autobiográfica para modificar su identidad femenina de un modo anticonvencional y liberador' (2002: 66).

---

8   As Toril Moi explains and warns when she writes about Kristeva's theory, '[it] is masculine rationality that has always privileged reason, order, unity and lucidity, and that it has done so by silencing and excluding the irrationality, chaos and fragmentation that has come to represent femininity. [...] To impose names is, then, not only an act of power, an enactment of Nietzsche's "will-to-knowledge"; it also reveals a desire to regulate and organize reality according to well-defined categories. If this is sometimes a valuable counter-strategy for feminists, we must nevertheless be wary of an obsession with nouns' (1985: 160).

The protagonist also uses sexuality as a weapon to change her position with respect to men. At the beginning of the novel, the voice of a more mature narrator foretells that when the narrator is writing and after their divorce, that is, in the future within the narrative we are reading, she will use el Traidor as a lover in order to take revenge against him: 'Porque con el Traidor lo mío ya es como una venganza, una adicción incontrolable, unos deseos de humillarlo, de cobrarle una a una las que me hizo' (Valdés 1995: 30).

The protagonist chooses the name of el Traidor's muse, the one he uses in his poems: Yocandra. From their first encounter the relationship between the protagonist and el Traidor is presented as that between a hunter and his prey: 'luchando con un paraguas negro, en medio de la ventisca y debajo del aguacero torrencial estaba él, estudiándome como una fiera a su presa' (Valdés 1995: 36). This kind of image appears in Canetti's and Chaviano's novels in order to reflect male superiority in a patriarchal society, a situation that they later try to challenge. At the beginning in *La nada cotidiana* the protagonist also assumes the role of the victim: 'Yo estaba lista para sus mordiscos, un ser para traicionar. Nunca me vio bella, confesó en sobradas ocasiones, pero sí víctima, y eso era lo que él buscaba, lo que busca' (1995: 36). After changing her name she comes back to his home and is rejected by him once more, but this time because of her virginity:

Él no podía admitir aquello. Me amenazó con el dedo y me partió para arriba visiblemente airado. Si yo era virgen alguien tenía que desvirgarme, pero jamás él. Él era incapaz, no soportaba a las vírgenes, él no se atrevía a romper algo tan delicado y húmedo, ¡el himen! (¿Cómo iba a sospechar que mucho tiempo después, y muy a menudo, iba a desgarrar zonas más sensibles en mí: la dignidad, el alma, y toda esa mojonería tan importante para nosotras?) Yo tenía que irme otra vez y volver rota, y cuidadito con contarle cómo había sucedido. Sería horroroso para él entrar en detalles que nada aportarían a nuestra futura relación sexual. (Valdés 1995: 37–8)

In this novel, therefore, we have the reversal of the supposedly masculine fantasy of having sex with a virgin. In this novel the hymen is what man cannot break, what prevents sexual intercourse, that part of the body of a woman that the male lover fears. The female character rejects this connotation of the hymen and prioritizes other 'areas' of her female essence: her dignity and soul. Therefore, there is an opposition between what is important for men and for women in a relationship; their points of view are different. Virginity appears clearly as a male construct. What el Traidor will break is more delicate than the hymen. Moreover, the female character questions the concept of virginity itself as understood by men. She confesses to having had anal sex previously:

Yo podría haberle explicado que era señorita por la vagina, pero no por otros c'anal'es [*sic*]. Aunque en la escuela algunas muchachas comenzaron a meternos miedo con que por atrás también se salía embarazada, que con

sólo pasársela, si caía una gotita en el muslo la cosa podía embarrarse y ya
era el embarque. (Valdés 1995: 38)

Anal sex becomes a substitute for vaginal sex as a way of preventing preg-
nancy. The narrator, using explicit and direct language, rejects and avoids her
role as a mother, giving priority to the pleasure of eroticism. This rejection of
the traditional maternal role for the woman becomes a feminist gesture. In the
words of Lucía Guerra, the patriarchal system limits the woman to her reproductive role:

> Cuerpo, mujer, madre, mujer que no es nada más que madre, mujer con una
> identidad fijada en el espacio concreto e invisible de su útero. Verdadera
> matriz de mutilaciones impuestas por la organización patriarcal. [...] Otro
> que el sujeto masculino manipula a través de las trampas de la maternidad
> sublime, el pecado, y el eterno femenino. Mujer, cuerpo reproductor, que no
> tiene otra alternativa que ser madre o anti-madre. (Guerra 1990a: 21–2)

The narrator chooses the second option, to be anti-madre, which in this case
entails a feminist stance, and, through humour, she reveals another strategy
of patriarchy – to reduce women to their genitalia – when she states her new
condition as 'himen criminal' (Valdés 1995: 39). The female body is reduced
to a part, her hymen, which becomes a metonym of the protagonist's body.
But she declares it to be 'Un himen dispuesto a matar el primer pene que se
atravesara en su camino. Salvo el amado' (1995: 39). The female body acquires
subjectivity and agency. Reduced to the hymen as representative of the whole
body, she adopts an active role in opposition to the masculine organ; however, the 'murder' of the penis cannot be read as a complete rejection of the
law of men in this context, as she is following the order of a man, el Traidor,
who does not want to have sex with a virgin. From the beginning of the
novel, the way Valdés describes the female sexual organs is completely different from the ways in which Canetti and Chaviano describe them. In Valdés'
novel the hymen and the vagina play an active role; they are not broken or
penetrated, they decapitate, they kill.

  Sexuality is also connected to the process of learning for the protagonist.
Through sexuality, the female character is exposed to marginal, extra-official
sources of knowledge; she subverts the official literary canon and official history and questions social prejudices. The body becomes thus a site of knowledge.
Yocandra is learning from el Traidor, but Valdés fails to subvert the male literary canon; we find Yocandra reading only books written by men. She does not
rescue or attempt to create a parallel female literary canon.

  In this novel the protagonist's marginality is double: as a victim of an oppressive regime that she shares with men, and as a woman within a patriarchal
system that prevents her from producing any writing; it is el Traidor who 'writes'

and who is a famous writer, and it is not until the end of the novel that the protagonist can be a 'sujeto productor de la escritura',[9] challenging the asymmetry
created by the patriarchal writing. The subversive nature of her sexuality is
obvious. She challenges her father's racism by finding a black lover and the
state by selecting an ex-political prisoner:

> Yo esperaba el oscurecer para restregarme en el muro del Castillo de la
> Fuerza con un ex preso político de cincuenta años. Él acababa de obtener su
> libertad. [...] Fue una aventura hermosa, algo sufrí con ella, pero me inició
> en las lecturas diferentes. Por él conocí *La tregua*, de Mario Benedetti.
>   Bastó media vez que mi padre comentara que lo último que le podía pasar
> a él y a su familia, el golpe mortal, era enterarse de que su hija templaba con
> un negro, para que yo me metiera hasta el tuétano con un negrón de ojos
> verdes [...]. Por él conocí en anécdotas todos los puertos importantes [...].
> Del negrón ojiesmeralda tuve que salir huyendo porque no se contentó con
> la retaguardia y ya quería el frente único, y porque yo no era tan valiente
> en aquella época, ni poseía las condiciones económicas mínimas, para
> enfrentarme a los problemas raciales de mi padre. (Valdés 1995: 38–9)

The intertextual reference to Mario Benedetti's novel – in which a mature man,
who does not have a good relationship with his sons and daughters, falls in love
– is not arbitrary. The protagonist emphasizes the gap between her father and
herself when she mentions that her father, a supporter of the revolution, is a
racist. I agree with Faccini when she claims that through both the father and el
Traidor 'Valdés identifica discurso patriarcal/discurso político hegemónico en
estos personajes, que se presentan en la novela como metonímicos de la revolución' (2002: n.p.).

Yocandra loses her virginity in an episode that is described without euphemisms or poetic language. This differentiates Valdés from Canetti and Chaviano, whose protagonists' first sexual experience is of the utmost importance
for the female characters and has connotations of rape, occurring in relationships in which the man uses his superior position to 'get' what he wants. In
Valdés' novel, on the other hand, the protagonist reverses this position; she is
the one who uses the man to 'get' what she wants, she is even the one who
inflicts pain on him:

> En la parada de guaguas del muelle de Casablanca, un peludo esperaba solitario
> cualquier ómnibus. Tanta era la mariguana y el ron que había ingerido que no
> tenía idea de su destino, sólo sospechaba que tenía que salir de aquel marasmo.
> Le di un chapuzón en el agua turbia y apestosa del malecón, brillante de residuos
> de petróleo. Después me paré en el medio de la avenida y sacándome un pezón

---

⁹   I borrow this phrase from Diamela Eltit in relation to Latin American feminism and the
need for women to be able to create their own discourse (Eltit 1990: 22).

conseguí *botella* en el auto de un General. […] bajé arrastrando al peludo hasta
La Red, un *night-club* oscurísimo del centro del Vedado. Se llamaba Machoqui,
y en pleno año setenta y cinco se había propuesto ser hippie cuando ya nadie
en el mundo, y mucho menos en Cuba, lo era. Le di cuatro bofetones, lancé
dos jarras de agua fría en su imbécil cara y comencé a besarlo para no perder
la costumbre del romanticismo. […] él se abrió la portañuela, y se sacó el pito
bien tieso. Yo ya tenía el blúmer por los tobillos. Evoqué la guillotina, y de un
tirón me senté en la cabeza del rabo. Él chilló de dolor, yo no había lubricado lo
suficiente. Costó trabajo, pero lo decapité. Sólo hubo un mínimo de ardor y una
aguada sangrecita. Mi himen había cumplido su cometido: matar a un tolete.
Consumado el hecho, como experto criminal, desapareció sin dejar rastros. Y
con la misma, acotejé mis ropas, pagué y me fui. De Machoqui, mi destupidor,
nunca he vuelto a saber. (Valdés 1995: 39–40).

The first experience of sexual intercourse lacks any trace of romanticism. The man's
role is passive and merely functional and the eroticism becomes an anti-eroticism.
The man is called 'peludo', 'criminal' or 'destupidor' and is a puppet, a mere instrument of the protagonist. In the description of this scene the female gaze and
discourse occupy centre stage. The female character is active and the man a simple
object of 'desire'. The male genitalia are called *pito*, *tolete*, but become symbolically decapitated by the female genitalia that appear as a guillotine, as a symbol of
power. The narrator does not give any romantic connotation to her first relationship,
breaking with the stereotype that a woman's first sexual experience is the most
important one; and she reduces the man, with her feminine gaze, to a useful penis.
In opposition to Canetti and Chaviano, who, when they are describing sexual intercourse, tend to adopt a male gaze, Valdés' character succeeds in using an actual
feminine point of view in which the female body is not objectified. This sexual
experience is not dialogic; in fact, the protagonist adopts traditional patriarchal
discourse in order to stress her power as the subject of the action. Sexual intercourse
is not in this case a form of dialogism but rather a way of showing female power
in reversal of patriarchal power relations. In opposition between el Traidor and
Machoqui, the protagonist claims from an adult point of view:

El Traidor desvirgó mi inocencia, si hoy soy despiadada es por su culpa.
Era el destinado a violar mis sueños y lo hizo cruelmente. Era el que debía
mentirme y me mató a mentiras. Era el que marca, y aquí estoy cubierta de
cicatrices. Él nunca lo sabrá, no está preparado. Yo lo amé como sólo puede
hacerlo una adolescente. Dócil, y con la inteligencia abierta a cualquier
locura. Y sus locuras las tomé demasiado en serio. Fue el primero que quise,
y eso, de cierta manera, lo convierte en excepcional. (Valdés 1995: 41–2)

Thus in Valdés we find the traditional viewpoint that a woman's first love is the
most important one, but in this novel this does not coincide with her first sexual experience. El Traidor is a character with many negative connotations, like

almost all the men in Valdés' novels. He, like Machoqui and her black lover, suffers a kind of fixity; he is a flat character who does not evolve as the novel progresses – the men are monologic characters. This fixedness has to do with the crude denunciation of the patriarchal system and with el Traidor's affiliation with power, namely, with the revolution.

Cámara has noted the close relationship between patriarchy and the state: 'en la sociedad socialista ha ocurrido un traspaso de poderes en el cual el patriarcado ejercido tradicionalmente por el Padre y el Esposo ha quedado ahora en manos del Estado' (1995: 55). This is why the figures of the father, husband and state constitute in this novel the embodiment of patriarchal society and discourse. Therefore, it is not surprising that the three are presented with negative and repressive connotations. As el Traidor is an intellectual who represents the elite of the country, Valdés associates him with corruption: he blackmails Yocandra's teachers in order to buy her a university degree without her having to attend classes. Valdés uses el Traidor as a metaphor for a whole political system, that of the Cuban revolution of 1959 and its flaws. She uses humour and sarcasm to mock both male characters and the political system.[10]

The university is one of the institutions that the narrator criticizes most, since education has been one of the key elements used by the Cuban government as propaganda in order to demonstrate the revolution's success. Valdés opposes official education through Yocandra's process of education which she undertakes through her relationships with men; her process of learning will culminate in her capacity to write and assume her past and surroundings. However, I do not agree with Cámara when she claims that

> Como los antiheroes pícaros Yocandra no puede crecer, ni avanzar hacia proyecto alguno: sus reacciones son básicamente volitivas. En su narración parte del hecho de reconocer que su consciencia ha sido amputada, que le está prohibido pensar, que el Estado decide por ella, y entonces escoge la mejor filosofía dado el caso: la frivolidad, el presentismo de quien vive para los placeres físicos los goces inmediatos que nadie puede impedirle o confiscarle, los únicos que controla, y donde su poder de agencia como sujeto encuentra aún una realización. (2002: 68)

Rather, I believe Yocandra can and in fact does develop within the narrative, as at the end of the novel she achieves a self-knowledge that she did not have at the beginning. Her use of sexuality is not frivolous but rather she uses her sexuality as a means of encounter both with the Other and with herself, and as a form of resistance against patriarchy and oppression.

---

[10] Cámara states: 'El carácter testimoniante y desmitificador de una utopía histórica como la Revolución Cubana es uno de los elementos que sitúa a la obra de Valdés dentro del panorama de la literatura postmoderna' (2002: 68).

However, the process of learning undertaken by Yocandra under el Traidor's leadership does not have positive connotations. Yocandra pays for her 'degree' with her '"prisión fecunda" a su servicio' (Valdés 1995: 43–4). In this statement there is an intertextual reference to the book *La prisión fecunda* by Mario Mencía, in which he refers to the period of time that Fidel Castro spent in prison on what was then Isla de Pinos, today Isla de la Juventud. With this intertextual reference, the protagonist refers to her specific 'prison', the one that el Traidor creates, as she becomes a kind of slave to him. The adjective 'fecunda', with which the author refers to the events that took place after Castro's liberation, has another connotation in this novel as the narrator links her subjugation to el Traidor with the process of learning, the only positive connotation of this relationship. The irony of this statement gives the adjective 'fecunda' the opposite meaning when used to describe the Cuban revolution and the relationship between Yocandra and el Traidor.

El Traidor appears as a God who tries to mould his creation. The image of the first lover as a God is recurrent, as we see in Canetti's and Chaviano's novels, and reflects the subjugation of women to patriarchy and a female character moulded by and with reference to a male model. In the following paragraph we see how the two lovers erotically perform this process of learning:

> [Y]o llevaba seis meses tecleando en la vieja Remington y no había aprendido ni a usar todos los dedos. Un mediodía, el Traidor me desnudó y me sentó como vine al mundo frente a su espléndida Olympia. Tapó el teclado con una hoja en blanco, vendó mis ojos, comenzó a acariciarme el cuello, la espalda, las nalgas, las teticas, el ombligo. Mientras tanto me dictaba poemas de *En la calzada de Jesús del Monte*. Mi sudor corría a mares y sus manos larguiruchas y secas cortaban los chorros que corrían desde mi cuello a mis pezones, de mi espalda a la raja del culo, de mis sobacos a las caderas. Antes del anochecer, ya yo escribía ciento veinte palabras por minuto, imposible pero cierto. (Valdés 1995: 44)

Although this relationship becomes more and more of a power relationship wherein the woman stays in a position of subjugation, almost becoming a slave – 'él ordenaba y yo cumplía al pie de la letra. Yo era una extensión de su pensamiento' (1995: 44) – the narrator stresses how she had believed this role equivalent to love. Women appear as part of the patriarchal order as much as men: 'yo cumplía cada orden por amor. Para mí, así debía amarse, eso era el amor' (1995: 45). Moreover, the protagonist uses this process of learning with her lover once more to oppose and criticize the official educational system:

> Empecé a darme cuenta de su tiranía bien tarde, en realidad cuando ya había aprendido – o chupado – lo suficiente, porque aquélla sin duda alguna fue mi gran universidad. [...] Yo era la estudiante que recibía comida, cama, sexo, y una enseñanza grandiosa, exquisita. Muy pronto aprendí a manejar

el cuchillo y el tenedor a la manera francesa, y los palitos chinos. Antes yo comía con cuchara. Recibía una preparación muy diferente a la de las bobaliconas de la escuela. [...] Cuando meses después entré por la puerta de Ciudad Libertad, me bastaron tres semanas para darme cuenta de que sus aulas nada tenían que ver con el conocimiento. (Valdés 1995: 46)

Both official Cuban education and the private classes of el Traidor are similar patriarchal forms of subjugation for the protagonist. In her relationship with el Traidor, the protagonist enters a life of hypocrisy herself. The simulacrum that the protagonist carries out shows the abyss between what she must be in the Symbolic order, in social terms, and what she actually is:

El Traidor y yo preparamos un guión perfecto y con sus buenas relaciones con funcionarios de todo tipo de ministerios consiguió los documentos necesarios para lograr la mentira. Para mis padres, yo había hecho mi último año de preuniversitario con una beca especial para hijos de pinchos en Isla de Pinos, me habían captado en la escuela por mi inteligencia y buen comportamiento, pero por encima de todo por el excelente desenvolvimiento de mi progenitor, implacable dirigente sindical. Para mis padres, yo era militante (poseía hasta un falso carnet). Para mis padres, yo había matriculado [*sic*] la carrera de Educación Física y permanecía becada en Ciudad Libertad. En las vacaciones mentía diciendo que iba al campo a colaborar en los planes agrícolas. Para mis padres, yo era un modelo de hija. El Traidor era el maestro-guía que cada mes los visitaba para informarles de mis progresos y prodigioso rendimiento escolar. Para ellos, yo era dirigente estudiantil. Eso a mi papito lo ponía en el clímax del orgasmo paternal. (Valdés 1995: 47)

This simulacrum is used by Valdés in order to criticize corruption at all levels in the political system to which el Traidor belongs. The simulacrum is only possible because of corruption and therefore el Traidor and Yocandra become the embodiment of a whole nation that, according to Valdés, has turned into pure simulacra. In this sense, Valdés echoes Chaviano in denouncing this supposed simulacrum that Cuban society has become. Valdés also agrees with the viewpoint that I analysed in chapter 1 in connection with Arenas's *El color del verano* and in chapter 2 in connection with Padura's *Máscaras*. Both Valdés and Chaviano use their female protagonists to show lives lived through double standards and to illustrate the power of sexuality and eroticism to challenge repression. In Valdés' novel, her protagonist suffers repression on all levels, socially and in her relationship with el Traidor. The microcosm of the place where she lives with her lover mirrors wider patriarchal society: 'En verdad vivía prisionera como en un convento, mi religión era el amor y mi dios era el Traidor' (Valdés 1995: 47). There is a dichotomy, however, between the house where she lives and society, in that the repression exerted by el Traidor is accepted by the female character: 'para mí aquella vida no era humillación y no tenía puntos de referencia con otros estados de felicidad. Afuera el mundo era tan feo que aquel cuarto atestado de libros constituía mi palacio repleto de tesoros' (Valdés 1995: 47–8). Literature becomes a refuge for her. The simulacrum is part of her marriage too; as el Traidor states: 'Oye, tenemos que casarnos, hoy mismo, ya lo arreglé todo, hace falta que nos casemos… Necesito una mujer, digo, una "compañera"… Me dan un puesto importante en un país lejano, en Europa, y tengo que ir casado' (Valdés 1995: 50). The wedding is the opposite of romantic; marriage appears as another oppressive institution for the female character:

> Y yo queriendo contarle a esa señora extraña 'mire, compañera abogada, yo lo conocí menor, pero ya pasaron tres años de encierro, y soy mayorcita y sé lo que hago. Y lo que hago es lo que él ordene, porque él es un hombre de mundo y sabe lo que hace, y siempre le ha salido bien. Él va por el camino correcto y yo detrás. Para eso soy su novia, o amante, o secretaria, o criada – no, perdón, la compañera que trabaja en la casa, las criadas no existen desde que la Revolución triunfó – o…' (Valdés 1995: 51)

Here we find a mockery of hegemonic discourse in which the word 'criada' is eliminated, but not the position. The protagonist condemns the inequalities between the genders and shows marriage as a trap for the woman, who is dominated by her husband. The protagonist's wedding represents everything that she does not want:

> Casada por el Palacio. Sin traje, sin brindis. Pero con fotos. Sin mamá, sin papá. Pero con fotos. Despeinada, sudada, vestida a-lo-como-quiera. Lo importante es el papel, el certificado de matrimonio donde consta que el escritor futuro diplomático posee una mujer, digo, una 'compañera'. Y las fotos que son la prueba más evidente de nuestro feliz y auténtico casamiento. Yo con una cara víctima de filme de terror que no la brinca un chivo. Como Mía Farrow en aquella película donde ella es una ciega y matan a toda la familia de la casa y ella se queda solita dentro, trancada con el asesino. (Valdés 1995: 51–2)

The author forces the reader to read between the lines and to perceive that what the narrator is saying does not correspond with what she wants to say. The male point of view of the man requiring a wife is challenged here with the suspicious repetition that they have photographs to prove that they are married. The photographs symbolize what marriage really means for the female protagonist: an image captured on paper. The intertextual reference to the film and the identification of Yocandra with its protagonist could not be clearer: the husband is associated with a murderer. Her marriage, nonetheless, is consensual and allows her social mobility as she will now belong to a new elite. As the narrator claims with irony: 'Entré en la alta sociedad socialista tropical' (1995: 53). The narrator, once more, uses her position to question the identity of her husband, as he defines himself as a philosopher, and the reality of her country:

> Filósofos habrá en Alemania, pero no en este país, con tanto calor y hambre y guardias de comité y reuniones para reunirse en otras reuniones, consejillos, asambleas generales, asambleas populares, en las cuales se discute la misma bobada de siempre, por qué el pan no llega a su hora, si es que llega. En este país que no hay vergüenza, qué vergüenza va a ver [*sic*] si no hay desodorante, ni una malanga, ni un cariño… ¿Un filósofo, viviendo en una cuartería cochinísima, sin baño ni cocina? ¿Un filósofo, cargando cubos de agua? Aunque en verdad la que los cargaba era yo. No importa, él es filósofo. A costa de lo que sea. (Valdés 1995 53–4)

The hardship that surrounds the protagonists causes intellectual poverty for the inhabitants of the island themselves. The narrator again criticizes the bureaucracy of the institutions that appear in the novel, for they are as useless as philosophy itself. The female character makes fun of her husband when she calls him 'un Rambo del comunismo, un machista leninista' (Valdés 1995: 55); she ridicules and undermines him. This mockery of her husband helps her to denounce his opportunism, as he has become part of the elite in order to obtain privileges and not because of any revolutionary ideology. There is also a criticism of his machismo, which the narrator identifies with communist ideology. The protagonist challenges any attempt by her husband to define himself in heroic terms. The protagonist provides another image of el Traidor that contrasts with the image he and others have of him and prevents him from being defined as a dialogic character, presenting him instead as a finalized, monologic character. Through writing the narrator creates herself and her lovers. As I shall now illustrate, the protagonist stresses the idea that identity is the product of fiction, of narration, of words:

> A mí no me interesaba nada toda aquella sarta de heroicidades, nunca creí un ápice de aquel anecdotario. Lo escuchaba como se escucha la novela de las dos, en estado total de semivigilia, absolutamente embriagada con la sonsera cotidiana. Yo no amaba al héroe, yo creía amar al escritor. Y en cuanto al hombre, ¿cómo podía amar a ese hombre morboso que sólo lograba venirse cuando con las embestidas furibundas de su cabilla hacía sangrar mi sexo? Por eso me habitué a las pajas. Sólo a hurtadillas gozaba de un amor imaginario. De mi invención. Porque a él lo inventé yo. (Valdés 1995: 55–6)

Masturbation and imagination appear as the only escape for the protagonist. Sexual intercourse with her husband becomes painful, as is the relationship itself. The narrator takes revenge on the masculine character when she names his penis 'cabilla', denying any characteristic of maleness.

When they leave the country to go to Europe her situation does not improve. Hence her subaltern condition seems to be the same within and beyond the island. Patriarchal society is not limited to Cuba or its socio-political situation: 'Y seguí siendo la misma fea durmiente, la maltratada, la sin destino, siempre pendiente de la frase que podía destruirlo todo, del estruendo que me despertaría' (Valdés 1995: 57). Moreover, in their house abroad the female protagonist has no space to share with her husband. She cannot stay inside the house when he is there. Symbolically, the woman lacks both space and voice. Once she discovers that her husband's novel is the repetition of 'Todos me persiguen. No puedo escribir porque todos me persiguen' (Valdés 1995: 58) she claims: 'Lo que debiera hacer es ir ahora mismo a la Embajada americana y pedir asilo – no político – sino marital' (1995: 58–9). After learning that her husband has not been writing anything despite his claims, and despite the fact that she has been acting as his servant to help him get the time he needs to write, the female discourse occupies and invades the centre of the narrative in a stream of consciousness:

> Comiéndome la gran mierda del siglo, creyendo que con todo este sacrificio estoy contribuyendo a la gran obra de un escritor cubano, que además es mi marido. Aún es mi marido, porque debo señalar que, antes de salir en las mañanas, cuando ya estoy lista en la puerta, bañada, vestida con mi ropa limpia y planchada, el abrigo impecablemente sacudido, sin una basurita, peinada, perfumada, entonces es cuando a él se le antoja singarme con ropa y todo encima de la colcha blanca que suelta pelusitas, o de la alfombra polvorienta, porque él no se gastará un quilo en comprar el esprai limpialfombras […] A esa hora debo volver a quitarme la ropa, bañarme nuevamente, introducirme un óvulo de nistatina en la vagina porque parece que él ha tenido relaciones con una venezolana de la UNESCO que le ha pegado una trichomona del carajo. Ten paciencia y perfúmate de nuevo, repíntate los labios. (Valdés 1995: 59–60)

What is stated here undermines the male figure whose status as a husband is questioned implicitly when the protagonist describes their sexual relationship, which, far from being romantic or pleasurable, has become part of a routine. The narrator questions the sexual relationship with her husband as the basis of her marital status. As we see in the quotation below, the narrator uses and abuses the romantic language of lovers to challenge and question in comic terms the superiority of the male and her subjugation; the words in English add sarcasm to the scene. The author adopts patriarchal and macho discourse and reappropriates it in order to denounce and challenge it, as she parodies the language of women at the service of their male lovers:

> Y cuando parece que puedes salir a batirte con las oleadas gélidas de la mañana, él te procura, dulce, casi tierno e indefenso:
> – Amor, ¿dejaste mi comida preparada?

Of course, my dear, honey, darling, papito lindo, mi chini, mi coqui, papichuli, etc... Dejé la comida recontrapreparada, el almuerzo que devorarás sin acordarte de mí, sin dejarme ni las sobras. La cena que te jactarás hasta chuparte los dedos y ni las migajas del pan para tu niña, oh baby, sólo los platos amontonados en el fregadero, y las manchas de café por todas partes y las colillas de cigarros, y los ceniceros desbordándose. (Valdés 1995: 60)

It is when she identifies her husband with the protagonist of the film *The Shining* (Valdés 1995: 60), in an intertextual game that, again, links the figure of the husband to that of a murderer, that she decides to abandon him. We could apply the words of Ellen Rooney to the context of the last paragraph, as I suggest that here the novelist aims to expose 'a masculinist "narrative of femininity"' where 'stereotypes of woman and women appear as the effects of patriarchy, including, of course, of patriarchy's many stories' (Rooney 2006: 73). Valdés participates in feminist rewritings. As Rooney asserts: 'Feminism thus always involves a rewriting of femininity or femininities, of the categories that define women as women' (2006: 73).

In the scene of the abandonment, the male character is transformed into a sort of *fantoche*, ridiculed in a 'capítulo digno del más vil culebrón venezolano' (Valdés 1995: 62). After leaving her husband, the protagonist returns to Cuba where she later remarries twice. From the perspective of the mature narrator, the protagonist tells us:

El avión, el divorcio. Me enamoré una segunda vez. Me casé y enviudé a los dos años. Sí, también soy viuda joven. Lo perdí en un accidente de avión. Ése podría ser otro libro de amor, el que tal vez nunca escribiré. Porque no se puede escribir toda la vida toda, y porque el dolor sigue aún profundo y latente. ¿O sí podré escribirlo? Lo perdí. Tardé mucho en enamorarme de nuevo, pero pude. ¿Olvidé? No, no olvidé, pero me dio una manía de enamorarme. Ya no soy aquella muchachita llorona y templona. (Valdés 1995: 62)

The process of writing becomes a symbol of the maturity of the narrator. The narrator is always forcing us as readers to be aware that we are confronting a piece of fiction. The protagonist, alter-ego of the author, writes and rewrites herself to assume control of her past and, although she prefers to avoid certain painful aspects of it, she uses writing as a process of self-discovery.

Memory is a key element in this process of writing developed in the novel, but love constitutes the protagonist's form of resistance. The process of writing is the confirmation of her authority, her agency, her capacity to name and to create and recreate herself. This attitude is connected to her sexuality:

El Traidor me tocó a la puerta una mañana, era domingo y habían transcurrido varios años, en sus manos se marchitaba una orquídea:

– Toma, es una catleya. – Apuntó a la orquídea de montaña, haciéndose el Proust.

Y yo estaba sola. Y quise salvar la sedienta flor. Y él daba pena lo malmacho que se había puesto, flaco, calvo y encorvado, los dientes cariados y flojos. Y yo sabía – porque venía de verme en el espejo del cuarto – que lucía radiante con mis treinta años. Y, ¿por qué no? Lo dejé pasar. (Valdés 1995: 63)

This is a turning point in the novel. The protagonist has inverted her relationship with el Traidor. With her pun of 'la sedienta flor' she is now the one who rules the relationship; even the physical erosion of el Traidor confirms her as the subject, not the object. She is now the one who chooses her lovers. She assumes patriarchal language to reconceptualize it in feminine terms.

Another female character is la Gusana, a nickname that is highly significant because 'gusano' (worm) is the label used by the Cuban government for those who are dissidents, that is, those opposed to the recent Cuban political system. La Gusana is a marginal character, a *jinetera* (prostitute) who decides to go into exile in Spain after marrying a Spanish man. Although she can be seen as an economic migrant in the global context, she asserts her own exile by stating that she has left Cuba because of its economic and political situation (Valdés 1995: 96):

La Gusana estaba ya harta de bretes políticos, y antes de que el jineterismo fuera agua común, ella lo ejerció desenfrenadamente. Tenía vísceras de precursora. Un buen día arregló los papeles, se casó con un viejo gordo español y se largó, nombrándome guardiana del apartamento. (Valdés 1995: 85)

I agree with González Abellás when he states that

esa temática femenina, en concreto de las experiencias femeninas relacionadas con la soledad del exilio, es lo que permanece como un hilo común en la narrativa de Valdés […] Es por eso que este tema impregna su poética, al ser la clave que subyace bajo toda la variedad temática de la obra de Valdés. (2008: 27)

With la Gusana prostitution becomes a right and, as she was a prostitute before the Special Period – the period of hardship – in the case of la Gusana it also becomes a choice. Her sexuality represents her freedom to choose.[11] In the

---

[11]   I agree with Almudena Olondo when she stresses the subversive nature of *jineterismo* in the Cuba of the Special Period. I believe that this is the connotation that Valdés clearly wants to give to prostitution in this novel. Olondo claims: 'el tema de la prostitución en la isla supera el mero ámbito económico y adquiere una connotación social e ideológica particular. La necesidad económica no explica suficientemente el auge del jineterismo. La prostitución se presenta tanto como un medio de acceder a un estilo de vida no accesible a todos, como una forma soterrada de *oposición al régimen*. Dado que las autoridades consideran que la prostitución y los delitos a ella

chapter entitled 'La Gusana' the protagonist starts talking to her, evoking her from a distance, and recalling their moments together. Both characters challenge social prejudices. Above all, the function of the character of la Gusana is as the embodiment of a Cuban generation disenfranchised after they had expected to be better off than the rest of Latin America, having had a revolution. Thus she claims: 'es cierto que en toda la América Latina se pasa un hambre de pinga, pero ellos no hicieron la Revolución' (Valdés 1995: 91).

Moreover, la Gusana is the protagonist's connection with her earlier years. The protagonist asks her friend, in a dialogue in which we only hear the protagonist's voice, a series of questions, all of which start with '¿Te acuerdas…?' These questions appear over the course of three pages and constitute a narrative technique through which the narrator stresses the differences between a present characterized by hardship and a better past. History seems to be a process in which everything goes missing and the protagonist is right in the centre of history; she is the protagonist, as are all the characters of this novel, of history. She ends this repetition with the sentences 'Sobrevivimos con el estómago encharcado o cerrado por reparación. Nada existe. Sólo el Partido es inmortal' (Valdés 1995: 93); this is a clear critique of the only thing that has remained constant over time, the Communist Party. Again, the author links the economic situation of Cuba with its political system.

In opposition to this description of the Cuban situation, we find a letter written by la Gusana to Yocandra from Spain. This letter is no more positive. The author uses la Gusana's letter to reflect on her life abroad where the promise of a better life becomes a trap as well. The Spanish man who takes her to Spain is, of course, depicted only in negative terms, a monologic character characterized only by the sexual repulsion that he provokes in la Gusana. Sexuality for the *jinetera* who lives in Spain is now a new trap:

asociados "son inadmisibles en una sociedad socialista" y las prostitutas son catalogadas como casos de "peligrosidad social" en el Código Penal recientemente modificado, el ejercicio del jineterismo se convierte en un ataque directo al corazón del sistema, dado que "…los casinos, casas de juego, los centros de prostitución masculina y femenina y otras muchas formas de actividades relacionadas con la pornografía y el sexo, ninguna de las cuales existen en Cuba y son ajenas a la cultura revolucionaria de nuestro pueblo" [Discurso de Fidel Castro, 26 de junio de 2004]. […] De este modo el ejercicio de la prostitución constituye un modo de sorda oposición al sistema vigente, toda vez que atenta contra el régimen machista imperante pese a todo, contra el énfasis en el trabajo productivo, contra los valores anticonsumistas y contra la moral puritana de la Revolución' (Olondo 2005: 158–9). Olondo continues: 'aunque el Código Penal vigente no contempla la prostitución como delito, sí la incluye dentro de la categoría de "estado peligroso" (definido como la tendencia de una persona a cometer delitos que están en contradicción con la moral socialista). La prostitución es recibida como un comportamiento antisocial, que causa perturbaciones a la comunidad y por ello objeto de apertura de expediente por "conducta peligrosa", de acuerdo con las nuevas modificaciones introducidas en dicho Código, tras la segunda advertencia a la jinetera para que voluntariamente deje su actividad' (2005: 167–8).

A este viejo gordo, calvo, colorado y refunfuñón – rima con bugarrón – no se lo tiempla ni la mismísima María Magdalena con diez varas de hambre. Además, no tenía tanto dinero como se nos pintaba en La Habana. [...] En fin, mi cielo, que estoy harta de este viejo tirapeos, que no se preocupa por evitar los eructos más escandalosos ni en casa de la madre que lo parió, y menos en sitios públicos. (Valdés 1995: 95–6)

The Spanish man is turned into an *esperpento*, as are all Spanish men, whose manliness is constantly questioned by la Gusana. The author tries to destabilize the idea of the Spanish *macho* in order to question fixed concepts of maleness:

Aquí los amantes cuestan carísimos, o en el mejor de los casos es a la americana, a pagar mitad y mitad. [...] La mayoría son homosexuales, no quieren cuento con una. Porque si al menos le metieran mano a los dos bandos, tú sabes que yo no estoy en ná, y que no tengo prejuicios. Pero ellos son recalcitrantes con los pipis. Las totas, vaya, no hay quien se las haga poner delante, lo de ellos son los rabos. Y de eso estamos todas en falta. (Valdés 1995: 97)

La Gusana reveals that sexuality is a cultural construct and calls for a more fluid sexuality, although in doing so she reveals her own sexual prejudices with reference to homosexuality:

No creas, ahora seguro te desmayarás, que hasta he pensado meterme a lesbiana. Una ve aquí tantas películas con tetas enormes y paradas, nalgas duras, mujeres toqueteándose que se te moja el blúmer y sin quererlo te viniste mirando a dos tipas chupándose los pezones y los clítoris. Y figúrate, ése es el cine que alquila en vídeo mi Bayoya. Pero el sexo con las mujeres – cuentan algunas revistas – es más peligroso con respecto al sida, porque con los tipos le encasquetas el preservativo y ya, pero todavía para las perillas no se han inventado las cámaras antiefluvios, o comoquieran [*sic*] llamarle, y el agüita cremosita cuando sale puede venir haciéndose la inocentita, pero, ¿y si está cundía de cualquier bacteria asesina de esas de filmes de terror? ¡P'allá, p'allá! (Valdés 1995: 97–8)

In a comic tone the narrator connects lesbianism with pathology; the female fluids have connotations of danger and terror. The female body is again dismembered and reduced to concrete parts that have sexual connotations. I suggest that this terror of lesbian sex has to do with the very traditional idea that homosexuality is unhealthy and contagious, an illness in itself. The connection between lesbianism and HIV is repeated by la Gusana, exposing her homophobia. Valdés uses this discourse to parodic effect.

La Gusana also makes fun of Spanish women, who appear as victims of traditional patriarchal society; they are cheated on by their husbands and are constantly ill-treated by them. The narrator shows neither pity for nor any kind of identification with these women. However, in a more serious tone she considers the ill-treatment received by Cuban prostitutes in Spain:

> Aquí vienen a visitarme, muy discreticas ellas, mulaticas casi niñas, o negritas cabezas de clavos, abandonadas por sus Pepes, o escapadas de ellos. Varias ejercen la prostitución clandestina, viven ilegales y lloran de terror, hambre y frío. Porque una cosa es putear en verano y otra bajo una nevada que pela. (Valdés 1995: 99–100)

The exploitation of these women is evident within and beyond Cuba. In Valdés' narrative exile does not seem to show a better future for women, who have to face ill-treatment, hunger and cold. The comparison between Cuba's and Spain's weather is ambiguous enough to raise the implicit question of where is the better place to live. Capitalism is not immune from the critiques of la Gusana, although she makes a pun with the Cuban slogans against capitalism, reversing them – capitalism is not only the enemy of socialism but also the enemy of one's pocket:

> En eso les doy la razón a los hablacáscaras [*sic*] de allá, la propaganda es realmente enemiga, pero enemiga del bolsillo. Oye, que te va envolviendo y enloqueciéndote: hoy una marca de champú, mañana el acondicionador y pasado mañana la cera depiladora, y los helados, los dulces, el jabón éste y el otro y el de más allá con leche de cabra y glicerina, y el perfume de mañana y el de tarde y el de noche, que le pararían la cabilla hasta al viejo don Rafael del Junco, el de *El derecho de nacer*, la radionovela. (Valdés 1995: 101)

Eventually, the narrator reverses the identification of exile with nostalgia and identifies Cubanness as a condition that continues even abroad; that is, it is intrinsic to all Cubans and cannot be erased by bureaucracy. There is an opposition between nationality, which is just a formality, a part of bureaucracy, and Cubanness, which is the essence of the person:

> Al casarme con el Viejo perdí mi nacionalidad, pero sólo significó unos cuantos trámites burocráticos, no sufrí como para cortarme las venas. Yo por dentro soy más cubana que las palmas, eso nadie me lo va a poder arrancar. Tampoco soy una patriotera extremista. Yo digo que Martí vivió la mayor parte de su vida en el extranjero, y más cubano que él hay que mandarlo a hacer. (Valdés 1995: 102)

Above all, la Gusana challenges all attempts to impose an image of a stable and fixed reality, which always appears as an imposture. She also defies homogeneous concepts of identity and, more specifically, of masculinity:

> Allá sí que no me iba a quedar. ¡Nada más de acordarme de aquella consigna que incitaba a morirse parado me entra un dolor de pies! ¿A

quién se le ocurrió tamaña sandez? Que si los cristales son los únicos que tienen derecho a rajarse, que si 'los hombres mueren de pie'. Yo estoy más intacta que nunca y pretendo morirme como la mayoría de los humanos, en horizontal. Una vez alguien me reprimió comentándome que esa frase pertenecía a Martí, pues si es así, él también pudo haber tenido frases equivocadas, que no siempre y a toda hora la gente está obligada a ser brillante e intachable.

Oye, que esas especies en extinción siguen viviendo su pedacito de lo irreprochable, irrevocable, indispensable, inevitable... Y no acaban de darse cuenta de lo insoportables que resultan, de lo invisible que es esa impuesta realidad. ¡Coño, la vida es civil! (Valdés 1995: 102–3)

La Gusana in the previous discourse criticizes the monolithic idea of masculinity. The figure of Martí represents the icon of masculinity, Cubanness and exile; he is usually venerated by both exiles and Cubans on the island and the narrator denounces the way in which his figure has been treated as monolithic and homogeneous. She condemns the imposition of such rigid concepts on humankind. Thus, she also challenges hegemonic discourses about national identity and denounces them as impositions that are distant from the essence of the Cuban people. La Gusana only has a voice through her letters; writing is the only way that she can liberate herself from her entrapment in exile and express how she feels. This character helps the author to criticize another reality, a reality that is not the Cuban one, and thus tries to neutralize the inside/outside the island dichotomy. Moreover, through la Gusana, Valdés exposes the difficulties of being in exile and, as Reinaldo Arenas also does in his texts, disrupts the representations of ideal paradises both within and beyond the island.

In the eighth chapter of the novel, entitled 'Las noches del Nihilista', the author establishes an intertextual reference with the famous chapter 8 of Lezama Lima's novel *Paradiso*. The author stresses the subversive nature of eroticism and creates a parallel between the novel we are reading and that of Lezama Lima: she conjectures that her novel will be censored as *Paradiso* was. She advances two main subjects in this chapter: the erotic nature of her relationship with el Nihilista, and censorship in Cuba, of which el Nihilista is a victim. He is a marginal independent filmmaker because his films try to portray a Cuba that is kept hidden from the media. It is not gratuitous that the narrator nicknames him 'nihilist', that is, a person who does not believe in any religious, political or social principle. He is a drug user, and with drugs he and the protagonist distance themselves from reality. It is not by chance that this marginal male character is the one who the protagonist really loves; he is not identified with the political system; he is a victim of it and therefore appears in this narration as a dialogic character, the only one of her lovers with whom the protagonist can have a dialogic erotic relationship. The historical, socio-political, economic and erotic repression is subverted by Yocandra with el Nihilista from this chapter until the end of the novel.

In this chapter Valdés disrupts an erotic scene through the use of humour. The narrator, naked, waits for her lover; however, while this scene could be erotic, the narrator, rather, makes it hilarious:

> Miro el reloj, ya son las ocho y media de la noche y desde las siete y media estoy encuera a la pelota, bañada, perfumada, el pelo sobre los hombros. Hasta encendí el aire acondicionado, por suerte parece que no quitarán la luz esta noche, ya lo hicieron por la mañana. Estoy congelándome desnuda, esperando al Nihilista, con los pezones erizadísimos, los pies arrugados, contraída, la carne de gallina. Y Peter Frampton cantando *Show me the way*. (Valdés 1995: 130)

Again, the narrator creates a counter-erotic discourse, using humour to destroy any possibility of romanticism, and even the intertextual reference becomes hilarious in this context. As I shall illustrate below, in a flashback the narrator recalls her encounter with el Nihilista and she describes her first sexual experience with him. Once more, Valdés uses a different language to describe the erotic scene. The scene adopts the female point of view in which the man is objectified. In contrast to previous scenes, with el Nihilista the narrator shows respect. He is not ridiculed and the power relationship disappears. It is an erotic scene per se in which the bodies communicate and reach the unity that according Bataille (1962) is the aim of erotic encounter:

> El beso duró el resto de la película, pero no exclusivamente en la boca. Él fue descendiendo con experimentada lentitud por mi cuello, me lengüeteó desde la barbilla hasta los pezones, donde permaneció minutos de goce interminable. Al rato fue aún más despacio, de mis senos a las costillas y de ellas al ombligo, y la punta de su lengua hizo estragos en mi vientre. Mi vientre bailaba la danza persa, por no decir que me remendaba desaforada como una negra en un barracón. Después, con sus dedos largos, apartó mis pendejos y relució, rojo y erguido, mi clítoris. Allí estampó el beso que lo consagró para la eternidad, el Nobel del cunilingüismo. Su nombre debiera aparecer en el *Guinness* como el mamalón más profesional que haya conocido la historia de la civilización. Tuve siete orgasmos, o mejor, me vine siete veces. (Valdés 1995: 136–7)

Valdés again uses a direct language in which erotic descriptions are detailed, and also employs vocabulary specific to Cuba. Humour is still an important element in the erotic description; it is used to highlight and exaggerate the positive qualities of her lover. This use of humour is in contrast to that employed to ridicule el Traidor. With the use of humour the erotic scene is demystified and the narrator foregrounds popular, informal language that subverts the seriousness of any official monologic language. The narrator continues her description of the erotic scene, moving her female gaze across the male body:

Cuando él se desnudó, su cuerpo griego me dejó pasmá, boquiabierta, baba
incluida. Espaldas ligeramente más anchas que las caderas, puro lomito
ahumado, tostadas por el 'indio', nuestro sol nacional. Caderas estrechas,
nalgas perfectas, lisas, el vello surge debajo de la punta y agrede los
muslos. Muslos parejos, musculosos, piernas tensas, tobillos gruesos, pies
elegantísimos y bien proporcionados – lo que es un buen augurio – hasta
con el detalle del dedo del medio más largo que el gordo, y eso es, sin
discusión de ningún tipo, un pie ático. El cuello con la exacta medida, ni
muy ancho, ni muy largo. El pelo encrespado, rizos fresquísimos adornan
su frente. Nariz prominente y recta. Labios como el milo, malteados. Brazos
musculosos, pero sin aspavientos, muñecas fuertes, manos suaves y largas
[…] Este hombre se me antojaba una exquisita obra de arte por fuera y por
dentro. Porque es tierno, paciente y pacífico. Su voz nunca se altera en lo más
mínimo. Es mi amante, no mi verdugo. (Valdés 1995: 137)

Here the female gaze does not have as its function the production of pleasure
for female readers, as is sometimes the case in the erotic narratives of male
writers who attempt to produce a certain pleasure in male readers through
the description of the female body. I posit that the female narrator adopts the
traditional position of the male in erotic fiction in order to assert her right to
be the subject of an enunciation of this type, and, in more general terms, to
be the subject of a central discourse within society. She uses the patriarchal
ideal of masculinity to recontextualize it in feminine terms. The description
of el Nihilista's body ends with a detailed depiction of his penis which becomes personified. Humour appears once more to emphasize the sexual en-
dowment of el Nihilista, who appears as the embodiment of maleness from
a female perspective:

La pinga, ¡ay, San Lázaro bendito, mi Babalú Ayé! El toletón del Nihilista
es la octava maravilla del mundo. ¡Y cuida'o no ocupe el primer escaño en
el escalafón de las fortunas de este siglo! Porque portar un rabo como ése es
como poseer una cuenta de millones y millones de dólares en un banco suizo.
Debo señalar, antes de que lo olvide, que junto al ombligo tiene un lunar
negro y redondo. Y desde allí le emerge de los poros la sedosa pendejera que
es un sueño acariciarla. Cuando la mano tropieza con la raíz del miembro –
nada que ver con un miembro del cedeerre – no puedes evitarlo, la boca se te
hace agua, las comisuras espuman.
    Es liso. Mide catorce centímetros sin erección, el doble erecto. Pero
no sé si porque soy amplia de cavidad, o porque él se mueve sabiamente,
nunca me ha dolido ni me ha lastimado. Incluso ni en el palo del pespunte,
el que va de la vulva al ano y a la inversa. Es rosado como la piel de un
recién nacido, debajo de los tejidos brillan miles de venitas rojas, parece
un diminuto jardín de Príncipes Negros, que en cubano son las rosas rojas.
El pellejo es dócil, cubre y descubre cuando es menester hacerlo, como un
mantón *belle époque*. Al tacto tiene la calidez de la jalea real, ese vigor que

cura la más emperrá amigdalitis. El centro es sólido, a prueba de derrumbes, apuntala'o desde siglos inverosímiles a.n.e., semejante a una columna del Partenón. La cabeza es – como un ordenador con el software más avanzado y eficaz – putona y cerebral, porque va justo al punto álgido, al del triunfo. No descansa hasta agotar las vías a la solución perfecta, la posición cómoda, la operación adecuada. Ejecuta febrilmente. Ella, la picha, 'no busca, encuentra', como Picasso. Es vibrante y sabrosona. Exhala un perfume a piel lavanda con *Mon savon*, ese jabón francés a base de extractos de fórmulas de perfumes antiquísimos, pachulí, jazmín, rosas, leche de cabra. [...] ¡Leche, leche de mi corazón! La savia de este hombre es como cuando ordeñan a una Holstein jovenzuela, y el chorro cae en la vasinilla igualito al maná celestial. Ése es precisamente el sabor de la esperma de este extraterrestre, un buche estrellado, luminoso, interplanetario, vía satélite. Un ponche repleto de una turba de saludables, deportivos y preñadores espermatozoides. (Valdés 1995: 137–9)

The erotic value of el Nihilista is focused on his penis, that is, his body and not his psyche. The depiction of the penis is presented through many comparisons and references that create a hypertext, a web of references in which the penis is not the important referent, as what is important here is what the penis represents. The male sign opens up multiple meanings and processes of signification. The penis is described using the five female senses and in terms related to technology and the study of art. The male genitals are both the instrument that produces pleasure and the instrument used to create a new language. Thus, male genitalia become part of the text itself; the source of pleasure and the producer of language. The narrator uses a pun to break any possible connection between el Nihilista's 'member' and the members of the CDR (*cedeerre*) – Comités de Defensa de la Revolución – and hence the erotic scene serves to challenge official discourses.

We, as readers, know very little about el Nihilista and his relationship with the protagonist; eroticism is the key element. Through the description of their sexual experiences together there is an opposition established between el Nihilista and el Traidor:

Él se quita la ropa y corre detrás de mí, falseando la carrera, jugando a los cogidos, obstaculizando el trayecto con muebles para emocionarnos más. Decide cogerme y me besa mordiéndome cerca de diez minutos [...] El pellizco hizo el efecto de un latido en su morronga, los testículos endurecidos se le recogen. Mis tetas se aprietan contra ellos y mi lengua da la bienvenida a la monárquica cabeza del animal, al rey de aquella selva que forman los pelos del pubis. Succiono hasta quedar exhausta. [...] Vómito y placer, arqueadas y mareo jubiloso. Mi clítoris se tensa, mi vulva mojada se encarrancha. [...] Entiendo perfectamente que debo enterrar su sexo en el mío y moverme de un lado a otro [...] o simplemente erguir mi espalda para que los pezones den exactos con su boca y él pueda de esta forma chuparlos hasta el hartazgo. Ahí tengo mi primer orgasmo. Lento, gozándolo centímetro a centímetro, con los ojos idos en los suyos y los pelos de su pecho rascando mis paradas tetas. [...] El rabo descansa entre mis nalgas, él las aprieta, y como yo me meneo, aquello resulta ser una masturbación sensacional, como cuando se hace entre los senos [...] al introducir sólo la puntica el dolor es tan agudo que casi me desmayo. Sin embargo, ni eso me despoja del deseo fulminante que siento de ser ensartada por detrás [...] Mi licor vaginal, natilla grumosa, se desliza por mis muslos como nunca, hacia las rodillas. El escozor ancestral remueve mis labios inferiores, ¡necesito ahí dentro el relleno viril! Me arde la piel y él me pasa un trozo de hielo por las axilas, por los calcañales, por la entrepierna. Tengo fuego uterino y él introduce dos cuadritos gélidos que derrito al instante. [...] Así, latiente y mentolada, él me penetra hasta la altura del ombligo, mi papaya coge aire y de su sexo se esparce un fuego intermitente, se extingue, vuelve a inflamarse, resultado de la mezcla del vaposán con la pomada del Tigre. Es como si me rayaran una caja de fósforos familiar completita dentro, y cada uno de los fósforos rayados fuera un orgasmo que debilita mis sentidos y me expone con mayor docilidad al goce. Ahí pierdo la cuenta. No sé cuántas veces son, infinitas. Casi a punto de perder el conocimiento, él pega sus labios a los míos y me besa atontado. Un escalofrío en el centro de gravedad nos recorre a los dos. Segundos después, su esperma inunda mi raja. Tengo visiones fantasmagóricas, de realidad virtual. (Valdés 1995: 143–7)

For the first time in the novel, through eroticism, the lovers attain a unity in which the boundaries between their bodies disappear. The sexual act becomes a form of resistance and a way of evading reality. Both the female and the male are in the same position and hand in hand. It is in the erotic encounter with el Nihilista that Yocandra finds an encounter with the Other. In this scene humour disappears and eroticism acquires transcendental nuances. There are no hierarchies or power relationships. These two characters become dialogic voices in a constant process of becoming.

   In the last chapter of the novel, entitled 'Y yo que lo tenía en un altar', el Traidor enters the protagonist's flat, breaking the balance she had achieved between herself and her two lovers. It is here that the masks fall away. The protagonist must explain to her lovers the nicknames she has given them, and thus we see the importance of naming. In a way, both el Traidor and el Nihilista reject the nicknames that she has given them, but the contrast between her lovers is obvious. The explanation of el Traidor's nickname reveals the true nature of his character. Her revenge is to unmask him, as she states:

No creas que te guardo rencor por los tarros que me pegaste, ya eso no tiene ninguna importancia para nadie. [...] Lo que hago, lo hago por humanidad, porque la venganza también es humana. [...] ese apodo en nada tiene que ver con alguna pasión personal. [...] ¿No te das cuenta, no te miras en un espejo? ¿Cuándo vas a dejar de traicionarte a ti mismo? ¿Cuándo acabarás de ser coherente con tus propios pensamientos? ¿Cuándo dejarás de inventarte a ti mismo, haciendo creer que estás escribiendo un libro? [...] Tú vives en la traición. Eres el traidor de ti mismo. Necesitas traicionar las pequeñas cosas de la vida. [...] Si acepté seguir la relación contigo, si permití que regresaras, fue para vengarme, y creo que incluso te estoy ayudando. (Valdés 1995: 153–4)

When the mask falls away the male character has to face himself. The process of learning is now reversed: now the male character, in a relationship with his lover, undergoes a process of self-discovery and is forced to face himself without any mask. The narrator gains control of the situation. This is her real revenge:

Eres adicto a la lástima. Dudé mucho cuando quise rebautizarte, tenía dos opciones: la Víctima o el Traidor. Escogí la última porque es más abarcadora, y porque a la larga un traidor siempre es víctima de algo, de alguien, ni que sea de sí mismo. Se acabó. Ni siquiera te odio. [...] Si te queda una gota de vergüenza te largas, si no, puedes quedarte. Aquí tendrás un refugio. Pero la siguiente condición: terminó tu dictadura. (Valdés 1995: 155)

It is in this last chapter that the narrator assumes her new position as female subject. There is a kind of epiphany in which the narrator is aware of herself and of her surroundings, and of her need to act and acquire agency through her writing:

Mis ojos casi sangran de lágrimas. Los aprieto y el líquido salado despega mis pestañas con gruesos goterones. Me estoy muriendo, me muero. No pueden ocurrirme tantas cosas al mismo tiempo. Y sin embargo, parece como si nada ocurriera, como si desde que nací hiciera lo mismo, callarme, estallar, llorar. Callarme, estallar, llorar. He roto mi pasividad. (Valdés 1995: 156)

The protagonist places herself within the context of a whole nation and emerges as the representative of its suffering. She appears alienated by those who represent power and by those who state in homogeneous and monolithic terms what an individual must be like:

Ser melancólica es mi protesta, la huelga que soy capaz de hacer para independizar mi tristeza de la tristeza colectiva, para ganar que me rebajen el horario de angustia asalariada, pagada con el salario del deber. Como si con el deber se pudiera comprar, por ejemplo, azúcar o petróleo. Nací marcada por el deber transcendental. Debí ser fiel a mis progenitores. Debí ser fiel a la patria. Debí ser fiel a la escuela. Debí ser fiel a las organizaciones de masas y a las otras. Debí ser fiel a los símbolos patrios. Debí ser fiel a mis 'compañeros'. Debí ser fiel a todo lo que no me fue fiel. Por exceso o por defecto. Queridos paternalistas, miren cómo me mata la fidelidad. (Valdés 1995: 157)

Against these 'paternalistas', she clearly identifies the force that oppresses her as masculine. She states: 'Lloro infiel, y ésa es mi cobarde prueba de coraje. Saber que lloro porque no creo en nada' (Valdés 1995: 157). She declares herself unfaithful and an unbeliever; she is also a nihilist. And the process of self-discovery reaches the end when 'Hoy me cae encima toda la vida de golpe: mi infancia, mis padres, la Gusana, el Lince, el Traidor, el Nihilista, la oficina, el mar… el país' (1995: 157). The process of writing becomes the only manner of reflecting on a genuine self, as in society she must wear a mask in order to survive:

> Para ser sincera y no engañar a nadie, mucho menos a mí, podría quitarme toda esa cagalera de la cabeza y dedicarme a mi otro yo ficticio. Sacar la careta reservada para la supervivencia: yo, jefa de redacción de una prestigiosa revista literaria. Asisto lo mismo a asambleas, consejillos, reuniones, que a recepciones en embajadas. Mantengo la boca cerrada, porque en boca cerrada no entran moscas. (Valdés 1995: 158)

The boundaries between reality and fiction blur. Her life appears as the constant loss of material goods and her loved ones. Writing seems to be the only way she can resist 'la nada cotidiana', nothingness, and is also a way to negotiate her identity, her Cubanness, her gender; a means to negotiate between what she is meant to be and what she really is. The fact that the protagonist starts writing when she has her two lovers in her flat and when she has faced her own feelings towards them shows the connections established in the novel between sexuality and the process of writing:

> Estoy ante un cuaderno rayado, devanándome los sesos. […] Busco cualquier pretexto en cada mínimo objeto que me rodea para no seguir pensando más. Para no comprometerme con algo que no sé si podré hacer, si tendré ovarios: describir la nada que es mi todo. […] Invoco a mis orishas: ¡Denme fuerzas! […] Porque tengo el miedo más grande del mundo. Por eso chachareo y chachareo. Para impedirme comenzar. Para evitarme iniciar la frase. Para autocensurar las palabras que, como unas locas, unas putas, unas hadas, unas diosas, explotan desaforadas con la tinta de la pluma que mis dedos aprietan. Porque hay amigos muy grandes que murieron, otros que se fueron y otros que se quedaron. Todos aquí, dentro de mí. Dentro de las palabras que no sé más si soy yo quien las escribe. O si son ellas las que me escriben a mí. (Valdés 1995: 167)

This polyphonic character will start writing the novel we have already read. The process of writing means a process of self-discovery, of scripting her subjectivity, and implies also the knowledge of her surroundings. As the protagonist/narrator/author becomes the voice of those who lack one, she evolves into being the representative of a whole nation and of collective memory. I agree with Cristina Ortiz Ceberio when she states:

Ambos nación y sujeto [...] se presentan identificados en los textos de la escritora. De esta manera el erotismo, el placer, el deseo son las marcas que se reclaman y entretejen el discurso narrativo en las obras de Valdés. En ellas se presenta un discurso en el cual se define lo erótico-popular, el hedonismo, el placer como oposición al discurso estatal, a la cartilla de racionamiento y a la asamblea. El placer, la noche, el cuerpo, se introducen en la narración como las instancias de las que emana un discurso que quiere ser disperso en sus contenidos, plural, ambiguo: Discurso que desenmarque el imaginario colectivo del discurso nacional clausurante y lo devuelva a la apertura. De esta manera, podríamos decir que, en su narrativa, Valdés aboga por la construcción de un discurso sobre el imaginario colectivo que se haga desde un ángulo que podríamos llamar la 'memoria del cuerpo' [...] Si la emergencia de un discurso alternativo se hace desde la reivindicación de lo carnal, es importante resaltar que ésta se hace desde un *locus femenino*. [...] Así, en las primeras páginas de La nada cotidiana, la primera descripción de las emociones de la narradora/protagonista indican las dos palabras claves en la narrativa de Valdés: cuerpo y resistencia, que en la narración se disuelven en un concepto único: resistencia corporal. (1998: 120–1)

The narrator rewrites herself in her version of her sexual relationships and in her social context. Throughout her sexual experiences we witness the personal development of the protagonist who exercises an active role against patriarchal oppression. With and within her writing the woman moves from a marginal position to occupy a central position. In *La nada cotidiana* the author questions what it means to be Cuban and female and challenges any stable and established notion of identity. The female narrator, even after painful sexual relationships, seeks to complement herself by meeting the Other through her sexual experiences with a man. This encounter is expressed through a large part of the narrative we are reading. Writing shows her importance as producer of a feminine discourse in the process of creation itself. The protagonist rejects the use of sexuality for reproduction but projects her erotic energy into her creative act, the act of writing. Humour also permeates the novel; the female narrator uses it in order to subvert official and hegemonic discourses, and to demystify sexuality. She eliminates romanticism and creates an anti-erotic discourse that serves to show her version of a crude reality without romantic idealism and euphemisms. The narrator asks her readers to be active in order to read between the lines and to decode the different levels of reading generated in her text. As Susan Sellers explains in relation to Luce Irigaray's feminist philosophy:

She [Irigaray] suggests that at present there are two paths women might take. One is for women to endeavour to become men's 'equal', in which case we would enjoy the same economic, social and political rights as men, but would, she believes, still be required to adopt the 'masquerade' of femininity as this has been prescribed by the masculine. The other is for women to reject the masculine system of (self-) representation, and to 'become speaking

subjects as well' and in our own way. She believes this production of an
other symbolic would have radical implications for both sexes, undermining
the foundations of the patriarchal schema and opening this to the possibility
of change. (1991: 80)

In *La nada cotidiana* we find elements of both paths, but with an emphasis on
the creation of 'an other symbolic', where female discourse moves to the centre
of the narration and the female protagonist becomes a dialogic speaking subject
who creates a new language in order to represent herself and to validate her
position of equality within Cuban society at least. When Yocandra becomes a
speaking subject she can express her real self and transforms the place that
patriarchal society has given to women. In sum, through her erotic encounters
Yocandra creates a dialogic relationship with el Nihilista and inserts herself into
the Symbolic but with her female voice.

Conclusion

I have argued in this study that dialogism is at the core of the Cuban literature produced in the 1990s, having a particular fluidity that had not been seen in earlier decades. I have posited that the decade that I study here represents a narrative junction, in part as a response to the hardship and social changes following the 1980 Mariel boatlift and particularly during the Special Period in the early 1990s. The latter is especially relevant for the writers studied here, except for Reinaldo Arenas who left Cuba during the Mariel boatlift. His response was more politically motivated from the very beginning, but I have used his work to indicate the turning point that led to more dramatic narrative changes in the Cuban novel of the 1990s. Indirectly, I have studied similarities and differences in a selection of writers from this decade, starting with Arenas, who died in 1990, but whose novel *El color del verano* was published posthumously in 1991 and prepared the ground for a new era of writing. I have studied issues concerning dialogism and polyphony, carnival and simulacra, intertextuality, the rewriting of history and the resulting palimpsest, erotic discourse, the body as a feminine strategy used by women authors and the use of language to particular effect between the Semiotic and the Symbolic. It has been my aim to allow the texts to suggest new readings. I have favoured close critical readings in combination with relevant theoretical approaches that shed light on the texts, particularly because the writers themselves seem to adapt to current literary trends. The topos of transtextuality, for example, is central to all six writers studied in this book, but they approach it from different angles, mostly with reference to intertextuality, the palimpsest and rhizomatic writing.

I have studied the ways in which Cuban writers have developed different narrative techniques in order to challenge and subvert fixed notions of identity, reality and the text itself. I also claim that during the 1990s there was an increase in the production of polyphonic novels. Following Bakhtin's terminology, I have interpreted polyphonic novels as those in which there is a 'plurality of equally-valid consciousnesses, each with its own world' (Bakhtin in Morris 1994: 89). As Sue Vice states, '[p]olyphony is dialogic in form' and '[w]ithout polyphony, dialogism is impossible' (1997: 112, 113). The authors who I have analysed create dialogism by means of the interactions between the different voices that constitute the polyphony; in many of these texts even the narrator's voice interacts with the other characters' voices; '[t]he polyphonic novel is a democratic

one, in which equality of utterance is central' (Vice 1997: 112). In the novels I
have studied, dialogism is also created by the use of intertextuality, heteroglossia and irony, the carnivalization and eroticization of discourse and the constant
use of masks. I have also argued that these texts, as representatives of particular
tendencies in the Cuban novel of the 1990s, focus on the concept of subjectivity. As is characteristic of dialogic characters, the Cuban writers that I have
studied, in accordance with the Bakhtinian concept of the subject, create dialogic subjects whose 'identity is always experienced as dispersed, unfinished
process, *self* consciousness is always unboundaried' (Morris 1994: 88, her italics). As I have shown, these dialogic characters contribute to an undermining
of the hegemonic official discourse of power that in these novels appears as
monologic and monolithic; that is, in the narratives selected here the discourse
of characters that represent power is an authoritative discourse. As Pam Morris
explains in reference to Bakhtin's dialogic theory:

> Any ruling class will attempt to monologize the word, imposing an eternal
> single meaning upon it, but a living ideological sign is always dialogic. Any
> word can be reaccentuated – a curse can be spoken as a word of praise – and
> any word can provoke its counter-word' (1994: 13).

Morris argues that, according to Bakhtin:

> Within language there is always at work a centripetal force which aims at
> centralizing and unifying meaning. Without this impulse the shared basis of
> understanding necessary for social life would disintegrate. This centripetal
> force in discourse is put to use by any dominant social group to impose its own
> monologic, unitary perceptions of truth. However, always working against
> that centralizing process is a centrifugal force – the force of heteroglossia –
> which stratifies and fragments ideological thought into multiple views of the
> world. (1994: 15)

This is the reason why the Cuban authors whose texts I have examined here
have chosen heteroglossia, polyphony and intertextuality as their subversive
strategies against the discourse of power. As Vice explains, polyphony means
'multi-voicedness', while 'heteroglossia' means 'multi-languagedness' (1997:
113). As Morris explains:

> [A]ny monologic truth claims made by one social language will be relativized
> by the existence of other views of the world. Thus the dialogic relations
> within heteroglossia bring about the 'destruction of any absolute bonding
> of ideological meaning to language' [...] this is nothing less than 'a radical
> revolution in the destinies of human discourse: the fundamental liberation of
> cultural-semantic and emotional intentions from the hegemony of a single
> language... as an absolute form of thought'. (1994: 16)

In the novels that I have examined we can see the constant clash between the discourse of those characters who represent power and the rest of the characters who embody different social classes, professions and genders. For example, Mario Conde in *Máscaras* speaks in a different manner than Faustino Arayán; the main character of *La nada cotidiana* speaks differently than her father; and the nameless protagonist of *Al otro lado* speaks differently than the Oráculo or Torquemada, to cite just a few examples. This clash is even sharper when we speak about feminine discourse because, as I have argued, feminine discourse, in this case erotic discourse, presents a fluid feminine, interstitial subject in-between spaces. I have explored the use of erotic discourse in Chaviano, Canetti and Valdés as a dialogic mechanism to present the female subject as one who rejects her erotic objectivization and stresses her agency as a producer of discourse. In the novels that I have analysed, feminine discourse is permeated by the effects of the Semiotic over the Symbolic. Within a patriarchal society, women's discourse has as its origin the female body. The female protagonists that I have analysed are in a constant search for themselves and this search is pursued through eroticism. The female body appears as a site where unconscious drives open up and expand the limits of the concepts of femininity established by the phallocentric system. By means of eroticism the protagonists recreate themselves through the intertextual game, the use of masks and the encounter with the Other. In the novels of Chaviano, Canetti and Valdés the feminine discourse destabilizes fixed notions of identity and questions the role of women within society.

With the exception of *Casa de juegos*, the novels that I have included in this study share a a common interest in the process of writing itself, best exemplified by Abilio Estévez's *Tuyo es el reino*. As I have argued, these novels create a Barthesian infinite text through the conscious use of intertextuality. Writing appears as a strategy of resistance against the official discourse. Through writing, the subaltern occupies the centre of the discourse and generates and rewrites her or his own version of both history and the official literary tradition. The process of writing itself serves as a space in which marginal voices can be heard, and assumes the form of a palimpsest in order to undermine and expand the imposed limits of national and cultural identity. All these novelists recreate the island of Cuba in their narratives and use memory as a mechanism to analyse Cuban socio-political reality. The protagonists assume the role of the representatives of collective memory.

The use of masks is another narrative strategy used by the six authors studied here. This is closely related to the notion of the unfinalizability of the subject proposed by Bakhtin. The masks allow the deployment of intertextuality and identity appears as a social construct. In these novels the construction of identity is produced by discourse and by the endless playing of (gender) roles. The mask also reveals identity as fluid; the subject appears in a constant process of becoming – a process that challenges monologic notions of subjectivity. Through the use of masks, the authors studied here blur the boundaries between reality and performance. The masks become a plurivalent sign that covers as well as uncovers the true self of the individual. Thus, they is employed as a narrative strategy. Overall, the novels studied here denounce Cuban society as pure simulacra, in which the individual has to use a mask in order to survive by remaining camouflaged.

This concept of simulacra is pushed to the limits in Arenas's creation of the carnival and Padura's use of the figure of the transvestite. Arenas creates a Bakhtinian chronotope, the carnival, the upside-down world, in which Arenas's *locas* can be heard and can create their own history. But, contrary to Bakhtinian carnival, Arenas's carnival achieves the dethroning of the leader. Arenas transforms Cuban society into a mere carnival in which everybody is homosexual. Through the carnivalization of discourse Arenas denounces Castro's regime and parodies the official Cuban literary canon. Padura, on the other hand, uses the figure of the transvestite as a product of intertextuality. The transvestite appears as an in-between being who challenges the concept of Cubanness. He inserts the Other within the project of the creation of a national identity. The transvestite appears in this novel as the actor *par excellence*.

It has been the intention of this study to demonstrate that Cuban literature is not simply divided along political lines or binary cultural divides, and that the literature produced by Cuban writers in exile belongs to the discourse of the nation and to recreations of the island from multiple shores. All six writers are concerned with issues of *cubanía*, which direct their writing enterprises. Thus I would conclude that, at a time of social crisis, authors have responded by subverting official discourses and participating in the postmodern possibilities that allow for more fluid texts, without aspiring to ultimate signifieds. Nonetheless, it is true that all of them have Cuba at the core of their writing project, and questions of nationhood and identity have not escaped them. All six writers studied here have contributed to opening up new narrative spaces in which to analyse the nation dialogically.

Appendix 1

First Interview with Leonardo Padura Fuentes (8 March 2004)[1]

Ángela Dorado-Otero: Según aparece en *La nota del autor* en su novela *Máscaras* usted define a Mario Conde como una metáfora; ¿podría aclarar este punto?

Leonardo Padura Fuentes: Mario Conde no es ni puede ser un personaje real —aunque trato de que lo parezca. Como individuo es demasiado débil, melancólico, alcohólico y fatal. Como policía —viéndolo en la realidad de lo que debería ser un policía de verdad— es un desastre, porque casi es el antipolicía, por su rechazo a la violencia, al uso de la fuerza, a la prepotencia. Pero su trabajo como policía de ficción lo hace bien, y como personaje novelesco es una expresión de las preocupaciones, modos de ser y de vivir, esperanzas y frustraciones de mi generación, y al ser un compendio de todos esos propósitos es que lo considero una metáfora: es una solución literaria, un recurso retórico, para lograr mi propia comunicación con la realidad y expresarla.

ADO: Teniendo en cuenta su novela *Máscaras* y la figura tan recurrente del travesti, ¿qué lugar ocuparía éste en el proceso de creación del Hombre Nuevo? ¿Qué función le asignaría a esta figura del travesti dentro de dicha novela?

LPF: Bueno, en la creación del Hombre Nuevo el travesti sería un marginado, supongo, aunque no soy especialista en los componentes y condiciones del Hombre Nuevo, pues creo que no lo he visto nunca. Respecto a la función del travesti en la novela es más metafórica aun que la de Mario Conde: el travesti es la representación máxima de la ocultación, de la transformación, de la transmutación que muchas personas han debido adoptar —y no sólo en Cuba— para sobrevivir en una sociedad que por diversas vías lo obliga a ocultar sus verdaderos deseos y pensamientos.

---

[1]   This interview was published as part of the series 'Hoy conversamos con: Leonardo Padura Fuentes', http://literaturacubana.com/boletins/sept (8 March 2004); this website is no longer active.

ADO: Algunos críticos han negado la posibilidad de que el Marqués en su novela *Máscaras* haya sufrido represalias por su sexualidad. ¿Qué opina usted de esta lectura de la novela? A mi entender, el Marqués sufre represalias tanto por su obra, la estética travesti de su teatro, como por su sexualidad.

LPF: Estoy de acuerdo contigo. El Marqués —vaya, él también es metafórico— sufre el mismo destino que muchos artistas cubanos que a principios de los 70 fueron marginados no sólo por lo que hacían o escribían, sino también por lo que eran: religiosos, homosexuales, apáticos políticos...

ADO: ¿Cree usted en la teoría de que el lector participa activamente en la fijación del significado de la novela?

LPF: Creo que sí, pues el lector es quien completa el ciclo de la obra literaria. Al menos yo escribo para que me lean y lo que fija el lector de mis obras es parte de ellas, sin duda.

ADO: En su novela *Máscaras* hay constantes referencias a otros autores y a sus obras: Virgilio Piñera, Calderón, Artaud, Miller... etc. ¿Qué función tiene para usted dicha intertextualidad en su novela?

LPF: Yo creo que a estas alturas de la historia y de la literatura todo es intertextual: siempre existe un pre-texto del que partimos, un pre-texto que nos armó de una idea de estructura, del uso de un adjetivo, de la técnica para delinear un personaje. Sólo que no siempre se reconoce que se está siendo intertextual. En esta novela, sin embargo, yo me apropio libre y casi descaradamente de textos de otros autores y los engarzo con la historia que voy narrando, pues es una novela sobre la literatura, sobre los artistas, y asumí los patrimonios literarios como una parte del arsenal que podía y quería utilizar.

ADO: ¿Consideraría al personaje del Marqués como un ser carnavalesco? ¿Por qué?

LPF: Varios teóricos de la literatura, en las décadas finales del siglo pasado estudiaron lo carnavalesco, la carnavalización y otras carnavalidades semejantes en las obras de varios escritores, y esto puso de moda entre algunos escritores 'lo carnavalesco'. En el caso del Marqués creo que sí, que se pudiera considerar carnavalesco, pero mi intención es que fuera un personaje que se valiera de lo teatral —era su oficio— para representar sus papeles en la vida, antes y después, de su defenestración. Por otro lado, es un hombre con un sentido del humor muy cáustico, un tipo irónico y autosuficiente, que se disfraza para sentirse por encima del mundo y de esa manera esconde sus propios miedos e incertidumbres.

ADO: En *Máscaras*, el teatro del Marqués aparece como un producto de la transculturación en la que se mezclan elementos de teatro griego, japonés, o del teatro bufo cubano, además de aparecer la sociedad cubana como híbrida y heterogénea cultural y racialmente. ¿Considera usted que éstos son los rasgos definitorios de 'lo cubano'?

LPF: No, porque yo sería incapaz de decir cuales son esos rasgos definitorios. Son tantos los elementos que intervienen en la formación de lo cubano, en épocas y situaciones tan diversas, que sólo enunciarlos sería esquemático. Aunque, por supuesto, el carácter mestizo, híbrido, multicultural, multirracial y multirreligioso del cubano, de lo cubano, es indiscutible. Somos, con toda seguridad, una de las naciones más 'mulatas' del mundo, gracias a una conjunción histórica, geográfica, social y cultural muy especial. Y creo que esa ha sido la gran fortuna del ser cubano, de 'lo cubano': la capacidad para integrarlo todo y dar algo nuevo.

ADO: En su novela *Máscaras*, exceptuando a Mario Conde, creo que los personajes que representan la voz del poder como Faustino Arayán son personajes monológicos y monolíticos, personajes fijos que no sufren ningún cambio a lo largo de la novela y que se niegan a contrastar sus puntos de vista con el resto de los personajes, mientras que personajes como Conde o el Marqués mantienen un diálogo constante entre ellos y a través de este diálogo se constituye su identidad; sus puntos de vista se intercambian, se oponen y se complementan sin llegar a transformarse uno en el otro pero influyendo uno en el otro. ¿Por qué este constraste entre las voces que representan el poder y las demás voces?

LPF: No había advertido ese detalle, pero es posible que así sea. Quizás estaba en mi subconsciente que así ocurriera en las novelas. Y en el caso específico de Faustino Arayán se trata de un personaje malévolo, en todos los sentidos, y no me interesaba que cambiara, mejorara, dialogara: debía ser así, pues en la vida hay tipos así... y, pensándolo un poco, quizás esta actitud que se refleja en mi construcción del personaje tenga que ver con mi poca simpatía por las personas como él, ¿no te parece?

Second Interview with Leonardo Padura Fuentes (18 July 2006)

Ángela Dorado-Otero: Como usted bien dice en la NOTA DEL AUTOR tanto de *Máscaras* como de *Adiós, Hemingway*, usted practica en sus novelas 'la licencia poética y posmoderna' de la intertextualidad. ¿De qué manera esta práctica afecta a su concepción de lo que es un texto, un autor o un lector y hasta qué punto afecta a las relaciones que se establecen entre éstos?

Leonardo Padura Fuentes: Pienso que los estudiosos de la literatura (yo lo he sido, todavía lo soy) vemos este tipo de procesos, fenómenos, estrategias desde una perspectiva diferente a la que tiene el escritor a la hora de ejecutarlos. Y es lógico: si uno, al parafrasear, utilizar, o hasta copiar un texto de otro autor se preguntara por todas estas 'afectaciones', sencillamente no escribiría. Por lo tanto todo se produce desde una perspectiva más utilitaria, o lúdica, o sensorial que desde una postura científica y racional, y apenas tiende una relación textual con otro autor para cumplir una necesidad del propio texto. Al menos así lo siento yo cuando estoy del lado de acá.

ADO: Aunque no es algo nuevo dentro de la literatura cubana, en la narrativa cubana de los años noventa existe un incremento en el uso de la figura del homosexual y/o travesti, (su novela *Máscaras* forma parte de esta nueva tendencia). ¿A qué factores atribuiría el (ab)uso de esta(s) figura(s)?

LPF: Sin duda al hecho de que había sido una figura marginada, escamoteada, discriminada en la sociedad y en la literatura, y eso le aportaba no sólo una posibilidad de explotación artística, sino, y sobre todo, un dramatismo intrínseco generado por la marginación, el escamoteo y la discriminación de marras, que se producen en una sociedad esencialmente machista, pero además oficialmente marxista, que por años consideró al homosexual no sólo como un enfermo pervertido, sino también como un ser no compatible con la ideología oficial.

ADO: A lo largo de las novelas que tienen como protagonista a Mario Conde aparece reiteradamente la idea del mundo del teatro y del teatro del mundo. Incluso el travesti se ensalza como el actor por antonomasia, Hemingway se crea a sí mismo como un personaje dentro de un teatro. El asesinato de Alexis Arayán es comparado con una tragedia griega. ¿Podría comentar acerca de esta idea de la teatralidad dentro de sus novelas?

LPF: El teatro es la representación de los dramas de la vida y lo teatral es una exacerbación de esa representación de lo real–vivido. Esa es la dimensión primera en que me interesa la teatralidad. Luego, el teatro es también la imitación, el fingimiento, el ser otro que asume el actor. Y esa duplicidad puede tener diversas connotaciones, desde sexuales y políticas, como ocurre en *Máscaras*, hasta literarias y éticas, como en *Adiós, Hemingway*, según el Hemingway que yo elaboro. Con esa duplicidad se produce un enmascaramiento del ser real, que se refugia o transfigura detrás del ser teatral que es el visible. Y esa necesidad humana, política, social de esconderse tras la máscara es la que me hace atractivo este recurso. ¿Por qué alguien se enmascara, se oculta, se difumina detrás de otro-yo visible? Eso es lo que busco explicar en algunas de mis novelas.

ADO: La memoria colectiva versus la memoria individual constituye uno de los temas más recurrentes dentro de sus novelas. Incluso Mario Conde aparece como un maldito recordador. ¿Me podría hablar del papel que juega la memoria en sus novelas y en este caso en particular?

LPF: En mis libros hay una doble polaridad memorística, si pudiéramos llamarla así. Por un lado está el rescate de una memoria digamos que tradicional, una memoria del pasado, que se va perdiendo por diversas razones: el tiempo, los cambios del mundo, etc., pero también por ser relegada a favor de otra memoria que, desde la propaganda oficial, se privilegia, en la medida en que el pasado se convierte en soporte del presente, cuando se destaca de él lo que le interesa a quienes actúan desde el presente y lo moldean. Pero hay otra memoria rescatada y esta es, precisamente, la más compleja, pues la memoria de la contemporaneidad, la memoria de lo que estamos viviendo hoy y que, al no tener demasiados asideros textuales, varios escritores cubanos tratamos de rescatar y establecer desde la cercanía de los hechos, para fijarla. Ese doble juego está muy presente en mis libros, pues me muevo siempre entre un pasado pretérito y un presente no oficial, pero que en ambos casos son reales, existieron y existen y tienen derecho a ser fijados y reelaborados.

Esta práctica está presente en todas las novelas de mi serie policial, encarnada especialmente en la nostalgia, la melancolía, la constante evocación del pasado del personaje de Mario Conde; pero es la sustancia misma de *La novela de mi vida*, un libro en el que coloco al presente en el espejo del pasado y, acercándolos casi hasta tocarse, hago un recorrido por 200 años de vida, cultura, poesía y nacionalidad cubanas.

ADO: Leyendo *Máscaras* me pregunto si hay algún motivo especial para que usted escogiera la *Electra Garrigó* de Virgilio Piñera como la obra teatral que provoca la defenestración y el exilio interior del Marqués, sobre todo cuando Piñera por tanto tiempo fue visto como un escritor maldito.

LPF: No especialmente-especial: sólo que esa obra es emblemática del teatro cubano, es la que marca el salto a la modernidad, y porque, al ser una de las tantas recreaciones del mito de Electra, trabaja la relación entre padre–hijo, entre ciudadano–poder, pero desde una perspectiva totalmente cubana, sin que se refiera a un contexto preciso, a una época específica. Todo ese carácter universal del mito y su reelaboración me parecían un punto de apoyo inmejorable para hablar después de padres e hijos, artistas y poder en el contexto cubano contemporáneo.

ADO: En *Máscaras* Alexis Arayán es católico, el día de la Transfiguración de Cristo, día de su muerte, se identifica con Cristo. Además también aparecen otros personajes católicos como Candito el Rojo o Eligio Riego. ¿Qué papel y qué función tienen para usted estos personajes dentro de la novela?

LPF: En unos casos es simbólico, como ocurre en Alexis; en otros es consustancial al personaje, como Eligio Riego; y en otros es un reflejo de una vida social cubana en la que la religiosidad se convierte en un asidero, como ocurre con Candito. El más notable es, por supuesto, el caso de Alexis, donde, como hice con Electra, me apoyé en el mito cristiano de la Transfiguración, pero sobre todo para trabajar esa traumática relación entre padre poderoso e hijo que es sacrificado por la decisión paterna. El hecho de que Cristo haya venido al mundo más a morir que a vivir siempre me ha parecido cruel y dramático, una especie de castigo divino que su padre le endilga sin él tener la menor posibilidad de escoger. Y eso es muy literario, altamente dramático, y por eso siempre me ha atraído, y no por razones místicas. Como dijo Buñuel, gracias a Dios soy ateo.

ADO: Debo confesar que desgraciadamente me ocurre como a Conde y, tras varias lecturas de *Máscaras* le tengo que preguntar: ¿Quién es el Otro Muchacho?

LPF: Es cualquiera y es nadie: es el oportunista, simplemente, ese tipo que hemos padecido tanto en tantas partes del mundo, pero que en Cuba ha sido un látigo, una constante, pues existe un terreno especialmente propicio para su procreación.

ADO: En sus novelas aparece el tema de la literatura como venganza, como resistencia ante la opresión y el olvido. ¿Es ésta su visión personal de la literatura?

LPF: Es una de mis concepciones de la literatura. Es que no sé si por suerte o por desgracia, tengo muy arraigada la conciencia de que la literatura tiene una función social que siempre debe cumplir. Por eso no imagino sentarme a escribir una novela (dos, tres años), o un relato (una, dos semanas) y no tener como primera prioridad la intención de decir algo sobre mi sociedad, mi tiempo, mis desilusiones con respecto a ellas, en fin, algo que comunique mis obsesiones, preocupaciones, frustraciones respecto al mundo en que vivo. Para eso escribo, y lo demás, todo lo demás, viene después. Por eso entre mis ideas sobre la función de la literatura está la resistencia: contra el olvido, contra la manipulación y la mentira, contra el oportunismo. Y trato de hacer todo esto, además, sin escribir una literatura abiertamente política, sin proponerme participar en el juego político de manera directa y sin afiliarme a un partido en específico que no sea el partido de la realidad en que vivo, de las experiencias que acumulo (por vivirlas o por verlas, oírlas, sentirlas), de lo que entiendo como la verdad.

ADO: En su novela *Adiós, Hemingway*, en contraposición con las anteriores, Conde es incapaz de descubrir la verdad del caso que está investigando, verdad que sólo el/la lector/a conoce a través de un narrador omnisciente. ¿A qué se debe este cambio y hasta qué punto es relevante en el ciclo de las novelas de Mario Conde?

LPF: En las cuatro novelas anteriores Conde logra descubrir una verdad policial que le ayuda a cerrar su caso como investigador. Pero en todas ellas saber esa verdad no lo satisface demasiado, incluso más de una vez hubiera preferido no conocerla, para no desgarrarse más. Por otro lado, en los argumentos de esas novelas la investigación estrictamente policial no es demasiado importante y, cada vez lo es menos. La verdad que Conde quiere saber, la que busca con más énfasis, no es quién asesinó a quién, sino por qué… Y en *Adiós, Hemingway* llevo esta noción a su extremo, pues la verdad policial le pasa por el lado sin que él pueda atraparla y, como ves, no le importa demasiado, porque mientras la perseguía, aprendió otras verdades más importantes sobre Hemingway, la condición del escritor, la amistad, la verdad y la mentira, la muerte que lo conmueven muchísimo más.

ADO: En *Adiós, Hemingway* ante la pregunta de Manolo '¿Y qué estás escribiendo ahora?' Conde responde 'La historia de un policía y un maricón que se hacen amigos'. Ante tal respuesta no puedo evitar pensar que *Máscaras* se convierte entonces en la obra de Mario Conde. ¿Tiene sentido lo que propongo? Y si no es así, ¿cuál es la función que tiene este guiño que usted le hace al lector?

LPF: De alguna forma Conde es una creación del propio Conde, y esto no es una pose. Conde es un personaje que se me ha escapado de las manos constantemente, que se ha empeñado en tener vida propia, con independencia de mis posibilidades de mandarlo a un sitio u otro, de hacerlo pensar de un modo u otro. Es un personaje diría que rebelde, que desde el inicio de nuestra relación fue estableciendo reglas y colocando las cosas en el sitio que correspondían según su carácter y personalidad. Más que un personaje creado, yo veo en él un hijo, también creado por mí, sobre el que tengo paternidad, influencia, cierto control, pero no todo el control, pues hay un gran porciento de él que creció con su propia dialéctica interna, con su lógica propia y ahí es donde Conde se comienza a escribir a sí mismo. Para reafirmar esa posibilidad, totalmente literaria, es que llega a afirmar algo como lo que citas o, al final de *Paisaje de otoño*, se encierra a escribir la primera novela de la serie y cierra un círculo de fuego en cuyo interior está él, solo, independiente, escribiéndose a sí mismo, dándose forma definitiva por sí solo.

ADO: Al final de *Adiós, Hemingway* Conde, el Flaco y el Conejo le mandan a Andrés, uno de sus mejores amigos que decidió irse a vivir a EEUU, un mensaje dentro de una botella de cristal que arrojan al mar. Veo esta imagen como una metáfora del diálogo que se debe establecer entre las 'dos orillas', la gente en exilio y la gente que vive en la isla. ¿Qué opina al respecto?

LPF: Mi propósito no era tan 'global', como se dice ahora, pero está implícito en ese que tú ves. El mensaje que va dentro de mi pequeña botella tiene que ver con la amistad: la necesidad de salvar ese pedacito que nos pertenece, en medio de las adversidades políticas, sociales, geográficas y todas las que se puedan citar. Creo que la amistad y la familia han sido las víctimas mayores del exilio cubano, pues de una y otra parte han existido históricamente posiciones muy extremas que han afectado a esos valores humanos. Hoy, desde Estados Unidos y con el regocijo de una parte de la comunidad cubana, se controla los viajes a la isla de los cubanos residentes en ese país; ayer, en Cuba, podías ser considerado incluso un desafecto si mantenías relación con los familiares que se habían ido. Así de terrible.

Por otra parte, estoy de acuerdo, totalmente, en la necesidad de un diálogo reconciliatorio, en la necesidad de olvidar rencores, en la necesidad de acercarnos, los cubanos de dentro y de fuera, por el bien de todo un país.

ADO: En todas sus novelas aparecen personajes femeninos pero ninguno tiene un papel relevante dentro de la narración, es decir, o son meros objetos sexuales o llevan a cabo papeles muy estereotipados, como son el de la mujer madre, hija o prostituta o amante. ¿Refleja esto el papel tradicional que la mujer pueda seguir ejerciendo dentro de la sociedad cubana actual?

LPF: Una novela no tiene que ser necesariamente el reflejo de una realidad tal y como es la realidad. Es un hecho que el papel social de las mujeres en Cuba ha tenido un crecimiento vertical en estas últimas décadas, del mismo modo que en otros países del mundo, pero incluso con mayores derechos y protecciones que en otras partes, por ejemplo, España, donde es frecuente que una mujer gane menos que un hombre por realizar el mismo trabajo, algo que es impensable en Cuba… porque los gritos de esa mujer se oirían en China. Hoy en día en las universidades, en los trabajos más calificados, el porciento de mujeres es incluso mayor que el de los hombres en muchos sectores. Todo esto no quiere decir que una herencia cultural machista (hispánica y africana, judeo cristiana y occidental) pueda ser borrada con leyes sociales y con el paso de cuatro décadas. Es algo profundo, que está arraigado incluso en la mentalidad de muchas mujeres cubanas. Ahora bien, en mis novelas, por ser de carácter policial, por tener que ver con la violencia, la corrupción, el abuso de poder, de un lado, y el trabajo policial, por otro, es lógico (creo yo) que exista una mayor presencia masculina, y que muchas de las mujeres que aparecen en ellas estén relacionadas con los personajes por vía filial o amorosa. Pero el peso específico de esas mujeres en la vida de esos hombres es enorme si te fijas: la madre de Carlos es el sostén de una familia, más aun, de una tribu —la de los amigos de su hijo; Tamara, la mujer que pretende Conde, es el ideal de belleza, la encarnación del amor posible; Míriam, el personaje femenino más fuerte de *Paisaje de otoño* es un carácter fortísimo, que cuando es utilizada es porque cae en manos de un manipulador profesional como su difunto marido… Y, en lo que a mí respecta, como persona, respeto demasiado a las mujeres: las respeto y les temo.

ADO: ¿Por qué creyó necesario que Mario Conde dejara de ser policía?

LPF: Desde la primera novela de la serie Mario Conde resultó un policía demasiado increíble, debido sobre todo a su sensibilidad e inteligencia, pero también a su incapacidad para la violencia y oír su falta de cultura como presunto policía investigador. A medida que avanzaba en las novelas me fui dando cuenta de que había creado un personaje que me satisfacía mucho, pero que estaba forzado en un trabajo que poco tenía que ver con él, hasta que decidí liberarlo en *Paisaje de otoño*, la cuarta y última novela de 'Las cuatro estaciones'. Creo que el personaje me lo agradeció y que las otras dos novelas que he escrito después también: desde fuera de la policía Conde tiene una libertad de actuar y pensar que es imposible dentro de un cuerpo represivo y pienso que esa posibilidad lo hace crecer como personaje, algo que es importante para él y para mí, de cara a estos últimos proyectos y, sobre todo, a los que seguro vendrán en un futuro no demasiado lejano, pues si le di la libertad a Conde de renunciar a la policía, la que sí no le daré es la de no volver conmigo para hacer otras novelas.

Bibliography

Primary Sources

Arenas, Reinaldo, 1991. *El color del verano* (Miami: Universal).
Canetti, Yanitzia, 1997. *Al otro lado* (Barcelona: Seix Barral).
Chaviano, Daína, 1999. *Casa de juegos* (Barcelona: Planeta).
Estévez, Abilio, 1997. *Tuyo es el reino* (Barcelona: Tusquets).
Padura Fuentes, Leonardo, 1997. *Máscaras* (Barcelona: Tusquets).
Valdés, Zoé, 1995. *La nada cotidiana* (Barcelona: Emecé).

Secondary Sources

Abel, Elizabeth, ed., 1982. *Writing and Sexual Difference* (Chicago: University of Chicago Press).
Abel, Elizabeth, Marianne Hirsch and Elizabeth Langland, eds, 1983. *The Voyage In: Fictions of Female Development* (Hanover: UP of New England).
Abreu, Juan, 1994. 'Presencia de Arenas', in Sánchez 1994: 13–20.
Ackroyd, Peter, 1979. *Dressing Up* (New York: Simon and Schuster).
Aguilú de Murphy, Raquel, 1989. *Los textos dramáticos de Virgilio Piñera y el teatro del absurdo* (Madrid: Pliegos).
Ahmed, Aijaz, 1987. 'Jameson's Rhetoric of Otherness and the "National Allegory"', *Text*, 17: 3–27.
Aiello Fernández, Antonio J., 2010. 'Presencia de la epísteme [*sic*] posmoderna en el discurso narrativo hispanoamericano de los umbrales del siglo XXI: Carlos Fuentes Macías, Mario Vargas Llosa y Leonardo Padura Fuentes'. PhD diss. [2009], The Univ. of Arizona. In *Dissertations and Theses: AandI*, ProQuest pub. no. AAT 3402943.
Alanís, Armando, 1998. 'Entrevista / Abilio Estévez / La literatura como salvación', *Reforma* (Mexico City), 12 September, <http://www.accessmylibrary. com> (accessed 14 July 2010).
Alcides Jofré, Manuel, 1990. 'El estilo de la mujer', in Berenguer et al. 1990: 53–72.
Allen, Graham, 2000. *Intertextuality* (London: Routledge).
Alonso Gallo, Laura P., and Fabio Murrieta, eds, 2003. *Guayaba Sweet: Literatura cubana en Estados Unidos* (Cádiz: Aduana Vieja).
Alter, Robert, 1975. *Partial Magic: The Novel as a Self-Conscious Genre* (Berkeley: U of California P).

Álvarez Borland, Isabel, 2004a. 'A Reminiscent Memory: Lezama Lima, Zoé Valdés, and Rilke's Island', *MLN*, 119.2: 344–62.

——, 2004b. 'La lengua nómada: Orígenes y la diáspora de los 90', *Encuentro*, 33: 265–75.

——, 2007. 'Fertile Multiplicities: Zoé Valdés and the Writers of the 90s Generation', in O'Reilly Herrera 2007: 253–67.

Amorós, Celia, 1991. *Hacia una crítica de la razón patriarcal* (Barcelona: Anthropos).

——, 1997. *Tiempo de feminismo* (Madrid: Cátedra).

Araújo, Nara, 1995. 'Literatura femenina, feminismo y crítica literaria feminista en Cuba', *Letras femeninas*, 21.1–2: 165–71.

——, 2005. 'Los límites del deseo: Sexualidad y erotismo en la literatura cubana contemporánea', in Ochoa 2005: 203–17.

Arenas, Reinaldo, 1994 [1992]. *Antes que anochezca*, 4th edn (Barcelona: Tusquets).

Arrabal, Fernando, 1983. *1984. Carta a Fidel Castro* (Madrid: Playor).

Arrufat, Antón, 1990. 'El nacimiento de la novela en Cuba', *Revista Iberoamericana*, 56: 747–57.

Artaud, Antonin, 1999. *El teatro y su doble* (Barcelona: Edhasa).

Babcock, Barbara, 1974. 'The Novel and the Carnival World', *MLN*, 89: 911–37.

Bachelard, Gastón, 1997. *El derecho de soñar* (Madrid: FCE).

Bakhtin, Mikhail M., 1981. *The Dialogic Imagination: Four Essays*, ed. Michael Holquist, tr. Caryl Emerson and Michael Holquist (Austin: U of Texas P).

——, 1982. *Estética de la creación verbal*, tr. Tatiana Bubnova (Mexico City: Siglo XXI).

——, 1984. *Problems of Dostoevsky's Poetics*, ed. and tr. Caryl Emerson (Manchester: MUP).

——, 1986. *Speech Genres and Other Late Essays*, tr. Vern McGee, ed. Caryl Emerson and Michael Holquist (Austin: U of Texas P).

——, 1987. *La cultura popular en la Edad Media y el Renacimiento: El contexto de François Rabelais*, tr. Julio Forcat and *César Conroy* (Madrid: Alianza).

——, 1989. *Teoría y estética de la novela*, tr. Helena S. Kriúkova and Vicente Cazcarra (Madrid: Taurus).

——, 1994. *El método formal en los estudios literarios: Introducción crítica a una poética sociológica*, tr. Tatiana Bubnova (Madrid: Alianza Universidad).

Barchino, Matías, 2001. 'El peso de la isla en la literatura cubana actual: pervivencia conjunta de las figuras de Virgilio Piñera y José Lezama Lima', in *La isla posible*, III Congreso de la Asociación Española de Estudios Literarios Hispanoamericanos (Tabarca, Alicante, 1998), ed. Carmen Alemany Bay, Remedios Mataix, José Carlos Rovira, with the collaboration of Pedro Mendiola Oñate (Alicante: U de Alicante), <http://www.cervantesvirtual.com/obra/la-isla-posible--0/> (accessed 1 July 2010).

Barnet, Miguel, 1968. *Autobiography of a Runaway Slave*, tr. Jocasta Innes (New York: Pantheon).

——, 1983. 'La novela-testimonio: socioliteratura', in *La fuente viva* (Havana: Letras Cubanas), pp. 12–42. [First publ. 1968, *Unión*, 4: 99–123].

Barquet, Jesús J., 1994. 'Rebeldía e irreverencia de Reinaldo Arenas', in Sánchez 1994: 27–38.

Barrett, Michèle, 1985. 'Ideology and the Cultural Production of Gender', in *Feminist Criticism and Social Change: Sex, Class, and Race in Literature and Culture*, ed. Judith L. Newton and Deborah Rosenfelt (New York: Methuen), pp. 65–85.

Barthes, Roland, 1975. *The Pleasure of the Text*, tr. Richard Miller (New York: Hill and Wang).

——, 1977. *Image Music Text*, tr. Stephen Heath (London: Fontana).

——, 1979. *A Lover's Discourse: Fragments*, tr. Richard Miller (New York: Hill and Wang).

——, 1987a. *Mythologies*, tr. Annette Lavers (New York: Hill and Wang).

——, 1987b. *El susurro del lenguaje: Más allá de la palabra y la escritura*, tr. C. Fernández Medrano (Barcelona: Paidós). ['La muerte del autor', pp. 65–71].

——, 2005. *El grado cero de la escritura. Seguido de Nueve ensayos críticos*, tr. Nicolás Rosa (Madrid: Siglo XXI).

Bataille, Georges, 1962 [1957]. *Eroticism*, tr. Mary Dalwood (London and New York: Marion Boyars).

Baudrillard, Jean, 1983. *Simulations*, tr. Paul Foss, Paul Patton and Philip Beitchman (New York: Semiotext(e)).

——, 1998. *Cultura y simulacro*, tr. Antoni Vicens and Pedro Rovira, 5th edn (Barcelona: Kairós).

——, 2000. *De la seducción*, tr. Elena Benarroch, 8th edn (Madrid: Cátedra).

Beauvoir, Simone de, 1953. *The Second Sex*, tr. and ed. H. M. Parshley (London: Jonathan Cape).

Behar, Sonia, 2009. *La caída del Hombre Nuevo: Narrativa cubana del Período Especial* (New York: Peter Lang).

Béjar, Eduardo, 1994. 'Reinaldo Arenas o la angustia de la modernidad', in Sánchez 1994: 53–61.

——, 2002–03. 'Abilio Estévez: Entrevisto: La salvación por la literatura', *Encuentro de la Cultura Cubana*, 26–7: 91–7.

Bejel, Emilio, 1991. *Escribir en Cuba* (Ríos Piedras: U de Puerto Rico).

——, 2001. *Gay Cuban Nation* (Chicago: U of Chicago P).

Bengelsdorf, Carollee, 1994. *The Problem of Democracy in Cuba* (Oxford: OUP).

Benítez Rojo, Antonio, 1987. *La textualidad de Reinaldo Arenas* (Madrid: Playor).

——, 1998. *La isla que se repite* (Barcelona: Casiopea).

Benjamin, Jessica, 1990. *The Bonds of Love* (London: Virago).

Benson, Renate, 1984. *German Expressionist Drama* (London: Macmillan).

Benstock, Shari, ed., 1988. *The Private Self: Theory and Practice of Women's Autobiographical Writing* (Chapel Hill, NC, and London: U of North Carolina P).

Berenguer, Carmen, Eugenia Brito, Diamela Eltit et al., eds, 1990. *Escribir en los bordes (Congreso Internacional de Literatura Femenina Latinoamericana, 1987)* (Santiago de Chile: Cuarto Propio).

Berenschot, Denis Jorge, 2003. 'Cubanía(s): Alternativa intertextual en la narrativa y el teatro cubanos del siglo XXI', *Revista Iberoamericana*, 69: 909–26.

Bergmann, Emilie, et al., eds, 1990. *Women, Culture and Politics in Latin America* (Berkeley: U of California P).

Bernstein, J. M., 1984. *The Philosophy of the Novel: Lukács, Marxism and the Dialectics of Form* (Minneapolis: U of Minnesota P).

Bersani, Leo, 1988. 'Is the Rectum a Grave?', in *AIDS: Cultural Analysis, Cultural Activism,* ed. Douglas Crimp (Cambridge, MA: MIT P), pp. 197–222.

Bertot, Lillian, 1994. 'Figuras y tropos de la opresión en la obra de Reinaldo Arenas', in Sánchez 1994: 63–75.

Bethke Elshtain, Jean, 1982. 'Feminist Discourse and its Discontents: Language, Power, and Meaning', *Signs,* 7: 603–21.

Bianchi Ross, Ciro, 2010. 'Marianano', *Juventud Rebelde,* 24 April, <http://www.juventudrebelde.cu/columnas/lectura/2010-04-24/marianao/> (accessed 1 June 2010).

Biblia de Jerusalén, 1976 (Bilbao: Desclée de Brouwer).

Blavatsky, Helena Petrovna, 1971. *The Voice of the Silence* (Pasadena, CA: Theosophical UP).

Bloch, Ernst, 1988. *The Utopian Function of Art and Literature* (Cambridge, MA: MIT P).

Bobes-Naves, María del Carmen, 1993. *Teoría general de la novela* (Madrid: Gredos).

Bolinger, Dwight, 1980. *Language, the Loaded Weapon. The Use and Abuse of Language Today* (London and New York: Longman).

Booker, M. Keith, 1996. *A Practical Introduction to Literary Theory and Criticism* (White Plains, NY: Longman).

Booth, W. C., 1974. *La retórica de la ficción* (Barcelona: Bosch).

Borinski, Alicia, 1975. 'Re-escribir y escribir: Arenas, Menard, Borges, Cervantes, Fray Servando', *Revista Iberoamericana,* 41: 605–16.

Bourdieu, Pierre, 2000 [1998]. *La dominación masculina,* tr. Joaquín Jordá (Barcelona: Anagrama).

Bristow, Joseph, 1997. *Sexuality* (London and New York: Routledge).

Brooksbank Jones, Anny, and Catherine Davies, eds, 1996. *Latin American Women's Writing: Feminist Readings in Theory and Crisis* (Oxford: OUP).

Brown, Joan L., 1991. *Women Writers of Contemporary Spain. Exiles in the Homeland* (Newark, DE: U of Delaware P).

Buckwalter-Arias, James, 2010. *Cuba and the New Origenismo* (Woodbridge: Támesis).

Burke, Peter, 1978. *Popular Culture in Early Modern Europe* (New York: New York UP).

Buruma, Ian, 1984. *Behind the Mask* (New York: New American Library).

Butler, Judith, 1993. *Bodies that Matter: On the Discursive Limits of 'Sex'* (New York: Routledge).

——, 1997. *The Psychic Life of Power: Theories in Subjection* (Stanford, CA: Stanford UP).

——, 1999a [1987]. *Subjects of Desire: Hegelian Reflections in Twentieth-Century France* (New York: Columbia UP).

——, 1999b [1990]. *Gender Trouble: Feminism and the Subversion of Identity* (New York: Routledge).

——, 2005. *Giving an Account of Oneself* (New York: Fordham UP).

Cabrera-Infante, Guillermo, 1998. *Vidas para leerlas* (Madrid: Alfaguara).

Cabrera, Lydia, 1988. *Los animales en el folklore y la magia de Cuba* (Miami: Universal).

——, 1992 [1954]. *El monte: Igbo-Finda; Ewe Orisha. Vititi Nfinda. Notas sobre las religiones, la magia, las supersticiones y el folklore de los negros criollos y el pueblo de Cuba*, 7th edn (Miami: Universal).

Calvo Peña, Beatriz, 2003. 'Entre la memoria y el deseo: Daína Chaviano y la creación de *puentes de encuentro* cubanos', in Alonso Gallo and Murrieta 2003: 331–49.

Cámara, Madeline, 1995. 'Feminismo vs totalitarismo: Notas para un estudio de textos y contextos de mujeres, en Cuba contemporánea (1989–1994)', *Bordes,* 2: 54–64.

——, 2002. *La letra rebelde: Estudios de escritoras cubanas* (Miami: Universal).

——, 2003. 'Novelistas cubanas en Estados Unidos: Entre la memoria y la invención', in Alonso Gallo and Murrieta 2003: 53–71.

Campuzano, Luisa, 1988. 'La mujer en la narrativa de la Revolución: ponencia sobre una carencia' (Trabajo presentado en el Primer Forum de Narrativa Cubana, dic. 1984), in *Quirón o del ensayo y otros eventos* (Havana: Letras Cubanas), pp. 66–104.

Capasso, Ruth Carver, 1998. 'The Empress Eugénie in *Malgrétout*', in *Le Siècle de George Sand*, ed. David A. Powell (Amsterdam: Rodopi), pp. 253–9.

Cardona, Rodolfo, and Anthony N. Zahareas, 1970. *Visión del esperpento: Teoría y práctica en los esperpentos de Valle-Inclán* (Madrid: Castalia).

Cardoso, Dinora, 2001. 'Bosch and Arenas: Two Gardens of Delights', *Journal of Humanistic Studies and Literature*, 1.1: 62–8.

Caruth, Cathy, 1995. 'Trauma and Experience: Introduction', in *Trauma: Explorations in Memory*, ed. Cathy Caruth (Baltimore, MD: Johns Hopkins UP), pp. 3–12.

Casal, Julián del, 1963. *Julián del Casal: Poesías* (Havana: Consejo Nacional de Cultura).

Castillo, Debra A., 1992. *Talking Back: Toward a Latin American Feminist Literary Criticism* (Ithaca, NY: Cornell UP).

Castle, Terry, 1986. *Masquerade and Civilization: The Carnivalesque in Eighteenth-Century Culture and Fiction* (Stanford, CA: Stanford UP).

Castro, Fidel, 1961. *Palabras a los intelectuales* (Havana: Ediciones del Consejo Nacional de Cultura).

——, 1991. 'Discurso de clausura', *Casa de las Américas*, 65–6: 21–33.

Cervera Salinas, Vicente, 2001. 'Esto no es una isla, sino el reino del Verbo', in *La isla posible,* III Congreso de la Asociación Española de Estudios Literarios Hispanoamericanos (Tabarca, Alicante, 1998), ed. Carmen Alemany Bay, Remedios Mataix, José Carlos Rovira, with the collaboration of Pedro Mendiola Oñate (Alicante: U de Alicante), <http://www.cervantesvirtual.com/servlet/SirveObras/27849280532309117471902/not0051.htm> (accessed 10 February 2010).

Chen-Sham, Jorge, and Isela Chiu-Olivares, eds, 2004. *De márgenes y adiciones: Novelistas latinoamericanas de los 90* (San José, Costa Rica: Perro Azul).

Chover Lafarga, Anna, 2006. '*Casa de juegos*: El erotismo como ética de la sub-versión', *Cuadernos de ALEPH: Revista de Literatura Hispánica*, 1: 59–72.
——, 2010. 'El cuarto de Tula. Erotismo y sexualidad en las narradoras cubanas del Periodo Especial'. PhD thesis, Univ. de València.
Christ, Carol P., 1980. *Diving Deep and Surfacing. Women Writers on Spiritual Quest* (Boston: Beacon).
Ciplijauskaité, Biruté, 1988. *La novela femenina contemporánea (1970–1985): Hacia una tipología de la narración en primera persona* (Barcelona: Anthropos).
Cirlot, Juan, 1982. *Diccionario de símbolos* (Barcelona: Labor).
Cixous, Hélèle, 1980. 'The Laugh of the Medusa', in *New French Feminisms: An Anthology*, ed. Elaine Marks and Isabelle de Courtivron (Amherst: U of Massachusetts P), pp. 245–64.
Cixous, Hélène, and Catherine Clément, 1993. *The Newly Born Woman*, tr. Betsy Wing (Minneapolis: U of Minnesota P).
Clark, Stephen J., 2000. 'Conversación con Abilio Estévez', *Caribe: Revista de Cultura y Literatura*, 3.1: 85–97.
Cole, Johnnetta B., 1988. 'Women in Cuba: The Revolution within the Revolution', in *Anthropology for the Nineties: Introductory Readings*, ed. Johnnetta B. Cole (New York: Free Press; London: Macmillan), pp. 532–48.
Condé, Lisa P., and Stephen Hart, ed., 1991. *Feminist Readings on Spanish and Latin American Literature* (Lewiston, NY: Mellen).
Coward, Rosalind, 1984. *Female Desire: Women's Sexuality Today* (London: Paladin).
Cruz, Manuel, 1892. *Cromitos cubanos (bocetos de autores hispanoamericanos)* (Havana: Biblioteca El Fígaro).
Culler, Jonathan, 1976. 'Presupposition and intertextuality', *MLN*, 91.6: 1380–96.
Danow, David, 1991. *The Thought of Mikhail Bakhtin: From Word to Culture* (New York: St. Martin's).
Davies, Catherine, ed., 1993. *Women Writers in Twentieth-Century Spain and Spanish America* (Lewiston, NY: Mellen).
——, 1997. *A Place in the Sun? Women Writers in Twentieth-Century Cuba* (London: Zed).
De Ferrari, Guillermina, 2004. 'Las palabras y las cosas: El lenguaje de la revolución en *El siglo de las luces*, de Alejo Carpentier, y *Los palacios distantes*, de Abilio Estévez', in *Nuevas lecturas de Alejo Carpentier*, ed. Alexis Rodríguez (Caracas: U Central de Venezuela), pp. 231–58.
De Lauretis, Teresa, ed., 1986. *Feminist Studies/Critical Studies* (Bloomington: Indiana UP).
——, 1987. *Technologies of Gender: Essays on Theory, Film, and Fiction* (Bloomington: Indiana UP).
Deleuze, Gilles, and Félix Guattari, 2000. *Rizoma: Introducción*, tr. José Vázquez Pérez and Umbelina Larraceleta, 3rd edn (Valencia: Pre-Textos).
Del Risco, Enrique, 2003. 'Reinaldo Arenas: Víctima imposible, literatura posible', in Alonso Gallo and Murrieta 2003: 255–79.
De Man, Paul, 1983. *Blindness and Insight: Essays in the Rhetoric of Contempo-*

rary Criticism, 2nd rev. edn (Minneapolis: U of Minnesota P).

——, 1989. 'Dialogue and Dialogism', in *Rethinking Bakhtin*, ed. Gary S. Morson and Caryl Emerson (Evanston, IL: Northwestern UP), pp. 105–14.

Derrida, Jacques, 1979. 'Living On: Border Lines', in *Deconstruction and Criticism*, ed. Harold Bloom et al. (New York: Seabury; London: Routlege), pp. 75–176.

——, 1982. *Margins of Philosophy*, tr. Alan Bass (London: Harvester).

Díaz, Roberto Ignacio, 2007. 'The Spirit of Cuba and the Ghost of Opera', *Symposium*, 61.1: 57–74.

Díez-Cobo, Rosa M., 2007. '*El color del verano o Nuevo jardín de las delicias*, de Reinaldo Arenas: Humor negro y carnaval narrativo', *Espéculo: Revista de Estudios Literarios*, 35: n.p.

Docter, Richard F., 1988. *Transvestites and Transsexuals: Toward a Theory of Cross-Gender Behavior* (New York: Plenum).

Doležel, Lubomír, 1997. *Historia breve de la poética*, tr. Luis Alburquerque (Madrid: Síntesis).

Dorado-Otero, Ángela, 2009. 'Entre Ovidio y Víctor Hugo: El exilio cubano dentro y fuera de los discursos oficiales' (CD ROM: 53 Congreso Internacional de Americanistas; symposium: Nuevas formas de conocer y reconocer los exilios europeos y americanos) (Mexico City: U Iberoamericana).

Dore, Elizabeth, and Maxine Molyneux, eds, 2000. *Hidden Histories of Gender and the State in Latin America* (Durham, NC, and London: Duke UP).

DRAE, 2004. *Diccionario de la lengua española*, 22nd edn, 2 vols (Madrid: Real Academia Española).

Dumont, René, 1973. *Is Cuba Socialist?*, tr. Stanley Hochman (London: Viking).

DuPlessis, Rachel Blau, 1985. *Writing Beyond the Ending. Narrative Strategies of Twentieth-Century Women Writers* (Bloomington: Indiana UP).

Eagleton, Mary, 1986. *Feminist Literary Theory: a Reader* (Oxford: Blackwell).

Eagleton, Terry, 1989. *The Rape of Clarissa: Writing, Sexuality and Class Struggle in Samuel Richardson* (London: Blackwell).

Eckstein, Susan, 1991. 'More on the Cuban Rectification Process: Whose Errors?', *Cuban Studies*, 21: 187–92.

Eco, Umberto, 1976. *A Theory of Semiotics* (Bloomington: Indiana UP).

——, 1984. 'The Frames of Comic "Freedom"', in *Carnival!*, ed. Thomas A. Sebeok (Berlin and New York: Mouton), pp. 1–9.

Edelman, Lee, 1994. *Homographies: Essays in Gay and Cultural Theory* (New York: Routledge).

Efundé, Agún, 1996 [1979]. *Los secretos de la santería* (Miami: Universal).

Eisenstein, Hester, and Alice Jardine, 1980. *The Future of Difference* (Boston: Hall).

Eliade, Mircea, 1975. *Iniciaciones místicas*, tr. José Matías Díaz (Madrid: Taurus).

——, 1985. 'Masks: Mythical and Ritual Origins', in *Symbolism, the Sacred, and the Arts*, ed. Diane Apostolos-Cappadona (New York: Crossroad), pp. 64–71.

Elliott, Patricia, 1991. *From Mastery to Analysis: Theories of Gender in Psychonalytic Feminism* (Ithaca, NY: Cornell UP).

Elster, Jon, 1986. *Karl Marx* (Cambridge: CUP).

Eltit, Diamela, 1990. 'Las artistas del congreso', in Berenguer et al. 1990: 17–19.

Epps, Brad, 1995. 'Proper Conduct: Reinaldo Arenas, Fidel Castro, and the Politics of Homosexuality', *Journal of the History of Sexuality*, 6.2: 231–83.

——, 1996. 'Estados de deseo: homosexualidad y nacionalidad (Juan Goytisolo y Reinaldo Arenas a vuelapluma)', *Revista Iberoamericana*, 62: 799–820.

Erauso, Catalina de, 1996. *Lieutenant Nun: Memoir of a Basque Transvestite in the New World*, tr. Michele Stepto and Gabriel Stepto (Boston: Beacon).

Escobedo, María, 2010. 'Abilio Estévez: "La patria no es más que lo que los políticos de cualquier signo nos quieren hacer creer"', *Cuadernos Hispanoamericanos*, 721–2: 163–73.

Esterrich, Carmelo, 1997. 'Locas, pájaros y demás mariconadas: el ciudadano sexual en Reinaldo Arenas', *Confluencia*, 13.1: 178–93.

Estévez, Abilio, 2010. 'Un delicioso peligro', *Cuadernos Hispanoamericanos*, 723: 7–11.

Ette, Ottmar, 1992. *La escritura de la memoria* (Frankfurt: Vervuert).

Evola, Julius, 1997. *Metafísica del sexo*, tr. Francesc Gutiérrez, series Sophia Perennis, no. 47 (Palma de Mallorca: Olañeta).

Faccini, Carmen, 2002. 'El discurso político de Zoé Valdés: *La nada cotidiana* y *Te di la vida entera*', *Ciberletras: Revista de crítica literaria y de cultura*, 7: n.p., <http://www.lehman.cuny.edu/ciberletras/v07/faccini.html> (accessed 8 September 2010).

Falcón Martínez, Constantino, Emilio Fernández-Galiano and Raquel López Melero, 1980. *Diccionario de la mitología clásica*, 2 vols (Madrid: Alianza).

Fernández Diego, Alejandro, 2003. 'Abilio Estévez y *Los palacios distantes*', *Lateral: Revista de Cultura*, 99 (March), <http://www.circulolateral.com/revista/revista/espejo/099abilioestevez.htm> (accessed 15 March 2010).

Fernández-Guerra, Ángel Luis, 1971. 'Recurrencias obsesivas y variantes alucinatorias en la obra de Reinaldo Arenas', *Caravelle. Cahiers du Monde Hispanique et Luso-Brésilien*, 16: 133–8.

Fernández Retamar, Roberto, 1989. *'Caliban' and Other Essays,* tr. Edwards Baker (Minneapolis: U of Minnesota P).

Fernández Robaina, Tomás, 1994. *Hablen paleros y santeros* (Havana: Editorial de Ciencias Sociales).

Fernández-Vázquez, Antonio, 2004. 'Humor y erotismo en las novelas de Yanitzia Canetti Duque', in *De márgenes y adiciones: Novelistas latinoamericanas de los 90*, ed. Jorge Chen Sham and Isela Chiu Olivares (San José, Costa Rica: Perro Azul).

Folkenflik, Robert, ed., 1993. *The Culture of Autobiography: Constructions of Self-Representation* (Stanford, CA: Stanford UP).

Fornet, Ambrosio, 2009. 'Cuba: Nation, Diaspora, Literature', *Critical Inquiry*, 35.2: 255–69.

Foster, David William, 1991. *Gay and Lesbian Themes in Latin American Writing* (Austin: U of Texas P).

——, 1997. *Sexual Textualities. Essays on Queer/ing Latin American Writing* (Austin: U of Texas P).

Foucault, Michel, 1972. *The Archaeology of Knowledge*, tr. A. Sheridan (New York: Pantheon).

——, 1981. *Un diálogo sobre el poder y otras conversaciones*, tr. Miguel Morey (Madrid: Alianza).

——, 1989. 'How Much Does It Cost For Reason to Tell the Truth?', in *Foucault Live*, ed. Sylvère Lotringer, tr. John Honston (New York: Semiotext[e]).

——, 1990. *The History of Sexuality*, Vol. I: *An Introduction*, tr. Robert Hurley (New York: Vintage).

——, 1999. 'About the Beginning of the Hermeneutics of the Self', in *Religion and Culture*, ed. Jeremy Carrette, tr. Thomas Keenan and Mark Blasius (New York: Routledge), pp. 158–81.

——, 2007. *Historia de la sexualidad*, Vol. I: *La voluntad de saber*, ed. Juan Almela, tr. Ulises Guiñazú, 31st edn (Mexico City: Siglo XXI).

Fowler, Víctor, 1998. *La maldición: una historia del placer como conquista* (Havana: Letras Cubanas).

——, 2001. *Historias del cuerpo* (Havana: Letras Cubanas).

Franken K[urzen], Clemens A., 2009. 'Leonardo Padura Fuentes y su detective nostálgico', *Revista Chilena de Literatura*, 74: 29–56.

Franzbach, Martin, 2000. 'La re-escritura de la novela policíaca cubana', in Reinstädler and Ette 2000: 69–77.

Frappier-Mazur, Lucienne, 1988. 'Marginal Canons: Rewriting the Erotic', *Yale French Studies*, 75: 112–28.

Freud, Sigmund, 1970. *Tótem y tabú*, tr. Luis López Ballesteros y de Torres, 4th edn (Madrid: Alianza).

——, 1973. *El yo y el ello*, tr. Ramón Rey Ardid and Luis López Ballesteros y de Torres (Madrid: Alianza).

——, 1997. *El malestar en la cultura*, tr. Ramón Rey Ardid (Madrid: Alianza).

——, 2000. *El chiste y su relación con el inconsciente*, tr. Luis López Ballesteros y de Torres (Madrid: Alianza).

——, 2005. *Psicoanálisis del arte*, tr. Luis López Ballesteros y de Torres (Madrid: Alianza).

Friedman, Norman, 1955. 'Point of View in Fiction: The Development of a Critical Concept', *PMLA*, 70: 1177.

Fuentes, Carlos, 1969. *La nueva novela hispanoamericana* (Mexico City: Joaquín Mortiz).

Fuentes, Yvette, 2002. 'Beyond the Nation: Issues of Identity in the Contemporary Narrative of Cuban Women Writing (in) the Diaspora'. PhD diss., Univ. of Miami. In *Dissertations and Theses: AandI*, ProQuest pub. no. AAT 3056613.

——, 2003. 'En medio de dos aguas: Yanitzia Canetti y la literatura cubana en los Estados Unidos', in Alonso Gallo and Murrieta 2003: 197–216.

Garber, Marjorie, 1992. *Vested Interests: Cross-Dressing and Cultural Anxiety* (New York: Routledge).

García Méndez, Luis Manuel, 2009. 'El navegante despierto: Abilio Estévez entrevisto por Luis Manuel García', *Encuentro de la cultura cubana*, 51–2: 116–22.

García Negroni, María Marta, and Marta Tordesillas Colado, 2001. *La enunciación en la lengua: de la deixis a la polifonía* (Madrid: Gredos).

García-Obregón, Omar, 2006a. *Cultural Cyclothymia in the Face of Dystocia: (De)constructing a National Identity in Exile. The Cuban Case* (Miami: CERA).

——, 2006b. 'Perspectivas transnacionales: Poéticas de resistencia en la creación de una identidad en exilio. La poesía de Reinaldo Arenas, Choman Hardi y Mahmud Darwish', CD ROM: *Lugares dos discursos* (Rio de Janeiro: ABRALIC, Associação Brasileira de Literatura Comparada), pp. 1–18.

——, 2009. 'Partículas de azogue: Movilidad y desplazamientos sígnicos del exilio cubano' (CD ROM: 53 Congreso Internacional de Americanistas; symposium: Nuevas formas de conocer y reconocer los exilios europeos y americanos) (Mexico City: U Iberoamericana).

García-Sánchez, Franklin, 1993. 'El dionisismo paródico-grotesco de *La loma del ángel*, de Reinaldo Arenas', *Revista Canadiense de Estudios Hispánicos*, 17.2: 271–8.

Gardiner, Michael, 1992. *The Dialogics of Critique: M. M. Bakhtin and the Theory of Ideology* (London: Routledge).

Garrido, Antonio, 1993. *El texto narrativo* (Madrid: Síntesis).

Genette, Gérard, 1972. *Figures III* (Paris: Seuil).

——, 1980. *Narrative Discourse*, tr. Jane E. Levin (Ithaca, NY: Cornell UP).

——, 1997. *Palimpsests: Literature in the Second Degree*, tr. Channa Newman and Claude Doubinsky (Lincoln, NE: U of Nebraska P).

Gilbert, Sandra M., and Susan Gubar, 1979. *The Madwoman in the Attic: The Woman Writer and the Nineteenth Century Literary Imagination* (New Haven: Yale UP).

——, 1989. *No Man's Land. The Place of the Woman Writer in the Twentieth Century* (New Haven: Yale UP).

Gillespie, Richard, ed., 1990. *Cuba After Thirty Years: Rectification and the Revolution* (London: Frank Cass).

Giudicelli, Christian, ed., 2004. *Utopies en Amérique latine* (Paris: Presses de la Sorbonne Nouvelle).

Giuliano, Maurizio, 1998. *El caso CEA: Intelectuales e inquisidores en Cuba ¿Perestroika en la Isla?* (Miami: Universal).

Gómez, Ivette Miriam, 2009. '(Dis)enchanted Writings: The Poetics of Ruins in Cuban Contemporary Narrative'. PhD diss., Univ. of California, Irvine. In *Dissertations and Theses: AandI*, ProQuest pub. no. AAT 3364943.

——, 2010. 'La invención de la historia: Abilio Estévez y las ruinas de un teatro', *Revista Iberoamericana*, 76: 695–712.

Gómez-Cabia, Fernando, 1998. *Estructura y actualidad del pensamiento de Mijail Bajtin* (Madrid: UAM).

González Abellás, Miguel, 2000. 'Aquella isla: Introducción al universo narrativo de Zoé Valdés', *Hispania*, 83.1: 42–50.

——, 2008. *Visiones de exilio: Para leer a Zoé Valdés* (Lanham, MD: UP of America).

González Echevarría, Roberto, 1989. 'Cuban Criticism and Literature: A Reply to Smith', *Cuban Studies*, 16: 101–6.

González-Freire, Natividad, 1961. *Teatro cubano (1927–1961)* (Havana: Ministerio de Relaciones Exteriores).

Goytisolo, Juan, 1984. 'Twenty-Six Rue de Biévre', *Partisan Review*, 51: 680–91.

Grace, Daphne, 2009. 'The Uneasy Masculinities of Dissidence and Exile: Reinaldo Arenas's Fight for Textual-Sexual Freedom', *Journal of Postcolonial Writing*, 45.3: 309–19.

Grosz, Elizabeth, 1989. *Sexual Subversions: Three French Feminists* (Sydney: Allen and Unwin).

Guerra, Lucía, 1990a. 'Entre la sumisión y la irreverencia', in Berenguer et al. 1990: 21–7.

——, 1990b. 'Silencios, disidencias y claudicaciones: los problemas teóricos de la nueva crítica feminista', in Berenguer et al. 1990: 73–83.

Guevara, Ernesto, 1986. 'El hombre nuevo', in *Ideas en torno de Latinoamérica*, ed. Leopoldo Zea, vol. 1 (Mexico City: UNAM).

——, 1997. *Textos revolucionarios* (Nafarroa: Txalaparta).

Gunew, Sneja, ed., 1991. *A Reader in Feminist Knowledge* (London and New York: Routledge).

Harlow, Barbara, 1987. *Resistance Literature* (New York: Methuen).

Harpham, Geoffrey G., 1982. *On the Grotesque: Strategies of Contradiction in Art and Literature* (Princeton, NJ: Princeton UP).

Hart, Stephen, 1993. *White Ink: Essays on Twentieth-Century Feminine Fiction in Spain and Latin America* (Madrid and London: Támesis).

Heilbrun, Carolyn, 1979. *Reinventing Womanhood* (New York: Norton).

Heras-León, Eduardo, 1986. *Teatro del siglo XIX* (Havana: Letras Cubanas).

Hernández-Miyares, Julio E., and Perla Rozencvaig, eds, 1990. *Reinaldo Arenas: alucinaciones, fantasía y realidad* (Glenview, IL: Foresman / Montesinos).

Hirsch, Marianne, 1979. 'The Novel of Formation as Genre: Between Great Expectations and Lost Illusions', *Genre*, 12.2: 293–311.

Hitchcock, Peter, 1993. *Dialogics of the Oppressed* (Minneapolis: U of Minnesota P).

Holquist, Michael, 2002. *Dialogism. Bakhtin and His World*, 2nd edn (London: Routledge).

Horno-Delgado, Asunción, 2006. 'Entrevista con Abilio Estévez', *Confluencia*, 22.1: 154–65.

Howe, Linda S., 2004. *Transgression and Conformity: Cuban Writers and Artists after the Revolution* (Madison: U of Wisconsin P).

Hughes, Alex, and Kate Ince, eds, 1996. *French Erotic Fiction: Women's Desiring Writing, 1880–1990* (Oxford: Berg).

Hughes, Sarah S., 1992. 'Beyond Eurocentrism: Developing World Women's Studies', *Feminist Studies*, 18.2: 389–404.

Huizinga, Johan, 2000. *Homo ludens*, tr. Eugenio Imaz (Madrid: Alianza Emecé).

Hunt, Lynn, ed., 1991. *Eroticism and the Body Politic* (Baltimore, MD: Johns Hopkins UP).

Hutcheon, Linda, 1980. *Narcissistic Narrative. The Metafictional Paradox* (Waterloo, ON: Wilfrid Laurier UP).

——, 1985. *A Theory of Parody* (New York: Methuen).

——, 1988. *A Poetics of Postmodernism: History, Theory, Fiction* (London: Routledge).

Ilie, Paul, 1968. *The Surrealist Mode in Spanish Literature: An Interpretation of Basic Trends from Post-Romanticism to the Spanish Vanguard* (Ann Arbor: U of Michigan P).

——, 1980. *Literature and Inner Exile: Authoritarian Spain, 1939–75* (Baltimore, MD: Johns Hopkins UP).

Irigaray, Luce, 1980. 'When Our Lips Speak Together', *Signs*, 63.1: 69–79.

——, 1985a. *Speculum of the Other Woman*, tr. G. C. Gill (Ithaca, NY: Cornell UP).

——, 1985b. *This Sex Which Is Not One*, tr. Catherine Porter (Ithaca, NY: Cornell UP).

——, 1987. *Sexes et parentés* (Paris: Minuit).

——, 1993. *Je, tu, nous. Toward a Culture of Difference*, tr. Alison Martin (New York: Routledge).

——, 2002. *The Way of Love*, tr. Heidi Bostic and Stephen Pluháček (London: Continuum).

——, 2008. *Sharing the World* (London: Continuum).

Iser, Wolfgang, 1974. *The Implied Reader: Patterns of Communication in Prose Fiction from Bunyan to Beckett* (Baltimore, MD: Johns Hopkins UP).

——, 1978. *The Act of Reading: A Theory of Aesthetic Response* (Baltimore, MD: Johns Hopkins UP).

Ishikawa, Jun, 1998. *The Legend of Gold and Other Stories* (Honolulu, HI: U of Hawaii P).

Jacobus, Mary, 1986. *Reading Woman: Essays in Feminist Criticism* (New York: Columbia UP).

Jakobson, Roman, 1990. *On Language*, ed. Linda R. Waugh and Monique Monville-Burston (Cambridge, MA: Harvard UP).

Jameson, Fredric, 1991. *Postmodernism* (London: Verso).

Jardine, Alice A., 1981. 'Pre-Texts for the Trasatlantic Feminist', *Yale French Studies*, 62: 220–36.

——, 1985. *Gynesis: Configurations of Woman and Modernity* (Ithaca, NY: Cornell UP).

Jauss, Hans Robert, 1982. *Towards an Aesthetic of Reception*, tr. Timothy Bahti (Brighton: Harvester).

Jed, Stephanie H., 1989. *Chaste Thinking: The Rape of Lucretia and the Birth of Humanism* (Bloomington: Indiana UP).

Kaebnick, Suzanne, 1997. 'The *loca* freedom fighter in *Antes de que anochezca* and *El color del verano*', *Chasqui*, 26.1: 102–14.

Kaminsky, A., 1993. *Reading the Body Politic: Feminist Criticism and Latin American Women Writers* (Minneapolis: U of Minnesota P).

Kamuf, Peggy, 1982. *Fictions of Feminine Desire. Disclosures of Heloise* (Lincoln, NE: U of Nebraska P).

Kapcia, Antoni, 1982. 'Revolution, the Intellectual and a Cuban Identity: The Long Tradition', *BLAR*, 1.2: 63–78.

Keppler, C. F., 1972. *The Double in Literature* (Detroit: Wayne State UP).

Kleinbord Labovitz, Esther, 1986. *The Myth of the Heroine: The Female Bildungsroman in the Twentieth Century* (New York: Peter Lang).

Kristeva, Julia, 1974. *La Révolution du langage poétique* (Paris: Seuil).

——, 1980. *Desire in Language: A Semiotic Approach to Literature and Art*, tr. T. Gora, A. Jardine and L. Roudiez (New York: Columbia UP; Oxford: Blackwell).

——, 1981. 'Word, Dialogue and Novel', in *Desire in Language*, ed. Leon S. Roudiez, tr. Thomas Gora, Alice Jardine and Leon S. Roudiez (Oxford: Blackwell), pp. 64–91.

——, 1982. *Powers of Horror. An Essay on Abjection*, tr. Leon S. Roudiez (New York: Columbia UP).

——, 1984. *Revolution in Poetic Language*, tr. Margaret Waller (New York: Columbia UP).

——, 1987. *Tales of Love*, tr. Leon S. Roudiez (New York: Columbia UP).

——, 2001. *Semiótica 1*, tr. José Martín Arancibia (Madrid: Espiral / Fundamentos).

Kumaraswami, Par, and Niamh Thornton, eds, 2007. *Revolucionarias* (Oxford: Peter Lang).

Kundera, Milan, 1998. *The Art of the Novel* (New York: Harper).

Kutzinski, Vera M., 1993. *Sugar's Secrets: Race and the Erotics of Cuban Nationalism* (Charlottesville: U of Virginia P).

Lacan, Jacques, 1977. 'The Significance of the Phallus', in *Écrits: A Selection*, tr. Alan Sheridan (New York: Norton), pp. 281–91.

——, 1992. *The Seminar of Jacques Lacan*. Book 7: *The Ethics of Psychoanalysis (1959–1960)*, tr. Dennis Porter (New York: Norton).

——, 1998. *The Seminar of Jacques Lacan*. Book 20: *On Feminine Sexuality: The Limits of Love and Knowledge, Encore (1972–1973)*, tr. Bruce Fink (New York: Norton).

Lachmann, Renate, 1987. 'Bakhtin and Carnival: Culture as Counter-culture', *Center for Humanistic Studies*, 14: 3–34.

Lahr-Vivaz, Elena, 2010. 'Timeless Rhetoric, Special Circumstances: Sex and Symbol in *La nada cotidiana*', *Revista Canadiense de Estudios Hispánicos*, 34.2: 303–21.

Lauter, Estella, and Carol Schreier-Rupprecht, eds, 1985. *Feminist Archetypal Theory. Interdisciplinary Re-Visions of Jungian Thought* (Knoxville: U of Tennessee P).

Leenhardt, Jacques, 1975. *Lectura política de la novela* (Mexico City: Siglo XXI).

Lefebvre, H., 1991. *The Production of Space* (Oxford: Blackwell).

Leiner, Marvin, 1994. *Sexual Politics in Cuba. Machismo, Homosexuality and AIDS* (Boulder, CO: Westview).

Levine, Suzanne Jill, 1976a. 'Borges a *Cobra* es barroc(o) (exé)gesis: Un estudio de la intertextualidad', in *Severo Sarduy*, ed. Julián Ríos (Madrid: Espiral / Fundamentos), pp. 87–105.

——, 1976b. '*Cobra*: el discurso como bricolage', in *Severo Sarduy*, ed. Julián

Ríos, tr. Graciela Colombo and Mariano Aguirre (Madrid: Espiral / Fundamentos), pp. 123–34.

Lévi-Strauss, Claude, 1985. *The Way of the Masks*, tr. M. Modelski S. (London: Cape).

Lezama Lima, José, 1969. *La expresión americana* (Madrid: Alianza).

Lichtheim, George, 1961. *Marxism* (New York: Frederick A. Praeger).

López-Cruz, Humberto, 1997a. 'Subversión en el discurso histórico de *El color del verano* de Reinaldo Arenas', *South Eastern Latin Americanist*, 41.1–2: 1–8.

——, 1997b. 'Desesperanza y continuidad en 'Orfeo Negro' y *El color del verano*', *Catálogo de Letras: Revista Cubana de Divulgación Cultural*, 11–12: 15.

——, 1998. 'La proyección apocalíptica areniana en *El color del verano*: subversión y libertad', *Monographic Review*, 14: 112–21.

——, 1999. '*El color del verano* de Reinaldo Arenas: Subversión social', in Sánchez and López Cruz 1999: 23–30.

Lotman, Iuri, 1996. *La semiosfera*, tr. Desiderio Navarro, 3 vols (Madrid: Cátedra).

Lotti, Alina M., 2009. 'Verdadero templo cultural', *Trabajadores* [Órgano de la Central de Trabajadores de Cuba], 5 January, <http://www.trabajadores.cu/materiales_especiales/coberturas/aniversario-50-del-triunfo-de-la-revolucion-cubana/verdadero-templo-cultural> (accessed 10 January 2010).

Lovelock, James, 1979. *Gaia: A New Look at Life on Earth* (Oxford: OUP).

——, 1988. *The Ages of Gaia: A Biography of our Living Earth* (New York: Norton).

Ludmer, Josefina, 1984. 'Tretas del débil', in *La sartén por el mango: Encuentro de escritoras latinoamericanas*, ed. Patricia Elena González and Eliana Ortega (Río Piedras, PR: Huracán), pp. 47–54.

——, 1999 [1991]. 'Tricks of the Weak', in *Feminist Perspectives on Sor Juana Inés de la Cruz*, ed. Stephanie Merrim (Detroit: Wayne State UP), pp. 86–93.

Lugo Nasario, Félix, 1995. *La alucinación y los recursos literarios en las novelas de Reinaldo Arenas* (Miami: Universal).

Lugo-Ortiz, Agnes, 1999. *Identidades imaginadas: Biografía y nacionalidad en el horizonte de la guerra (Cuba 1860–1898)* (San Juan: U of Puerto Rico).

Luis Reyes, Dean, 2001. 'Abilio Estévez: Vecino de la isla. Entrevista con el autor de *Tuyo es el reino*', <http://www.librusa.com/entrevista11.htm> [28 February 2001; no longer available online].

Lúkacs, Georg, 1920. *The Theory of the Novel*, tr. Anna Bostock (Cambridge, MA: MIT P).

Lumsden, Ian, 1996. *Machos, Maricones and Gays. Cuba and Homosexuality* (Philadelphia: Temple UP).

Lyotard, Jean-François, 1984. *The Postmodern Condition: A Report on Knowledge*, tr. Geoff Bennington and Brian Massumi (Minneapolis: U of Minnesota P; Manchester: MUP).

Machover, Jacobo, 2001. *La memoria frente al poder. Escritores cubanos del exilio: Guillermo Cabrera Infante, Severo Sarduy, Reinaldo Arenas* (Valencia: U de València).

Mack, John, ed., 1994. *Masks and the Art of Expression* (New York: Abrams).

Magee, Bryan, 1997. *The Philosophy of Schopenhauer*, rev. edn (Oxford: OUP).

Manzor-Coats, Lillian, 1995. 'Performative Identities: Scenes Between Two Cubas', in *Bridges to Cuba / Puentes a Cuba,* ed. Ruth Behar (Ann Arbor: U of Michigan P), pp. 253–66.

Mañach, Jorge, 1962. 'Indagación del choteo', in *Los mejores ensayistas cubanos,* ed. Salvador Bueno (Lima: Festival del Libro Cubano), pp. 79–89.

——, 1969. *Indagación del choteo* (Miami: Mnemosyne).

Margulis, Lynn, and Dorian Sagan, 1987. *Microcosmos: Four Billion Years of Evolution from Our Microbian Ancestors* (New York: Summit).

Marquis, Rebecca, 2006. 'Daughters of Saint Theresa: Authority and Rhetoric in the Confessional Narratives of Three Twentieth-Century Spanish and Latin American Women Writers'. PhD diss., Indiana Univ. In *Dissertations and Theses: AandI*, ProQuest pub. no. AAT 3240037.

Martin, Alison, 2000. *Luce Irigaray and the Question of the Divine* (London: MHRA).

Martínez, Sanjuana, 1997. 'Abilio Estévez, revelación en la Feria de Francfort con su primera novela, dice que Cuba vive un esplendor literario, pero no editorial' (Interview), *Proceso*, 7 December, <http://www.accessmylibrary.com> (accessed 14 July 2010).

Martínez-Fernández, José Enrique, 2001. *La intertextualidad literaria* (Madrid: Cátedra).

Martín Gaite, Carmen, 1987. *Desde la ventana* (Madrid: Espasa Calpe).

Mayor Marsán, Maricel, 2004–05. 'Entrevista con la escritora cubana Daína Chaviano: Entre la ciencia y lo sobrenatural', *Baquiana: Revista Literaria*, 6: 193–9.

McCard, Victoria L., 2008. '*Compañera* or *Ciudadana*? The Double Life of the *Jinetera* in Daína Chaviano's *El hombre, la hembra y el hambre*', *Hispanet Journal*, 1: 1–22.

Meltzer, Françoise, 1987. *Salome and the Dance of Writing: Portraits of Mimesis in Literatura* (Chicago: U of Chicago P).

Méndez-Soto, Ernesto, 1977. *Panorama de la novela cubana de la revolución (1959–1970)* (Miami: Universal).

Menton, Seymour, 1978. *La narrativa de la revolución cubana* (Madrid: Nova Scholar).

Merrim, Stephanie, ed., 1991. *Feminist Perspectives on Sor Juana Inés de la Cruz* (Detroit: Wayne State UP).

Michelena, José Antonio, 2006. 'Aportes de Leonardo Padura a la literatura policial cubana', in Uxó 2006: 38–53.

Milner, George B., 1972. 'Homo Ridens: Toward a Semiotic Theory of Humor and Laughter', *Semiotica*, 5: 1–30.

Mitchell, Juliet, and Jacqueline Rose, eds, 1982. *Feminine Sexuality: Jacques Lacan and the 'école freudienne'* (Basingstoke: Macmillan).

Moi, Toril, 1985. *Sexual / Textual Politics: Feminist Literary Theory* (New York: Methuen).

——, 1988. *French Feminist Thought. A Reader* (Oxford: Blackwell).

——, 1989. *The Kristeva Reader* (Oxford: Blackwell).

Molinero, Rita, 1994. 'Arenas en el jardín de las delicias', in Sánchez 1994: 129–37.

——, 1995. 'De asaltos, furias y falos: en donde Arenas descubre "otro" de los mundos posibles', *Apuntes Posmodernos*, 6.1: 66–75.

Money, John, 1988. *Gay, Straight and In-Between: The Sexology of Erotic Orientation* (New York: OUP).

Moreno, Fernando, and Alain Sincard, eds, 1990. *Escritura y sexualidad en la literatura hispanoamericana* (Madrid: Fundamentos).

Morris, Pam, ed., 1994. *The Bakhtin Reader: Selected Writings of Bakhtin, Medvedev, Voloshinov* (London: Arnold).

Moya Fábregas, Johanna I., 2010. 'The Cuban Woman's Revolutionary Experience: Patriarchal Culture and the State's Gender Ideology, 1950–1976', *Journal of Women's History*, 22.1: 61–84.

Muecke, D. C., 1969. *The Compass of Irony* (London: Methuen).

Müller, Erika, 2000. 'Abilio Estévez, Virgilio Piñera y la claustrofobia: el espacio dramático cerrado y la Isla', in Reinstädler and Ette 2000: 143–51.

Napier, David, 1986. *Masks, Transformation and Paradox* (Berkeley: U of California P).

Navajas, Gonzalo, 1987. *Teoría y práctica de la novela española posmoderna* (Barcelona: Edicions del Mall).

Nuez, Iván de la, 1998. *La balsa perpetua: Soledad y conexiones de la cultura cubana* (Barcelona: Casiopea).

——, ed., 1999. *Paisajes después del muro: disidencias en el poscomunismo diez años después de la caída del muro de Berlín* (Barcelona: Península).

Ochoa Fernández, María Luisa, ed., 2005. ¡Ay, qué rico! *El sexo en la cultura y la literatura cubana* (Valencia: Aduana Vieja).

Olivares, Jorge, 1985. 'Carnival and the Novel: Reinaldo Arenas' *El palacio de las blanquísimas mofetas*', *Hispanic Review*, 53.4: 467–76.

——, 2000. '¿Por qué llora Reinaldo Arenas?', *MLN*, 115.2: 268–98.

Olney, James, 1972. *Metaphors of Self. The Meaning of Autobiography* (Princeton, NJ: Princeton UP).

Olondo, Almudena, 2005. 'Economía sumergida, prostitución emergente', in Ochoa 2005: 147–68.

Oppenheimer, Andrés, 1992. *Castro's Final Hour* (New York: Simon and Schuster).

O'Reilly Herrera, Andrea, ed., 2007. *Cuba: Idea of a Nation Displaced* (Albany, NY: SUNY P).

Orr, Mary, 2003. *Intertextuality: Debates and Contexts* (Cambridge: Polity).

Ortega, Eliana, 1990. 'Y después de todo aquí estamos', in Berenguer, et al. 1990: 29-35.

Ortiz, Fernando, 1940. *Contrapunteo del tabaco y el azúcar* (Havana: Jesús Montero).

——, 1991a. *Estudios etnosociológicos*, ed. Isaac Barreal Fernández (Havana: Editorial de Ciencias Sociales).

——, 1991b. 'Los factores humanos de la cubanidad', in Ortiz 1991a: 10–30.

Ortiz, Ricardo L., 1998. 'Pleasure's Exile. Reinaldo Arenas's Last Writing', in *Borders, Exiles, Diasporas*, ed. Elazar Barkan and Marie-Denise Shelton (Stanford, CA: Stanford UP), pp. 92–111.

——, 2007. *Cultural Erotics in Cuban America* (Minneapolis: U of Minnesota P).

Ortiz Ceberio, Cristina, 1998. 'La narrativa de Zoé Valdés: Hacia una reconfiguración de la na(rra)ción cubana', *Chasqui*, 27.2: 116–27.

Padilla, Heberto, 1989. *La mala memoria* (Barcelona: Plaza and Janés).

Padula, Alfred, and Lois Smith, 1996. *Sex and Revolution: Women in Socialist Cuba* (Oxford: OUP).

Padura Fuentes, Leonardo, 1993. *El submarino amarillo (Cuento cubano 1966–1991)* (Mexico City: UNAM).

——, 1999. 'Modernidad y postmodernidad: la novela policial en Iberoamérica', *Hispamérica*, 84: 37–50.

Pastor, Brígida M., 2003. *Fashioning Feminism in Cuba and Beyond: The Prose of Gertrudis Gómez de Avellaneda* (Oxford: Peter Lang).

Paz, Octavio, 1993. *La llama doble: amor y erotismo* (Barcelona: Seix Barral).

Pelayo, Antonio, ed., 1973. *Andrzej Wajda, testigo y conciencia de una generación*, XIII Conversaciones Internacionales de Cine, 1972 (Valladolid: Semana Internacional de Cine).

Pérez-Firmat, Gustavo, 1978. 'Apuntes para un modelo de la intertextualidad en literatura', *Romanic Review*, 69: 1–14.

——, 1986. *Literature and Liminality. Festive Readings in the Hispanic Tradition* (Durham, NC: Duke UP).

Piñera, Virgilio, 1960. *Teatro completo* (Havana: Ediciones R).

——, 2005. *La vida entera (1937–1977). Antología poética*, ed. Joaquín Juan Penalva (Madrid: Signos, Huerga y Fierro).

Ponzio, Augusto, 1998. *La revolución bajtiniana* (Madrid: Cátedra).

Pratt, Annis, 1981. *Archetypal Patterns in Women's Fiction* (Bloomington: Indiana UP).

Pujalá, Grisel, 1993. *Cuatro ensayos sobre poesía cubana* (Coral Gables, FL: La Torre de Papel).

Radford Ruether, Rosemary, 1993. *Gaia and God: An Ecofeminist Theology of Earth Healing* (London: SCM).

Radhakrishnan, Rajagopalan, 1996. *Diasporic Mediations. Between Home and Location* (Minneapolis: U of Minnesota P).

Rama, Ángel, 1982. *La novela en América Latina: Panoramas 1920–1980* (Bogotá: Instituto Colombiano de Cultura).

Ramblado Minero, María de la Cinta, 2006. 'La isla revolucionaria: El dilema de la identidad cubana en *Fresa y chocolate* y *La nada cotidiana*', *Letras Hispanas*, 3.2: 86–94.

Ramos Collazo, José Antonio, 2010. 'Detective Novel in Puerto Rico and Cuba: The Cases of Wilfredo Mattos Cintrón and Leonardo Padura Fuentes'. PhD diss., Univ. of Puerto Rico, Río Piedras. In *Dissertations and Theses: AandI*, ProQuest pub. no. AAT 3365016.

Randall, Margaret, 1974. *Cuban Women Now* (Toronto: Women's Press).

——, 1975. *Mujeres en la revolución* (Mexico City: Siglo XXI).

——, 1981. *Women in Cuba. Twenty Years Later* (New York: Smyrna).

——, 1982. *Breaking the Silences* (Vancouver: Pulp Press).

——, 1992. *Gathering Rage. The Failure of 20th Century Revolutions to Develop a Feminist Agenda* (New York: Monthly Review Press).

Reinstädler, Janett, and Ottmar Ette, eds, 2000. *Todas las islas la isla: Nuevas y novísimas tendencias en la literatura y cultura de Cuba* (Madrid: Iberoamericana; Frankfurt: Vervuert).

Resik Aguirre, Magda, 2001. 'Abilio Estévez: De lo que se habla no se escribe', *La Jiribilla*, <http://www.lajiribilla.cu/2001/n10_julio/277_10.html> (accessed 8 September 2013).

Reyes, Graciela, ed., 1989. *Teorías literarias en la actualidad* (Madrid: El Arquero).

Richard, Nelly, 1990. 'De la literatura de mujeres a la textualidad femenina', in Berenguer et al. 1990: 39–52.

Ricoeur, Paul, 1978. *The Rule of Metaphor: Multi-Disciplinary Studies of the Creation of Meaning in Language*, tr. Robert Czerny, with Kathleen McLaughlin and John Costello (London: Routledge).

——, 2004. *Memory, History, Forgetting*, tr. Kathleen Blamey and David Pellauer (Chicago: U of Chicago P).

Rivero, Eliana, 2005. *Discursos de la diáspora* (Cádiz: Aduana Vieja).

Riviere, Joan, 1986. 'Womanliness as a Masquerade', in *Formations of Fantasy*, ed. Victor Burgin, James Donald and Cora Kaplan (London: Methuen), pp. 35–44.

Rodríguez, Alicia, 1994. 'La mujer en la obra de Reinaldo Arenas', in Sánchez 1994: 151–9.

Rodríguez Coronel, Rogelio, 1986. *La novela de la revolución cubana (1959–1979)* (Havana: Letras Cubanas).

Rodríguez-Mangual, Edna, 2005. 'Un caos lúcido: Delimitaciones de la ciudad antillana en *Tuyo es el reino* de Abilio Estévez', *La Torre: Revista de la Universidad de Puerto Rico*, 10.35: 121–33.

Rodríguez Monegal, Emir, 1972. *El boom de la novela latinoamericana* (Caracas: Tiempo Nuevo).

——, 1976. 'Las metamorfosis del texto', in *Severo Sarduy*, ed. Julián Ríos (Madrid: Espiral / Fundamentos), pp. 35–61.

——, 1980. 'The Labyrinthine World of Reinaldo Arenas', *Latin American Literary Review*, 8.16: 126–31.

Rogers, Robert, 1970. *The Double in Literature* (Detroit: Wayne State UP).

Rojas, Rafael, 1995. *Cuba: la isla posible* (Barcelona: Destino).

Romeu, Raquel, 1999. *Voces de mujeres en la literatura cubana* (Madrid: Verbum).

Rooney, Ellen, 2006. 'The Literary Politics of Feminist Theory', in *Feminist Literary Theory*, ed. Ellen Rooney (Cambridge: CUP), pp. 73–95.

Rorty, Richard, 1989. *Contingency, Irony and Solidarity* (New York: Cambridge UP).

Ros, Enrique, 2004. *La UMAP: El Gulag castrista* (Miami: Universal).

Rosell, Sara, 2000. 'La (re)formulación del policial cubano: La tetralogía de Leonardo Padura Fuentes', *Hispanic Journal*, 21.2: 447–58.

Roudiez, Leon S., 1980. 'Introduction', in Kristeva 1980: 1–20.

——, 1984. 'Introduction', in Kristeva 1984: 1–10.

Rozencvaig, Perla, 1981. 'Reinaldo Arenas, entrevista', *Hispamérica*, 10.28: 41–8.

——, 1986. *Reinaldo Arenas: narrativa de transgresión* (Mexico City: Oasis).

——, 1994. 'Constantes dispersas en la narrativa del exilio', in *Lo que no se ha dicho*, ed. Pedro Monge (New York: Ollantay), pp. 144–54.

——, 1996. 'La complicidad del lenguaje en *La nada cotidiana*', *Revista Hispánica Moderna*, 49.2: 430–3.

Russo, Vito, 1987. *The Celluloid Closet: Homosexuality in the Movies* (New York: Harper).

Sánchez, Reinaldo, ed., 1994. *Reinaldo Arenas: Recuerdo y presencia* (Miami: Universal).

Sánchez, Reinaldo, and Humberto López Cruz, eds, 1999. *Ideología y subversión: Otra vez Arenas* (Salamanca: Centro de Estudios Ibéricos y Americanos de Salamanca).

Sánchez, Yvette, 2000. '"Esta isla se vende": proyecciones desde el exilio de una generación ¿desilusionada?', in Reinstädler and Ette 2000: 163–76.

Santarcangeli, Paolo, 2002. *El libro de los laberintos: historia de un mito y de un símbolo* (Madrid: Siruela).

Sarabia Acosta, Diana L., 2007. 'Sueños y desencantos en novelas y películas cubanas del Período especial'. PhD diss., Univ. of Ottawa, Canada. In *Dissertations and Theses: AandI*, ProQuest pub. no. AAT NR49396; published, Sarabia Acosta 2009.

——, 2009. *Sueños y desencantos de novelas y películas cubanas del Período especial* (Valladolid: Universitas Castellae).

Sarduy, Severo, 1973. 'Writing / Transvestism', *Review*, 9 (Fall): 33–50.

——, 1982. *La simulación* (Caracas: Monte Ávila).

——, 1987. *Ensayos generales sobre el barroco* (Mexico City: FCE).

Sargent, Lydia, ed., 1981. *Women and Revolution: A Discussion of the Unhappy Marriage of Marxism and Feminism* (London: Pluto).

Sartre, Jean-Paul, 1993. *Essays in Existentialism*, ed. Wade Baskin (New York: Citadel).

Saussure, Ferdinand de, 1945. *Curso de lingüística general*, tr. Amado Alonso (Buenos Aires: Losada).

Scholes, Robert, 1982. *Semiotics and Interpretation* (New Haven, CT: Yale UP).

Schopenhauer, Arthur, 1969. *The World as Will and Representation*, tr. E. F. J. Payne, 2 vols (Toronto: Dover Publications).

Schwartz, Kessel, 1984. 'Homosexuality and the Fiction of Reinaldo Arenas', *Journal of Evolutionary Psychology*, 5.1–2: 12–20.

Sedgwick, Eve K., 1985. *Between Men: English Literature and Male Homosocial Desire* (New York: Columbia UP).

Séjourné, Laurette, 1980. *La mujer cubana en el quehacer de la historia* (Mexico City: Siglo XXI).

Sellers, Susan, 1991. *Language and Sexual Difference: Feminist Writing in France* (London: Macmillan).

Shaw, Donald L., 1999. *Nueva narrativa hispanoamericana* (Madrid: Cátedra).

Showalter, Elaine, ed., 1986. *The New Feminist Criticism* (London: Virago).

——, 2001. *The Female Malady: Women, Madness and English Culture 1830–1980* (London: Virago), pp. 145–64.

Sierra Madero, Abel, 2006. *Del otro lado del espejo: La sexualidad en la construcción de la nación cubana* (Havana: Casa de las Américas).

Singer, June, 1977. *Androgyny: Towards a New Theory of Sexuality* (London: Routledge).

Skidmore, Thomas E., 1997. *Modern Latin America* (New York and Oxford: OUP).

Smith, Anthony, 1991. *National Identity* (London: Penguin).

Smith, Lois M., and Alfred L. Padula, 1988. 'Twenty Questions on Sex and Gender in Revolutionary Cuba', *Cuban Studies*, 18: 149–58.

——, 1996. *Sex and Revolution. Women in Socialist Cuba* (Oxford and New York: OUP).

Smith, Paul Julian, 1989. *The Body Hispanic: Gender and Sexuality in Spanish and Spanish American Literature* (Oxford: Clarendon).

Smith, Sidonie, 1987. *A Poetics of Women's Autobiography: Marginality and the Fictions of Self- Representation* (Bloomington: Indiana UP).

Smith, Verity A., 1989. 'Recent Trends in Cuban Criticism and Literature', *Cuban Studies*, 16: 81–99.

——, 1995. 'What are Little Girls Made of Under Socialism? Cuba's *Mujeres* and *Muchachas* in the Period 1980–1991', *Studies in Latin American Popular Culture*, 14: 1–15.

Snitow, Ann, et al., eds, 1984. *Desire: The Politics of Sexuality* (London: Virago).

Soto, Francisco, 1990. *Conversando con Reinaldo Arenas* (Madrid: Betania).

——, 1994. *Reinaldo Arenas: The Pentagonía* (Gainesville: UP of Florida).

——, 1995. 'El color del verano: innovaciones temáticas y aportaciones ideológicas a la novela del dictador', *Apuntes Posmodernos*, 6.1: 59–65.

——, 1998. *Reinaldo Arenas* (New York: Twayne).

Soto Fernández, Liliana, 2008. 'La sexualidad en La Habana de *La nada cotidiana* y de *El hombre, la hembra y el hambre*', *Hispania*, 91.2: 463–4.

Souza, Raymond D., 1976. *Major Cuban Novelists: Innovation and Tradition* (Columbia: U of Missouri).

Spivak, Gayatri Chakravorty, 1983. 'Displacement and the Discourse of Woman', in *Displacement. Derrida and After*, ed. Mark Krupnick (Bloomington: Indiana UP), pp. 169–95.

——, 1988. 'Can the Subaltern Speak?', in *Marxism and the Interpretation of Culture*, ed. Cary Nelson and Lawrence Grossberg (London: Macmillan), pp. 271–313.

——, 1999. *A Critique of Postcolonial Reason: Toward a History of the Vanishing Present* (Cambridge, MA: Harvard UP).

Staten, Henry, 1995. *Eros in Mourning. Homer to Lacan* (Baltimore, MD: Johns Hopkins UP).

Still, Judith, 1984. 'Lucretia's Silent Rhetoric', *Oxford Literary Review*, 6: 70–86.

Suleiman, Susan Rubin, ed., 1986. *The Female Body in Western Culture* (Cambridge, MA: Harvard UP).

Taplin, Oliver, 1978. *Greek Tragedy in Action* (London: Methuen).

Thiem, Anncgret, 2004. '*Al otro lado*: Yanitzia Canetti entre la mística y el postmodernismo', *Espéculo: Revista de Estudios Literarios*, 26 (March–June): n.p.

——, 2006. 'Ana Pizarro y Yanitzia Canetti: Memoria colectiva y mitología: ¿estrategias para la construcción de una identidad coherente?', in *Un continente en movimiento: Migraciones en América Latina*, ed. Ingrid Wehr (Madrid: Iberoamericana), pp. 169–76.

Thompson, William Irwin, 1987. *Gaia: A Way of Knowing: Political Implications of the New Biology* (Great Barrington, MA: Lindisfarne).

Timmer, Nanne, 2007. 'La crisis de representación en tres novelas cubanas: *La nada cotidiana* de Zoé Valdés, *El pájaro, pincel y tinta china* de Ena Lucía Portela y *La última playa* de Atilio Caballero', *Revista Iberoamericana*, 73: 259–74.

Tinajero, Araceli, ed., 2010. *Cultura y letras cubanas en el siglo XXI* (Madrid: Iberoamericana; Frankfurt: Vervuert)

Todorov, Tzvetan, 1977. 'The Typology of Detective Fiction', in *The Poetics of Prose*, tr. Richard Howard (Ithaca, NY: Cornell UP), pp. 42–52.

Tomás Fernández, Lourdes, 1994. *Fray Servando alucinado* (Miami: U of Miami, Letras de Oro).

Torrents, Nissa, 1991. 'Women Characters and Male Writers: A Cuban Approach', in *Feminist Readings on Spanish and Latin-American Literature*, ed. Lisa Condé and Stephen Hart (Lewiston, NY: Mellen), pp. 173–93.

Torres Rioseco, Arturo, 1963. *Precursores del modernismo: Estudios críticos y antología* (New York: Las Americas Publishing Company).

Tseëlon, Efrat, 2001. 'Reflections on Mask and Carnival', in *Masquerade and Identities*, ed. Efrat Tseëlon (London and New York: Routledge), pp. 18–31.

Turner, Victor, 1969. *The Ritual Process: Structure and Anti-Structure* (Chicago: Aldine).

Tyler, William Jefferson, 1981. 'The Agitated Spirit: Life and Major Works of the Contemporary Japanese Novelist Ishikawa Jun'. PhD diss., Harvard Univ. In *Dissertations and Theses: AandI*, ProQuest pub. no. AAT 8202207.

Unamuno, Miguel de, 1945. *En torno al casticismo*, 2nd edn (Buenos Aires: Espasa-Calpe Argentina).

Urbina, Nicasio, 1992. 'Horror en la obra de Reinaldo Arenas', *Hispanic Journal*, 13.1: 111–22.

——, 1994. 'De *Celestino antes del alba* a *El Portero*: historia de una carcajada', in Sánchez 1994: 201–23.

Uxó, Carlos, ed., 2006. *The Detective Fiction of Leonardo Padura Fuentes* (Manchester: MUP).

Vadillo, Alicia E., 2002. *Santería y vodú: Caminos que se cruzan sobre la narrativa cubana contemporánea* (Madrid: Biblioteca Nueva).

Valdés Zamora, Armando, 2009. 'La escritura imaginaria de Abilio Estévez', *Encuentro de la cultura cubana*, 51–2: 124–33.

Valero, Roberto, 1991. *El desamparado humor de Reinaldo Arenas* (Miami: U of Miami).

Valis, Noël, and Carol Maier, eds, 1990. *In the Feminine Mode. Essays on Hispanic Women Writers* (Lewisburg: Bucknell UP).

Vázquez Díaz, René, ed., 1994. *Bipolaridad de la cultura cubana* (Stockholm: The Olof Palme International Center).

Vera León, Antonio, 2000. 'Narraciones obscenas: Cabrera Infante, Reinaldo Arenas, Zoé Valdés', in Reinstädler and Ette 2000: 177–91.

Vice, Sue, 1997. *Introducing Bakhtin* (Manchester: MUP).

Vickroy, Laurie, 2005. 'The Traumas of Unbelonging: Reinaldo Arenas's Recuperations of Cuba', *MELUS: The Journal of the Society for the Study of the Multi-Ethnic Literature of the United States*, 30.4: 109–28.

Vilahomat, José Ramón, 2010. 'Sátira híbrida y sujeto menipeo: La literatura cubana y latinoamericana actual', *Espéculo: Revista de Estudios Literarios*, 44: n.p.

Vilaseca, David, 1997. 'On the Constitution and Uses of Homosexuality in Reinaldo Arenas's *Antes que anochezca*', *Bulletin of Hispanic Studies*, 74.3: 351–71.

Volek, Emil, 1985. 'La carnavalización y la alegoría en *El mundo alucinante* de Reinaldo Arenas', *Revista Iberoamericana*, 51: 125–48.

Voloshinov, Valentin N., 1976. *El signo ideológico y la filosofía del lenguaje*, tr. Rosa María Rússovich (Buenos Aires: Nueva Visión).

Wasserman, Carol, 2000. *La mujer y su circunstancia en la literatura latinoamericana actual* (Madrid: Pliegos).

Waugh, Patricia, 1989. *Feminine Fictions. Revisiting the Postmodern* (London and New York: Routledge).

Wehr, Ingrid, ed., 2006. *Un continente en movimiento: Migraciones en América Latina* (Madrid: Iberoamericana; Frankfurt: Vervuert).

Weinrich, Harald, 2004 [1997]. *Lethe: The Art and Critique of Forgetting*, tr. Steven Rendall (Ithaca, NY: Cornell UP).

Wells, Stanley, and Gary Taylor, eds, 1998. *The Oxford Shakespeare: The Complete Works* (Oxford: OUP).

Whitehead, Anne, 2009. *Memory* (London and New York: Routledge).

Whitfield, Esther Katheryn, 2001. 'Fiction(s) of Cuba in Literary Economies of the 1990s: Buying In or Selling Out?'. PhD diss., Harvard Univ. In *Dissertations and Theses: AandI*, ProQuest pub. no. AAT 3011510.

——, 2008. *Cuban Currency: The Dollar and 'Special Period' Fiction* (Minneapolis: U of Minnesota P).

Whitford, Margaret, 1991a. *Luce Irigaray. Philosophy in the Feminine* (London: Routledge).

——, ed., 1991b. *The Irigaray Reader* (Oxford: Blackwell).

Wiles, David, 1991. *The Masks of Menander: Sign and Meaning in Greek and Roman Performance* (Cambridge: CUP).

Wilkinson, Stephen, 2000. 'Detective Fiction in Cuban Society and Culture'. PhD thesis, Queen Mary, Univ. of London; published, Wilkinson 2006.

——, 2006. *Detective Fiction in Cuban Society and Culture* (Bern: Peter Lang).

Williams, Eric, 1970. *From Columbus to Castro. The History of the Caribbean 1492–1969* (London: André Deutsch).

Winks, Christopher, 2008. 'La isla a la deriva, con sus caras y sus culos. Lo tardío transgresor en *El color del verano*', in *Del alba al anochecer: La escritura en Reinaldo Arenas*, ed. María Teresa Miaja de la Peña (Madrid: Iberoamericana; Mexico City: UNAM), pp. 103–16.

Wyatt, Jean, 1990. *Reconstructing Desire: The Role of the Unconscious in Women's Reading and Writing* (Chapel Hill, NC: U of North Carolina P).

Yates, Frances A., 1966. *The Art of Memory* (Chicago: U of Chicago P).

Young, Allen, 1981. *Gays Under the Cuban Revolution* (San Francisco: Grey Fox).

Zavala, Iris, 1989a. 'Dialogía, voces, enunciados: Bajtin y su círculo', in *Teorías literarias en la actualidad*, ed. Graciela Reyes (Madrid: El Arquero), pp. 79–128.

——, 1989b. 'Poética de la carnavalización en Valle-Inclán', in *Formas carnavalescas en el arte y la literatura*, ed. Javier Huerta Calvo (Barcelona: Serbal), pp. 257–78.

——, 1990. *La musa funambulesca. Poética de la carnavalización en Valle-Inclán* (Madrid: Orígenes).

——, 1991. *La posmodernidad y Mijail Bajtin. Una poética dialógica* (Madrid: Espasa Calpe).

——, 1996. *Bajtin y sus apócrifos* (Barcelona: Anthropos).

Zea, Leopoldo, 1986. *Ideas en torno de Latinoamérica* (Mexico City: UNAM).

Zendegui, Ileana, 2004. *The Postmodern Poetic Narrative of Cuban Writer Reinaldo Arenas* (Lewiston, NY: Mellen).

Index

jineterismo   220, 220 n.11
jouissance   167, 169, 188

Kaebnick, Suzanne   21, 24, 30
knowledge (self)   3, 12, 79, 91, 99,
    135, 152, 156, 182, 213
Kristeva, Julia   12, 13, 14, 57, 103
    n.2, 144, 144 n.6, 145, 187, 188,
    190, 191, 192, 193, 204, 208 n.8

labyrinth   136, 143, 150, 156,
    160–2
language   5, 8, 10, 15, 18, 19, 34,
    57, 59 n.11, 63, 73, 74, 86, 94, 97,
    108, 109, 144 n.6, 169, 174,
    186–92, 201, 203, 204, 206, 207,
    227, 233, 234
    authoritative language   140
    childish language   192
    different language   225
    erotic language   14
    explicit and direct language   210,
        225
    feminine language   19
    fictional language   131
    fragmented language   19
    informal language   225
    innocent language   97
    maternal language   187
    monologic language   225
    multi-languagedness   234
    mystic language   161
    neutral language   94, 97
    new language   14, 162, 227, 232
    of the public square   36
    of women   218
    patriarchal language   14, 19, 148,
        220, 148, 220
    poetic language   57, 160, 171,
        211
    privileged language   23, 171
    revolutionary language   190
    romantic language   218

scatological language   37
sexual language   203
social language   234
surrealist language   146, 196,
    207
symbolic language   148
undialogized language   108, 140
unitary language   34, 86
vulgar language   14
laughter   184
    carnival laughter   37
    carnivalesque laughter   33, 38
    grotesque laughter   37
law, paternal   57
Lezama Lima, José   34, 35, 79, 92,
    100, 104, 224
literariness   10, 11, 99, 100
literature   3, 5, 10, 19, 45, 48, 55,
    59 n.11, 60, 78, 87, 99, 100, 103,
    104, 108, 111, 112, 114, 116, 117,
    133, 147, 147 n.8, 148, 196, 205,
    207, 216, 236
    clinical literature   129
    confessional literature   163
    contemporary Latin American
        Literature   68
    Cuban literature   6, 11, 17, 19,
        53, 72, 100, 129, 203, 233, 236
    French literature   154
    God of literature   132
    history of literature   14, 51
    literature in the second
        degree   99, 103
    male literature   183
    monolithic notions of literature
        11
    Spanish literature   149
    universal literature   110, 112
locas   24, 25, 26, 30, 34, 230, 236
López-Cruz, Humberto   21, 30, 38,
    38 n.9, 41
Lotman, Iuri   58 n.8, 152
Ludmer, Josefina   16, 154, 195, 202

Lightning Source UK Ltd.
Milton Keynes UK
UKOW05n1043180414

230231UK00004B/20/P